HONOURING THE DECLARATION

University of Regina Press designates one title each year that best exemplifies the guiding editorial and manuscript production principles of long-time senior editor Donna Grant.

HONOURING *the* DECLARATION

Church Commitments to Reconciliation and the United Nations Declaration on the Rights of Indigenous Peoples

edited by

DON SCHWEITZER *and* **PAUL L. GAREAU**

© 2021 University of Regina Press

All rights reserved. No part of this work covered by the copyrights hereon may be reproduced or used in any form or by any means—graphic, electronic, or mechanical—without the prior written permission of the publisher. Any request for photocopying, recording, taping, or placement in information storage and retrieval systems of any sort shall be directed in writing to Access Copyright.

Cover art: "Rock Dove (*Columba livia*) with wings raised in flight, in monochrome" by Panu Ruangjan / iStock
Cover design: Duncan Campbell, University of Regina Press
Interior layout design: John van der Woude, JVDW Designs
Copy editor: Ryan Perks
Proofreader: Alison Strobel
Indexer: Patricia Furdek

Library and Archives Canada Cataloguing in Publication

Title: Honouring the Declaration : church commitments to reconciliation and the United Nations Declaration on the Rights of Indigenous Peoples / edited by Dr. Don Schweitzer and Dr. Paul L. Gareau.
Names: Schweitzer, Don, 1958- editor. | Gareau, Paul L., editor.
Description: Includes bibliographical references.
Identifiers: Canadiana (print) 20210232897 | Canadiana (ebook) 20210236779 | ISBN 9780889778337 (hardcover) | ISBN 9780889778320 (softcover) | ISBN 9780889778344 (PDF) | ISBN 9780889778351 (EPUB)
Subjects: LCSH: Reconciliation—Religious aspects—United Church of Canada. | LCSH: United Nations. General Assembly. Declaration on the Rights of Indigenous Peoples. | LCSH: Civil rights—Religious aspects—Christianity. | LCSH: Race relations—Religious aspects—United Church of Canada. | LCSH: Indigenous peoples—Civil rights—Canada. | LCSH: Indigenous peoples—Legal status, laws, etc.—Canada. | LCSH: Decolonization—Canada.
Classification: LCC BT738.37 .H66 2021 | DDC 261.8—dc23

University of Regina Press, University of Regina
Regina, Saskatchewan, Canada, S4S 0A2
tel: (306) 585-4758 fax: (306) 585-4699
web: www.uofrpress.ca

We acknowledge the support of the Canada Council for the Arts for our publishing program. We acknowledge the financial support of the Government of Canada. / Nous reconnaissons l'appui financier du gouvernement du Canada. This publication was made possible with support from Creative Saskatchewan's Book Publishing Production Grant Program.

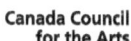  

CONTENTS

Acronyms **XI**
Foreword **XIII**
Don Schweitzer and Paul L. Gareau

Introduction **XV**
Sandra Beardsall, Sa'ke'j Henderson, and Don Schweitzer

CHAPTER 1
The Indigenous Imperative: The Role of Seminaries in the Realization of Reconciliation and Indigenizing **1**
Sa'ke'j Henderson

CHAPTER 2
What to Do with All These Canaanites? A Settler-Canadian Reading of Biblical Conquest Stories **31**
Christine Mitchell

CHAPTER 3
Restructured Feelings: Pitfalls of Settler-Christian Turns to Education **53**
Lynn Caldwell

CHAPTER 4
The Declaration and the Indigenous Ministries
of the United Church of Canada   75
Adrian Jacobs, Keeper of the Circle, Sandy-Saulteaux Spiritual Centre

CHAPTER 5
"Not Alone in This Struggle for Justice":
Project North and the United Church of Canada, 1975–87   101
Sandra Beardsall

CHAPTER 6
Storied Places and Sacred Relations:
Métis Density, Lifeways, and Indigenous Rights in the Declaration   131
Paul L. Gareau

CHAPTER 7
The Power and Practise of Indigenous Christian Rituals and Ceremonies   159
HyeRan Kim-Cragg

CHAPTER 8
Justification by Grace as a Spiritual Resource:
Non-Indigenous Christians Adopting the Declaration as the Framework
for Reconciliation with Indigenous Peoples in Canada   183
Don Schweitzer

CHAPTER 9
The Declaration and the Common Good   207
Jennifer Janzen-Ball

CHAPTER 10
Working from the Heart:
Considering Reconciliation/Mīnwastamātowin through the Lenses
of Miýo-Wāhkōtowin, Miýo-Pimātisiwin, and Gender   229
Iskwewuk E-wichiwitochik/Women Walking Together

Afterword   265
Sa'ke'j Henderson and Don Schweitzer

Appendix A
An Ecumenical Statement on the United Nations Declaration on the Rights of Indigenous Peoples: Responding to the Truth and Reconciliation Commission's Call to Action 48   273

Appendix B
Statement on UN Declaration on the Rights of Indigenous Peoples as the Framework for Reconciliation   277

Index   281

ACRONYMS

ANCC	All Native Circle Conference
CRGB Models	*Culturally Relevant Gender Based Models of Reconciliation*
DJSRC	Doctor Jessie Saulteaux Resource Centre
DMC	Division of Mission in Canada
FSTC	Francis Sandy Theological Centre
GCE	General Council Executive
IBNWT	Indian Brotherhood of the Northwest Territories
ICPOND	Interchurch Project on Northern Development (Project North)
IE	Iskwewuk E-wichiwitochik/Women Walking Together
MMIWG2S	missing and murdered Indigenous women, girls, and Two-Spirits
NCC	Northern Coordinating Committee
NIB	National Indian Brotherhood
NIMMIWG2S	National Inquiry into Missing and Murdered Indigenous Women, Girls, and Two-Spirits
NWAC	Native Women's Association of Canada

— ACRONYMS —

SPS	Saskatoon Police Service
SSSC	Sandy-Saulteaux Spiritual Centre
TRC	Truth and Reconciliation Commission of Canada
UCC	The United Church of Canada
UNDRIP	United Nations Declaration on the Rights of Indigenous Peoples

FOREWORD

On November 23 and 24, 2017, the contributors to this volume gathered at St. Andrew's College in Saskatoon, located on Treaty 6 territory and on the Métis Homeland. We congregated to present and discuss the outlines of our chapters and talk about the possibility of bringing them together into an edited collection. This meeting decisively shaped what you are now reading in several ways. We must first explain some of the terms and ideas from this book.

First Sa'ke'j Henderson, who spent years working along with others to draft what became the United Nations Declaration on the Rights of Indigenous Peoples, expressed an aversion to the acronym UNDRIP. Out of respect for him, in what follows we have used "the Declaration" as an abbreviation for this document instead, although "UNDRIP" does appear in quotations and references. Second, our authors use the term "Indigenous" to speak generally of the perspectives and experiences of the First Peoples of the land on which we live and where this book took shape. This term does not negate the importance of recognizing the term "Aboriginal," which in section 35 of the *Constitution Act, 1982* recognizes Treaty Rights of First Nations, Inuit, and Métis Peoples living in Canada. Our orientation is always toward Indigenous self-determination by naming Indigenous nations in our texts using Indigenous autonyms and languages where we can. In this way, we affirm Indigenous sovereignty in our writing by reflecting the experiences of Indigenous Peoples in place, as was well as in relations with other peoples and in other places.

Finally, the group did not want to have one or two editors making autocratic decisions about other people's chapters. So instead of having editors, two "timekeepers" were chosen, who were charged with keeping the project moving ahead. However, as these timekeepers, we found that some aspects of the work of making a collaborative, edited volume were unavoidable, and that "timekeeper" is not yet a recognized term in academic publishing. So, in a concession to convention, we are listed as "editors" in the book's front matter. However, in editing this book, we strove to adopt a deeply collaborative approach. Over the time of writing, authors were set into pairs to review and support each other's work. It was a helpful and relational way to find the critical voice of our chapters as well as to help one another in the collaborative editing process. Major editorial decisions such as chapter order were made by the group, and in that regard our role has indeed been more of timekeeping than a strictly top-down, editorial one. It has been an honour to have been entrusted with this responsibility.

—Don Schweitzer and Paul L. Gareau
(timekeepers/editors)

INTRODUCTION

by

SANDRA BEARDSALL, SA'KE'J HENDERSON,
AND DON SCHWEITZER

On March 30, 2016, seven Canadian churches issued "An Ecumenical Statement on the *United Nations Declaration on the Rights of Indigenous Peoples*."[1] The United Church of Canada was one of these. As parties to the Indian Residential Schools Settlement Agreement, it and other churches had promised to receive and act on the Calls to Action issued by the Truth and Reconciliation Commission of Canada (TRC). Call to Action 48 mandated them "to formally adopt and comply with the principles, norms, and standards of the United Nations Declaration on the Rights of Indigenous Peoples as a framework for reconciliation."[2] The "Ecumenical Statement" announced that its signees were doing this and gave a brief description of the Declaration, noting that the rights affirmed therein "constitute the minimum standards for the survival, dignity, security, and well-being of Indigenous peoples worldwide."[3] The statement indicated that these churches received this call to action as those who were implicated in the oppression of Indigenous Peoples, and it expressed their commitment to remedy this:

> Settlers in Canada have benefited, directly or indirectly, from the occupation and usurpation of Indigenous lands and resources. Indigenous peoples, however, have experienced impoverishment, oppression, dispossession from their lands, and the destruction of their cultures and spiritual practices. The root causes of this ongoing impoverishment and oppression of Indigenous peoples must be identified and, then, we must be willing to make it right.[4]

The statement added that the Declaration's emphasis on respecting the right of Indigenous Peoples to self-determination would help churches "address the root causes of this inequity,"[5] and ultimately correct them.

The following day, the United Church issued its own statement reiterating its commitment to comply with the Declaration.[6] It noted that it had been working toward reconciliation with Indigenous Peoples since apologizing in 1986 for its role in colonization and the destruction of Indigenous spirituality and practices.[7] The United Church's statement concluded as follows: "We are not sure what lies ahead as we complete this turn towards justice and deepen our commitment to a new identity, a new relationship, and a new way of being, both in the church and in the world. A new relationship is waiting, and we turn our faces towards it."[8] The 2019 version of the United Church's *Manual* reiterates this commitment and states that the church intends to develop mechanisms to report on its progress in living it out.[9]

Accepting the UN Declaration as a framework for reconciliation is a major undertaking for Canadian churches. As the "Ecumenical Statement" indicates, until recently Canadian society has operated on the assumption that Indigenous Peoples' lands were available "for the purposes of state formation, settlement, and capitalist development."[10] Up until the 1970s, Canadian churches were largely complicit in this. They continue to benefit from it. Adopting the Declaration as a framework for reconciliation requires that this assumption be replaced with respect for a wide range of Indigenous Rights, particularly the right to self-determination and to "use, develop and control" Indigenous Lands, as laid out in articles 3 and 26.[11] If Canadian churches follow through on this commitment, it will introduce fundamental changes into their relationships to Indigenous Peoples. Consultation with Indigenous Peoples, acknowledgement of their rights, respect for their traditions, practices, and teachings will have to become standard practice for Canadian churches. As the conclusion to the United Church's statement indicates, accepting the Declaration as a framework for reconciliation means that Canadian churches are seeking to enter into a new relationship with Indigenous Peoples, one with far-reaching implications for how the churches operate. Following through on this commitment will require all the resources that Canadian churches can muster.

This book is intended to provide an academic resource to help the United Church and other Canadian denominations follow through on this commitment. The TRC's Call to Action 60 calls on seminaries to develop curriculum addressing "the responsibility that churches have to mitigate ... [religious] conflicts and prevent spiritual violence."[12] This book can also be a resource for such curricula. An anonymous reviewer suggested that such resources have an analysis and understanding of theological violence. Accordingly, chapter 2 provides an analysis of this in the Hebrew Bible. Chapters 4 and 8 provide elements of this kind of analysis for Christian theology. Chapters 3, 5, and 10 provide critical reflections on the effectiveness of some reconciliation practices and recent attempts by the United Church to be in solidarity with Indigenous Peoples. However, the Indigenous contributors to this volume have chosen to affirm Indigenous self-determinacy and resiliency rather than focus on what white settlers have done to their peoples, in order to decentre white hegemony in this discussion.

Academics and theologians have a role to play as the churches think, work, and pray toward a new understanding of themselves and a new relationship to Indigenous Peoples. The authors in this book write from a variety of perspectives and engage a multitude of issues. This reflects the many kinds of questions that must be explored if the churches are to fulfill the commitment they have made. All the authors are located in Treaty 6 and Treaty 1 territories and the homeland of the Métis, on what we now call the Canadian Prairies. This is a response to the commitment the churches have made from this particular place. It is also a response at this time to a spiritual movement, one of the signs of the times that churches, theologians, and Christian social ethicists are called to attend to. This spiritual movement comprises the struggle for justice that has been and continues to be waged by Indigenous Peoples and their allies in Canada and beyond. This movement has awakened the United Church and other Canadian denominations to the need to repent of their colonial legacy. Hopefully, the following chapters will help them carry this repentance forward into constructive action.

The Declaration codifies the demand for recognition and respect for Indigenous Peoples that this spiritual movement made in the international forum of the United Nations. It is a word for this time. The churches have said they will listen to it. This listening needs to happen on two levels. First, in accepting the Declaration as a framework for reconciliation, the churches need to listen carefully to its forty-six articles and the joint statement issued at its implementation; the rights described therein need to be taken seriously and upheld by law. The churches must work to see that this happens. Equally important, though, is a recognition of the spirit that inspired the twenty years of struggle and negotiation that it took to develop the Declaration and get it implemented. The Declaration needs to be listened to on a second level as an expression of this spirit. It is fundamentally a call for settler societies to manifest a new love and respect for Indigenous Peoples. To speak for a moment in Christian terms, the churches are realizing that the Holy Spirit has addressed them through the movement that gave rise to the Declaration, calling them to respect Indigenous Peoples and their cultures, practices, traditions, religions, and lands. The Declaration codifies what this means in the language of human rights at this point in time. It establishes the basis for a new relationship between Indigenous and non-Indigenous people in which the old settler social order must give way to a new one. But respect, as it is a form of love, is deeper, broader, and more creative than any codification of it can ever be. Reconciliation is an ongoing, dynamic process. The compliance of settler societies and the churches with the articles of the Declaration are essential for reconciliation. But this needs to be undergirded and inspired by an acceptance

INTRODUCTION

of the underlying message that the Spirit is communicating to them through this document. In the future, as the new social order that the Declaration mandates develops, and as the Declaration becomes tradition, new needs and possibilities for the furtherance of reconciliation will become apparent— needs and possibilities that the Declaration's articles do not directly address. It will be this deeper listening that guides and inspires the continuing work of reconciliation beyond what the Declaration presently envisages.

What follows begins with a brief overview of the movement that led to the framing and adoption of the Declaration at the United Nations. We then survey the events in Canada that led to the establishment of the TRC, and finally, how this book was conceived. Following this, each contributor introduces themselves and their chapter, in the order in which they appear.

I

> *Empire has located its existence not in the smooth recurrent spinning time of cycles of the seasons but in the jagged time of rise and fall, of beginning and ends, of catastrophe. Empire dooms itself to live in history and plot against history. One thought alone preoccupies the submerged mind of Empire: how not to end, how not to die, how to prolong its era.*
> —J.M. Coetzee, *Waiting for the Barbarians*

A brief history of the Indigenous struggle to be human, a person, and peoples in various eras shows how urgent the need is for a better understanding of the relationship between Indigenous and Eurocentric forms of knowledge. It also illustrates some of the dilemmas in which we find ourselves as we seek to build some measure of trans-systemic understanding between these ways of viewing the world.

In the struggle for constitutional reforms that took place in Canada between 1978 and 1981, the Elders, leaders, and lawyers of the Aboriginal nations came to comprehend human rights. When First Nations raised the issue of the human rights covenants that had been ratified by Canada with the first ministers, they told us that those principles did not apply to us, that we were the wrong kind of people.

The first ministers' ideology was not new. For five generations Indigenous Peoples had been burdened with this ideology in many ways. The Catholic Church made the same arguments in the sixteenth century when it discovered that the Holy Bible mentioned neither the American continents nor its people. Catholic priests and scholars sought to determine whether, because of the gap in the God's knowledge system, the Indigenous Peoples of the continent should be considered as infidels, natural slaves, or humans. In 1512 and again in 1537, the Holy See decided that they were human beings who cannot be deprived of their liberty to possess property.[13] Despite its treaties with the British sovereign, one of the first acts of the new Canadian state was to declare in 1876 that Indians were made to be non-persons; this would not be amended until 1951.[14] The result was the same: as non-persons, we were denied our spirituality, our humanity, our knowledge system, our dignity, and access to our laws and systems of justice.

First Nations, in order to resist the first ministers' decision to deny our human rights, joined the Indigenous lawyers and leaders around the world at the United Nations in an attempt to have the international and national regimes respond to the growing crisis of systemic racism and colonialism, and to have our human rights affirmed. Eventually, the United Nations responded to our efforts and created the Working Group on Indigenous Populations in Geneva.

In the alien and expensive meeting places of Geneva, we articulated the meaning of our humanity and our vision of a fair and ethical society. The working group became the first international ceremony for Indigenous Peoples. It also became the venue for a strange, postcolonial journey to the heart of our darkness: we had to prove, after all the wretchedness of the last five hundred years, that we were people who had inherent dignity and who possess human rights. It was a hard, obsidian, degrading, and humiliating journey that entailed unravelling the worst of Euro-Christian thought about our ancestors and us. As we addressed the flaws in these arguments, the state representatives were practising their old privileges and challenging our traditions and visions and denying our aspirations. They rejected our understanding of humanity. They insulted our efforts to change the way the "world" thought about us. The arguments of the nation-states were familiar to us, as we had lived our lives under these oppressive regimes. What was new was that these governments had to hear our persuasive responses. Within the nation-states we were silenced and ignored; at the UN we forced a debate on the total denial of our humanity.

According to the teachings of our Oral Traditions, we explored the unknown territory of relationships with each other. In many Indigenous traditions, languages, and styles, we sought to initiate a creative, transformative vision of human rights in an otherwise complacent world order. We probed for agreements on how existing UN human rights covenants should be applied to Indigenous Peoples.

These debates, which took place over thirty years in Geneva, were an effort to crystallize our vision of a postcolonial order in ink. As the Lakota holy man Black Elk revealed in an ancient teaching, "A human being who has a vision is not able to use the power of it until after they have realized this vision on earth for people to see."[15] If we wanted a better life tomorrow, we had to have the courage to envision the impossible and translate it into text. We had to assume the task of conveying our visions within the six languages of the UN law to human rights experts and baffled government representatives.

When Indigenous delegates were killed, persecuted, and imprisoned upon their return from Geneva, state representatives mocked our efforts to bring the terrorists to justice. When these arguments were rejected, these representatives became complicit in this terror.[16]

In our great diplomatic movement, Indigenous Peoples left many ink trails or cognitive traces of our vision at the United Nations as we attempted to create a just tomorrow. This includes the 1989 International Labour Organization Convention on Indigenous and Tribal Peoples; the inclusion of Indigenous Peoples' Traditional Knowledge in the 1992 UN Convention on Biological Diversity; the establishment in 2000 of the UN Permanent Forum on

Indigenous Issues; and the 2003 Indigenous Peoples Programme of the World Council of Churches. The final achievement came in 2007, with the adoption of the UN Declaration on the Rights of Indigenous Peoples, a rearticulation of global Indigenous knowledge systems in the language of human rights. And yet, the legacy of colonialism and racism persists.

II

While this struggle was being waged at the United Nations, Indigenous Peoples in Canada were working to overthrow the colonial attitudes and practices of Canadian governments, business interests, and churches. Self-criticism within the United Church concerning its mission work with Indigenous Peoples began to appear as early as 1940.[17] But it was not until the 1960s that United Church leaders began to listen to and consult with Indigenous Peoples concerning their needs and aspirations.[18] As the United Church and other Canadian denominations began to listen to Indigenous Peoples, they also began to undertake advocacy work on their behalf.[19] As the United Church became involved with Indigenous struggles for justice, it experienced a loss of innocence. In 1984, Alberta Billy, an Indigenous delegate to the United Church's General Council Executive from Cape Mudge, British Columbia, demanded that the United Church apologize for its treatment of Indigenous Peoples.[20] In 1986, it issued an apology at its General Council meeting in Sudbury, Ontario. This was the first of a number of apologies that would be issued by churches that had been involved with running residential schools. The Kanesatake Resistance (i.e., the Oka Crisis) in the summer of 1990 led to the creation of the Royal Commission on Aboriginal Peoples. By the end of the decade, an ever-increasing number of residential school survivors were launching civil actions against the Canadian government and the churches that ran these schools. This led to the Indian Residential Schools Settlement Agreement, which went into effect in 2006–7. This provided for the establishment of a truth and reconciliation commission that would focus on Indigenous people's experiences of residential school and the impacts on their communities. At its closing event in June 2015, the TRC issued ninety-four Calls to Action

— INTRODUCTION —

detailing what was needed to effect reconciliation between Indigenous Peoples and settlers in Canada. Among these was Call to Action 48.

III

Shortly after the United Church and others announced their commitment to the UN Declaration as a framework for reconciliation with Indigenous Peoples, the faculty at St. Andrew's College, as educators in a theological school of the United Church of Canada, began a conversation about how teaching and research at the college could assist the church in fulfilling this important obligation.

The faculty members acknowledged that the United Church and its predecessor denominations had been deeply implicated in the denial of the rights of Indigenous Peoples in Canada for nearly two centuries, and that assimilationist and racist attitudes continue to thrive in settler society. The TRC's Principles of Reconciliation remind us that reconciliation is a process of healing relationships that requires public truth sharing (Principle 3) and "sustained public education and dialogue" (Principle 10).[21] This is work that members of the academy are well positioned to undertake. Faculty members recognized that to adopt a framework of Indigenous Rights in order to address these principles would involve acts of personal and intellectual repentance and would require a multi-faceted approach to the church and its life in the world.

The result of these acknowledgements and conversations was the decision to produce an academic resource that would address the United Church's commitments from the perspectives of the faculty members' various academic disciplines. However, the TRC defines "'reconciliation' as an ongoing process of establishing and maintaining respectful relationships."[22] The college's faculty members could not undertake this work of reconciliation on their own, and they invited Indigenous scholars and activists to participate in the project. A grant from the United Church's Justice and Reconciliation Fund enabled the prospective authors to meet in Saskatoon for a two-day symposium, where each author described their proposed chapter and the whole group was able to reflect on the proposal together. This symposium proved to be a rich gift to the participants. A hope-filled process of truth-telling and trust-building emerged as we wrestled with our common task. We also agreed upon the book title, committed to responding to each other's drafts, determined how we might organize the chapters, and appointed timekeepers to help us fulfill our writing commitments. We trust that the resulting volume manifests the personal and collective yearning for reconciliation and justice that motivated this project.

On December 3, 2020, Bill C-15 received its first reading in Parliament. If passed, the bill will commit the Government of Canada to ensuring that Canadian laws are consistent with the Declaration. The bill also calls for the development, within three years of its passage, an action plan by which the Canadian federal government will achieve the Declaration's objectives. The passage of this bill and the meeting its goals require tremendous political will and strong grassroots support. Hopefully, this book will help the United Church and other Christian denominations in Canada support Bill C-15's passage and help generate popular commitment to its stated goals.

We now turn to some brief self-descriptions of the contributors and their chapters.

IV

James (SA'KE'J) Youngblood Henderson, JD, IPC, FRSC

I have been a research fellow with the Native Law Centre of Canada at the University of Saskatchewan College of Law since 1993. I was one of the strategists who created Indigenous diplomacy in the UN system, and I took part in the drafting team in both working groups on the UN Declaration of the Rights of Indigenous Peoples. I have written about this experience in *Indigenous Diplomacy and the Rights of Peoples: Achieving UN Recognition* (2008). Additionally, I have co-authored with Marie Battiste *Protecting Indigenous Knowledge and Heritage: A Global Challenge* (2000). I have been a member of the Advisory Board to the Minister of Foreign Affairs, and a member of the Sectoral Commission

INTRODUCTION

on Culture, Communication and Information of the Canadian Commission for UNESCO and the Experts Advisory Group on International Cultural Diversity. I am currently a member of the Advisory Committee of the Centre for International Governance Innovation's International Law Research Program. My chapter outlines the framework of Indigenous imperatives deriving from both Canadian constitutional law and the UN Declaration on the Rights of Indigenous Peoples, and how seminaries can use this framework to realize an honourable reconciliation.

Christine Mitchell

A cradle United Church layperson, I was formed deeply in childhood by the so-called New Curriculum. This United Church education program exposed children and adults to the richness of the Christian intellectual tradition, and in my case, pointed to the beauty and depth of scripture. Until I came to Saskatoon in 2002 as professor of Hebrew scriptures at St. Andrew's College, I had lived and studied almost entirely in Ottawa, with a brief sojourn in southern Ontario for my undergraduate studies in Near Eastern archaeology. The present book project gave me the opportunity to explore problematic biblical texts from the perspective of both reading practice and contextual interpretation. In my chapter, I ground myself as a Euro-Canadian settler trying to show how biblical texts dealing with invasion, colonization, exclusion, and genocide operate within Canadian social and political discourse. I argue that while churches have one role to play in dismantling the biblical bases of the Doctrine of Discovery and *terra nullius* concepts, my guild of biblical scholars—both religious and secular—has just as important a role in informing Canadian public discourse. Some biblical texts give a road map for true reconciliation, which always consists of both repentance and reparation, and I suggest that this is a way forward in the Canadian context. I remain aware that my engagement in this work has led to academic and professional opportunities for me: I have benefited as a Euro-Canadian from colonization, and I am now benefiting as a scholar from the aftermath of the TRC. The work must be done—it cannot be left to Indigenous scholars alone to educate Canadians. But who is permitted to engage in such work must always be problematized.

Lynn Caldwell

My first experience of formal schooling involved catching a small yellow school bus from "town" to get to a building on Flying Dust First Nation every weekday afternoon, sometime in the early 1970s. I have many vivid memories that I carry from those days, and in recent years I have puzzled over those memories and that experience with more scrutiny as I realize how unusual it was for settler kids to be bussed to a First Nation for our schooling. I'd like to find out more about those circumstances. Maybe sometime I will. These days, my experience of education and schooling primarily involves my work as a professor of church and society at St. Andrew's College. I come to this work from my graduate studies in sociology and equity studies in education at the Ontario Institute for Studies in Education/University of Toronto, from my own master of divinity studies at St. Andrew's in the 1990s, and from my role as an educator in an ecumenical anti-racist project in southern Alberta, followed by time with the United Church of Canada Saskatchewan Conference Program Staff. As I note in my contribution to this collection, I now question many of my own practices as a social justice education facilitator in light of the TRC's Calls to Action and the calls to implement the UN Declaration. This perspective forms the basis for what I offer here, and for my hope for new conversations about the role and possibilities in education. I am deeply appreciative of the opportunity to contribute this reflection and to share in this project in these critical times.

Adrian Jacobs

Since 2012, I have been the Keeper of the Circle at Sandy-Saulteaux Spiritual Centre, the national Indigenous ministry training school of the United Church of Canada, in Beausejour, Manitoba, on Treaty 1 territory. I grew up at the Six

INTRODUCTION

Nations Reserve in southern Ontario, the largest in Canada. I am Ganosono, Turtle Clan, of the Six Nations Haudenosaunee Confederacy and live as guest in Anishinaabe territory. I have been mentored in Indigenous history, culture, ceremony, and Traditional Knowledge by Elders and colleagues across Turtle Island and internationally. I have pastoral education and twenty-plus years of pastoral experience in churches in Ontario. I have been involved in educating and mentoring leaders for Indigenous Christian ministry in Canada and the United States for over thirty-eight years. The United Church of Canada's embrace of the UN Declaration as a framework for reconciliation is a significant step in the development of self-governance among Indigenous communities of faith. The nine calls to the church endorsed at the General Council 43 in Oshawa, Ontario, in 2018 points the way forward for an Indigenous flourishing, and perhaps even a renewal in the rest of the church. My chapter explores the implications of these calls in the light of the UN Declaration and describes possibilities and hope espoused by our Elders.

Sandra Beardsall

I am both an ordained United Church minister and, since 1997, professor of church history and ecumenics at St. Andrew's College. I grew up in Brampton, Ontario, studied in Toronto, and lived in small towns in Newfoundland, Labrador, and eastern Ontario before moving to Saskatoon. When the United Church adopted the UN Declaration as a framework for reconciliation, I believe it invited church members into a challenging conversation about the intersection of rights, justice, repentance, healing, and solidarity. As a historian, I saw the story of the ecumenical coalition Project North as an ideal lens through which to enter this discussion. My chapter outlines how Project North was formed, what it did, and how United Church members reacted to its strong and unrelenting demand that Canadian society recognize Indigenous Rights. My chapter unpacks that story from a personal perspective—my own small engagement with that wider narrative—as a way to confront my own responsibilities and opportunities on the reconciliation journey.

Paul L. Gareau

My name is Paul L. Gareau. I am Métis and French Canadian, and I grew up in the hamlet of Bellevue, near Batoche, Saskatchewan. The Batoche region is an important, storied place for the Métis Nation that has long suffered the fragmentation of relations due to settler colonialism. This fragmented social and physical/spiritual geography has been at the centre of my identity and my life's work in understanding and resisting systemic racism as well as affirming Indigenous relations and Métis sovereignty. I am an assistant professor in the Faculty of Native Studies and past research fellow for the Rupertsland Centre for Métis Research at the University of Alberta. My research explores Métis experiences of religion, the influence of Catholicism on early and late-modern identity, the legacy of colonial discourses on Indigenous and ethnocultural minorities, youth agency and engagement, identity and religious conservatism, new religious movements, and the multiplicity of experience in rural spaces. As a Métis studies scholar, Indigenous/Native studies is the disciplinary focus that helps centre my work through theory and methodology on relationality, gender, Indigenous epistemologies, land, and sovereignty/peoplehood.

My chapter looks at the socio-religious elements of the Declaration as they relate to land and Indigenous sovereignty. It is necessary to hear the stories of Indigenous Peoples in order to affirm rights that are productive and meaningful. This work therefore focuses on understanding Métis experiences of religion at Catholic pilgrimage sites like Lac Ste. Anne in Alberta. My role in this chapter is to unpack Indigenous ways of understanding the sacred and relations with regards to the concepts of Indigenous density and lifeways, explicate Métis ways of knowing and being beyond the restrictions of settler colonial racialization, and affirm the Métis Nation's storied connections to place that makes Lac Ste. Anne "sacred" and that sustains Métis peoplehood.

INTRODUCTION

HyeRan Kim-Cragg (김혜란)

My name is HyeRan Kim-Cragg. I am a migrant from South Korea. My parents were refugees from North Korea. I carry my ancestors' experiences of colonialism under the Japanese occupation. I am an ordained minister of the Presbyterian Church in the Republic of Korea, a partner denomination of the United Church of Canada. I am a non-white racialized settler to Canada. I am honoured to be part of this book project as a former faculty member who used to teach worship and preaching at St. Andrew's College (until June 2019), and who now teaches preaching at Emmanuel College, Toronto. This book is an academic response to the TRC's Calls to Action as the church formally adopts the UN Declaration as a framework for reconciliation. I am especially thankful to this project's collaborative effort to join with Indigenous scholars. My essay examines article 12.1 of the UN Declaration, which addresses "the right [of Indigenous people] to manifest, practise, develop and teach their spiritual and religious traditions, customs, and ceremonies." It notes the importance of ritual and ceremony for Indigenous people. As a postcolonial scholar, I interrogate the ways in which Indigenous spiritual practices have been oppressed by European Christianity. My chapter analyzes how such oppression has relied on the notion that Western knowledge is superior to Indigenous forms of knowledge. I counter this colonialist notion by claiming that an Indigenous episteme is not only valid but also provides subversive resistance. I showcase Indigenous agency and resistance through the analysis of the hymn translation by Cree. Finally, the chapter demonstrates the wisdom of Indigenous Christians, who are able to embrace Christian traditions as their own while simultaneously decolonizing them.

Don Schweitzer

I grew up in the suburbs on the west side of Kingston, Ontario. My family attended St. Andrew's-by-the-Lake United Church, and my parents were very active in it. While attending university I became a candidate for the ministry in the United Church. I was ordained in 1982 and settled in Turtle River Larger

Parish, which is northwest of North Battleford and adjacent to Thunderchild First Nation. In 2000 I began to teach theology at St. Andrew's College, where I was eventually hired as the McDougald Professor of Theology. Adopting the UN Declaration as a framework for reconciliation sets a challenging mission goal for the United Church. My chapter explores how the doctrine of justification by grace can provide spiritual resources for the United Church that can guide and empower it as it seeks to live out this commitment.

Jennifer Janzen-Ball

I am an ordained United Church minister and have been director of the Designated Lay Ministry (DLM) Program since 2010. While engaged in ministry, in doctoral studies, and in various employment and teaching roles, I've lived on the Prairies (on the territories of Treaties 7, 2, 6), in New Brunswick (Mi'kmaq), and in Toronto (the historical territory of the Huron-Wendat, Petun, Seneca, and, most recently, the Mississaugas of the New Credit Indigenous Peoples, covered by the Dish With One Spoon Wampum Belt Covenant). I've since returned to Treaty 6 territory and the homeland of the Métis and to the South Saskatchewan River watershed (Saskatoon) and to my alma mater of St. Andrew's College, which now hosts the DLM Program. I believe the United Church's adoption of the UN Declaration as a framework for reconciliation challenges United Church members to re-examine critically our own theologies through an ethical lens that helps us to see the lived realities and consequences of such theologies (for instance, Indian residential schools and the Sixties Scoop). In my chapter, I suggest that the Christian ethical concept of the common good must be rethought in light of the ways in which Christianity and colonization (the sword and the cross) have malformed Indigenous and settler/newcomer relations.

Iskwewuk E-wichiwitochik/Women Walking Together

For over twelve years the women of Saskatoon-based activist collective Iskwewuk E-wichiwitochik (IE)—the name is Cree for Women Walking

Together—have been working to address the issue of missing and murdered Indigenous women, girls, and Two-Spirits (MMIWG2S). While IE not only supports but arguably exemplifies reconciliation between Indigenous and non-Indigenous people in Canada, we warn against the danger of official reconciliation becoming a neo-colonial project in benefiting non-Indigenous more than Indigenous Peoples. Thus, along with the Native Women's Association of Canada, we contend that *honourable* reconciliation must be framed in terms both gender-sensitive and culturally relevant to Indigenous people. Such reconciliation cannot occur without healing from the wounds of the historical and ongoing racism that has afflicted and continues to afflict both groups of people, and such healing can only proceed from decolonization. We further affirm the position taken by TRC commissioner Murray Sinclair—namely, that reconciliation will be a non-starter for many Indigenous people until the epidemic of murderous violence against IWG2S has been resolved. Our chapter expresses gratitude for the dedicated and principled work that resulted in the UN Declaration while recognizing that the TRC's Calls to Action enjoined the Canadian churches involved in Indian residential schools to adopt the Declaration as the framework for reconciliation. In light of women, girls, and Two-Spirited people's vulnerability to violations of their human rights, however, we urge the United Church of Canada to adopt a supplementary framework to the Declaration specifically to guard the human rights of IWG2S.

Finally, the book ends with an afterword by Sa'ke'j Henderson and Don Schweitzer reflecting on what we need to breathe in to empower us for the work that lies ahead.

Notes

1   The statement can be found at https://www.kairoscanada.org/wp-content/uploads/2016/03/Ecumenical-Statement-EN.pdf. It also reproduced in appendix A of this book.
2   Truth and Reconciliation Commission of Canada, *Honouring the Truth, Reconciling for the Future: Summary of the Final Report of the Truth and Reconciliation Commission of Canada* (Winnipeg: Truth and Reconciliation Commission of Canada, 2015), 327.

3   See appendix A, "An Ecumenical Statement on the *United Nations Declaration on the Rights of Indigenous Peoples*." Canadian Roman Catholic bishops issued their own statement of support for the Declaration as a framework for reconciliation on March 19, 2016.
4   Ibid.
5   Ibid.
6   See appendix B in this volume, "Statement on UN Declaration on the Rights of Indigenous Peoples as the Framework for Reconciliation."
7   The 1986 apology, as well as a response by Mrs. Edith Memnook, a representative of the All Native Circle Conference, at the United Church's 1988 General Council, are available at https://united-church.ca/social-action/justice-initiatives/reconciliation-and-indigenous-justice/apologies.
8   See appendix B, "Statement on UN Declaration."
9   United Church of Canada, *The Manual* (Toronto: United Church Publishing House, 2019), 10–11.
10 Glen Coulthard, *Red Skin, White Masks: Rejecting the Colonial Politics of Recognition* (Minneapolis: University of Minneapolis Press, 2014), 125.
11 UN General Assembly, Resolution 61/295, United Nations Declaration on the Rights of Indigenous Peoples, A/RES/61/295 (October 2, 2007), https://undocs.org/A/RES/61/295.
12 Truth and Reconciliation Commission of Canada, *Honouring the Truth, Reconciling for the Future*, 330.
13 Lewis Hanke, *The Spanish Struggle for Justice in the Conquest of America* (Philadelphia: University of Pennsylvania, 1949); Homer Noley, *First White Frost: Native Americans and United Methodism* (Nashville: Abingdon Press, 1991).
14 An Act to Amend and Consolidate the Laws Respecting Indians, SC 1876, c 18, s 12.
15 Cited in James (Sa'ke'j) Youngblood Henderson, *Indigenous Diplomacy and the Rights of Peoples: Achieving UN Recognition* (Vancouver: UBC Press, 2008), 48.
16 Marie Battiste and James (Sa'ke'j) Youngblood Henderson, *Protecting Indigenous Knowledge and Heritage: A Global Challenge* (Saskatoon: Purich Publishing, 2000), 271.
17 Loraine MacKenzie Shepherd, "The United Church's Mission Work within Canada and Its Impact on Indigenous and Ethnic Minority Communities," in *The Theology of the United Church of Canada*, ed. Don Schweitzer, Robert C. Fennell, and Michael Bourgeois (Waterloo, ON: Wilfrid Laurier University Press, 2019), 294.
18 Ibid.
19 Peter Hamel, "The Aboriginal Rights Coalition," in *Coalitions for Justice*, ed. Christopher Lind and Joe Mihevc (Ottawa: Novalis, 1994), 16–36.
20 J.R. Miller, *Residential Schools and Reconciliation: Canada Confronts Its History* (Toronto: University of Toronto Press, 2017), 3. Much of what follows in this paragraph is drawn from this source. Miller, based on an interview with Jim Sinclair, describes Alberta Billy's intervention as happening at the United Church's General Council meeting in 1984. Stan McKay and Janet Silman, meanwhile, describe it as occurring at a meeting of the United Church's General Council Executive. See Stan McKay and Janet Silman, *The First Nations: A Canadian Experience of the Gospel-Culture Encounter* (Geneva: WCC Publications, 1995), 31–2.

21 Truth and Reconciliation Commission of Canada, *What We Have Learned: Principles of Truth and Reconciliation* (Winnipeg: Truth and Reconciliation Commission of Canada, 2015), 3, 4.
22 Ibid., 121.

CHAPTER 1

THE INDIGENOUS IMPERATIVE

The Role of Seminaries in the Realization of Reconciliation and Indigenizing

by

SA'KE'J HENDERSON

We come from the land, the sky, from love and the body. From matter and creation. We are, life is, an equation we cannot form or shape, a mystery we can't trace in spite of our attempts to follow it back to its origin, to find out where life began, even in all our stories of when the universe came into being, how the first people emerged.
—Linda Hogan (Chickasaw), *Dwellings: A Spiritual History of the Living World*

Can we talk of integration until there is integration of hearts and minds? Unless you have this, you only have a physical presence, and the walls between us are as high as the mountain range.
—Chief Dan George (Tsleil-Waututh)

THE TRUTH AND RECONCILIATION COMMISSION OF CANADA (TRC) established that the minimum standards of the United Nations Declaration on the Rights of Indigenous Peoples (henceforth "Declaration")[1] are the appropriate framework for a holistic vision of reconciliation that provides the necessary principles, norms, and standards for reconciliation to flourish in twenty-first-century Canada. To gain the freedom to make reconciliation and to generate alternative futures for Canadian society with clarity and deliberation, we must be able to imagine these futures and to talk about them. Reconciliation is about translating hope into insight, and about transforming insight into action.

The guiding principle of reconciliation is comprehending the various Indigenous concepts relating to the inherent dignity of Indigenous people and their knowledge systems. Reconciliation is manifested in many ways: knowledge, cultural heritage and identity, spirituality, rights to languages, participation, and inclusion, gender equality, empowerment, and strengthening capacity. It is also reflected in self-determination, non-discrimination, equity, and equality. Education in the reconciliation framework is viewed as essential for the full development of Indigenous personalities, talents, and the mental and physical abilities that each person requires to reach their full potential. This reconciliation vision generated the Indigenizing imperative as a path we are meant to travel together in the context of post-secondary education.

Like the building of the national railway in the nineteenth century, or the agricultural project in the twentieth century, reconciliation is the largest national project of this century. It is a multi-actor, multi-site, multi-generational project. In 2012, when asked why the University of Saskatchewan had made Aboriginal education such a high priority, Provost Brett Fairbairn referred to what President Peter MacKinnon had called the university's "foundational imperative"—namely, that the institution should address the biggest social and economic issues facing the province. "In the early 20th century, that meant that we focused on agriculture," Fairbairn explained. "In the early 21st century, it means the success of aboriginal people because of the importance to the future of the province."[2]

1. THE INDIGENOUS IMPERATIVE

In 2015, the new president of the University of Saskatchewan, Peter Stoicheff, in an address to the university and assembled politicians, announced that he would make Indigenization his top priority for the university.[3] President Stoicheff described a vision in which the university and its colleges would act as the agent of the Aboriginal imperative: "I think of it this way: if not us as a university leading the way, then who; and if not now in the wake of the recent TRC recommendations, then when?" He stated that the university's "future rests on its great potential to inquire, to inform, to innovate and to indigenize." "None of the rest of it [the university mission of research, scholarly, and artistic work, teaching, and community outreach] matters at this point in our nation's history if we do not achieve this."[4] The university must be a leader in closing the various gaps between Aboriginal and non-Aboriginal people, he continued, calling this a "moral imperative."

I would suggest the same commitment applies to seminaries. The United Church of Canada has already adopted the UN Declaration as a framework for reconciliation between Indigenous Peoples and non-Indigenous Canadians.[5] The task is now realizing the commitment.

After twenty-five years of technical meetings, diplomatic negotiations, and promotional activities (such as the UN International Year and Decade), in which Indigenous Peoples' organizations played a visible and decisive role, the UN General Assembly adopted the Declaration.[6] It affirmed an emergent global consensus by signalling the nation-states' resolve to accept the UN's systemic obligations of decolonization and human rights, and it extended human rights and fundamental freedoms to Indigenous Peoples. The Declaration also rejected the existing grand narratives of empire and colonialism of the settler nations. But more important for the university and its colleges is the way in which the Declaration advanced a new narrative of how these poor, defeated, powerless peoples—the vulnerable bottom of global humanity—had developed, through their diplomacy, ethical allies in the international arena, with its complex structures and protocols.

For thousands of linguistically and culturally distinct societies, deep in history and abundant in knowledge, who had for the most part been denied and sidelined by the national and imperial projects of the last five centuries but who refused to disappear, the Declaration was a monumental achievement. How was it possible for such diverse peoples united in solidarity around the principles of the Declaration to transform the nation-state narrative of Indigenous deficiency into an assertion of their human rights and a reconciliation of Eurocentric and Indigenous legal traditions?

For seminaries, one challenge is comprehending and teaching this most intriguing and inspiring movement in Indigenous diplomacy and renaissance as an emerging grand narrative of liberation. It is a narrative equal on par with that of anti-slavery movements, the Black liberation struggle, the women's movement, the Velvet Revolution, to the undoing of apartheid. In each of these movements, the people had been stripped of external power by the nation-state but drew inspiration from the spirit of their inner consciousness and knowledge systems—an inherent dignity no one could take from them—in a disciplined and dedicated way. However, most seminaries have not embraced or celebrated this liberation narrative or sought to implement the Declaration.

The Declaration is notable in that it combines many elements of international law and policy that had not previously resided together in a single programmatic instrument: collective self-determination and territorial integrity; sustainable development; equality and non-discrimination; the progressive attainment of healthier, better fed, and better educated communities; custody and control of culturally significant properties; ownership of art and scientific knowledge; and more. In combination with the UNESCO World Declaration on Higher Education for the Twenty-First Century: Vision and Action;[7] the International Labour Organization's Indigenous and Tribal Peoples Convention;[8] UN Resolution 69/2, from the World Conference on Indigenous Peoples;[9] the Truth and Reconciliation Commission of Canada's Final Report;[10] and the Organization of American States' American Declaration on the Rights of Indigenous Peoples,[11] the UN Declaration has generated the Indigenous imperative in education.

In scope and vision, the Declaration is a global charter reflecting Indigenous people's status, rights, and responsibilities in the current international order.

1. THE INDIGENOUS IMPERATIVE

It addresses every concern raised by Indigenous people themselves, but it is couched in general language, leaving the details, as so often is the case in the international arena, to negotiations and agreements yet to be made within each member state. The Declaration affirms the UN human rights instruments ratified by Canada as well as the UNESCO World Declaration on Higher Education, and it shows how these rights must relate to Indigenous people's specific conditions. It presents to the governments, civil society, and universities and seminaries a *map of action* for respecting and protecting Indigenous people's inherent human rights, and in doing so, it fosters a new consciousness.

The Declaration itself refers to implementation by institutions, international organizations, and UN agencies, and there has been concrete action on moving the rights outlined in the Declaration into constitutional and national laws in the Americas. Moreover, the leverage and influence of NGOs, the corporate sector, and "partnerships" in generating the new norm or concept of shared value in the knowledge economy have emerged. Indeed, the restructuring of global power since 1990 all point to the potential for knowledge-based institutions such as universities, colleges, and seminaries to assert much-needed leadership. Each of these movements requires effective reconciliation and Indigenizing to assert and maintain the potentiality of the knowledge economy.

Harmonizing the Declaration with the Constitution of Canada

As a signatory of international human rights treaties, Canada has made a full commitment to the defence and implementation of human rights both at home and abroad.[12] Successive governments have affirmed Canada's commitment to international human rights standards and to the mechanisms that interpret and apply them. Canada's statements of support vis-à-vis the UN Declaration reaffirms its commitment to promoting and protecting the rights of Indigenous Peoples, without exceptions, at home and abroad. Canada has stressed that the constitutional rights framework, enriched by the principles of the Declaration, will continue to be the cornerstone of its efforts to promote and protect the rights of Aboriginal people.[13]

Canada has declared that it is now confident that the principles and rights expressed in the Declaration can be interpreted in a manner that is consistent with the constitutional framework protecting the Treaty Rights of Aboriginal Peoples laid out in section 35[14] and section 52(1) of the *Constitution Act, 1982*. The inherent human rights enshrined in the Declaration can be shielded against individual rights in sections 25,[15] 26,[16] and 27[17] of the *Charter of Rights and Freedoms*. This protection limits a person's freedom to choose or practise his or her religion, consciousness, belief, thought, and expression in section 2 of the *Charter*.[18] Together, sections 25–27 of the *Charter* constitutionally protects Aboriginal spirituality from an abrogation or derogation by individuals, seminaries, churches, and corporations, while section 35 limits governmental interference in the exercise of Aboriginal spirituality.

In fully endorsing the Declaration as part of the Constitution, Canada reaffirms its commitment to building a positive and productive relationship with First Nations, Inuit, and Métis Peoples based on our shared history, respect, and a desire to move forward together. It promises to harmonize federal laws with the shaping principles and rights expressed in the Declaration. At the broadest level, the Constitution and the Declaration created the imperative framework for reconciliation. Canadian universities, colleges, and seminaries are appropriate institutions to assist Aboriginal people in fully developing their Indigenous personality, talents, and mental and physical abilities, and in practising their self-determination without discrimination.

The Shaping Principle of Inherent Human Dignity

The principle of respect for inherent human dignity holds a prominent position in UN and intergovernmental instruments. It is the "shaping" or "overarching principle" of the law of human rights. Far from representing a style or orientation, the higher profile accorded to this principle is a genuine shift in substance that needs to be carefully understood and unpacked. It is opposed to most of the Judeo-Christian idea of original sin.

1. THE INDIGENOUS IMPERATIVE

International human rights law has explicitly enshrined the principle of inherent human dignity. The preamble of the Universal Declaration of Human Rights of 1948 declares that "the inherent dignity" of all members of the human family is "the foundation of freedom, justice and peace in the world." This is a principle that replaces the idea of sovereignty and the power of the culture of war. Inherent human dignity generates human rights and justice. The concept of inherent human dignity has been at the heart of the significant human rights instruments, beginning with the two international covenants on human rights adopted in 1966—the International Covenant on Civil and Political Rights and the International Covenant on Economic, Social and Cultural Rights—as well as most treaties banning torture, slavery, and inhuman and degrading treatments and discriminations of all sorts.[19]

The enactment of the Declaration signalled the nation-states' resolve to accept the UN's systemic obligations of decolonization and human rights, and it extended human rights and fundamental freedoms to Indigenous Peoples. The Declaration rejected the settler nations' grand narratives of empire and colonialism. In their place, the Declaration generated a reconciliation between Indigenous Peoples and the nation-state. But more important for the universities, colleges, and seminaries is the new narrative of how these poor, defeated, powerless peoples—the vulnerable bottom of global humanity—had developed ethical allies in the global arena, with its complex structures and protocols, through their peaceful voice and diplomacy. Indigenous people may say that we have overcome our national and global humiliation and belittlement. There is scarcely anything new that can wound our inherent dignity, pride, or degrade our heritages that we have not already experienced. We have suffered through constant and unabashed violations of our inherent dignity.

Although the principle of inherent human dignity is at the core of the major international human rights instruments, many Eurocentric academics are concerned that inherent human dignity is never explicitly defined in international law.[20] Instead of definitions, a careful analysis of human rights law and intergovernmental policy documents, and of the discussions that led to their adoption, shows that the recourse to human dignity reflects an ominous concern about the need to ensure respect for the inherent worth of every human being. The Declaration and the covenants of human rights provide valuable guidance for the comprehension of inherent dignity as a foundation of justice in the world: they declare the principles that (1) dignity is "inherent...to all members of the human family";[21] (2) that all human beings are "free and equal in dignity and rights";[22] and (3) that human rights "derive from the inherent dignity of the human person."[23]

Based on these three principles, the use of inherent human dignity as the source of human rights is an attempt to animate a more profound concept of inherent dignity. It is an attempt to ameliorate the legacy of the Eurocentric ideological constructs of cognitive imperialism,[24] cultural genocide,[25] or epistemicide.[26] To promote an external standard of minimum protection necessary for human dignity, international law and human rights covenants recognized the rights of all people to self-determination. By virtue of that right, they freely determine their political status and freely pursue their economic, social, and cultural development. Self-determination was the hard-won recognition and consensus that inherent dignity is at the heart of human society. The Supreme Court of Canada has affirmed that the existence of a people's right to self-determination is now a general principle of international law.[27]

The Eurocentric knowledge systems of law and higher education have a difficult time defining "inherent."[28] In Eurocentric legal systems, either God, monarchs, or the assemblies of the nation delegate rights to humans—humans do not derive these rights from the inherency of the human condition. The principle that human rights and fundamental freedoms are derived from inherent human dignity has important practical consequences. Since this dignity and the related human rights are not delegated by any authority but are pre-existing values that are inherent in every human being, they cannot be legitimately waived, diminished, or taken away by any humans, governments, courts, or societies.[29] It goes to the heart of humanness. Thus, nation-states and their education systems have a positive obligation to recognize, respect, and progressively affirm and realize inherent human dignity as the source of human rights and cognitive justice in its laws.

1. THE INDIGENOUS IMPERATIVE

The Indigenous imperative in education is based on the inherent human dignity and rights of every woman and man, who are the ultimate beneficiaries and stakeholders of humanity. Human dignity and rights are not only the starting point but also the measure of the success of education and the culture of peace.

Purpose and Intent of the UN Declaration

There is a global consensus behind the many articles in the Declaration that describe, articulate, and distribute inherent human rights. Self-determination is the manifestation of the inherent dignity of Indigenous Peoples laid out in the Declaration. The inherent dignity, as it is inseparable from the human condition, is the same for all, and it cannot be gained or lost and does not allow for any degree.

In its preamble, the Declaration "affirm[s] that Indigenous peoples are equal to all other peoples while recognizing the right of all peoples to be different, to consider themselves different, and to be recognized as such." Because of their equality with other *peoples*, Indigenous Peoples enjoy the right to various levels of collective decision-making. This includes "self-determination" and the right to "promote their [own] development in accordance with their aspirations and needs." It includes partnership with national authorities in the management of their territories and in the education and well-being of their children, and prior consultation on any matter that affects them.

The preamble of the Declaration speaks to the status of individuals. Individuals must be "free from discrimination of any kind, and be able to enjoy all of the human rights that international law secures to all persons." Also, they must enjoy those "rights inherent in their cultures and histories" as Indigenous people. Enjoyment of Traditional Territories and the exercise of inherent rights reserved explicitly by treaties are highlighted in the preamble. Hence the Declaration intends that every Indigenous person, as an individual, share freely in the traditional lands, spiritual traditions, cultural legacies, and treaty commitments of her ancestors. At the same time, article 5 of the Declaration aspires to a balance between cultural distinctiveness and equality of opportunity within national societies: "Indigenous peoples have the right to maintain and strengthen their distinct political, legal, economic, social and cultural institutions, while retaining their right to participate fully, if they so choose, in the political, economic, social and cultural life of the State."

It is also significant that the Declaration is an "operational" instrument. In its preamble and several substantive articles—namely, articles 37, 39, and 41—it directs the member states and the UN system itself to promote the Declaration and to transfer resources, including financial aid, to Indigenous Peoples to assist them in the realization of their rights. It also, in article 40, affirms the role of international institutions in enforcing treaties and agreements between states and Indigenous Peoples. Moreover, the UN system has generated the role of Indigenous Peoples themselves, through their representatives at the UN Permanent Forum on Indigenous Issues,[30] in consulting and collaborating with UN operational agencies and programs (as laid out in article 42 of the Declaration) such as UNESCO, the International Labour Organization, and the World Health Organization, among others, as well as those nations that ratified the Declaration.

The TRC's Calls to Action require a new order for the expression of ethical and honourable principles. Nêhiyaw (Cree) scholar Willie Ermine's[31] concept of "ethical space" is a guiding theoretical framework of the Declaration and for honourable reconciliations. It exists at the meeting point between the Eurocentric and Indigenous knowledge systems. Ermine viewed this convergence of knowledge systems or world views as an essential precondition for protracted engagement with ethical dialogues and honourable reconciliations.

The development of the concept of ethical space is particularly important because of the rifts existing between knowledge systems and the lack of comprehension on the part of the Eurocentric knowledge systems of Indigenous lifeways and spirituality. The ethical space represents one pathway to the unknown terrain of reconciliation and how the unknown future will be configured. Generating a trans-systemic ethical space is essential for respectful and collaborative reconciliation to unfold and exist among future generations. An honourable reconciliation represents a braiding of Indigenous knowledge and spirituality that must be respected and honoured in its own right through the creation of an innovative and trans-systemic ethical space.

Situated Responsibility

The Declaration presents a unique humanistic and holistic approach to education. Article 14 expressly secures the right of "Indigenous individuals, especially children...to all forms of education," including, "where possible," education "in their own culture and provided in their own language," even outside of their communities. Article 15 declares that Indigenous Peoples have "the right to the dignity and diversity of their cultures, traditions, histories and aspirations which shall be appropriately reflected in education." These articles attempt to end Indigenous students' sense that they have to hide their spiritual beliefs in Eurocentric education systems. It seeks to ensure that education and learning systems are inclusive and rights-based, and that they reflect the diversity of all learners by fostering the development of a balanced education system in which everyone has equal opportunity for meaningful, lifelong learning delivered through multiple formal and informal pathways.

The Declaration states that Indigenous people's rights as individuals include the freedom "not to be subjected to forced assimilation" (articles 8.1 and 8.2(d)). This right ends the fatalistic ideology of forced assimilation in compulsory education. The fundamental freedom of Indigenous students to retain their cultural identity must necessarily include the exercise, on an individual level, of the following rights ascribed by the Declaration to "peoples," especially the rights of Aboriginal Peoples recognized by the Constitution of Canada:

- To "practice and revitalize...cultural traditions and customs (article 11).
- Redress with respect to "religious and spiritual property taken without their free, prior and informed consent or in violation of their laws, traditions and customs" (article 11(2)).

- To "manifest, practice, develop and teach their spiritual and religious traditions customs, and ceremonies and maintaining their religious and cultural sites together with repatriation of their human remains" (article 12).
- To "revitalize, use, develop and transmit to future generations their histories, languages, oral traditions, philosophies, writing systems and literatures," and to "retain their own names" (article 13).
- To "maintain, control, protect and develop their cultural heritage, traditional knowledge and traditional cultural expressions," such as their "oral traditions, literatures, designs, sports and traditional games and visual and performing arts" (article 31).

These human rights ensure that the struggle for social justice includes the search for cognitive[32] or knowledge justice in pursuit of inclusive education and society.

These rights recognize and affirm the plurality of knowledge systems and the right of these distinct knowledge systems to coexist.[33] South African scholar and UNESCO education expert Catherine Odora Hoppers and Mi'kmaw scholar Marie Battiste propose the imperative of cognitive justice in educational systems. They argue that all knowledge systems are valid and should coexist in a dialogic relationship with each other. Cognitive justice implies the strengthening of the "voice" of the oppressed and marginalized Indigenous knowledge systems and the decolonizing of the Eurocentric education system. They argue that Indigenous knowledge system have to be included in the dialogues of knowledge in all education systems without having to fit in the structures and standards of Eurocentric (or Western) knowledge systems. When Indigenous knowledges are treated equally and legitimately in educational curricula, they can play their role in achieving a more dialogical and trans-systemic orientation that remains connected to the livelihoods and survival of all peoples.[34] Cognitive justice is a crucial concept both for decolonizing and Indigenizing higher education.[35] No global justice can exist without cognitive justice.[36] Importantly, "cognitive justice does not imply that all Western forms of knowledge are of no use and that all indigenous forms of science need privileging.... On the contrary, dialogic standards... must continue to judge between what is beneficial and what is evil in both western and indigenous knowledges."[37]

It is difficult to imagine how such cognitive justice can be realized fully in education *without* Indigenous families and students steadfastly asserting them, regardless of whether they live in a self-governing Aboriginal community, an urban neighbourhood, or at a campus or seminary. It is impossible to conceive of a program to "revitalize" and sustain Indigenous Peoples' knowledge systems, languages, cultures, spirituality, medicine, artistic works, and literatures without the co-operation of K–12 and post-secondary education systems.

Neither the Declaration nor cognitive justice holds that everyone must have the same education. Cognitive justice sees the fundamental right to education in Indigenous and European knowledge systems as a manifestation of inherent dignity, given the pivotal role of compulsory education in securing human capabilities and the meaning and exercise of constitutional rights. However, if education is to enable Indigenous Peoples, especially the young and those with different abilities, to develop their human potential, then the minimum offered must be ample enough; at the very least, that minimum amount must be delivered in a way that respects the inherent dignity of Indigenous people and their right to an equal opportunity to know who they are and to understand their Indigenous heritage. Education plays an integral role in maintaining the fabric of any society and in sustaining its members' spiritual sensibilities and cultural heritage.

Practising Trans-systemic Cognitive Justice

Canadian universities and seminaries, through Universities Canada, have affirmed their responsibilities to work toward reconciliation and to Indigenize their curriculum and activities.[38] They have realized that Aboriginal education is the great imperative of the twenty-first century, in Canada and beyond.[39] They understand that the constitutional rights of Aboriginal people explicitly recognize and affirm the importance of education in the development of Aboriginal children. Each year, more Aboriginal youth (and many adults with children of their own) voluntarily seek insight, clarification, honest appreciation, certification, and, ultimately, empowerment from Canadian universities, colleges, and seminaries. This is an integral part of their efforts to create a meaningful life that blends the best of Indigenous and Eurocentric knowledge.

Aboriginal students are most often confronted with disappointingly real and complex forms of discrimination against their knowledge systems, spiritual beliefs, and languages, and such discrimination contains some ominous signs for the future. Universities, colleges, and seminaries will inevitably guide the realization of the Declaration: training the people that will interpret and apply it; giving (or not giving) Indigenous communities the intellectual resources to better seize and use the opportunities the Declaration affords; creating space for Indigenous youth to re-vision their communities and futures in productive ways; and explaining it all to everyone else.

Historically, the well-motivated efforts to introduce Christian religion and theology among Indigenous Peoples have served as an aid to Eurocentric colonialism, exploitation, and destruction, rather than representing a tradition of love. Settlers did not question or transcend their knowledge system, which they viewed as derived from God. The Truth and Reconciliation Commission introduced the term "spiritual violence" as a key component of the Indian residential school system, which the commission defined as occurring when "a person's spiritual or religious tradition, beliefs, or practices are demeaned or belittled."[40] The commission defines "reconciliation" as an ongoing process of revitalizing Indigenous spirituality, cultures, languages, laws, and governance systems in modern and dynamic contexts.

The curriculum of theological seminaries that educate students in theology, generally preparing them for ordination as clergy, for a career in academia, or for ministry should recognize that reconciliation requires different levels of complexity and commitments. In dealing with an Indigenous person, the seminaries need to determine what their spiritual and cultural commitments are and what the precise circumstances of the Indigenous person's complaint are, to take the measure of the burden that is or is not imposed. The concept of spiritual accommodation means that seminaries need to contain exceptions for people whose conscientious commitments it burdens. It therefore directs the administrators or faculty of a seminary to understand the nature of the Indigenous person's spiritual or cultural struggle, asking what that person can do and be, rather than imposing an exceptionless rule on everyone.

Reconciliation is built on a trust that begins asymmetrically. Reconciliation has to be identified, named, and acknowledged; the symmetrical nature of trust must be earned by actions. The curriculum of universities, colleges, and seminaries requires a comprehension that the Declaration clarified and affirmed existing Aboriginal and Treaty Rights. It also affirmed other human rights obligations in international instruments that Canada signed or endorsed pertaining to Aboriginal Peoples in Canada. Together, these human rights obligations provide a global consensus around an agenda of short-, medium- and long-term initiatives.

Reconciliation requires a commitment from theological seminaries to engage in some critical analysis of the historical and systemic persecution of Indigenous spirituality, and to consider the appropriateness of their educational goals and objectives. This initiative should be undertaken with humility and grace. The TRC stated that spiritual violence occurs in many situations: when a person is not permitted to follow her or his preferred spiritual or religious tradition; when a different spiritual or religious path or practice is forced on a person; when a person's spiritual or religious tradition, beliefs, or practices are demeaned or belittled; or when a person is made to feel shame for practising his or her traditional or family beliefs).[41] Any activities that create hatred, systematic discrimination, forced assimilation, or marginalization vis-à-vis Indigenous Peoples shall be avoided.

Seminaries should collaborate with Indigenous people in an evaluation of their ethos and their efforts at reform, and to avoid repeating the failures of the past. It is crucial that seminaries understand how and why they perverted Christian doctrine to justify their actions. Indigenous leadership is a critical component of this evaluation, and it must play an active role in generating symmetrical reconciliation. Seminaries should affirm Indigenous spirituality based on the biosphere in its own right. They should also recognize individuals' freedom to choose spiritual and religious coexistence, a freedom that must be respected if we are to generate a full and robust reconciliation.

The Declaration understood that Indigenous people's rights are fragile in most educational institutions, with their hegemonic Eurocentrism. They are in constant danger of being co-opted and obliterated by academic freedoms intent on preserving the dominance of Eurocentric knowledge systems. The Declaration recognizes the ameliorative and enriched concept of the Aboriginal people's right to establish and control their educational institutions by "providing education in their languages [and] culturally distinct pedagogies" alongside their right to access educational institutions. This right imagines complementary but related institutions promoting Aboriginal cultural and spiritual literacy, and the ability to participate fully in the best of their traditions alongside the Christian tradition. As the crucial first step, the churches should create and fund Indigenous centres devoted to working out the higher-order principles of respecting Indigenous spirituality within the churches. The development of these necessary principles frequently means hard and difficult translations, where the harmonizing of relevant factors must necessarily accompany a divergent sense of traditions and contexts. The development of these principles must also begin with an ethical space, a kind of experienced articulation and imagination of perspectives. The principles have to be derived from a confrontation of knowledge systems in a real and complex situation within which people can try to function as equals. In that way, the principles can be closely associated with ideas of context-sensitive reasoning embedded in spiritual traditions.

One significant but underdeveloped model that exists is the Sandy-Saulteaux Spiritual Centre. Although the centre is different from most seminaries and unequal in terms of tangible and intangible facilities, but it has nonetheless generated a trans-systemic combined capability when it comes to the development of its members spiritual lives. Its graduates and students are the vanguard of reconciliation and the future leaders of reconciliation activities. The centre comprehends Aboriginal people's situations in a way that brings obstacles to full reconciliation to light and exhibits a commitment to the precise and spiritually attuned teaching of reconciliation. The centre has demonstrated that seminaries that seem to treat Aboriginal and non-Aboriginal students in a similar way did not in fact promote substantively equal opportunities for personal development, but instead masked the historical perpetuation of white supremacy and the stigmas with which being Aboriginal people are too often associated.

These centres should be organized and managed by Aboriginal people, and they should be paired with seminaries that serve Aboriginal persons wherever they may live. Articles 7 and 8 of the Declaration express the basic principles applicable to these Indigenous spiritual centres and related seminaries. These principles aim to defend the integrity of Indigenous societies and their cultures in broad terms. The Declaration must be read alongside constitutional rights to comprehend and implement a larger constitutional framework. This symbiotic approach requires a trans-systemic understanding of Indigenous knowledge systems and an understanding of how these can be braided together with Eurocentric forms of knowledge in seminaries.[42]

The Supreme Court of Canada has stated that the purpose of affirming the Treaty Rights of Aboriginal people in section 35 of the *Charter* is a constitutional commitment to recognize, value, and to protect traditions, customs, and practices that were historically important features of these distinctive communities and that persist in the present day as integral elements of their ongoing and shared culture.[43] The Supreme Court in *Côté* has stated that a constitutional imperative exists, and that for every constitutional right of Aboriginal people, there is a corresponding constitutional duty to teach these rights.[44] The court decisions generated the framework of reconciliation with seminaries.

Another very important role for seminaries, as outlined in the Declaration, is helping Aboriginal people develop their own educational institutions within or in association with a seminary. Measures that the seminaries can take to combine their development with the development of Aboriginal educational institutions include the following:

- Establishing a College of Elders to guide the seminaries' reconciliation programs.
- Facilitating Aboriginal people's establishment of intellectual, cultural, and residential hubs within seminary campuses, and financing such hubs on a comparable level to other programs.[45]
- Strengthening the quality of the seminary training of Aboriginal professionals by incorporating Aboriginal languages and culturally distinct spiritual pedagogies.
- Increasing the opportunities for Aboriginal persons to acquire training and certification as teachers.
- Co-operating with other universities, colleges, seminaries, and Aboriginal educational institutions nationally—and if necessary, internationally[46]—to ensure the certification of courses in transfers and admissions.
- Co-operating with other universities, colleges, seminaries, and Aboriginal educational institutions to ensure that every Aboriginal language in Canada is taught and used on at least one campus to which Aboriginal youth have free access.
- Ensuring that Aboriginal youth have genuinely equal opportunity to access university degree programs, taking into account their linguistic and cultural characteristics, as well as their financial circumstances.
- Establishing boards, talking circles, and other advisory processes to ensure that Aboriginal students, staff, and communities guide the development of these activities.
- Contributing faculty and technical and financial assistance to Aboriginal educational institutions within Aboriginal communities, including reserves as well as urban areas and other settings within an Aboriginal or treaty territory in which Aboriginal parents organize for the education of their children.

1. THE INDIGENOUS IMPERATIVE

Core Responsibilities

The Declaration, like constitutional law, contemplates Aboriginal cultures as dynamic and changing, and it refers to the rights to "revitalize" and "develop" spiritual and cultural manifestations as well as the rights to protect, preserve, or maintain them. For the seminaries, this implies both negative and positive duties in horizontal collaborations with Aboriginal Peoples. The first duty is to generate an analytical framework for conserving and maintaining the spiritual and cultural manifestations in their possession, in consultation with Indigenous Peoples. The second duty is to afford access for Indigenous people to learn, enjoy, transmit, and add to this framework the parts of their spiritual and cultural legacies that may remain in the seminaries as solidaristic understandings.

Seminaries' core responsibility is to create an honourable reconciliation that respects constitutionally protected Aboriginal knowledge, traditions, spirituality, and rights in all their forms. These constitutional protections include various UN declarations and related documents. The honour of the Crown is a part of the constitutional supremacy of Aboriginal and Treaty Rights in Canada, and this doctrine applies to all legislative acts and the governance system that deals with Aboriginal Peoples.

Among the many specific rights and duties enumerated in the Declaration are the access-to-education principle outlined in article 14, which animates article 3(d) of the UNESCO World Declaration on Higher Education,[47] and the fair-representation-in-education principle articulated in article 15, which go hand in hand with various articles prohibiting discrimination of any kind against Indigenous persons. These principles govern some of the most basic functions of the seminaries: the admission of students, the hiring and promotion of faculty, the teaching and respectful inclusion of Aboriginal knowledge and languages in the curriculum.

The Declaration underscores the need for seminaries to condemn any use of their facilities in which Aboriginal people are maligned as intellectually inferior or morally irresponsible, or in which others advocate depriving Aboriginal communities of their rights or lands on account of their origins or cultures.

This requires careful examination of admissions and hiring procedures for possible sources of discrimination against Aboriginal students and scholars, and class offerings and curricula that take into account Aboriginal languages, cultural content, and the fair representation of Aboriginal Peoples. These are core responsibilities of the seminaries since it is impossible to run a post-secondary institution without encountering and resolving these issues. The obvious application of the Declaration and article 15(2) of the *Charter* to seminaries is the protection of Aboriginal students and faculty, and their communities, from any racist or discriminatory propaganda denying the application of their rights.

In any educational institution, a balance must be struck between assuring free expression and a free exchange of ideas, and protecting students from cruel, malicious, bullying, or threatening speech that intimidates, alienates, or marginalizes them or deprives them of the opportunity to enjoy fully the knowledge (and the certification) that academic studies afford. In particular, seminaries typically guard against "hate speech" directed against any group of students, inside or outside the classroom, including any teaching that singles out particular groups of students for ridicule, blame, or dehumanization.

Educational and public-information institutions must not only curb discriminatory speech, they must also help combat discrimination by acknowledging the "dignity and diversity of [Indigenous] cultures, traditions, histories and aspirations" in their administrations, classrooms, and events (as per article 15 of the Declaration). This duty necessarily implies consultation with a wide range of Aboriginal Elders and scholars, as well as the incorporation of Aboriginal people in all aspects of an institution's intellectual life—and not only as students, but also as faculty and staff, performers, artists, guest speakers and residents, program advisers, and members of governing bodies. This prospective spirit can be called spiritual emergence.

Article 8 of the Declaration and article 15(2) of the *Charter* refers to effective mechanisms of redress for violations, which casts the application of this principle into the past as well. Although a university or seminary may not condone or benefit from the dispossession or forced assimilation of Aboriginal people today, the question remains: Did it participate in, or benefit from, such actions

— 1. THE INDIGENOUS IMPERATIVE —

in the past? Did it train teachers and administrators for residential schools, for instance? Did it receive legacy gifts that arose from the extraction of natural resources on unpurchased Aboriginal lands? Many Canadian seminaries have benefited at least indirectly from dispossession, through their benefactors or government subsidies. And many of them contributed to forced assimilation by training the agents of assimilation (from Indian agents to residential school staff), by conducting research that facilitated or justified dispossession and assimilation, and by justifying government policies of dispossession and assimilation in textbooks and teaching.

It is not morally or legally sufficient for the seminaries merely to defer to government commissions or legislation to redress such grievances. What most advances the aims of the Declaration is for seminaries to remedy the harm of residential schools to Aboriginal people by welcoming them and their spirituality into their day-to-day activities. They can invest more resources in programs that help Aboriginal students achieve genuinely equal opportunity in education. They can provide tuition waivers to children of residential school survivors. And they can celebrate and strengthen Canada's Aboriginal foundations by fostering Aboriginal educational, artistic, and scientific institutions both on campus and off. Indeed, seminaries should be mindful of the essential role that they can play in improving the broad socio-economic conditions of Aboriginal people in contrast to other Canadians (as outlined in articles 20-4 of the Declaration). They have a significant role in unpacking the Eurocentric taxonomies, classifications, and other social constructions that generated privilege for some and disadvantages for Aboriginal people and others.

The seminaries must uplift the Aboriginal knowledge systems and spirituality associated with the land on which their campuses are located, as well as in the various regions where Aboriginal spirituality may differ in critical dimensions despite their shared elements of "Indigenousness."[48] Collapsing the diversity of Aboriginal cultures into generalizations can quickly become another form of stereotyping.

Similarly, the seminaries engage in research, build museums, and amass collections of ethnographic materials (objects and data as well as recordings, art, and literature). The Declaration recognizes that Aboriginal people have the right to control the disposition of all of the past, present, and future manifestations of their cultures—material, scientific, or artistic. These manifestations include "archaeological and historical sites, artifacts, designs, ceremonies, technologies and visual and performing arts and literature" (article 11); "their histories, languages, oral traditions, philosophies, writing systems and literatures [and] the names of persons and places" (article 13); "traditional medicines and...vital medicinal plants, animals and minerals" (article 24); and "manifestations of their sciences, technologies and cultures, including human and genetic resources, seeds, medicines, knowledge of the properties of fauna and flora, oral traditions, literatures, designs, sports and traditional games and visual and performing arts" (article 31).

The Declaration refers to the access and use of spiritual sites and mechanisms for the repatriation of culturally significant objects and human remains (article 12). The seminaries must regard the collections and data associated with Aboriginal cultures—indeed, with any Indigenous culture worldwide—at the very least as subject to consultation with the group concerned over disposition, use, and interpretation (article 18).

The seminaries' ongoing research programs are also impacted by the Declaration—albeit not explicitly. For while the Declaration does not speak to the conduct of research activities as such, a right to control research on any manifestation of Indigenous cultures is implied in the individual and collective rights to protect and enjoy those manifestations (articles 11, 12, 13, 24, and 31). Likewise, a right to privacy for communities is implied in their rights to "own, use, develop and control" their territories (article 26), and to govern their "internal and local affairs" (article 4) and their members under their own laws (articles 33–5). This right is also implied in Indigenous communities' right to control any use of their lands, resources, or Traditional Knowledge (articles 21–31). These norms should be respected by institutional review boards and incorporated into the acquisition policies of museums and other university depositories of materials and data (article 31).[49]

A third layer of responsibilities relates to the role that seminaries play as investors, employers, land developers, and commercial enterprises.

Discrimination based on Aboriginality is prohibited, particularly in the matter of employment and labour standards (article 17). Where seminaries operate as owners, builders, or developers of real estate—or as investors or beneficiaries of energy or resource extraction—they may also be expected to abide by the provisions of the Declaration that prohibit any activities on the traditional lands of Aboriginal Peoples without free and informed consent (articles 26, 29, 32). This norm is also retroactive, requiring redress for involuntary loss of lands and resources in the past (article 28), which could, for example, include the campus of a seminary, its research stations, or lands that form a part of its endowment. Although in Canada the duty of redress for land claims has rested with the government, it is not so limited in the Declaration, which suggests that the beneficiaries of past takings at least share the responsibility for making remedies.

In addition to its impact on seminaries' core functions, the Declaration also informs other responsibilities and obligations, such as non-discrimination and instruction in Aboriginal knowledge systems and languages. Many of these obligations assume a structural, programmatic, or remedial form, regardless of whether a seminary has achieved a fair representation of Aboriginal Peoples in education, public information, and the media.

A Summary Outline of Trans-systemic Reconciliations

Principles Applicable to Aboriginal Students' Well-Being

- A duty to contribute to the livelihoods of Indigenous students, so that they can pursue their studies freely, to the extent of their visions and abilities.
- A commitment to allocate reasonable space and resources on campus for Indigenous students to manifest, practise, develop, share, and teach their spiritual, religious, and cultural traditions, as they deem appropriate.

Principles Applicable to Teaching and Speech about Aboriginal Peoples

- A duty to secure classrooms, and the campus as a whole, against hate speech directed at Indigenous students and their communities.
- An obligation to review cultural elements such as artifacts, designs, ceremonies, music, art, literature, customs, and spiritual knowledge with appropriate experts and custodians within the Aboriginal communities concerned, before sharing and interpreting them in classroom, exhibits, or publications.
- A duty to respect, in teaching and other academic activities, the right of all Indigenous Peoples to privacy in matters of religion, culture, art, and belief.

Principles Applicable to Research Activities with Aboriginal Peoples

- A duty to help Aboriginal communities improve their health and livelihoods through co-operative research and programs that strengthen Aboriginal studies and educational institutions.
- An obligation to give priority to the documentation and survival of Indigenous languages in co-operation with native speakers, their communities, and schools.
- A commitment to revisit, review, and, where called for, revise the interpretation, storage, and display of cultural materials in consultation with the families and communities from which these materials originated.
- A duty to return culturally important materials to the families and communities from which they originated, under agreements that will ensure the future enjoyment of these materials by the relevant Indigenous Peoples, and a greater appreciation and respect for them within Canadian society as a whole.
- A duty to share the proceeds of discoveries (including patents, registered designs, and plant varieties) and copyrighted materials

with Aboriginal communities whose cultural knowledge, arts, and technologies contributed to those discoveries and publications.

Principles Applicable to Investments, Donations, and Lands

- A responsibility to recognize, honour, and uplift the Aboriginal Peoples upon whose Traditional Territories the campus is located.
- An obligation to review university investments and revenue periodically to ensure that no income arises from lands or resources acquired involuntarily from Indigenous Peoples.
- A commitment to contribute to reparations for past dispossessions, lost resources, and forcible assimilation, to the extent that the seminary participated in or benefited historically from these actions.

Conclusion

To ethically address the global shift in consciousness reflected in the UN Declaration requires a cognitive unravelling of the legacy of Eurocentric colonialism and racism and a shift away from Eurocentric religion, philosophy, humanity, and law and toward trans-systemic reconciliations. Laws can move human consciousness and sensibilities in the direction of justice, but to make that shift, our spirits must be engaged. Indigenous people have hoped that revealing these harmful legacies would lead to good-faith efforts to reach a trans-systemic reconciliation, one that is open to Indigenous systems of knowledge and spirituality, as well as the concept of inherent dignity. As usual, good-faith reconciliations present complicated cognitive challenges. Success or failure cannot be measured on one axis alone; reconciliation requires contingent, dynamic, and ongoing dialogue. To this end, I can only agree with Pierre Teilhard de Chardin when he said that "The day will come when, after mastering the ether, wind, the tides and gravitation, we shall harness for God the energies of love. And, on that day, for a second time in the history of the world, we will have discovered fire."[50]

Notes

Guidance was provided by *ababinilli*, *ma'heo'o*, and *niskam*, although I assume full responsibility for interpretation. Before any other sounds are expressed, I silently extend blessings to the biosphere. These blessings come before all words. Because the biosphere is, life exists, therefore we are. I have discussed the negotiation and meaning of the UN Declaration in my book *Indigenous Diplomacy and the Rights of Peoples: Achieving UN Recognition* (Saskatoon: Purich Publishing, 2008).

1. UN General Assembly, Resolution 61/295, United Nations Declaration on the Rights of Indigenous Peoples, A/RES/61/295 (October 2, 2007), https://undocs.org/A/RES/61/295.
2. Ishmael Daro, "University Looks to Boost Reputation over Next Four Years: Third Integrated Plan Emphasizes Research, Aboriginal Engagement," *The Sheaf*, February 16, 2012, https://thesheaf.com/2012/02/16/university-looks-to-boost-reputation-over-next-four-years-third-integrated-plan-emphasizes-research-aboriginal-engagement/.
3. "President's Address to University," *On Campus News*, 28 August 2015, https://news.usask.ca/on-campus-news/2015-08-28.pdf.
4. Ibid.
5. See appendix A in this volume, "An Ecumenical Statement on the *United Nations Declaration on the Rights of Indigenous Peoples*"; United Church of Canada, "United Church Responds to Calls to Actions on the UN Declaration," March 31, 2016, https://united-church.ca/sites/default/files/undrip-united-church-statement.pdf; and appendix B in this volume, "Statement on UN Declaration on the Rights of Indigenous Peoples as the Framework for Reconciliation."
6. UN General Assembly, Resolution 61/295.
7. UNESCO, World Declaration on Higher Education for the Twenty-First Century: Vision and Action, ED.98/CONF.202/3 (October 9, 1998), https://unesdoc.unesco.org/ark:/48223/pf0000113878.
8. International Labour Organization, Convention 169, Indigenous and Tribal Peoples Convention, C169 (June 27, 1989), https://www.ilo.org/dyn/normlex/en/f?p=NORMLEXPUB:12100:0::NO::P12100_INSTRUMENT_ID:312314.
9. UN General Assembly, Resolution 69/2, Outcome document of the high-level plenary meeting of the General Assembly known as the World Conference on Indigenous Peoples, A/RES/69/2 (September 25, 2014), https://undocs.org/en/A/RES/69/2.
10. See *Final Report of the Truth and Reconciliation Commission of Canada*, 6 vols. (Montreal and Kingston: McGill-Queen's University Press, 2015).
11. OAS General Assembly, Resolution 2888, American Declaration on the Rights of Indigenous Peoples, AG/RES. 2888 (XLVI-O/16) (June 15, 2016), http://www.oas.org/en/sla/docs/AG07239E03.pdf.
12. Government of Canada, "Implementing the United Nations Declaration on the Rights of Indigenous Peoples in Canada," last modified December 16, 2020, https://www.aadnc-

aandc.gc.ca/eng/1309374407406/1309374458958; Department of Justice, "Principles Respecting the Government of Canada's Relationship with Indigenous Peoples," last modified February 14, 2018, http://www.justice.gc.ca/eng/csj-sjc/principles-principes.html.

13 Government of Canada, "Implementing the United Nations Declaration"; Department of Justice, "Principles."

14 Most of the Georgian treaties with the Mi'kmaw nation provide specifically for freedom of religion for Mi'kmaw families, although the king retained authority to provide for the missionaries, as outlined in the Elikawake Treaty of 1726. Moreover, in the negotiations of the Victorian Treaty 8, the royal commissioners reported that the Wood Cree, the Beaver, and the Chipewyan negotiators "seemed desirous of securing educational advantages for their children, but stipulated that in the matter of schools there should be no interference with their religious beliefs." Extracts from the Commissioners' Report are reproduced in *Benoit v Canada*, 2003 FCA 1 at para 8, 228 DLR (4th), 242 FTR 159.

15 Section 25 of the *Charter* reads: "The guarantee in this Charter of certain rights and freedoms shall not be construed so as to abrogate or derogate from any aboriginal, treaty or other rights or freedoms that pertain to the aboriginal peoples of Canada including (a) any rights or freedoms that have been recognized by the Royal Proclamation of October 7, 1763; and (b) any rights or freedoms that now exist by way of land claims agreements or may be so acquired."

16 Section 26 of the *Charter* reads: "The guarantee in this Charter of certain rights and freedoms shall not be construed as denying the existence of any other rights or freedoms that exist in Canada."

17 Section 27 of the *Charter* reads: "This Charter shall be interpreted in a manner consistent with the preservation and enhancement of the multicultural heritage of Canadians."

18 Section 2 of the *Charter* reads: "Everyone has the following fundamental freedoms: (a) freedom of conscience and religion; (b) freedom of thought, belief, opinion and expression, including freedom of the press and other media of communication."

19 Consequently, inherent dignity was enacted in the major UN conventions—namely, the UN Convention on the Rights of Child (1989), the International Convention on the Protection of the Rights of All Migrant Workers and Members of Their Families (1990), and the International Convention for the Protection of All Persons from Enforced Disappearance and the Convention on the Rights of Persons with Disabilities (both 2007). The second paragraph of the preamble to the Vienna Declaration and Programme of Action (1993) affirms that "all human rights derive from the dignity and worth inherent in the human person and that the human person is the central subject of human rights and fundamental freedoms, and consequently should be the principal beneficiary and should participate actively in the realization of these rights and freedoms." After the Vienna Declaration, human dignity was constitutionally protected in many national constitutions.

20 The undefined nature of the principle is similar to all basic moral and legal principles (justice, freedom, autonomy, etc.), which usually are not defined by law. The old Roman dictum *omnis definitio in iure periculosa est* (every definition in law is perilous) applies to the principle of inherent human dignity. Defining of inherent human dignity is a perilous

act because of the impossibility of finding a precise definition of such fundamental concepts that satisfy everyone, especially in trans-systemic knowledge systems. It is also precarious because lawmakers are well aware that rigid definitions may in some cases lead to unsolvable difficulties in the implementation of legal norms.

21 This comes from the preamble of the Universal Declaration, specifically the first and fifth paragraphs (my emphasis): "Whereas *recognition of the inherent dignity* and of the equal and inalienable rights of all members of the human family is the foundation of freedom, justice and peace in the world," and "Whereas the peoples of the United Nations have in the Charter reaffirmed their faith in fundamental human rights, *in the dignity and worth of the human person* and in *the equal rights of men and women and have determined to promote social progress and better standards of life in larger freedom*." See UN General Assembly, Resolution 217 A(III), Universal Declaration of Human Rights, A/RES/217 (December 10, 1948), https://undocs.org/A/RES/217(III).

22 As laid out in article 1 of the Universal Declaration of Human Rights. The Supreme Court of Canada has declared that the promotion of inherent human dignity is one of the lodestars for the protection of all of the rights guaranteed by the *Canadian Charter of Rights and Freedoms*. The *Charter* "guarantees the rights and freedoms set out in it subject only to such reasonable limits prescribed by law as can be demonstrably justified in a free and democratic society" (article 1). Additionally, the guarantee in this *Charter* of individual "rights and freedoms shall not be construed to abrogate or derogate from any aboriginal, treaty or other rights or freedoms that pertain to the aboriginal peoples of Canada" (article 25). Chief Justice Dickson said in *R v Oakes*, [1986] 1 SCR 103 at 136: "The Court must be guided by the values and principles essential to a free and democratic society which I believe embody, to name but a few, respect for the inherent dignity of the human person..."

23 From the preambles of the International Covenant on Civil and Political Rights and the International Covenant on Economic, Social and Cultural Rights.

24 Marie Battiste, *Decolonizing Education: Nourishing the Learning Spirit* (Saskatoon: Purich Publishing, 2013).

25 See Truth and Reconciliation Commission of Canada, *Honouring the Truth, Reconciling for the Future: Summary of the Final Report of the Truth and Reconciliation Commission of Canada* (Winnipeg: Truth and Reconciliation Commission of Canada), 1, 57, 134.

26 See Boaventura de Sousa Santos, *Epistemologies of the South: Justice against Epistemicide* (Boulder, CO: Paradigm, 2014).

27 *Reference Re Secession of Quebec*, [1998] 2 SCR 21 at para 114.

28 The Eurocentric dictionaries usually define "inherent" as a "permanent or characteristic attribute of something." Indeed, the concept of inherent human dignity has been denied in the past and present and may be open to abuse and misinterpretation in the future.

29 Oscar Schachter, "Human Dignity as a Normative Concept," *American Journal of International Law*, no. 77 (1983): 853; Samuel Moyn, *The Last Utopia: Human Rights in History* (Cambridge, MA: Harvard University Press, 2012).

30 An advisory council with sixteen voting members (half of them Indigenous persons) established by Resolution 2000/22 of the United Nations Economic and Social Council before the adoption of the Declaration; it has met annually since 2002.

31 Willie Ermine, "The Ethical Space of Engagement," *Indigenous Law Journal* 6, no. 1 (2007): 193.

32 In *Epistemologies of the South*, Santos writes that "social injustice is based on cognitive injustice" (240), therefore, "there is no global social justice without global cognitive justice" (13).

33 Indigenous scholars and activists have used this concept in the debates over the Draft Declaration on the Rights of Indigenous People in the UN Working Group on Indigenous Populations. The concept was applied to education by Catherine A. Odora Hoppers, "Education, Culture, and Society in a Globalising World: Implications for Comparative and International Education," *Compare: A Journal of Comparative and International Education* 39, no. 5 (2009): 601–14. See also Battiste, *Decolonizing Education*, and Truija Veintie, "Coloniality and Cognitive Justice: Reinterpreting Formal Education for the People in Ecuador," *International Journal of Multicultural Education* 15, no. 3 (2013): 45. In science, Indian scholar Shiv Visvanathan used the concept for a democracy of knowledge in *A Carnival of Science: Essays on Science, Technology and Development* (Delhi: Oxford University Press, 1997). Boaventura de Sousa Santos refers to the epistemic dominance of Eurocentrism as "abyssal thinking" and the need for recognition of epistemic diversity and cognitive justice; see *Cognitive Justice in a Global World: Prudent Knowledges for a Decent Life* (Lanham, MD: Lexington, 2007). The authors calling for cognitive justice can be found in a growing variety of fields, such as ethnobiology, technology and database design, and in information and communication technology for development (ICT4D).

34 Professor Visvanathan writes that cognitive justice recognizes the right of different forms of knowledge to coexist, but he adds that this plurality needs to go beyond tolerance or liberalism to an active recognition of the need for diversity. Visvanathan demands recognition of knowledges, not only as methods but as ways of life. "[K]nowledge is embedded in an ecology of knowledges in which each knowledge has its place, its claim to a cosmology, its sense as a form of life. In this sense, knowledge is not something to be abstracted from a culture as a life form; it is connected to livelihood, a life cycle, a lifestyle; it determines life chances." See Shiv Visvanathan, "The Search for Cognitive Justice" accessed February 8, 2021, http://www.india-seminar.com/2009/597/597_shiv_visvanathan.htm.

35 Marie Battiste, Lynne Bell, and L.M. Findlay, "Decolonizing Education in Canadian Universities: An Interdisciplinary, International, Indigenous Research Project," *Canadian Journal of Native Education* 62, no. 2 (2002): 82–95; Linda Tuhiwai Smith, *Decolonizing Methodologies: Research and Indigenous Peoples* (London: Zed Books, 1999).

36 As Santos writes in *Epistemologies of the South*, "there is no global social justice without global cognitive justice" (13).

37 Visvanathan, "The Search for Cognitive Justice."

38 See Universities Canada, "Universities Canada Principles on Indigenous Education," June 29, 2015, http://www.univcan.ca/media-room/media-releases/universities-canada-principles-on-indigenous-education/.

39 "Forging New Relationships: The Foundational Document on Aboriginal Initiatives at the University of Saskatchewan," University of Saskatchewan Integrated Planning

(October 2003), https://www.usask.ca/ipa/documents/planning/aboriginal_foundationaldoc_2003.pdf.

40   Truth and Reconciliation Commission of Canada, *Final Report*, 6:96–8.
41   Ibid., 96.
42   In 1987, the national leaders of nine denominations and major church organizations issued *A New Covenant: Towards the Constitutional Recognition and Protection of Aboriginal Self-Government in Canada: A Pastoral Statement by the Leaders of the Christian Churches on Aboriginal Rights and the Canadian Constitution*, which is available at http://home.istar.ca/~arc/english/new_cov_e.html. In a ceremony in Winnipeg in 2007, the churches marked the twentieth anniversary of the *New Covenant* by renewing and reaffirming their 1987 commitment.
43   *R v Van der Peet*, [1996] 2 SCR 507 at para 31; *R v Powley*, [2003] 2 SCR 207 at paras 13, 17, 33.
44   *R v Côté*, [1996] 3 SCR 139 at para 56: "to ensure the continuity of aboriginal practices, customs and tradition, a substantive aboriginal right will normally include the incidental right to teach such a practice, custom and tradition to a younger generation." This would also apply to the various treaty rights to education.
45   Article 16 of the Declaration (on mass media) suggests that universities should give particular attention to sponsoring newspapers, journals, radio stations, websites, and other media programs that target Aboriginal audiences, especially in Aboriginal languages.
46   Article 36 of the Declaration directs states to facilitate international contacts of this nature.
47   Article 3(d) provides that "Access to higher education for members of some special target groups, such as indigenous peoples, cultural and linguistic minorities, disadvantaged groups, peoples living under occupation and those who suffer from disabilities, must be actively facilitated, since these groups as collectivities and as individuals may have both experience and talent that can be of great value for the development of societies and nations. Special material help and educational solutions can help overcome the obstacles that these groups face, both in accessing and in continuing higher education."
48   Articles 44 and 46 of the Declaration and section 35(4) of the *Constitution Act, 1982* prohibit gender bias in the enjoyment of Aboriginal rights; however, the traditional status of women is a sensitive issue, and frequently a contested one in some Aboriginal cultures. Fair representation requires acknowledging this reality and its historical roots while recognizing the conflict with international and national norms.
49   See Siegfried Wiessner and Marie Battiste, "The 2000 Revision of the United Nations Draft Principles and Guidelines on the Protection of the Heritage of Indigenous People," *St. Thomas Law Review* 13, no. 1 (2000–1): 383; Marie Battiste and James (Sa'ke'j) Youngblood Henderson, *Protecting Indigenous Knowledge and Heritage: A Global Challenge* (Saskatoon: Purich Publishing, 2000).
50   Pierre Teilhard de Chardin, *Toward the Future*, trans. and ed. René Hague (New York: Harcourt Brace Jovanovich, 1975), 84–5.

CHAPTER 2

WHAT TO DO WITH ALL THESE CANAANITES?
A Settler-Canadian Reading of Biblical Conquest Stories

by

CHRISTINE MITCHELL

Importance of the Issue

On February 9, 2018, a white farmer was acquitted in Saskatchewan of the murder of a young Indigenous man on August 25, 2016. Regardless of the fact that the defence's version of events was physically impossible—they claimed the farmer's gun accidentally misfired as he struggled to remove the keys from the ignition of the young man's car—the all-white jury chose to acquit on the charge of second-degree murder and the lesser but still serious charge of manslaughter. Importantly, the farmer's lawyers did not argue self-defence: they did not claim that the young Indigenous man had threatened the white farmer. Instead, the defence argued that it was an accident; that the farmer's gun malfunctioned. The gun, they claimed, was being used only to try to frighten the young man and his friends, not to harm them. The mere presence on the farm of Indigenous individuals had led the farmer to retrieve that handgun—a weapon with no purpose other than to harm human beings. According to the farmer's own testimony, the mere presence of Indigenous individuals signalled danger to him; their presence had to be eliminated by a threat of violence. Although we cannot know for certain the reasoning that led the jury to acquit, they must have accepted the premise that brandishing a handgun at Indigenous individuals is an appropriate response to the presence of those individuals in a white farmer's yard.[1]

What does this anecdote have to do with the Bible or with biblical conquest narratives? For me, the parallels are clear: there are indigenous folks and settler-invader folks, there is land, and from the settlers there is clear anxiety over what to do with all the leftover Indigenous folks. Those leftover folks are the ones who did not have the good manners to either vacate or die. Instead, they remain a constant reminder that the conquest is incomplete and contested. So, what to do with all these Canaanites?

Context as a Reader

A number of biblical books—primarily Deuteronomy, Joshua, and Judges—attempt to work through this very serious question of what to do with all these Canaanites. This question is phrased as an allusion to a 1989 essay by Robert Allen Warrior, "Canaanites, Cowboys, and Indians," which is the earliest scholarly article that I know of that reads the biblical conquest stories in an explicitly suspicious hermeneutic that is contextual and reader centred. In that essay, Warrior positions himself as an American Christian Indigenous man who identifies far more with the Canaanites than with the Israelites, the chosen people that his faith tells him he should identify with. He demonstrates that for an Indigenous person in the Americas, it is not a big leap to read the biblical conquest narratives as directly applicable to his experience.[2]

I cannot position myself as a Canaanite when I read these texts. My ancestors came to what is now Canada at various points between the 1630s and the 1920s. Some of them came to Manitoba in the late nineteenth century, fleeing famine in Iceland. Some of them were brought in the 1750s from Württemberg (then part of the Holy Roman Empire, in what is now Germany) by the English to populate Nova Scotia in the wake of the expulsion, also by the English, of my Acadian ancestors (the one surviving branch of this side of the family ended up in Prince Edward Island). Others came to Toronto in the wave of immigration from the United Kingdom after World War 1. All of them benefited from the removal of Indigenous people from the land, whether gradually in the Maritimes throughout the seventeenth and eighteenth centuries, or rapidly by means of the Numbered Treaties on the Prairies in the late nineteenth century. How are the biblical conquest narratives applicable to my experience and the experience of other settler Canadians? As a biblical scholar, a Canadian biblical scholar, what are my responsibilities when I read and teach these stories?[3]

Doctrine of Discovery, *Terra Nullius*, Genocide

In its Calls to Action, the Truth and Reconciliation Commission of Canada (TRC) called for all governments and all faith and social justice groups in Canada to adopt and implement the United Nations Declaration as the framework for reconciliation.[4] In its preamble, the Declaration "recogniz[es] and reaffirm[s] that indigenous individuals are entitled without discrimination to all human rights recognized in international law, and that indigenous peoples possess collective rights which are indispensable for their existence, well-being and integral development as peoples." Article 1 of the Declaration reaffirms that statement.[5] The TRC's Calls to Action also implore the Government of Canada, as well as churches and faith groups, to repudiate concepts such as the Doctrine of Discovery and *terra nullius*, which were used to justify the European colonization of Indigenous Lands.[6] Standard histories of these concepts trace them to fifteenth-century papal decrees, and ultimately back to Augustine's concept of just war (especially in his *Questions on the Heptateuch*, where he deals particularly with the book of Joshua).[7] While the legal basis of these concepts may be explained this way, their continued moral force may be best understood through the history of North American colonization by largely British Protestants.[8]

Protestantism, with its emphasis on scripture and its rejection of the authority of the Roman Catholic magisterium, is key to understanding how and to what extent the biblical texts behind the Doctrine of Discovery, *terra nullius*, and the policy of genocide continue to remain operational in Canadian settler consciousness. Because of the Protestant argument that scripture interprets itself and that its meaning may be discerned by individuals of faith, there is no fence around those texts that justify conquest and genocide. They remain present for anyone to read and use. Even though the fifteenth-century papal decrees on the colonization of the Americas can be traced back through Aquinas and Augustine to the biblical book of Joshua, for Protestants, the line is direct and immediate. This direct availability is true of all biblical texts that assume an androcentric slave-holding culture, and it was not so very long ago that subjugation of women and ownership of slaves found their moral basis in biblical texts. The qualitative difference, I suggest, is the difference between a set of cultural discourses and practices that are *described* and *regulated* as part of everyday life, and practices that are *prescribed* and have a particular applicability to unique situations. That is, it is one thing to assume that women are handed over from father to husband in exchange for a bride price in keeping with general cultural practice, and quite another to be commanded to exterminate entire groups of people every once in a while. The fact that one set of texts demands this extermination, while many other texts implicitly acknowledge that the extermination was messy and incomplete, is a rupture or discontinuity that helps us see the artificial and fantastic nature of the command to exterminate.

The TRC used the term "genocide" to refer to the general relationship between Canada and Indigenous Peoples. However, the TRC could not use the term "genocide" with respect to the Indian residential schools, since the concept has a specific legal definition under international law, and in its mandate the TRC was explicitly barred from conducting a formal legal process.[9] In its place, the commission used the term "cultural genocide" to refer to the "destruction of those structures and practices that allow the group to continue as a group."[10] It found that "the Canadian government pursued this policy of cultural genocide because it wished to divest itself of its legal and financial obligations to Aboriginal people and gain control over their land and resources,"[11] and that "residential schooling was always more than simply an educational program: it was an integral part of a conscious policy of cultural genocide."[12] However, I am not bound by the legal stricture to avoid the concept "genocide." It is a useful category of analysis, and so I would like to examine it before turning to biblical texts.

The legal definition of "genocide" was developed in the aftermath of World War II, and the analysis of genocide was largely confined to the sphere of legal scholarship until the 1990s. Since then, historians and sociologists have turned to genocide as a category of scholarly analysis. These efforts have worked to broaden the field in order for us to understand the dynamics of genocide and to develop definitions that are more useful in looking at the phenomenon beyond the strict legal interpretations. A particularly useful one is Martin Shaw's: "Genocide is a form of violent social conflict, or war, between armed power organizations that aim to destroy civilian social groups and those groups and other actors who resist this destruction." The ensuing "genocidal action [is]...action in which armed power organizations treat civilian social groups as enemies and aim to destroy their real or putative social power, by means of killing, violence, and coercion against individuals whom they regard as members of the groups."[13] This definition is useful because it includes the possibility of resistance, and because it allows for genocide in "peacetime." The former recognizes that the victims of genocide are not necessarily passive; the latter recognizes that genocide is in itself an act of war, regardless of whether it has been formally declared.[14] Both are germane to our examination of biblical texts and Canadian contexts.

In the book *Purify and Destroy*, the sociologist of non-violence Jacques Semelin looks at the dynamics of genocide rather than legalities or definitions. He uses the word "massacre" to refer to organized mass killing, and examines three cases: the Holocaust, the Balkans in the 1990s, and Rwanda in the 1990s. From his analysis, he finds three ideal-types of massacres. The first is subjugation: "to annihilate a group partly in order to force the rest into total submission." The second is eradication: "to eliminate a community.... This process involves 'cleansing or 'purifying' the area." And the third is insurrection: "to provoke an intense traumatic shock likely to influence" state policies, otherwise known as terrorism.[15] Eradication is what is typically meant when we use the word "genocide," but subjugation and eradication "complement each other by targeting different groups."[16] Eradication uses the language of "purify and destroy." Semelin uses Mary Douglas's foundational work on purity and pollution, extending it to analyze the logic of twentieth-century genocides: "the need to defend the purity of civilisation against the corruption of modernity."[17] His summary of this logic is worth quoting at length:

> Identity-based purity...in fact tends to result in the formation of a separate enemy figure. This "them" perceived as basically different from "us" becomes an "other in excess." This figure of the enemy proceeds from a magnified vision of a difference on to which "our" anxiety will adhere to the point of wishing his destruction. This "Other in excess" is of course different from "us" from a qualitative standpoint: he does not have the same blood as we do, or the same customs; he does not have the same nose or the same body shape, he is taller or shorter, his skin is a different colour. In fact, did he not arrive in this land after we did? He thus has no right to remain here and his presence is literally unbearable: he spreads his stench over this territory that belonged to our ancestors, our nation, our God.... As he tends to multiply, proliferate, pullulate, he may well submerge us if we are not careful.... Radical measures must therefore be taken to defend ourselves against these vile and perverse creatures.[18]

Role of Biblical Scholarship

Given all the above, and given the fact that we have biblical texts that command colonization and extermination, and a history in North America of exactly these actions taken upon the Indigenous Peoples of the land, what are we to do? Ignoring these texts, or refusing to deal with them, is not a viable strategy, as it leaves these texts available to others. Ignoring racism does not make it go away. Leaving the texts to religious communities to remedy ignores the question of a broader responsibility for how these texts continue to function in the public sphere. Canada is increasingly a secular country, and it has a large non-Christian population, but a majority of Canadians still identify as Christian—67 percent, according to Statistics Canada.[19] Yet with weekly church attendance below 20 percent, even if churches do careful and assiduous work to decolonize these texts, most Canadians will not be part of those conversations (only about 15 percent will be), even though, paradoxically, they are nominally Christian. Because these texts undergird the legal and moral basis for colonialism, they cannot be left to churches alone.[20] Working to decolonize these texts in the public sphere is the only responsible option. All biblical scholars in Canada, whether employed in public or church-related schools, have a responsibility to lead the efforts to dismantle the biblical bases of the Doctrine of Discovery, *terra nullius*, and genocide.

Troubling Texts

There are two bodies of texts to deal with. One set is largely from Deuteronomy, Joshua, and Judges, while the second is from Chronicles and Ezra-Nehemiah. The first set deals largely with the invasion and settlement of the Promised Land by the Israelites, and the second set with the Judahites' removal from and return to the land after the Babylonian conquest. It is historically unlikely that the invasion and settlement of the land took place as it was described in Joshua, while biblical scholars and historians agree that the destruction of Jerusalem and its surrounding territory in 586 BCE and the forced migration of the Judahite elite to Babylon is a historical fact that lies behind Chronicles and Ezra-Nehemiah. Nevertheless, in the self-understanding of the authors of these biblical texts, the Israelite conquest of Canaan did happen. Since it has only been settled by scholars in the last thirty years that the Joshua conquest stories are not historical in the modern sense, we can safely assume that the vast majority of readers, from antiquity to the present day, have seen these texts as a reflection of historical events. What is important today is the rhetorical and ideological effect of these stories, not whether historians agree on their historicity.[21]

Troubling Texts: Discovery and Conquest

The text that prescribes invasion, conquest, and extermination of the indigenous Canaanites is Deuteronomy 20:10–18, also known as one of the texts justifying Holy War:

> When you approach a city to make war against it, you may call out to it in peace. If it answers you in peace and opens its gates to you, then all the people found in it may be enslaved to you as your forced labour. But if it does not make peace with you, and makes war with you, then you may besiege it. When the LORD your god gives it into your power, then you may strike down every male with the sword's edge. As for the women, and the children, and the livestock, and everything else in the city, all its spoil, you may take it as your booty. You may consume the spoil of your enemies that the LORD your god has given you. Thus you may do to all the cities that are very far away from you, which are not among the cities of these nations here.
>
> As for the cities of these peoples which the LORD your god is giving to you as an ancestral possession, you may not allow anything that breathes remain alive. Instead, you may consecrate to destruction the Hittites and the Amorites, the Canaanites and the Perizzites, the Hivites and the Jebusites, just as the LORD your god has commanded you, so that they may not teach you to do all the abominable things that they do for their gods, and you thereby sin against the LORD your god.[22]

There are two prescriptions here: the first, for towns and territories outside the area claimed by God for the Israelites, calls for the pacification of these peoples by surrender or by conquest. Those who surrender enter into servitude, while those who resist are punished but not exterminated. The second prescription

2. WHAT TO DO WITH ALL THESE CANAANITES?

relates to those towns and territories inside the land claimed by God for the Israelites, and it calls for extermination, regardless of whether these populations resist or not. The reason for both of these prescriptions is made clear at the end: the mere presence of the indigenous inhabitants in the Promised Land is a danger because they *may* teach the Israelites abhorrent and sinful practices. The indigenous inhabitants of the non–Promised Land do not pose the same risk. What is important to note is that it is only a risk: the indigenous inhabitants of the Promised Land are only theoretically dangerous. Yet their presence cannot be tolerated. As Cherokee scholar Laura Donaldson has demonstrated, English, especially Puritan, settlers in the seventeenth and eighteenth centuries used the rhetoric of the Promised Land in a number of ways: to speak of their own sense of redemption from persecution, to be sure, but also to justify their occupation of and domination over the original inhabitants of the land.[23] The two are opposing sides of the same coin: liberation and occupation. The idea that Indigenous people are dangerous, not because they might resist being dispossessed of their lands and settlements, but simply by virtue of their potential for corrupting the settlers comes right from Deuteronomy 20.

The books following Deuteronomy—Joshua and Judges—are an extended reflection on the impossibility of fully realizing the vision of Deuteronomy in all its aspects.[24] The story of the trickery of the Hivites living in the settlement of Gibeon in Joshua 9 provides the best example pertaining directly to the prescriptions of Deuteronomy 20:

> Joshua called [the Hivites of Gibeon] to him, and spoke to them: "Why did you deceive us by saying, 'We are very far away from you,' when you are living nearby to us? Now, be cursed! There shall never fail to be slaves from among you, hewers of wood and drawers of water for the temple of my god." They answered Joshua and said, "Indeed it was told to us your slaves that which the LORD your god had commanded his slave Moses, to give to you all the land, and to destroy all the inhabitants of the land before you. We were very afraid for our lives because of you. So we did this thing. Now, see, we are in your power. Do to us whatever you think is right and proper." So

this is what he did: he saved them from the power of the Israelites, and they did not murder them. But on that day Joshua made them hewers of wood and drawers of water for the congregation and for the altar of the LORD, until today, at the place that he should choose. (Josh. 9:22–27)

Somehow, the Gibeonites have discovered the exact wording of the commands in Deuteronomy 20, and they cleverly disguise themselves as indigenous inhabitants from outside the Promised Land and ask to make a treaty. Joshua, Moses's successor, agrees, but later learns of the trick. Because they have entered into a treaty—a sacred agreement—he decides not to kill them but instead to make them slaves. Two things stand out here for me. First, he does not back out of the treaty: he had guaranteed their lives (Josh. 9:15) (but remember that the prescription regarding the indigenous inhabitants outside the Promised Land commanded that such people become forced labourers). Therefore, Joshua makes them forced labourers on their own land. The second thing that stands out is the phrase "hewers of wood and drawers of water," which is often used in the Canadian context to connote the country's resource-based economy. It was introduced into the Canadian lexicon in Minister of Finance Leonard Tilley's 1879 budget speech,[25] and the phrase continues to be used in this manner to this day.[26] However, it has also been used to describe the position of the majority of Québécois and their exploitation by anglophone Canada.[27] Never have I seen this phrase used to refer to Indigenous people or groups in Canada, and yet in Joshua 9, the phrase applies to the indigenous inhabitants. It says a lot about Canada when either Canadians as a whole or the Québécois see themselves as being colonized and subjugated, condemned to servitude in the land they see as their own, while comfortably ignoring the original inhabitants of the land.

Joshua 11 demonstrates that obedience to divine command led to the extermination of most of the indigenous inhabitants of the Promised Land, but also that some survived:

All the cities of these kings, and all the kings themselves, Joshua captured, and he struck them with the edge of the sword, consecrating them to

2. WHAT TO DO WITH ALL THESE CANAANITES?

destruction, just as Moses, slave of the LORD had commanded.... All the spoil and the livestock of these cities the Israelites took as booty for themselves, but they struck down all the human life with the edge of the sword, until they had destroyed them all; they did not spare any who breathed.

Joshua made war against these kings for a long time. Not one city made peace with the Israelites, except the Hivites living in Gibeon; they took all of them in battle. It was the LORD's doing to strengthen their will to approach Israel in battle, when favour might have been shown to them, so that Israel might consecrate them to destruction and might destroy them just as the LORD had commanded Moses. (Josh. 11:12, 14, 18–20)

By continually referring to the Hivites of Gibeon, the story subtly reminds us that they gained their safety through trickery and therefore cannot be trusted. They are always in the land, potentially dangerous and contaminating, yet cannot be exterminated because of the sacred treaty.

The end of the book of Joshua has Joshua's farewell speech:

"When you crossed over the Jordan River and came to Jericho, the leaders of Jericho fought with you, also the Amorites, the Perizzites, the Canaanites, the Hittites, the Girgashites, the Hivites, and the Jebusites, and I gave them into your power. I had sent the plague before you, and it drove out before you the two kings of the Amorites, not your sword or your bow. I gave you a land on which you had not laboured, and cities that you had not built, and you lived in them, eating from vineyards and olive groves that you had not planted."

The people answered, and said... "For the LORD our god is the one who brought our ancestors and us up out from the land of Egypt, from the house of slavery... the LORD has driven out all the peoples before us, the Amorites living in the land; so also we will serve the LORD, for he is our god." (Josh. 24:11–13, 16–18)

Two points are relevant here: first, a reminder that God had prepared the land for the people by destroying the indigenous inhabitants by plague. Second, that the Promised Land was a gift to people who had not done the work to make it suitable for human habitation, and who in fact profited by the labour of others. The parallels to the Canadian experience are obvious. However, the text makes a point, here and elsewhere, of the very fact of the profiting. The people's response is to promise to serve the God who had made this gift. As a settler myself, can I believe that God made me a gift of this land? Clearly our forebears believed it, and the Doctrine of Discovery is a part of that belief. But can I continue to believe that today? No, I cannot. And the text of Joshua does not believe it either. If the land were truly a gift, it would have been empty of indigenous inhabitants, and war would not have been required in order to occupy it. The text of Joshua contains a paradox: the land is a gift, but it must be taken and guarded with extreme vigilance. Joshua's paradox shows up in Canadian stories and justifications for the settlement of the land: it is a gift—perhaps these days not from God, but from the technological advantages enjoyed by seventeenth-century Europeans—but it must be taken and guarded from the remaining Indigenous inhabitants.

The book of Judges adds one little additional component to the narrative of occupation:

> These are the nations that the LORD left to test Israel, those who had not known war in Canaan—it was only so that the generations of the Israelites might know how to fight war; it was only for them who had no experience—the five lords of the Philistines, all the Canaanites and the Sidonians and the Hivites living on Mount Lebanon, from Mount Master-of-Hermon to Approach-to-Hamath. They were for the testing of Israel to know whether they would obey the commandment of the LORD which he had commanded their ancestors through Moses. The Israelites lived near the Canaanites, Hittites, Amorites, Perizzites, Hivites, and Jebusites. They took their daughters as wives for themselves, and their own daughters they gave to their sons, and they served their gods. The Israelites did evil in the sight of the LORD. (Judg. 3:1–7)

2. WHAT TO DO WITH ALL THESE CANAANITES?

The indigenous inhabitants had not been eradicated. Their presence is now explained as part of God's plan. Their presence has two purposes: first, to give the people practice in forms of violence; and second, to be the means by which the people's own worthiness might be measured. The people fail, of course, but by presenting them with the temptation that leads to failure, the failure is softened somewhat. There is the unspoken wish that, if only we had wiped them out, they would not be causing us to sin. This first set of texts, from Deuteronomy, Joshua, and Judges, provides a theological and moral justification for genocide; through allegorical reading—the dominant mode of reading until the eighteenth century, and the primary mode of reading as practised in faith communities today—genocide of the "Other in excess" remains legitimated.

Troubling Texts: Empty Land

The second set of biblical texts gives the rationale for empty land theology, and in turn for *terra nullius*. The conquest of Jerusalem, its destruction by the Babylonians under Nebuchadnezzar, and the removal of the elites to Babylon in 586 BCE is explained in two ways across the corpus of biblical texts. One is familiar from our brief examination of Deuteronomy, Joshua, and Judges: the people sinned and they were punished. A remnant of the population was left, according to 2 Kings 25. The other explanation posits a build-up of cultic impurity in the land as described in the abrogation of the command in Leviticus 26 to give the land its rest, its Sabbath:

> [God] brought up the king of the Babylonians against them. He murdered their young noblemen by the sword in the sanctuary. He did not spare young man or young woman, the aged or the feeble. [God] gave all of them into his power.... They burned the temple of God, and they broke down the wall of Jerusalem. All the strongholds they burned with fire, and all its precious vessels they destroyed. He deported to Babylon those spared by the sword, and they became slaves to him and his sons, until the advent of the Persian kingdom, in order to fulfill the word of the LORD by the mouth of Jeremiah,

until the land had satisfied its Sabbaths. All the time of its devastation it kept Sabbath, to fulfill seventy years. (2 Chron. 36:17, 19–21)

When applied to the story of the destruction and forced removal, 2 Chronicles 36 has the land remaining completely empty of human life. The descendants of those who had been forced to move to Babylon are those who are chosen by imperial decree to repopulate the land. The land was empty, just waiting to be inhabited:

In the first year of Cyrus, King of Persia, to complete the word of LORD by the mouth of Jeremiah, the LORD roused the spirit of Cyrus, King of Persia, and he caused a spoken word and also a written edict to travel around his kingdom, saying: "Thus says Cyrus, King of Persia: The LORD, god of heaven, has given all the kingdoms of the earth to me. He has appointed me to build him a temple in Jerusalem, which is in Judah. Whoever among you is from all his people, may the LORD his god be with him. Let him go up!" (2 Chron. 36:22–23 = Ezr. 1:1–3a) "to Jerusalem, which is in Judah, and build a temple of the LORD, god of Israel. He is the god who is in Jerusalem." (Ezr. 1:3b)

However, early in the book of Ezra the returning elites soon find that there are in fact people living in the land; it was not empty at all. Not only was it not empty, the people in it claimed kinship and ethnic ties to the returning elites. They were Judahites and Israelites. The rhetorical and ideological trick for dealing with them is quite neat:

When these things were finished, the officers approached me, saying: "The people Israel, the priests, and the Levites, have not separated themselves from the peoples of the lands, whose abominations are like those of the Canaanites, the Hittites, the Perizzites, the Jebusites, the Ammonites, the Moabites, the Egyptians, and the Amorites. For they take up from their daughters as wives for themselves and for their sons. They have mixed the holy seed with the peoples of the lands. The officers and officials have been the leaders in this sacrilege." When I heard this report, I tore my garment and my mantle, I pulled hair from my head and beard, and I sat down in horror. (Ezr. 9:1–3)

The "peoples of the lands" are equated with the indigenous inhabitants in Deuteronomy. (Some translations obscure this equation, and make it seem as if the Canaanites, Hittites, etc., are still in the land.) Once the equation is made, the ideological basis exists for erasing the Judahites who did not share the Ezran community's experience of forced migration. Their claim to the land has been negated by equating them with the indigenous inhabitants. Ideologically, the land is now empty. So, too, was Canada made an empty land because its Indigenous Peoples had not made "proper" use of it by farming.[28]

Hermeneutics of Suspicion or Reparative Reading?

The mode of reading that Paul Ricoeur termed the "hermeneutics of suspicion" has become the dominant one in the humanities over the past forty years. It assumes that texts and other cultural products mask their own ideological biases, or if these attitudes are not masked, they are at least repressed. A text may seem to be about one thing, but it is really about something else. This mode of reading assumes that the objects we study are un-trustable, but that the astute reader can see through the mask or the repression and point to the text's meaning.

Recently I have been pondering Eve Kosofsky Sedgwick's essay on "paranoid reading," which has been increasingly cited since its print publication in 2003. Her take on the hermeneutics of suspicion is to call it paranoid reading. Two quotations from the essay are striking. First, she notes that "it's strange that a hermeneutic of suspicion would appear so trusting about the effects of exposure."[29] This is true! Once we have peeled back the mask to expose the pernicious violence of the text's ideology, our work is done, right? Simply airing it out will put an end to it. However, as Sedgwick argues, this is manifestly not the case. Further, she goes on to ask, "What does a hermeneutics of suspicion and exposure have to say to social formations in which visibility itself constitutes much of the violence?"[30] As we saw in looking at the biblical texts, most of the violence is highly visible. In Joshua 9, the Israelites' presence is what spurs the Hivites of Gibeon to action. We had to do some careful reading to pick up the subtle construction of Ezra's Judahite opponents as equivalent to Canaanites, but it was not hidden. The violence is visible: there is nothing to suspect or expose. I might gently suggest that the reaction of many well-intentioned settler Canadians to the TRC is congruent: we have heard the Truth, so that alone is enough to lead to Reconciliation. I think Sedgwick was right, and the hermeneutics of suspicion and exposure alone cannot address the deep and systemic injustices and racism of Canadian colonial society.

So what to do? Sedgwick went on in her essay to argue for a turn to "reparative reading." While the hermeneutics of suspicion is negative and paranoid, "the desire of a reparative impulse on the other hand, is additive and accretive.... It wants to assemble and confer plenitude on an object that will then have resources to offer to an inchoate self."[31] She suggested that "what we can best learn from [reparative reading] practices are, perhaps, the many ways selves and communities succeed in extracting sustenance from the objects of a culture—even of a culture whose avowed desire has often been not to sustain them."[32] She did not say much more about reparative reading, and her premature death cut off anything else she might have said. Scholars who have taken up the challenge have gone in two different directions: first, so-called surface reading that celebrates the aesthetics of a text (but I think there are significant ethical problems with this approach);[33] and second, reading with empathy and love.[34] The latter is more consistent with Sedgwick's work as a queer theorist.[35] As a queer theorist, Sedgwick was positioned to locate and celebrate how her community was able to find something in the surrounding culture to sustain it. However, as a settler Canadian, I do not think I am positioned to prescribe to Indigenous people how sustenance may be extracted from settler culture. I can provide a small example from my observations of the results of the trial of Raymond Cormier in the murder of Indigenous girl Tina Fontaine in Winnipeg in February 2018. According to media reports, after the not-guilty verdict was announced, family members of Tina Fontaine huddled, and someone began reciting the Lord's Prayer.[36] As an observer, and given my remarks in this chapter, this act seems to me to be an example of sustenance extracted from a culture whose avowed desire has been not to sustain Indigenous selves and communities.

So as a settler, what options do I have? One option is to turn to other biblical texts to look for models of reparation. One of my favourites is a text from Leviticus, which is directly concerned with something that is stolen:

> When a person sins and commits sacrilege against the LORD by deceiving someone with whom the person is in relationship...if one swears falsely about one of all the things a human being may do to sin in these matters—when one has sinned and feels guilt, and would return the stolen thing or the extorted thing or the deposited thing that had been entrusted, or the lost thing that one found, or anything else about which the person swore falsely, the person shall make restitution and add a fifth part to it. The person shall pay it to its owner upon realizing the guilt. Then the person shall bring as a guilt-penalty to the LORD, a ram without blemish from the flock, or its equivalent, as a guilt-penalty to the priest. The priest shall make expiation on the person's behalf before the LORD, and the person shall be forgiven for whatever one may have done to incur guilt thereby. (Lev. 5:21–26; English 6:2–7)

Considering that one epithet for Canada is "stolen Indigenous land," this text is particularly appropriate. However, there is a series of broader principles at play in the logic of the text, applicable beyond the case of theft. First, it is a sin to deal deceitfully (it is also a sin to swear falsely, but that is not new). Second, one has to feel guilty about the sin. Third, one has to pay reparation in excess of what was gained through deceit. Forgiveness can happen only after the recognition of guilt and the making of reparation. When we apply this logic to the Canadian case, we can see that as a society, we have recognized that we have dealt deceitfully, and we feel guilty. However, that is not enough to gain forgiveness, or even reconciliation: we settlers need to make reparation. Without making right the wrong, right relationships will not happen. The text from Leviticus suggests it is for God to forgive, not the wronged party.[37] Perhaps we should be holding up this text, and instead of insisting upon extracting forgiveness, as settler readers we can be asking, "What do *we* need to do?" Perhaps one way forward is to actually heed the call of the TRC, and to read the conquest texts through the lens of the UN Declaration, with its affirmation of human rights for Indigenous Peoples.

Layered Places, Layered Texts

In 2015 and 2017, I had the opportunity to spend time in Berlin, which of course has its own problematic history of oppression and violence. As a site of memory, the city seems to be a layering of effects, or as Sedgwick calls it, it is accretive and additive. Examples include the nineteenth-century Victory Column in the Tiergarten park, with its Nazi-era additions but also its unrepaired damage from Soviet shelling in 1945; the Topography of Terror memorial site on the ruins of the Gestapo headquarters; the Memorial to the Murdered Jews of Europe next to the site of Hitler's Chancellery; the juxtaposition of the statue of Frederick the Great with the Bebelplatz book-burning memorial; the East Side Gallery, with its post-1991 paintings on one of the few remaining sections of the Berlin Wall. The past is not eradicated, nor is it celebrated. It is remembered. Is this a way forward for dealing with biblical texts that call for the eradication of the indigenous inhabitants of a Promised Land? Already the biblical text is layered: the prescriptions in Deuteronomy are not fully actualized in Joshua, then reinterpreted in Judges, and reapplied in Ezra. Can I add—can we add—more layers to these texts, to the extent that it becomes impossible to strip away those layers? I do not know. I do know that simply exposing these texts is not an option, nor is simply ignoring them.[38]

All I have to deal with are texts. They give a rhetorical picture of some ancient scribes' views on the construction of Israelite and Judahite identity. We can be almost certain that in Persian- and Hellenistic-period Judaea, they were not enacted. They are almost certainly fantasies. As biblical scholar Shawn

Kelley states, "once the discipline of biblical studies gets past the notion that genocidal ideology produces genocide, we would be in a better position to see how the Bible, biblical scholars and theologians, genocidal ideology, and genocidal actions all interact with each other."[39] However, understanding the ancient context—what I do as a scholar of these texts—does not solve the problems of "plain reading" today. The most acute problem of "plain reading" is that the reader who is looking for meaning, who has some notion of scriptural authority, however vague, will ignore the obvious context in favour of an uncritical allegorization of the text. Such an uncritical allegorization might suggest that because ancient Israelites were commanded to exterminate the Canaanites, so modern European-heritage settlers of Canada should feel justified in exterminating the Indigenous Peoples of this land. "Plain readers" do not even realize, in my experience, that they are making this step. Jacques Semelin, in his analysis of genocide, says that moving from fantasy to actuality is difficult and not necessarily a natural step.[40] As readers, we are called now more than ever to contextualize these texts as fantasies, and to resist any attempts to use them to justify an actuality. We are also, I think, ethically bound to raise up texts that call for reparations to those who have been wronged. That may be the best contribution we can make to Canada's work of reconciliation.

Notes

1 In lieu of a trial transcript, the live tweets of CBC reporters Charles Hamilton and Jason Warick and CTV reporter Angelina Irinici form the basis of my analysis. See Charles Hamilton, Twitter posts, January 29–February 9, 2018, twitter.com/_chamilton; Jason Warick, Twitter posts, January 29–February 9, 2018, twitter.com/WarickCBC; Angelina Irinici, Twitter posts, January 29–February 9, 2018, twitter.com/angelinaiCTV.

2 Robert Allen Warrior, "Canaanites, Cowboys, and Indians: Deliverance, Conquest, and Liberation Theology Today," *Christianity and Crisis* 49, no. 12 (September 11, 1989): 261–5. For comparison, see Jace Weaver, "Premodern Ironies: First Nations and Chosen Peoples," in *The Calling of the Nations: Exegesis, Ethnography, and Empire in a Biblical-Historic Present*, ed. Mark Vessey, Sharon V. Betcher, Robert A. Daum, and Harry O. Maier (Toronto: University of Toronto Press, 2011), 291–304.

3 See Charles William Miller, "Negotiating Boundaries: Israelites and Canaanites Receive Help from a Russian," *Journal of Religion and Society*, no. 12 (2010),

https://dspace2.creighton.edu/xmlui/bitstream/handle/10504/64583/2010-1. pdf?sequence=1, who asks similar questions while contextualizing himself as a professor in North Dakota.

4   Truth and Reconciliation Commission of Canada, *Truth and Reconciliation Commission of Canada: Calls to Action* (Winnipeg: Truth and Reconciliation Commission of Canada, 2015), http://trc.ca/assets/pdf/Calls_to_Action_English2.pdf, Calls to Action 43 and 48.

5   UN General Assembly, Resolution 61/295, United Nations Declaration on the Rights of Indigenous Peoples, A/RES/61/295 (October 2, 2007), https://undocs.org/A/RES/61/295.

6   Truth and Reconciliation Commission of Canada, *Calls to Action*, especially Calls to Action 45 and 49.

7   Jennifer Reid, "The Doctrine of Discovery and Canadian Law," *Canadian Journal of Native Studies* 30 (2010): 335–9; Wilcomb E. Washburn, *Red Man's Land/White Man's Law: The Past and Present Status of the American Indian*, 2nd ed. (Norman: University of Oklahoma Press, 1995), 3–23.

8   The reality of French colonization, the French being mostly Catholics, is restricted both geographically and temporally. Due to the insular nature of various French-Canadian cultures until well into the twentieth century, the general influence of Catholicism upon Canadian society outside Quebec was restricted, although this began to change with immigration from southern Europe in the late nineteenth century. In other words, while I am not denying or downplaying the role of French colonization of North America—it is crucial in the formation of Métis identity, for example—I am highlighting the role of British Protestants.

9   See "Indian Residential Schools Settlement Agreement, Schedule 'N': Mandate for the Truth and Reconciliation Commission," accessed February 10, 2021, http://www.residentialschoolsettlement.ca/SCHEDULE_N.pdf; David B. MacDonald, "Coming to Terms with the Canadian Past: Truth and Reconciliation, Indigenous Genocide, and the Post-war German Model," in *Replicating Atonement: Foreign Models in the Commemoration of Atrocities*, ed. Mischa Gabowitsch (Cham, CH: Palgrave Macmillan, 2017), 163–83, notes that the chair of the TRC, Justice Murray Sinclair, has stated publicly his view that the Indian residential school system was a violation of the United Nations Convention on Genocide.

10   Truth and Reconciliation Commission of Canada, *What We Have Learned: Principles of Truth and Reconciliation* (Winnipeg: Truth and Reconciliation Commission of Canada, 2015), 5.

11   Ibid., 6.

12   Ibid., 25.

13   Martin Shaw, *What Is Genocide?* (Cambridge: Polity, 2007), 154.

14   Ibid., 155.

15   Jacques Semelin, *Purify and Destroy: The Political Uses of Massacre and Genocide* (New York: Columbia University Press, 2007), 327–61.

16   Ibid., 343.

17   Ibid., 12.

18 Ibid., 37–8.
19 Statistics Canada, 2011 *National Household Survey*, accessed February 10, 2021, https://www12.statcan.gc.ca/nhs-enm/2011/dp-pd/dt-td/index-eng.cfm.
20 Benjamin Wormald places *monthly* attendance at worship services for Canada-born Canadians at 22 percent in 2011—a slow but steady decline from 31 percent in 1998. Monthly attendance at worship services among first-generation immigrants has remained steady at 43 percent. See Benjamin Wormald, "Canada's Changing Religious Landscape," Pew Research Center, June 27, 2013, https://www.pewforum.org/2013/06/27/canadas-changing-religious-landscape/. Weekly attendance can safely be assumed to be lower, as even by 2005, weekly attendance was 21 percent, down from 31 percent in 1985. See Colin Lindsay, "Canadians Attend Weekly Religious Services Less Than 20 Years Ago," *Statistics Canada, General Social Survey: Matter of Fact No. 3*, https://www150.statcan.gc.ca/n1/pub/89-630-x/2008001/article/10650-eng.pdf. A more recent survey places *monthly* attendance at religious services (not necessarily Christian) at 20 percent. See Angus Reid Institute, "A Spectrum of Spirituality: Canadians Keep the Faith to Varying Degrees, but Few Reject it Entirely," April 13, 2017, http://angusreid.org/wp-content/uploads/2017/04/2017.04.12_Faith_Wave_1_Part_1.pdf. For an excellent discussion of the trends in Canadian Christianity, see Brian P. Clarke and Stuart Macdonald, *Leaving Christianity: Changing Allegiances in Canada since 1945* (Montreal: McGill-Queen's University Press, 2017), especially their observation that "[churches'] norms were embedded in Canadian law, and a wide array of social institutions…socialized Canadians into their values and world view. Since the 1960s, these churches have lost their position of dominance in Canadian culture" (234). As I am arguing, because Christian norms are embedded in Canadian culture and law, it is incumbent upon biblical scholars, no matter their affiliation, to work with the texts in the public sphere.
21 For a thorough review of scholarship on the (Christian) Bible and genocide, see Shawn Kelley, *Genocide, the Bible, and Biblical Scholarship* (Leiden, NL: Brill, 2016).
22 All biblical translations from Hebrew are my own.
23 Laura E. Donaldson, "Joshua in America: On Cowboys, Canaanites, and Indians," in *The Calling of the Nations: Exegesis, Ethnography, and Empire in a Biblical-Historic Present*, ed. Mark Vessey, Sharon V. Betcher, Robert A. Daum, and Harry O. Maier (Toronto: University of Toronto Press, 2011), 273–90; see also Alfred A. Cave, "Canaanites in a Promised Land: The American Indian and the Providential Theory of Empire," *American Indian Quarterly*, no. 12 (1988): 277–97.
24 Robert Polzin, *Moses and the Deuteronomist: A Literary Study of the Deuteronomic History, Part 1: Deuteronomy, Joshua, Judges* (New York: Seabury Press, 1980).
25 C.M. Wallace, "Tilley, Sir Samuel Leonard," *Dictionary of Canadian Biography*, vol. 12, University of Toronto/Université Laval, accessed April 7, 2021, http://www.biographi.ca/en/bio/tilley_samuel_leonard_12E.html.
26 See, for example, Barrie McKenna, "Hewers of Wood, Maybe; but Good at It: Report," *Globe and Mail*, March 26, 2017, https://www.theglobeandmail.com/report-on-business/economy/economy-lab/hewers-of-wood-maybe-but-good-at-it-report/article610507/.

27 See, for example, Léon Dion, *Quebec: The Unfinished Revolution* (Montreal: McGill-Queen's University Press, 1976), 99.
28 Truth and Reconciliation Commission of Canada, *What We Have Learned*, 18.
29 Eve Kosofsky Sedgwick, *Touching Feeling: Affect, Pedagogy, Performativity* (Durham, NC: Duke University Press, 2003), 138. See also Bruno Latour, "Why Has Critique Run Out of Steam? From Matters of Fact to Matters of Concern," *Critical Inquiry*, no. 30 (2004): 225–48.
30 Sedgwick, *Touching Feeling*, 140.
31 Ibid., 149.
32 Ibid., 150–1.
33 Stephen Best and Sharon Marcus, "Surface Reading: An Introduction," *Representations*, no. 108 (2009): 1–21.
34 Heather Love, "Truth and Consequences: On Paranoid Reading and Reparative Reading," *Criticism*, no. 52 (2010): 235–41.
35 Robyn Wiegman, "The Times We're In: Queer Feminist Criticism and the Reparative 'Turn,'" *Feminist Theory*, no. 15 (2014): 4–25.
36 Karen Pauls (@karenpaulscbc), #RaymondCormier being led out. Thelma yelled at him before he left, now crying "My baby." Supporters have circled her and are praying the Lord's Prayer. #mmiwg, Twitter, February 22, 2018, 6:16 p.m., twitter.com/karenpaulscbc/status/966813946391838720.
37 See MacDonald, "Coming to Terms," 170, which points out that in contrast to the South African TRC, "Christian notions of forgiveness…were notably avoided in the Canadian TRC, where, in a sense, Christianity was itself on trial for having co-founded and managed the residential schools."
38 But see Mischa Gabowitsch, "Replicating Atonement: The German Model and Beyond," in *Replicating Atonement: Foreign Models in the Commemoration of Atrocities*, ed. Mischa Gabowitsch (Cham, CH: Palgrave Macmillan, 2017), 1–21, who notes that "foreign models can be instructive and inspiring, but they need to be studied in detail and in context—and alongside local cultural resources" (17).
39 Kelley, *Genocide*, 63.
40 Semelin, *Purify and Destroy*, 1–2.

CHAPTER 3

RESTRUCTURED FEELINGS
Pitfalls of Settler-Christian Turns to Education

by

LYNN CALDWELL

> We are not sure what lies ahead as we complete this turn towards justice
> and deepen our commitment to a new identity, a new relationship,
> and a new way of being, both in the church and in the world.
> A new relationship is waiting, and we turn our faces towards it.
> —From the United Church of Canada's
> "Statement on the UN Declaration," March 2016[1]

Calls to Education

IF EDUCATION IS A PATH TOWARD JUSTICE THROUGH NEW WAYS of being, relationships, and identities, it is a path that bears much scrutiny for its promise of such transformative outcomes. This chapter is a form of that scrutiny. In it, I consider some implications of calls to education as a response to the United Church of Canada (UCC) statement on the adoption of the UN Declaration as a framework for reconciliation. This critical attention to invocations of education contributes to discussion about the role of education in the stated desires for new relationships, identities, and ways of being. The specific discussion that I hope to initiate with this analysis concerns the ways in which a focus on the scrutiny rather than on the promise of education's claims could contribute to the realization of relationships and justice as envisioned in the UCC statement. Calling for such discussion is not to argue against the role of education in non-Indigenous and Indigenous relations and futures, nor in response to this statement. It is, rather, an argument against overstating what education about difference, about injustice and oppression, or about reconciliation and justice can achieve. It is an argument for scrutinizing settler-Christian turns to such education, and for clearly positioning settler education as a preliminary aspect, rather than a composite part, of the stated outcomes for adopting the Declaration as a framework for reconciliation.

There are pitfalls and problems in settler turns to education in the work of addressing the ongoing injustices of colonialism; I recognize these problems from my own participation in them. The pitfalls and problems I address here involve the framing of reconciliation as a learning outcome for white-settler subjects. This chapter names and addresses the pitfall, for settler subjects, of identifying desires for allyship, solidarity, and reconciliation as learned structures of feeling or as transformative moral outcomes for the learners. By "structure of feeling," I refer to a concept from the cultural theorist Raymond Williams. Structures of feeling can be understood as a way that a social idea is experienced, or felt, personally.[2] In my use of the term, I am interested in the way that outcomes of education directed toward political or social change and engagement are accounted for through the felt experiences of participants. By "transformative moral outcomes," I refer more specifically to such educational efforts accounted for or assessed in terms of an expressed change of quality in the moral life of the learner or learners. The pitfall I want to bring into scrutiny, through what I offer in this chapter, and through the discussion and reflection that I hope to provoke, is that of assessing or expecting outcomes of educational effort in such terms. Particularly, I am concerned about settler[3] education.

In the fragment from the UCC statement cited at the opening to this chapter, there is no direct mention of education. The statement's most direct reference to education is found in one of the bullet points describing the work of a task group established to implement the principles of the UN Declaration in the church. The first point on that list of actions is to "engage the church in learning more about the UN Declaration on the Rights of Indigenous Peoples and the meaning of its 'principles, norms, and standards.'"[4] The rest of the statement, including the remainder of that list of actions for implementing the Declaration, focuses on institutional and identity change, and on efforts for alignment with the Declaration. Indeed, the statement conveys a commitment to a broad scope in such efforts:

> [the UN Declaration] requires us to review all aspects of our life as a church, from how we worship and build community to our human resources and finance policies to how we practise advocacy. It requires us to revisit our identity as a church, and how that identity does or does not foster relationships of mutuality, equality and respect, both within and beyond the walls of the church.[5]

My reading of a call to education through this statement and the subsequent letter to the church[6] is grounded in and responds to a much broader context than the words themselves. The claim of education as a path toward justice and better relations is widespread enough[7] that I place this analysis of settler-Christian education for reconciliation alongside the United Church statement in anticipation of and based on my own experiences of the calls to education that accompany statements about justice in this context. I hope to encourage a discussion about education, out of a concern for the contexts in which the UCC statement will be taken up, more so than the content of the statement itself. Again, I do not present this concern as a dismissal of education, or of contexts in which education is invoked as a path to justice, nor as a dismissal of settler

Christians or settler-Christian actions for solidarity; it is a call for scrutiny, and it is an argument for actively de-escalating the claims regarding what such education can achieve.

The Good of Education

Much research and scholarship on decolonization and anti-racism names and documents the pitfalls of white-settler moves toward solidarity, allyship, coexistence, decolonization, and reconciliation. This chapter *begins* with the knowledge that such moves are problematic and that they ought not to be the endpoint of white-settler endeavours toward justice. I specifically argue that the task for settler social justice educators is to relinquish the assessment of our own learning, or of our affective experience, as a measure of progress in the dismantling of colonialism. Calls for that relinquishment predate this chapter and this anthology. My argument is for framing any turn to education occasioned by the UCC statement in relation to such calls.

Education is not a self-evident, singular, inherent good. After all, residential schools were part of what was called "education," and there is much activism and scholarship contesting any assurance that education in its various forms is inevitably good.[8] Education is a site and process that always involves power relations, uneven histories, and all the effects of institutions and culture. It is a social phenomenon. To invoke education as a path to justice or transformed relationships and identities must be to invite a conversation, and a conversation attentive to the debates about what education does. When we encourage education in the context of settler-Indigenous relations, or specifically in response to a Canadian church's affirmation of the implementation of the Declaration, the resulting conversations can benefit from recognizing, at a bare minimum, the existing knowledge and direction from settler-colonial studies, Indigenous and anti-racism scholarship, and related activism. There is existing knowledge about the problems of taking education as a given, and also specifically about settler participation in anti-oppressive, reconciliatory, or anti-racist educational efforts.

At issue here is the structuring of learning, education, and feeling as themselves a form of reconciliation, and of reconciliation as a form of affect. Such structuring is an example of "settler moves to innocence," identified by Tuck and Yang in their analysis of what happens when decolonization is used to describe things other than "the repatriation of Indigenous land and life."[9] These settler moves to innocence, which operate in claims of or calls for decolonization as other than such repatriation, are forms of evasion that attempt to preserve settler futures. One of the evasions, or moves to innocence, that Tuck and Yang identify is in the form of an attitude we might call "free your mind and the rest will follow."[10] This occurs when the development of critical consciousness is prioritized over repatriation:

> We agree that curricula, literature, and pedagogy can be crafted to aid people in learning to see settler colonialism, to articulate critiques of settler epistemology, and set aside settler histories and values in search of ethics that reject domination and exploitation; this is not unimportant work. *However, the front-loading of critical consciousness building can waylay decolonization,* even though the experience of teaching and learning to be critical of settler colonialism can be so powerful it can feel like it is indeed making change.[11]

Protestant projects of reconciliation that focus on a structuring of settler feelings as the learned affect can helpfully be reconsidered in the terms of Tuck and Yang's ethic of incommensurability, and as a form of harm reduction rather than a form of reconciliation.[12] In an ethic of incommensurability, the measure of settler education about colonization would not be taken or offered in the terms of decolonization. These are not the same things; settler conscientization, or learning the details of colonization, are not the same as decolonization.

In the most direct terms, I am advancing an argument to explicitly resist naming Protestant social justice education as reconciliatory, as decolonizing, or even as transformative. It is possible to resist the notion that these endeavours are liberatory, or that the measure of them can even be taken in such terms. It is possible to locate this work differently: as preliminary and foundational, rather than as interventionist or of a determined moral value. I will return to describe this possibility below, in the section on reconsidering the place of education.

For now, it is important for me to first be specific about the pitfalls contained in settlers' claims of education. One such pitfall in the context of settler social justice education is the notion of goodness. This manifests in relation to the achieved or expected outcomes from settler education, and in relation to the effects on learner participants. There is a significant literature on how "being good" is a problem in relation to white-settler, and in many ways particularly Christian-settler, allyship, solidarity, and anti-racism. This is taken up, for example, by Mahrouse and by Schick and St. Denis, as discussed below.[13]

As a faculty member at a theological seminary in which attention to the Truth and Reconciliation Commission of Canada's Calls to Action is a frequent topic of conversation—indeed, they form an integral part of many of our curriculum and other institutional planning discussions—we function with a tacit understanding and an often explicit commitment to education motivated by accountability for the church's implications in colonialism. In this and in many other contexts, I have designed, organized, and facilitated educational events I would identify in terms of social justice to engage settler Christians in learning about oppression and social inequalities, and particularly through learning about colonialism and racism. I have observed and experienced moments in all those efforts that I would have considered transformative, and that I frequently found myself relating to in terms of moral outcomes for myself or the learners with whom I worked. At times I have advanced that naming of outcomes myself, and at times have found that framework ascribed to these efforts by others. I have experienced many conversations in these contexts in which participants or students have struggled to align what they have experienced during a given course or event with some assurance or evidence that their learning has made some transformative impact.

It is possible to relinquish the assessment of these educational practices, pedagogies, forms of learning in terms of reconciliation as an outcome, or in terms of affect as an outcome. It is possible to do so without relinquishing the educational efforts themselves. Sara Ahmed's attention to the non-performativity of anti-racism is informative here. In her study of "diversity" policy initiatives, she describes how policies and reports are interpreted as "doing" something that creates the effect that they describe.[14] She draws attention to how policy statements, or stated commitments to social action, are "nonperformative":

> In my model of the nonperformative, the failure of the speech act to do what it says is not a failure of intent or even circumstance, *but is actually what the speech act is doing.* Such speech acts are taken up *as if* they are performatives (as if they have brought about the effects they name), such that the names come to stand in for the effects. As a result, naming can be a way of not bringing something into effect.[15]

In accounting for the limited effects of institutional policy initiatives on diversity, or in recognizing "the unfinished nature of a social action,"[16] Ahmed is not arguing against diversity initiatives or policies; she is, rather, arguing for a commitment to questioning "what we are doing"[17] as itself an integral part of taking the action intended in such initiatives. In a related way, turning the stated "good" of education as a path to justice into a question is to turn away from assessing the effects of that education in terms of its stated intent. This may be difficult, even counterintuitive for educators and learners committed to change and to responding to calls for action. However, it is not only *possible* to relinquish the assessment of this education in the terms of transformational outcomes for learners or as some measure of moral goodness—it is also repeatedly identified as important to do so.

Critical scholarship and activism related to education, race, and settler colonialism is one source for questioning the stated goods of settler social justice education in relation to Indigenous calls to action. This is evident, for example, in the work of Tuck and Yang cited above, and the work of critical race scholars, to which I turn below. Such knowledge can usefully impact the interpretation and experience of settler Christians learning how to respond to calls to action, such as those embedded in a commitment to the implementation of the UN Declaration; and, it requires careful consideration of both settler learner and educator intent, and also of education itself.

Allyship and Solidarity as Outcomes for Social Justice Learners

Critical scholars and educators have detailed the effects of settler or white participation in anti-racist, solidaristic, or reconciliatory education and activism. Some of the specific studies I draw attention to here demonstrate ways that participants' intentions or outcomes have taken the form of, say, feelings about or regard for oneself, or assessments of one's own moral qualities in relation to racism. In their analyses and practices, these studies address the challenge of educating settlers and white-identified learners, both when we are resistant to and also when we are openly invested in anti-racist education and active solidarity, and these analyses productively turn the stated "good" or "performativity" of settler social justice education into a question. As I will return to in my conclusion to this chapter, situating such a question as part of an educational commitment and practice can contribute constructively toward the justice envisioned by the UCC statement.

In an analysis of their many years of teaching an integrative anti-racist education course as part of a teacher education program, Carol Schick and Verna St. Denis[18] identify ideological assumptions about inequality in Canada that operate in white students' understandings of themselves as relating to Indigenous people as cultural "Others."[19] They raise a caution about the ways that education in such contexts can unintentionally reinforce racist power relations if the teaching does not examine these ideologies and how they impact the practice of anti-racist education. This account of ideological assumptions,[20] and what happens in the anti-racism course, informs my argument about the problem of centring moral outcomes for churches or "settler Christians" in education for reconciliation. One key piece of Schick and St. Denis's analysis concerns student responses that express how the course "challenges [their] self-images as already knowledgeable and sympathetic to difference," and is therefore "an affront to their self-perceptions as supportive liberals."[21] A self-perception as knowledgeable, sympathetic, and supportive implies moral value and a positive assessment of one's personal goodness; the students' experiences of having these valued perceptions challenged impacts their assessment of the course.

3. RESTRUCTURED FEELINGS

The course itself strives to encourage students to question the basis of these self-perceptions, and the impulse to preserve them, in relation to race and racism. The course, and Schick and St. Denis's analysis of it, explains how dominant messages about being good or innocent in regard to racism emerge from and preserve the racial status quo, and specifically the meanings of whiteness. Schick and St. Denis's work with pre-service teachers is grounded in broader accounts of how such messages function in Canada. They write that "the concepts and ideological assumptions that we describe are embedded in the social fabric of our schools, communities, and the history of our nation; they are not unique to our preservice teachers."[22] Further, Schick and St. Denis detail how discourses of learning about culture and cultural difference, as expressed by students who come to the course "thinking they are going to learn of the other,"[23] secure and centre the white learner as the norm in relation to the perceived cultural Other about whom and about whose concerns they expect to be learning. In the case of students in the anti-racism course, this is embedded in an understanding that the purpose of their learning is to become good teachers. I recognize, having taught this very course myself, and having observed and analyzed similar educational contexts as a facilitator or participant, that for white-identified or white-settler learners, the notion of becoming a good teacher in the context of this learning rests in a similar ideological framework to that of becoming a good ally, or good at anti-racist solidarity, as an outcome of what I have referred to as settler-Christian education for social justice.

Where students in the course addressed by Schick and St. Denis "recoil at the suggestion that they are members of a dominant group,"[24] the UCC statement on the Declaration assumes a starting point in which the church as addressed in the statement is likely to engage that suggestion more openly. This is consistent with my experience as an educator: in the UCC social justice education frameworks/practices I encounter, there are many acknowledgements of the need to confront such self-perceptions. There are many examples of calls for and resources devoted to an examination of the dominant culture, white privilege, and colonialism in histories of settler-Christian and anti-racist education within the UCC. This is the context in which the UCC statement on implementing the Declaration as a framework for reconciliation, as well as the call to a "new way of being" and "new relationship" on paths toward justice, is made.²⁵ This is currently evident, for example, on the UCC website, which contains many "anti-racism" resources.²⁶ These resources and initiatives, including a mandatory anti-racism training program for all ministry personnel, include explicit work on whiteness, colonialism, and studies of settler privilege. This is not to say that individuals or groups among the letter's intended recipients would not recoil at the call to action and accountability as members of a dominant group, just as the teacher candidates in Schick and St. Denis's study would not all respond alike. It is to say, rather, that the framing of the UCC call to response is not unprecedented in its context. The UCC statement on the Declaration itself names the "settler church" as the focus for change and accountability, both in terms of this current commitment as well as throughout its history:

> The United Church has been on a journey towards reconciliation for more than 30 years. In 1986 the settler church responded to the long-standing call of Indigenous Peoples to apologize for its role in colonization and the destruction of their cultures and spiritual practices. This Apology was acknowledged by the Indigenous church two years later, with the expressed hope that the church would live out the Apology in "action and sincerity."²⁷

The call for response identifies an audience in the form of the church, and specifically the settler church.

While such references to "the settler church" invoke a context of critique, that discourse can also have the effect of naturalizing an identification of whiteness with Christianity in the course of framing an anti-racist commitment and practice. In the quote above, "church" and "settler church" are used without clear distinction. I encounter this as a persistent and significant challenge in my own work, one that can also accompany explicit intentions to grapple with the problem of whiteness. Throughout this chapter, I have been using the terms "settler education" and "settler-Christian education" to describe the focus of my call for scrutiny. A problem with this is the potential conflation of white

3. RESTRUCTURED FEELINGS

with settler and with "non-Indigenous" in ways that can both neglect racialized people not positioned as settlers and make the term "settler" appear as an "empty signifier."[28] Rachel Flowers, an Indigenous scholar whose analysis of some settler moves toward solidarity informs my own attention to this term, stresses the importance of deploying it with an understanding of its political and historical meanings and the necessary specifics of colonial relations in its use. In my use of it to describe a particular call to education, I am recognizing that there are forms of education designed to address "settlers" in ways that critically engage that careful use, and also in ways that do not. My intent is to draw attention to pitfalls that exist in both instances. There remain challenges to address when we come to education identifying or addressed as settlers, both when this is done with critical awareness and intent, and also in those instances when "settler" is used inaccurately or with less precision. These are challenges in educational efforts addressed to or organized by settler-identified individuals and groups, however carefully we approach that identification, however consciously we approach our efforts to address the relations of colonialism and the "responsibilities and action"[29] called for of settlers, and however committed we may be to solidarity as allies against colonialism.

Gada Mahrouse's work on "cross-racial solidarity activism" or "race-conscious transnational activism" as shown in some solidarity campaigns looks at activists who are "aware of whiteness as an identity and a category and [who] consciously deploy the status or privilege associated with it."[30] She writes about "a conscious and purposeful deployment of the dominant positioning that 'whiteness' inscribes onto some bodies,"[31] and specifically about how this functions among individuals who volunteer in positions variously understood as "protective accompaniers, witness-observers, 'unarmed bodyguards,' or 'human shields.'"[32] Mahrouse uses the term "race-conscious" to describe attempts to negotiate that awareness in practices of solidarity specific to the contexts she studies. She also notes how many of these activists are "self-conscious about how their interventions may in fact contribute to furthering *injustice*."[33] Part of Mahrouse's argument involves analysis and discussion of the activists' strategies and ethical negotiations in making decisions about how to visually represent the suffering of others. Drawing on the work of Hannah Arendt, she argues that "racialized global relations that transnational activism is embedded within serve to draw compassion for the activists and pity for the suffering Other, thereby reinstating unequal relations rather than disrupting them."[34] This pity for the suffering Other emerges from a similar self-perception as pre-service teachers expressing anti-racist education as a form of learning to relate to a cultural Other through their experience of the course.

Mahrouse considers the implications of white/Westerners[35] as mediators of the suffering they witness as international solidarity activists who travel to sites of conflict away from their home places. In terms of the UCC statement and the contexts of UCC social justice education, I interpret calls to education as a call to both race consciousness and to a presumed audience of race-conscious respondents. Mahrouse describes throughout her book the ways that international solidarity activists enter into and experience their actions with *expressed awareness* of the role of race and, more specifically, the intrinsic role of whiteness, even as they position themselves in the reinforcement of whiteness as a protected subject position globally. In the material publicized by the organizations involved in the solidarity action described in Mahrouse's study, "declarations of awareness of privilege and articulations of power imbalances abound."[36] The activists positioning themselves as bringing their perceived or experienced security and "antiracist intentions"[37] to solidarity with others who face violent oppression are not necessarily resistant to drawing attention to the privileges they embody in relation to others.

In her analysis of solidarity organizations and activist discourse, Mahrouse "explores how individuals constitute themselves as moral subjects through their actions and through the meanings they attribute to their actions."[38] As with the conclusions posed by Schick and St. Denis in their study of student resistance to anti-racist education, these accounts by Mahrouse of race-conscious activism reveal how the affective and ideological basis for subjects to secure a place for themselves as doing or being good in relation to the world's injustices relies on a strong affiliation with a purportedly well-intentioned collective subjectivity, in this case with Canadianness. Mahrouse's work exposes how affiliation with this subjectivity of good intention also reinforces notions of victimhood and vulnerability and continues to secure the moral and knowing subject as the white/Westerner; it "inscribes morality to the noble white/Western activist telling the story.... Assigning humanity to the Other is, after all, whiteness in its finest form."[39] These are instances of individuals acting out of a consciousness of their own privilege and at the same time confronting the limitations of those actions, of that consciousness, and of their intentions. Mahrouse's work on this is a difficult challenge to those of us who seek to counter racism and colonialism through endeavours to educate ourselves and others as allies or solidarity-seekers.

The challenges posed in these studies, of an anti-racism classroom and of race-conscious solidarity activists, represent a broad field of study and engagement with teaching and learning; this is critical work to address how those of us who have benefited from the structures and histories of race and racism can understand and act on the difficult knowledge of these benefits. When the church is asked, as in the letter regarding the UCC's commitment to the Declaration, to join "in thinking critically about the nature of the relationship between Indigenous and non-Indigenous peoples in the church and in Canada,"[40] it is a turn to this challenging and deeply studied terrain of education. It is possible for the outcomes for the participants, or subjects, that the UCC statement does identify as "settlers," as for pre-service teachers or international solidarity activists, to be assessed in relation to their good intentions or to an impact that their participation as learners might have on some broader achievement of justice—sometimes called "reconciliation"—in historically unjust relations. As I identified at the outset, this is the pitfall of assessing settler turns to education in terms of moral outcomes or structures of feeling for the learners.

Earlier I referred briefly to Rachel Flowers and her attention to the use of the term "settler." The fuller discussion she presents includes in part an account of "the problematics in conceptualizations of allyship, as well as notions of co-existence, by those purporting to act in solidarity with Indigenous peoples [and] an analysis of the settler desire for recognition by the colonized."[41] In this account of the settler desire for recognition, I recognized myself, as an educator and as a participant, in the endeavours toward justice I have been concerned with in this chapter. Flowers, naming ways that settlers interfere in Indigenous movements toward freedom, and in this description also referring to Tuck and Yang's account of moves to innocence, describes a manifestation of settler self-interest: "In the city, in the classroom, or at a protest, there is always a settler seeking my recognition. She wants me to recognize that she is distanced from the others. She is innocent. Through her look, the Other wants me to see that she is a good settler, an ally."[42] I have often participated in, and facilitated, conversations at social justice education events that are evaluative in terms of what action the education we have participated in will actually produce. I have learned, and offered, a lot of practices to elicit ideas about things to do as outcomes from whatever the activities and content of that education has been. The deep concern I am repeating in this chapter is for the ways that such conversation and such education produces the types of moments Flowers describes. She follows that description with her response to the settler seeking recognition: "But my only thought is: *Don't smile at me.*"[43]

I see that as a kind of moment that embodies the need and possibility to actively resist and relinquish the inclination to turn a desire for allyship and solidarity into a measure for the outcomes we seek in settler education. Part of the work required in settler education is to shift from conversations that situate calls to new action within our own coming to awareness or our new consciousness, and rather to situate the action, ourselves, and our learning, as supplementary to the actions of decolonization. This requires a relationship to the action of decolonizing, it requires our education, but it challenges us to resist championing our own learning as having discernible effect.

Conclusions: Reconsidering the Place of Education

A tremendous amount of brilliance, mobilization, organization, and resistance went into having any brown, black, or red bodies on the land right now at all.
—Leanne Betasamosake Simpson[44]

Leanne Betasamosake Simpson describes how current Indigenous existence results from centuries of "resistance against all odds"[45] and through long histories of mobilization, through the practices of Indigenous political systems, and through long-established forms of relating, organizing, and sharing knowledge and resources. She also identifies the initial actions and naming of the Idle No More movement in the fall and winter of 2012–13 as "only the latest mass mobilization *visible* to white Canada."[46] Simpson details how Idle No More's ability to maintain a high level of visibility through public action and online organizing relates to that long and continuous history of Indigenous survival, despite Canada's presence.

The calls for action toward which the UCC statement identifies its response exist in this long history of Indigenous mobilization. The time that we live in, and in which we strive to confront, repair, and cease the injuries and violence of Canada and colonialism, situates us all in relation to the Indigenous present Simpson describes. What I have been naming as "settler education," and specifically settler-Christian education in response to the UCC statement on the Declaration, takes place in relation to this present and to all that makes it possible. The questions I pose about any political and transformative claims that could be made about such education is not to negate or render unnecessary the feelings that settler participants or facilitators might seek or experience as outcomes from learning about how and why we exist in this present. The questions that call for a scrutiny of this education *do* advocate for detaching such feeling from itself being a measure of attaining the social or political transformation that the Declaration and other Indigenous calls to society and church require.

Barbara Applebaum, an anti-racism scholar and educator, makes a related observation. "The point," she writes, "is not to transcend 'bad feelings' but rather to fashion a new relationship to such feelings. As a result, the development of better possibilities for listening and speaking will become possible. Such an approach to being 'a problem' that does not dwell on feeling bad may inspire whites to be receptive to the point that they will be changed by what they hear."[47] Applebaum makes this point in response to George Yancy's question, posed by Yancy in the title of the anthology in which Applebaum contributes a response: "How does it feel to be a white problem?" Applebaum aligns her response with Yancy's argument that whites should "tarry" with the feeling of being a problem, and urges "whites to be skeptical of their desires for redemption,"[48] a desire which may take the form of wanting particular feelings or associating an experience of learning or awakening to injustice as a fulfilment of justice itself.

To learn about Canada *is* to learn about residential schools; how can Canada be taught without that history and the conditions that make it possible? To study and learn about Canada involves learning about the rights of Indigenous Peoples, and about the violations of these rights; it involves learning about Indigenous forms of governance and the historical relationships of Indigenous sovereignties and European colonial incursions. To learn about Canada is to learn about histories of immigration, about legislated exclusions, unequal labour practices, about the displacement of Black communities, about Black lives, about many forms of community struggle and survival in the midst of and in opposition to the establishment of Canada as a nation. There is no definable moral outcome of learning about Canada, or about the United Church of Canada, with attention to the presence of these histories. Education about residential schools, the Doctrine of Discovery, displacements from the land, Indigenous sovereignties, preservation of languages, and anything else that might be identified as part of a curriculum of learning for the purposes of those desires outlined in the UCC statement on the UN Declaration do not themselves produce reconciled subjects or forward movement on the path to justice. It is possible to continue to call for education about Canada, about colonialism, about Indigenous sovereignties and futures, without attaching such education to effects on learners, or those effects to outcomes of reconciliation, justice, or transformation.

As I consider experiences I have named here, and others, many settler Christians come out "intact" from our engagements tagged as learning about racism, reconciliation, Canada, even as consciousness and relationships shift, and even as knowledges form. There are effects and often they are experienced by learners in immediate ways. However, these are not effects to be measured in the terms of reconciliation, social justice, or decolonization. In Ahmed's terms, the effects are non-performative. The work of settler-Christian education is relational and political; however, very specific to the context I am addressing, in the interests of the justice we seek, and the new relations and politics aspired to in the church's statement on the Declaration, there is no claim to be made for a transformative moral outcome in this education. There *is* a politics that emerges in learning to relinquish that claim. For settler Christians it is a politics that requires abiding with and accepting a loss of empowerment that might otherwise come through our turns to education.

To posit a framework for education in response to the calls to learn a new path, a framework that situates its potential in what may be a more positive frame, and that accounts for the pitfalls examined above, is to imagine this call to education as a call to study and learn "the workings" or "structures" of how social life is constituted. Learning about oppression, power, culture, whiteness, race, and privilege is (like) learning an anatomy; it is like learning how a nation is held together and how it functions. Studying anatomy and learning how a body is structured and functions is incredibly valuable, but the moral outcome and the ethical imperative is different from that often invoked for social justice education. The measure of learning in relation to any ethical or moral imperatives likely shifts as we consider the content of social justice learning and that of anatomy. There are indeed ethical considerations in the study of anatomy; however, it doesn't really make you a good person to learn about how a body is structured and moves. The health of your body or anyone else's isn't immediately, nor even necessarily, affected by this knowledge. Such learning certainly can be a part of a path to health, but in and of itself the outcome of learning anatomy in the ways I am conceiving it here, is just that—the knowledge of anatomy. This is the argument I am making about a framework for education in response to the UCC statement on adopting the Declaration.

This is a framework that can be applied to multiple educational practices that would engage settler Christians in response to the UCC statement, to the Declaration, to the present in its many contexts. The church and its statement, and the United Nations and its Declaration, are more than abstract in their content or intentions. There are moments in time, events, documents, ideas, individuals, and relationships to learn about. An example that some in the intended audience of the UCC statement and letter would be familiar with, as a form of education related to the Declaration and to UCC commitments to reconciliation, is known as the KAIROS "blanket exercise."[49] As an interactive and facilitated experience of education about Indigenous and Canadian histories, the blanket exercise involves participants using blankets placed on a floor to experience simulated re-enactments of the making of Canada through violence toward Indigenous Peoples and lands. Participants experience, through a narrated and enacted account, specific events and impacts of Canadian colonial nation making and specific related forms of resistance, survival, and loss for Indigenous Peoples. The experience of such an exercise entails certain describable impacts. This would be the case for participating in a university or seminary course on race, colonialism, racism, church history, intercultural ministry, or contextual theology, or for attending an anti-racism workshop. Experiences, ideas, conversations, feelings, questions, observations, can of course be described and shared from such practices.

In a quotation from Tuck and Yang I shared in an earlier section of this chapter, they support the notion that settler education that teaches the histories of settler colonialism can "aid" in a change in values and in learning new ethics. Calls for this education, specific to learning the impacts of settler colonialism and white supremacist ideologies in multiple forms, are widespread.[50] Christianity, churches, and in specific ways white-settler-Canadian Christians, are embedded in histories and ongoing traditions that include race, racism, and colonialism. The studies of anti-racist education described in Schick and St. Denis's and in Mahrouse's analyses also clearly advocate for a type of education, and specifically for the teaching of white-identified people about whiteness and about the histories of race and racism, that impacts how we live and how we understand who we are. The educational efforts and solidarity activism referred to in these studies, as with something like participation in a blanket exercise or a seminary course or workshop on race and racism, do impact the self-perception of white-identified learners or activists in critical ways. However, it is a pitfall of settler education to equate these impacts with reconciliation, or to take them as a measure of justice, or of individual moral improvement. To tarry with being a problem, to recognize the incommensurability and non-performativity of settler-Christian education, requires us to learn new ways to ask and respond to questions about what we are doing and to practise responding to our own and others' inquiries about the effects of our education with a lot more certainty in saying "I don't know." It is possible to say that we don't know the effects, and at the same time to describe what we are learning and what we are doing, and to share and teach that knowledge in ways that turn us toward a more just future.

What we can learn, in studying the anatomies of colonialism and racism, and in learning about and seeking out the knowledges and teachings that lead to health, to the justice and new relations of the Declaration, is to recognize ourselves and the places from which we act. We can learn the intent and history and impetus for the Declaration and learn the specific histories of Indigenous governance and community in which these rights have been practised and honoured. We can study the theological praxis of the United Church of Canada, the diverse histories of Indigenous Christians, the various uses of the term "settler," the many different practices of teaching and learning anti-racism, and the different analyses and forms of decolonization globally. We can learn that whiteness impacts Christianity, and that Christianity is not white. To de-escalate the claims to transformational or moral outcomes for myself or those with whom I participate in settler-Christian social justice education, to diminish and relinquish the assessment of this teaching and learning as a discernable step on a path to justice, to scrutinize this educational work in light of abundant and accessible critique, and to situate it in, but not of, the decolonizing and Indigenous present, is itself an educational task.

Notes

1   The statement—the full title of which is "Statement on UN Declaration on the Rights of Indigenous Peoples as the Framework for Reconciliation"—is available at

https://united-church.ca/sites/default/files/undrip-united-church-statement.pdf; it is also reproduced in appendix B of this volume.

2. Williams used this concept throughout his work, and it is drawn on and further developed by other cultural theorists to understand and explain ways that social realities are encountered as felt experiences. See, for example, Raymond Williams, *Culture* (London: Fontana, 1981).
3. I address my use of the term "settler" later in the chapter.
4. United Church of Canada, "Statement on UN Declaration."
5. Ibid.
6. Moderator of the United Church of Canada, "Commitment to UN Declaration on the Rights of Indigenous Peoples," September 8, 2016, https://united-church.ca/sites/default/files/letter_undrip.pdf
7. This is evident in the long history of engagement with social justice issues through education in the United Church of Canada.
8. Critical scholarship on education in its foundations and practices is of course extensive and draws from a wide range of knowledges, theoretical traditions, and forms of critique. Examples of addressing the singularity or affiliations of education with good intent and outcome include extensive work in critical race theory and education, the critical pedagogies tradition emerging from Paulo Freire, Indigenous knowledges and practices, and postcolonial critiques of education. For contemporary educational theory, see especially Ivan Illich, *Deschooling Society* (New York: Harper Colophon, 1983); Gert J.J. Biesta, *The Beautiful Risk of Education* (New York: Routledge, 2016).
9. Eve Tuck and K. Wayne Yang, "Decolonization Is Not a Metaphor," *Decolonization: Indigeneity, Education, and Society* 1, no. 1 (2012): 21.
10. Ibid., 19.
11. Ibid. Emphasis added.
12. Ibid. Here Tuck and Yang are referring to Anna Jacobs's 2009 master's thesis on white harm reduction. See Jacobs, "Undoing the Harm of White Supremacy" (MA diss., Gallatin School, New York University, 2009).
13. See also George Yancy, ed., *White Self-Criticality beyond Anti-racism: How Does It Feel to Be a White Problem?* (Lanham, MD: Lexington Books, 2015).
14. Sara Ahmed, *On Being Included: Racism and Diversity in Institutional Life* (Durham, NC: Duke University Press, 2012).
15. Ibid., 17. Emphasis in the original.
16. Ibid., 11.
17. Ibid., 17.
18. Carol Schick and Verna St. Denis, "What Makes Anti-racist Pedagogy in Teacher Education Difficult? Three Popular Ideological Assumptions," *Alberta Journal of Educational Research* 49, no. 1 (2003): 55–69.
19. Ibid., 60.
20. Ibid. Schick and St. Denis identify three popular assumptions in student responses to the course—namely, that "race does not matter," that "everyone has equal opportunity," and that "individual acts and good intentions can secure innocence and superiority" (60).

21   Ibid., 57.
22   Ibid., 67.
23   Ibid., 65.
24   Ibid., 57.
25   United Church of Canada, "Statement on UN Declaration."
26   The UCC's official website hosts these resources under the "Justice Initiatives" heading, and they are prefaced with a statement reiterating the church's commitment to being an "anti-racist denomination." These resources are available at https://www.united-church.ca/social-action/justice-initiatives/anti-racism.
27   United Church of Canada, "Statement on UN Declaration."
28   Rachel Flowers, "Refusal to Forgive: Indigenous Women's Love and Rage," *Decolonization: Indigeneity, Education & Society* 4, no. 2 (December 17, 2015): 33.
29   Ibid.
30   Gada Mahrouse, *Conflicted Commitments: Race, Privilege, and Power in Solidarity Activism* (Montreal: McGill-Queen's University Press, 2014), 88.
31   Ibid.
32   Ibid., 19.
33   Ibid., 88.
34   Ibid., 88–9.
35   Mahrouse's explanation for her use of this term is clear and extensive in her text, in relation to the fuller analysis that she engages. See in particular her discussion of this on p. 19.
36   Ibid., 95.
37   Ibid., 104.
38   Ibid., 89.
39   Ibid., 99.
40   Moderator of the United Church of Canada, "Commitment to UN Declaration."
41   Flowers, "Refusal to Forgive," 33.
42   Ibid., 38.
43   Ibid. Emphasis in the original.
44   This line comes from Leanne Betasamosake Simpson, Rinaldo Walcott, and Glen Coulthard, "Idle No More and Black Lives Matter: An Exchange (Panel Discussion)," *Studies in Social Justice* 12, no. 1 (2018): 77.
45   Ibid.
46   Ibid.
47   Barbara Applebaum, "Flipping the Script...and Still a Problem: Staying in the Anxiety of Being a Problem," in *White Self-Criticality beyond Anti-racism: How Does It Feel to Be a White Problem?*, ed. George Yancy (Lanham, MD: Lexington Books, 2015), 16.
48   Ibid.
49   Some background is available at KAIROS Canada's website, at https://www.kairosblanketexercise.org/about/#history.
50   See Jennifer Harvey, *Dear White Christians: For Those Still Longing for Racial Reconciliation* (Grand Rapids, MI: Eerdmans, 2014), for one detailed account that directly considers the pitfalls of education "as" reconciliation.

CHAPTER 4

THE DECLARATION and the INDIGENOUS MINISTRIES of the UNITED CHURCH OF CANADA

by

ADRIAN JACOBS, KEEPER OF THE CIRCLE,
SANDY-SAULTEAUX SPIRITUAL CENTRE

T HE UNITED NATIONS DECLARATION ON THE RIGHTS OF Indigenous Peoples[1] is fundamentally about Indigenous Peoples' self-governance and the sustainability afforded through their ability to access their traditional land base. These two themes run throughout the document's preamble and forty-six articles. The United Church of Canada (UCC), in its embrace of the Truth and Reconciliation Commission of Canada's (TRC) Calls to Action, has adopted the Declaration as a framework for reconciliation between Indigenous and non-Indigenous people in Canada, including members of the UCC.[2] To live out this commitment, and to ensure that the viability of a thriving national Indigenous community of faith work is realized, the church will need to evidence Indigenous self-governance and embrace a reparations approach to land-based assets.

Further to a realized self-governance, the TRC's Call to Action 48 asks that churches ensure that their "policies, programs, and practices comply with the [Declaration]." This means that Indigenous governance needs to be centred on Indigenous values and priorities for a truly Indigenous expression of Christian faith in the UCC. This requires a centring of peoplehood rather than a denominational policy of assimilation.

An embodied faith means a tangible addressing of land issues. Indigenous Lands are mentioned or implied in six of the twenty-five paragraphs of the Declaration's preamble. Indigenous Lands are mentioned or implied in sixteen of the Declaration's forty-six articles. Indigenous Peoples' connection to the land for sustenance, spirituality, culture, and ceremony is recognized and affirmed repeatedly in the document. Without land and its ability to provide sustenance and resource, Indigenous Peoples are severely hampered in their identity and ability to function as distinct societies. The UCC is asset-rich; it regularly decommissions and disposes of properties, and therefore has the capacity to support Indigenous ministries for the foreseeable future.

These are what article 43 of the UN declaration refers to as the "minimum standards for the survival, dignity and well-being of the indigenous peoples." These are required for Indigenous communities of faith in the UCC. Indigenous folk have survived assimilation into the UCC and Indian residential schools, have asserted their dignity, and now it is time for them to flourish in all aspects of their Indigenous cultural milieu.

Denominational Identities

Belonging to a denomination and being colonized into an iteration of a Euro-Western culture are the result of very similar processes. Becoming a member of a denomination requires a subversion of one's idiosyncrasies and an affirmation of denominational commonalities. Historically, this has primarily been a

4. THE DECLARATION AND THE INDIGENOUS MINISTRIES

matter of belief and polity. In a creed or statement of faith, members declare, "We believe..." In addition to a formal creed, there is also an agreement to abide by the ethos of the denomination. These are the unwritten "family values" by which members recognize each other as parts of a unique group that differs from others.

To enter the polity of a denomination, the candidate for membership agrees to submit to the constituted authorities and the accepted decision-making process. Denominations differ as to the arrangement of authorities in their structure of decision-making. Episcopal systems emphasize the rule of bishops or overseers. Presbyterian systems feature a Council of Elders. Congregational groups vote in their workers and leaders. The UCC created a polity that combined all the sensibilities of their merging denominations in 1925.[3]

The UCC utilizes a conciliar model for its governance.[4] This is where congregational and clergy representatives from around the country gather as the highest decision-making body to determine the direction of the church at large. An influential elected moderator and a constitutionally established general secretary preside over an executive that leads the church between national gatherings. From its foundation in 1925 until 2018, conferences, composed of several presbyteries, govern in similar fashion with annual and semi-annual gatherings. Churches choose their representatives to attend presbytery, conference, and general councils. General Council 43 saw a reorganization that basically organized most of the work of the conferences and presbyteries into regions, with some work going to the national denominational body and some work to individual communities of faith.[5]

Also at General Council 43, nine Calls to the Church from the Caretakers of Our Indigenous Circle were embraced.[6] This direction arises out of the long struggle for identity and self-governance among Indigenous communities of faith and a pursuit of the responsibilities arising from the Declaration. In these Calls to the Church, the UCC affirms that "all doctrines, policies and practices based on or advocating superiority of peoples or individuals on the basis of national origin or racial, religious, ethnic or cultural differences are racist, scientifically false, legally invalid, morally condemnable and socially unjust."[7] The calls imagine the establishment and living out of the Declaration in Indigenous communities of faith. Teachings, policies, and procedures reflecting Indigenous identity, values, and Protocols are now centred in the broader Indigenous community.

Indigenous Invisibility

In any colonial enterprise, the erasure of Indigenous identity, nationhood, and land tenure are objects of colonial rule. The 1763 Royal Proclamation, for example, declares that, "whereas it is just and reasonable, and essential to *Our Interest* and the *Security of Our Colonies,* that the several Nations or Tribes of Indians, with who We are connected, and who live under *Our Protection* should not be molested or disturbed in the Possession of such *Parts of Our Dominions and Territories* as, not having been ceded to or *purchased by Us,* are reserved to them, or any of them, as *their Hunting Grounds*."[8] In 1763, the British Crown declared its dominion over Indigenous territories in what is now North America, with hunting rights remaining for Indigenous people. This assumption of radical underlying title on behalf of the Crown arises from the legal fiction of the Doctrine of Discovery, which was assumed to be valid by the US Supreme Court in its March 10, 1823, decision in *Johnson v M'Intosh*.[9] Indigenous nations were not accorded the standing and rights of European nations, including the right to own land and the attendant ability to sell it to other entities aside from the Crown.

Extermination, expulsion, or assimilation were colonial methods to eliminate the encumbrances of Indigenous Peoples' land-based, economic, and political sovereignty.[10] When Indigenous Peoples disappear as distinct entities, then the colonization project is complete. And yet, in spite of this genocidal effort, Indigenous people continue to thrive, and are now the fastest-growing ethnic community in Canada. This resilience is a result of the strength of Indigenous cultures and languages, and of Indigenous people's connection to the land.

4. THE DECLARATION AND THE INDIGENOUS MINISTRIES

While the Indigenous churches within the larger Methodist and Presbyterian Churches were included in the 1925 union that resulted in the creation of the UCC, they were not consulted on this matter. In fact, they were treated as though they had no voice; they were disappeared. General Council 41 recognized this inequity and revised the introduction to the 1925 Basis of Union to highlight this historical oversight. At that time, it also unveiled the new United Church crest, which features the common four colours of Indigenous communities and the Mohawk words *Akwe nia'tetewá:neren* (All Our Relations), as a demonstration of its sorrow over past injustices and its commitment to a better future.

Full Indigenous identity restoration would involve recognition of Indigenous claims to land, political structures, and the freedom to live as uniquely Indigenous nations capable of establishing relations with all other nations. In reference to the UCC, Indigenous communities of faith would have sustainable support from the land to ensure their flourishing, their own unique ecclesial structures, and the freedom to live as authentically Indigenous nations/communities in a peer relationship with the rest of the UCC. Failure to achieve this restoration is to maintain the colonial and denominational disappearance of Indigenous people.

Colonial Identity

European colonizers chose various methods of dealing with Indigenous nations. In some cases, the Spanish killed the ruling families and elites in what is now Latin America and inserted themselves into the resulting leadership vacuum. In other cases, Indigenous culture was sometimes tolerated if colonial forces were acknowledged and submitted to. The French were pragmatic and generally interested in trade and used intermarriage to establish advantageous relationships. The French policy of assimilation resulted in what Sophie White calls "Wild Frenchmen and Frenchified Indians."[11]

The English drew the borders of "New England" on the Eastern Seaboard of Turtle Island. They required Indigenous people within those borders to either leave or submit to assimilation. If Indigenous people resisted, then the English attempted to exterminate them. It is interesting that Indigenous people number in the scores of millions in Latin American, and that there are millions of mixed-blood and Métis people on Turtle Island. Originally numbering in the tens of millions, there remained only about a quarter of a million Indigenous people in 1900 in the English territories of Canada and the United States.

The English required the absorption of the Indigenous people within their assumed borders into colonial identity. This was achieved by the policy of assimilation. This colonial "civilization" project ran hand in hand with the "Christianization" mission of the churches. Indian residential schools applied this policy to Indigenous children stripped from their parental and community authorities and teachers. In 1986, the UCC apologized for its involvement in the assimilation project in its general church mission, and in 1998 it apologized for its role in running Indian residential schools for the Canadian federal government.[12] Indigenous communities replied that they received the apology but did not accept it as they needed to see what the apology means in practice.

Treaties

In 1613, the Haudenosaunee people made a treaty with the Dutch called Guswentah, or Two Row, and this was encoded into a Wampum Belt.[13] Wampum Belts are the sacred records of Haudenosaunee commitments in nation-to-nation agreements. This treaty making was not a new invention that started with European settlers; it came from a long line of tradition practised among Eastern Woodlands Indigenous nations.

The tubular beads making up the Wampum Belts were made from purple and white quahog shells. In order to establish sacred agreements between nations, these beads were arranged into symbols on beaded belts. Wampum Keepers maintained the memory of these belts by committing the stories to sacred retellings. Listening and reflecting were well-practised skills among

4. THE DECLARATION AND THE INDIGENOUS MINISTRIES

Indigenous folk. One event recorded by colonial scribes details an hour-long presentation by the colonial party, followed by silence and caucusing. A speaker then arose and recounted what the colonial party said for about forty-five minutes. Then there was a response to the colonial offer.

In the early 1600s, the Dutch became the world's leading colonizing power. They sailed up the Hudson River from New Amsterdam (now New York City) with a view to trade. They met the easternmost Haudenosaunee nation, the Mohawks, at the confluence of the Mohawk River and the Hudson, near the present-day city of Albany, New York. Our people treated with them and conveyed our values and how we saw the relationship. The Dutch attempted to call us children, and themselves fathers. The Mohawks immediately countered that and insisted that we would be brothers.

The Guswentah/Two Row Wampum Belt is a white belt standing for the common river of life our peoples travelled together. Two rows of purple beads parallel to each other and separated by three rows of white beads stood for the Dutch, who travelled the river in their ship of state with their people, their laws and ways, and their leaders, and the for the Haudenosaunee, who travelled the river in their canoe of state, with their people, their laws and ways, and their leaders. The three rows of white beads separating each vessel in the river represent the desire for friendship, the peace that comes from respect, and the strength that comes from right relations.

What is inherent in this Wampum Belt is the peer-to-peer nature of treaty— it is between nations. These agreements entail an unequivocal affirmation of distinct identity. Each party is respected by the other and there is no call for the conversion or colonization of the other. That each nation has their own laws and ways means that each distinct polity and culture are affirmed, and one nation is not better than the other.

At General Council 42, held in 2015 in Corner Brook, Newfoundland, I made a presentation as part of the Aboriginal Ministries Council Report in which I gave the history and principles of the Guswentah/Two Row Wampum Belt. I said to the United Church delegates, "You have stepped out of your boat and come into our boat and have taken over leadership and pushed us to the back of our own canoe. We are in the process of gently pushing your foot out of our boat and back into yours. This will be better for the both of us!" I was surprised by the applause this statement garnered.

Land and Reparations

The colonizers dealt with Indigenous people as they did in order to gain access to and then ownership over the land. The colonial record of treaties was written in English common law terms that emphasized the idea of the "final sale" in land transactions. In signing treaties with the colonizers, Indigenous nations had the understanding that they were sharing the land. The colonial justice system has relied on the Doctrine of Discovery for its assertion of underlying radical title to the land, with Indigenous Title resting upon Crown title, according to which only occupancy and use would be acknowledged for Indigenous people. The Doctrine of Discovery is a legal fiction, and the UCC has denounced and repudiated it as such.[14]

But these denunciations and repudiations are meaningless unless the UCC recognizes that they serve to undermine the Crown's underlying radical title. If this is the implication of this action, then when congregations decommission and sell their churches, they are selling an Indigenous asset on Indigenous Land. Although the UCC is in no position to change the laws of Canada in order to enforce Indigenous land rights, it can play a positive role by moving forward with a reparations approach to land issues. The UCC's Saskatchewan Conference, for example, is sending a portion of its resource revenues from the land to the All Native Circle Conference's Plains Presbytery. Knox United Church in Regina sold its church property in the city for over $1 million, of which it gave more than $100,000 to the Plains Presbytery and $40,000 to Sandy-Saulteaux Spiritual Centre in Beausejour, Manitoba.

The UCC's long-standing pursuit of justice and right relations with Indigenous people takes its logical next step with a tangible support for our Mother the Earth and the bounty it can provide for Indigenous communities of faith. Out of the billions of dollars of property assets owned by the UCC can come the millions of dollars needed to heal and rebuild the Indigenous communities destroyed by the policy of assimilation and land theft.

White Fragility and Indigenous Identity

The social media hashtag #BlackLivesMatter arose out of the many police shootings of Black people in the United States. It was vigorously countered by an #AllLivesMatter and a #BlueLivesMatter response. This either/or knee-jerk reaction assumed that proponents of the Black Lives Matter movement were saying that people who were not Black did not matter. This was not the movement's message, however. Rather, it sought an affirmation of Black dignity in the face of outrageous indignity.

A fragile identity mistook this emphasis on injustice and declared the primacy of a simple equality. This ethnocentric response has a long history in the colonial world. When white European missionaries first came to the Indigenous Peoples of Turtle Island, they had to assume the position of children. They didn't know the language. They didn't know how to survive. They didn't know the Indigenous culture. They didn't know the values of the people they depended on. They eventually learned the language and translated the Bible and gave it to Indigenous communities.

Indigenous people at first embraced the missionaries' spirituality since it spoke of great and mysterious matters. They interpreted it in the light of their own ways of thinking. Early on, there were many Indigenous lay leaders and gatherings, and these assumed the character of the people who attended. Later on, when the immigrant community grew larger than their Indigenous counterparts, the unique Indigenous character of the Christian experience was deemed suspect, and orthodoxy was imposed in its place. This meant the closing of special Indigenous training programs that often took place in Indigenous languages. The many Indigenous lay leaders were disincentivized and as a result became fewer in number. Other white missionaries came and took over the burgeoning missions and killed Indigenous initiatives. These Indigenous efforts resulted in what mission historian Ruth Tucker called "a noble failure," with the white missionary saviors running all around meeting everyone's needs.[15] A sullen Indigenous resentment permeates these mission churches, where there is little to no Indigenous ownership of the Christian enterprise.

Jesus Insisted on a People's Self-Governance

Before Jesus left this earth, he said another comforter would come and take his place as God's agent. Jesus did not hold on to his authority but gave it away. He trusted that his sometimes untrustworthy disciples would nonetheless "get it right" and carry on the liberation and healing he had begun. He had a faith in both the Holy Spirit and his followers' ability to do what needed to be done.

The apostle Paul had post-resurrection engagement with Jesus, and he maintained this same faith that those he influenced would carry the ball of leadership after he was gone. Paul's team helped the locals with the selection of good leaders and then left, only to return years later. The short discipleship tenure of both Jesus (about three years) and Paul (a few months to three years) expresses the idea that local leadership can be trusted to take over very important jobs.

The colonial and denominational insistence on an extensive and deep assimilation, followed by a lifelong allegiance to the colonial and denominational power structures, is the antithesis of the pattern laid down by Jesus and Paul. The kind of "discipleship" that Jesus mandated was not meant to result in the colonization of Indigenous nations. Nationhood expressed through languages was evidenced on the Day of Pentecost, the birthday of the church. Paul was the apostle to the Gentiles, or nations. The book of Revelation gives the picture of leaders in their splendour entering the City of God with the glory and honour of their nations. The discipleship of nations called for in the New Testament does not mean the end of nationhood and an assimilation into some universal church governance structure and culture.

The United Church *Manual*

The United Church has struggled with its *Manual*. Its development has paralleled that of the UCC's fundamental beliefs as articulated in the Twenty Articles of Doctrine statement, contained within the 1925 Basis of Union; the 1940 Statement of Faith; the 1968 New Creed; and the 2006 Song of Faith. The *Manual* has evolved from being a very prescriptive document to more of a set of guidelines in the larger church effort not to be restrictive and dodgy. There is a desire among UCC congregants to be more responsive to the sensibilities of the current times. Nevertheless, the UCC *Manual* remains a Western document, with its attendant difficulties when applied in the Indigenous context.

Indigenous leaders expressed their need for Indigenous ministry training in the 1970s. Under the supportive home missions' leadership of Reverend Doug McMurtry, candidates for training were chosen by Elders from Indigenous UCC churches in northern Manitoba and northwestern Ontario. They met for several weeks in the summer over several years, after which they were approved for ordination without the usual academic requirement of a master of divinity degree. These charter graduates became the backbone and eventual elder statesmen of the UCC Indigenous church. Reverend John Thompson was instrumental in fostering Indigenous self-governance by teaching these early leaders about liberation theology.

The UCC Indigenous churches of northern Manitoba and northwestern Ontario felt left out and at times completely ignored when it came time to meet in conference and presbytery, and so they decided to come away and establish their own Keewatin Presbytery in 1981. After a year of struggling through with the demands of the UCC *Manual*, the Keewatin Presbytery came back exhausted to the Conference of Manitoba and Northwestern Ontario, but this only furthered its members' feelings of exclusion. They decided they did not want to return to this and expressed the sentiment that "We are going to pull aside and find out who we are and then we will come back to you as ourselves."

Indigenous Ministry Training Development

This Indigenous church collective developed alongside a growing Indigenous ministry training effort. Dr. Jessie Saulteaux, from Carry-the-Kettle Reserve in Saskatchewan, had a dream about training "our own people for our churches." The Doctor Jessie Saulteaux Resource Centre (DJSRC) was born in 1984. DJSRC operated out of Prairie Christian Theological Centre at Calling Lakes Retreat Centre, in Qu'Appelle, Saskatchewan, before finally settling in Beausejour, Manitoba. UCC Indigenous lay leader Francis Sandy, from Christian Island Reserve in Ontario, wanted to see all Indigenous churches in Ontario with Indigenous ministers. To this end, Francis Sandy Theological Centre (FSTC) was established in 1987 and functioned out of Five Oaks Retreat Centre in Paris, Ontario.

Initially, DJSRC and FSTC each graduated people for ordained, commissioned, and designated lay ministry, but both organizations struggled financially and faced inadequate staffing. As a result, in September 2011, the two amalgamated into the Sandy-Saulteaux Spiritual Centre (SSSC). Representatives of DJSRC and FSTC, including board members, staff, and students, together with UCC representatives, met to discern the vision and future of an amalgamated school where a renewed Indigenous ministry mandate and adequate staffing could move the development of Indigenous ministry training forward. This amalgamation process was accomplished by the Wabung Group. *Wabung* is an Anishinaabe word for "the future."

DJSRC, FSTC, and SSSC were developed and vetted through a UCC recognition process to ensure that the church's ministry and educational parameters were met. Indigenous sensibilities were largely fulfilled by the Learning Circle model, the mentoring of Indigenous community Vision Keepers, the oversight of student development by Councils on Learning (presbytery and conference levels), and curricular selections that focused on Indigenous culture, history, and issues. The core curriculum was the same as the UCC's other clergy-training initiatives. Self-theologizing was limited to sociological issues, with some forays into core doctrines like Creation and the understanding of covenants in the history of Indigenous-Crown relations.

The need to foster of healing among Indigenous ministry candidates in the face of immense intergenerational trauma was addressed with various experimental efforts, and these were met with varying levels of success. The Indigenous church overseers and the ministry training staff knew the importance of addressing these personal healing issues, but they were limited by the training tools available. The *Wabung* process that shaped SSSC involved experimentation with ways of being and learning that were Indigenous in an effort to decolonize the training process. The Indigenous church is a dynamic, evolving community whose next stages of growth are indicated by past development.

All Native Circle Conference—Indigenous Self-Governance

At the August 1988 meeting of the UCC General Council in Victoria, British Columbia, the All Native Circle Conference (ANCC) was established, supporting a request by Aboriginal church members for their own conference, and for self-governance within the church.[16]

This momentous point in UCC history also affirmed that there would be no limitations on membership or leadership for people with same-sex attraction or relationships. ANCC, composed of sixty United churches ranging from Alberta to Quebec, became the thirteenth UCC conference. This took the initial Indigenous self-governance experiment of the Keewatin Presbytery to the conference level.

The Elders were excited and spoke of liberty to do things "our way." They hoped that adequate resources would now be devoted to real self-governance. The Learning Circle model of education and community gatherings formed the framework in which this would be accomplished. A Council of the Whole, a Council on Healing, a Council on Respect, a Council on Learning, and a Council on Sharing expressed an Indigenous methodology, in contrast to *Robert's Rules of Order*. However, this nascent autonomy devolved into an administrative effort to fulfill the demands of the UCC *Manual*.

UCC forms were difficult to fill out, but ANCC administrators did their best to interpret their meaning to the Indigenous faith communities who had to fill them out. Hand-written notes in the margins and text boxes of these forms were evidence of the cultural disconnect. ANCC Speaker Cheryl Jourdain said that United churches that displayed the new four-coloured UCC shield were attractive to Indigenous people, but when they went inside, they discovered all-white congregations. The style of service at these churches was expressive of the white UCC community's values, with pews, pulpits, preachers, hymnody, and processions. She also noted that the *Manual* had a beautiful Indigenous four-coloured background behind the new four-coloured UCC crest. She then opened it and facetiously said, "Inside, it's white!" The challenge to the Indigenous community is to open an Indigenous *Manual* and see Indigenous contents.

The Implications of the Declaration for the UCC

The UCC made a commitment to embrace the 2007 United Nations Declaration on the Rights of Indigenous Peoples. At a meeting of Indigenous and settler church leaders at Nottawasaga Inn Resort in Alliston, Ontario, a statement was released in response to Truth and Reconciliation Commission's Call to Action 48:

> Today [March 31, 2016], The United Church of Canada expresses publicly our commitment to honouring Call to Action #48, adopting and complying with the principles, norms, and standards of the United Nations Declaration on the Rights of Indigenous Peoples as the framework for reconciliation.[17]

This statement was delivered by moderator Jordan Cantwell in English and French and by Indigenous leaders in the Gitxsan, Mohawk, and Cree languages. Referring to the Declaration, it makes the following claims on behalf of the UCC:

> We understand the principles, norms, and standards of the Declaration to be reflected in:

4. THE DECLARATION AND THE INDIGENOUS MINISTRIES

- The right to self-determination
- The right to cultural and spiritual identity
- The right to participate in decision-making
- The right to lands and resources
- The right to free, prior, and informed consent
- The right to be free from discrimination

The TRC's Call to Action 48 says the UCC must ensure "that their institutions, policies, programs, and practices comply with" the Declaration.[18] To simply impose the UCC's traditional practices upon the Indigenous communities of faith is a colonial act and a violation of the Declaration. There can be no reconciliation until there is substantive recognition that Indigenous communities have their own structures and, in the words of British Columbia Elder Alberta Billy, "our own way of doing things."[19] Church policies, programs, and practices must reflect the kaleidoscope formed by the many Indigenous cultures in Canada.

Indigenous communities of faith require nothing less than an Indigenous church manual—one that looks Indigenous on the inside. This manual cannot be a one-size-fits-all rule book; rather, it must satisfy questions of appropriateness and accountability voiced by the many Indigenous communities of faith. These faith communities need to be able to address their fundamental concerns about responsibility and accountability through their own governance structures. These can then be relayed to the rest of the UCC.

Caretakers of Our Indigenous Circle

A representative group of individuals from the Indigenous ministries of the UCC (BC Native Ministries, All Native Circle Conference, ON QC Native Ministries, Aboriginal Ministries Council, and Sandy-Saulteaux Spiritual Centre) began a process of imagining what the further development of Indigenous ministries in the UCC would look like in light of the fundamental changes being imagined in the broader church. To this end, General Council 42 crafted eight remits outlining fundamental changes to the structure and practices of the UCC as a result of falling mission and service revenue and an aging and declining membership. These remits were brought forward in an effort to bring renewal to the church, and to allocate the church's budget in a way that reflects the changing times. The Aboriginal Ministries Council thus set out to negotiate with the UCC's General Council Executive on a proposal for changes in Indigenous communities of faith.

These were outlined in nine Calls to the Church, which took as their backdrop the long history of Indigenous ministry within the UCC:

1. Concerning an Office of Vocation—ensuring Indigenous ministry is overseen by competent and experienced Indigenous people and that policies arise from Indigenous sensibilities.

2. Concerning Indigenous Ministry Formation Accompaniment and Oversight—ensuring Indigenous ministry development is under the oversight and tutelage of competent Indigenous leaders and that non-Indigenous overseers are well versed in Indigenous ways of being and function.

3. Concerning Indigenous Communities of Faith Approved Ministry Placement—widening the door of what constitutes "ministry" placement to meet the evolving and growing needs in the Indigenous communities.

4. Concerning Indigenous Testamur—ensures that the approved program to prepare students for Indigenous ministry arises from Indigenous worldviews.

5. Concerning a National Indigenous Organization for Fellowship and Support—ensuring a vision for the leadership of elders and an ongoing development of self-governance compatible with Indigenous values and ways.

4. THE DECLARATION AND THE INDIGENOUS MINISTRIES

6. Concerning Belonging—ensuring the right for Indigenous communities of faith to choose their relationships with other church governing bodies.

7. Concerning Indigenous Community Leadership and Consensus Building—ensure the time and resources necessary to achieve consensus.

8. Concerning Sustainable Support—ensuring support for Indigenous ministry development.

9. Concerning Sexual Orientation and Diversity—ensuring inclusive care is taken of LGBTQ2A+ folk in the Indigenous communities of faith.

Each of the calls was preceded by a recounting of some of aspect of Indigenous ministry history. These historical points chronicled developments made in the area of each call. Building upon what Indigenous Elders have said over the years ensures development is made. Our Cree Elder from Fisher River Cree Nation, Manitoba, the Right Reverend Doctor Stan McKay, warned in light of the big changes happening in the UCC, "I hope we don't get colonized all over again."[20]

General Council 43 and the Calls to the Church

On the opening day of General Council 43, held at Durham College, in Oshawa, Ontario, the Calls to the Church were approved by an overwhelming margin. These calls did not go through the usual process for proposals brought before the General Council because the previous General Council decided that it would negotiate certain changes for Indigenous ministries. The General Council Executive had accompaniers who received the work of the caretakers and asked clarifying questions. When the calls were brought to General Council Executive in November 2017, they were approved for acceptance at General Council 43.

Extensive education and information sessions were held across the church prior to acceptance at General Council 43, and, given the special nature of the calls, they were embraced whole cloth. Now it is up to the Indigenous communities of faith to answer the "how" questions when it comes to implementing these calls.

Decolonization and Indigenous Self-Determination

The question of what an Indigenous UCC *Manual* could look like is perhaps the most intriguing and integral outcome of the church's embrace of both the TRC's Calls to Action and the UN Declaration. Dr. Patricia Vickers said, "Colonization is a spiritual act and cannot be decolonized, but must be transformed."[21] Decolonization can be viewed on a spectrum ranging from incremental change to dismantling and rebuilding. Transformation entails much more than this. Transformation is analogous to a fundamental structural change of one thing into another entity. This is the kind of restoration of Indigenous communities imagined by both the TRC and the Declaration.

Colonialism removed the locus of control from Indigenous communities and placed it in a colonial power centre or capital. This locus of control must be re-centred in Indigenous communities for all things: governance, education, culture, kinship, Protocols, ceremony, spirituality, land, et cetera. Anything less than a complete transformation is still an expression of the policy of assimilation.

Our traditional cultures still exist, in varying degrees of wholeness. Even where the cultural loss has created complete holes in our cultures, our communities have filled them, as all evolving, living entities do. The Mi'kmaq lost some of their ceremonies as a result of the Catholic Christianization of their communities, and they invited Lakota ceremonialists to teach them their pipe tradition. The number seven in their origin story related well to the Lakota Seven Ceremonies and Directions. As Indigenous people, we honour the decisions of Indigenous communities and respect their Protocols. We are not in a position to tell them they are doing things incorrectly. That is for their own people to decide.

4. THE DECLARATION AND THE INDIGENOUS MINISTRIES

Other communities have preserved most, if not all, of their traditional culture, language, teachings, and ceremonies. These communities must simply be helped to restore these elements to the rest of their members, who suffered loss through colonialism in general and Indian residential schools in particular. What a community may require in an Indigenous Testamur will remain a growing and developing dimension of Indigenous ministry training. sssc will have to find ways to honour these culturally specific dimensions as the Calls to the Church entrusts it to oversee Indigenous Testamur.

From previous conversations, and from looking forward to future developments, we know that we must focus on certain transformative elements. This includes restoring the locus of control to Indigenous communities, a move that will result in a kaleidoscope of diversity that expresses the Day of Pentecost announcement made by the Spirit through the many languages of the inauguration of the assembly of the followers of Christ.[22] This kaleidoscope of national glory will proceed into the great City of God one day![23]

Preamble over Prescription

Treaties were always accompanied by protracted negotiations and dialogue. Answering the questions that clarified the story of the treaty parties and the mutual pledges were more important than the individual commitments of the agreements. It is necessary to tell the overarching story of Indigenous communities of faith and how it has evolved prior to and as part of ucc history.

The story of exclusion and inclusion, the policy of assimilation in the Indian residential schools, the loss of language and culture, the resistance of Indigenous people, the apologies, the commitment to "living into right relations," the ministry training and recognition experiments, and the current call for continued development and reparations must be remembered by every generation. Never losing the sight of what has been is the way forward in an organic development of the healing relationship the Indigenous communities of faith have with the rest of the ucc.

This preamble story must precede any particular provisions itemized in a procedures and policy manual. This story is the most essential aspect of guiding the way forward and working together as Indigenous communities of faith and collectives and with the broader UCC. This story is of necessity a metanarrative. Indigenous communities must assemble this story and create ongoing opportunities to tell it if they are to pass it on to future generations. We need to tell the stories of Henry Bird Steinhauer, Peter Jones, Peter Jacobs, Alberta Billy, Dolly Lansdowne, Jim White, Francis Sandy, the 1970s Indian Ministry Training Program, the first Indigenous presbytery, et cetera.

Wampum Belts, Staffs, Symbols

Perhaps an even more Indigenous way than a formal manual would be to have a Wampum Belt or other Indigenous symbol serve as a mnemonic device. This symbol would act as a prompt for remembering and recounting the basic framework and responsibilities of the Indigenous faith community. This information will be committed to memory and preserved as an aspect of our Indigenous Oral Traditions.

Creating such a symbol would require a long, multi-community conversation, the aim of which would be arriving at a consensus on a framework story that captures the agreed-upon responsibilities of the member communities of faith. An appropriate symbol or symbols would then need to be assembled and kept in community or communities with assigned symbol-keepers who will recount the framework story on a periodic basis. This recounting must be done in community ceremony so that shared memory is fostered.

Membership in the Indigenous faith community/collective would require knowing and agreeing to keep the responsibilities of the framework story and understanding how the symbol expresses this. As this is reviewed and embodied in community ceremony, membership maintains vitality. The story is encoded in symbol and embodied in ceremony. This is essentially how Indigenous traditional communities have kept their cultures intact throughout more than five hundred years of concerted effort toward assimilation and extermination. Can there be a more tried and true way to keep the faith vital? Is this faith worth this kind of effort? If it isn't, then let's abandon it!

4. THE DECLARATION AND THE INDIGENOUS MINISTRIES

A True Consensus Methodology

The UCC has appropriated terms and methods used by Indigenous communities, but the spirit embedded in these have not truly been lived out. Consensus is not a flash of colour in a business meeting to measure the temperature of the room, but a deep, facilitated, and extensive community dialogue by which ways forward are brought forward from the grassroots. Colonial experience has so impacted Indigenous communities that anything that smacks of "orders from headquarters" is immediately deemed suspect; as such, it has little chance to be anything more than reluctantly and resentfully enacted, or it is ignored altogether.

Consensus is a systemic process that requires time. This process involves the presentation of issues and concerns, cultural interpretation, and the gathering of a community position that can be embraced by all. Certainly, in consensus societies, no one individual or group is forced to accept the agreements of the clear majority, and the dissenters do not undermine that community desire either. Consensus is not uniformity but an agreed way to move forward together.

By the time an issue reaches the broader community forum, little tinkering is done and a consensus on moving forward is more a matter of course. Because the preamble story is well-known, the fundamental question—"How does this action we take express our common values?"—is asked and answered. If consensus can't be reached, and the issue is a weighty matter, then it is sent back to communities of faith for further dialogue. Provisions can be made for voting in time-sensitive (by Indigenous assessment, and not because colonial people want an answer "right away!") matters or emergency situations.

Both/And, Not Either/Or

The Christian experience is a reconciling one, not one to bring destructive division. Theologizing and organizing in the Indigenous communities of faith must not be forced through an either/or grid. A both/and approach creates an open space of safe welcome. Indigenous spirituality in the Christian experience will not be a reproduction of Western systematic theology and practice, the fruit of the either/or approach.

The binary "this or that" approach of the historic missions must be scrapped. This methodology was used in the search for a "pure" orthodoxy or acceptable church experience. Debates over whether something is "pagan" or "Christian" need to be thrown on the junk pile. Even the word "Christianity" as applied to any one community's experience is misleading. The world is and should be recognized as full of different Christianities. No one community should claim their expression of the Christian experience as the standard for all others.

The gender binary is a unique Western contribution to our communities that often has no counterpart in our languages.[24] The Cree language does not have the pronouns "he" or "she." A Cree cishet[25] male student at SSSC said, "My wife is gone into town to go to the drug store. He will be back soon." When speaking in English he has to remember to include gender. His default when speaking in English is "he, him, or his." This is why he referred to his cishet female spouse as "he."

Exclusion and punishments for fundamental orientations, gifts, and abilities are foreign to many Indigenous cultures. Everything about a person in their uniqueness is a gift to the Indigenous community, regardless of whether anyone understands the gift. Litmus tests that form part of some oppressive world view must be abandoned in favour of the Indigenous primal acceptance of identity—personally and communally.

Jesus, an Anonymous Indigenous Person, a Missing or Murdered Indigenous Woman, the Cultural Transgressor

Indigenous men, women, and trans people have been killed at alarming rates by patriarchal colonial society. Jesus was so anonymous that it required a member of his inner circle to identify him in order to arrest him before his crucifixion. He was murdered by the hierarchical and patriarchal judicial system of his day. The rigid patriarchal Jewish religion and Roman Empire could not countenance someone who advocated for oppressed women and ordained a woman to be the first to proclaim his resurrection. This person who referred to themselves as a "hen desiring to gather her chicks under the feathers of her wings" for protection but was rejected and killed. This human, who, in a society marked by gender binaries, displayed gender-fluid expression, was the exception who challenged the norm and needed to be eliminated.

Jesus of the oppressed, of the rejected, of the norm-busting, of the marginalized, of the dispossessed, is an Indigenous Jesus. Jesus the slave liberator; healer of the broken heart; friend of sinners, strangers, sullied, and all stationed—this Jesus is an Indigenous Jesus. The Indigenous experience of the colonial project and the policy of assimilation orients our community to this Jesus of the margins. The days of the church as chaplain of the colonial empire are over!

Conclusion: An Apology Lived Out and Felt in the Indigenous Community

It was a significant thing for the UCC to apologize for colonization in 1986, and specifically for Indian residential schools in 1998, but the response of Indigenous Elders has been the most indicative of Indigenous concerns. During a 1984 General Council Executive meeting in British Columbia, Elder Alberta Billy broke meeting protocol and called on the church to apologize to the Indigenous community for what it did. When church leaders finally did, the answer was, "We receive the apology but we don't accept it. We need to see what this means."

When these apologies are felt in remote fly-in Indigenous communities, and the local church members can say what the UCC's apologies mean, then there will be acceptance of these words. Until then, an apology is an aspirational ideal without substance. Indigenous church members and Elders must be able to say, "I see all around me what the United Church means when it apologizes. I can feel their sincere love and good works. I can feel justice in their support and promotion of our ministries and our well-being. I know beyond doubt that the United Church of Canada loves us because of what they do and the respect they show us."

May it be so!

Notes

1. UN General Assembly, Resolution 61/295, United Nations Declaration on the Rights of Indigenous Peoples, A/RES/61/295 (October 2, 2007), https://undocs.org/A/RES/61/295.
2. The UCC's "Statement on UN Declaration on the Rights of Indigenous Peoples as the Framework for Reconciliation," from March 31, 2016, is reproduced in appendix B of this volume.
3. See United Church of Canada, *The Basis of Union*, First General Council, June 10, 1925, Toronto, Ontario, available at https://united-church.ca/sites/default/files/basis-of-union.pdf.
4. United Church of Canada, "Boards of Governance/Manual 2013," https://www.united-church.ca/sites/default/files/handbook_models-board-governance.pdf, 14.
5. Kathryn Dorrell, "Remit Enactment Means Major Structural Changes for the Church," United Church of Canada General Council 43, Oshawa Ontario, July 22, 2018, https://generalcouncil43.ca/news/remit-enactment-means-major-structural-changes-church.
6. Caretakers of Our Indigenous Circle, "Calls to the Church," United Church of Canada General Council 43, Oshawa, Ontario, July 23, 2018, https://united-church.ca/sites/default/files/06_caretakers_of_our_indigenous_circle_report_-_revised.pdf; Stephanie Strachan, "Being in Covenant with Mother Earth and All My Relations," United Church of Canada General Council 43, Oshawa, Ontario, July 23, 2018, https://generalcouncil43.ca/news/being-covenant-mother-earth-and-all-my-relations.
7. The United Nations General Assembly, *United Nations Declaration on the Rights of Indigenous People*, 2.
8. Crown-Indigenous Relations and Northern Affairs Canada, "The 250th Anniversary of the Royal Proclamation of 1763," last modified March 8, 2016, https://www.aadnc-aandc.gc.ca/eng/1370355181092/1370355203645#a6. Emphasis added.
9. Legal Information Institute, Cornell Law School, "Johnson and Graham's Lessee v. William M'Intosh," accessed February 19, 2021, https://www.law.cornell.edu/supremecourt/text/21/543.
10. "Colonialism is a form of control frequently characterized by the establishment of settler communities that result in the displacement, absorption, or destruction of pre-existing indigenous communities," Paul R. Bartrop, "Episodes from the Genocide of the Native Americans: A Review Essay," *Genocide Studies and Prevention: An International Journal* 2, no. 2 (2007): 190.
11. Sophie White, *Wild Frenchmen and Frenchified Indians: Material Culture and Race in Colonial Louisiana* (Philadelphia: University of Pennsylvania Press, 2013).
12. United Church of Canada, "1986 Apology to Indigenous Peoples," accessed April 7, 2021, https://united-church.ca/sites/default/files/apologies-response-crest.pdf.
13. See "Two Row History," Two Row Wampum Renewal Campaign, accessed February 19, 2021, http://honorthetworow.org/learn-more/history/.
14. See United Church of Canada, "Repudiation of the Doctrine of Discovery: Backgrounder," accessed April 7, 2021, https://united-church.ca/sites/default/files/doctrine-discovery-backgrounder.pdf.

4. THE DECLARATION AND THE INDIGENOUS MINISTRIES

15 Ruth Tucker, *From Jerusalem to Irian Jaya: A Biographical History of Christian Missions* (Grand Rapids, MI: Zondervan, 2011).
16 United Church of Canada, *General Council Archives Guide to Holdings Related to Residential Schools* (Toronto: Archives of the United Church of Canada, n.d.), https://www.unitedchurcharchives.ca/wp-content/uploads/2018/02/Public-Guide-to-Residential-Schools_2016.pdf, 11.
17 See appendix B in this volume.
18 Truth and Reconciliation Commission of Canada, *Truth and Reconciliation Commission of Canada: Calls to Action* (Winnipeg: Truth and Reconciliation Commission of Canada, 2015), http://trc.ca/assets/pdf/Calls_to_Action_English2.pdf.
19 Alberta Billy, unpublished remarks, Aboriginal Ministries Council, Quadra Island, British Columbia, October 17–19, 2014.
20 Unpublished remarks, Sandy-Saulteaux Spiritual Centre, Beausejour, Manitoba, January 19, 2018.
21 Unpublished remarks before the North American Institute for Indigenous Theological Studies Symposium at Wheaton College, Illinois, June 4–6, 2015.
22 Acts 2:1–11 records that on the Day of Pentecost, the Spirit spoke through many languages from many regions.
23 "The nations shall walk by its light and the rulers and leaders of the earth shall bring into it their glory.... They shall bring the glory (the splendor and majesty) and the honor of the nations into it" (Rev. 21:24–26, Amplified Bible, Classic Edition [AMPC]).
24 The term "gender binary" is used in this paragraph to highlight English-language usage and the lack of these terms in the Cree language.
25 The term "cishet" is used to refer to a person who identifies as the gender they were assigned at birth and has a heterosexual orientation. See "cishet," Dictionary.com, accessed April 7, 2021, https://www.dictionary.com/browse/cishet.

CHAPTER 5

"NOT ALONE IN THIS STRUGGLE FOR JUSTICE"
Project North and the United Church of Canada, 1975–87

by

SANDRA BEARDSALL

I T WAS, I THOUGHT, AN INNOCENT QUESTION. ON A FEBRUARY evening in 1986, a few of us were rocking gently on the black swivel chairs in the lounge of Toronto's Bond Place Hotel. I was one of a group of United Church members who had gathered to reflect for three days on the experience of church life in Canada's "North." We were that year's iteration of "Forum on the North," a small annual assembly intended to focus on the unique challenges facing the United Church of Canada in isolated communities in northern provincial regions and the territories. Although the group included Indigenous members, most of us were of white European extraction, living in resource and other northern towns. I was twenty-six years old and newly ordained. Originally from southern Ontario, I was now serving congregations in fishing outports along the southern Labrador coast. Access to these communities at that time was by two-hour ferry ride from northern Newfoundland in the summer, and by plane in the winter. To spend a few days back in an urban centre, but with people who understood northern life, seemed an ideal winter respite.

I posed my question, in this casual evening conversation, to a national United Church staff member: how did the Forum come into being? "Oh," he replied, "the Forum on the North was created to pacify white northern United Church members who were upset by Project North's privileging of 'native rights.'" Project North, formed in 1975, was an ecumenical coalition sponsored by all of Canada's largest Christian denominations, and a few smaller ones too. It involved church members (mostly in southern Canada) supporting the demands of Indigenous communities for justice across the Canadian North. It represents one of the earliest sustained actions by churches to stand in solidarity with the land rights of Indigenous Canadians. Its founders, Karmel Taylor McCullum and Hugh McCullum, had travelled extensively in the North, and they warned that a "new colonialism" was developing as "metropolitan power" moved into northern regions in quest of profit-making resources. As a young ordinand, I was supportive of Project North. It was a shock to hear that the Forum on the North stood somehow in opposition to this important activist organization. So it was that a pleasant winter gathering in Toronto served to "unsettle the settler within" me.[1]

The relationship between Project North and the United Church, including the Forum on the North, was indeed unsettling for many Canadians. It unfolded in a time of political awakening in Canadian Indigenous communities. It represented a radical change in the ways the Canadian churches related to Aboriginal Peoples. And it brought northern Aboriginal concerns into the boardrooms and furnace rooms of the South, rattling the cages of enterprise, industry, and "progress" as it travelled. Project North has been the focus of previous scholarly work.[2] The purpose of this chapter is not so much to rehearse the many projects and campaigns Indigenous communities and Project North undertook together, as to examine Project North as perhaps the earliest concerted attempt by some Canadian churches to be "allies" to Indigenous people. Before the word "reconciliation" had entered the Indigenous or settler lexicon,

5. "NOT ALONE IN THIS STRUGGLE FOR JUSTICE"

before there was yet a draft of an Indigenous rights declaration, before there were scholars attempting to describe processes of "decolonization," Aboriginal groups in northern Canada were putting their confidence in a church coalition based in the South, and a powerful partnership that would last over a decade was underway. What can we learn from that experience that might assist in understanding the principles (if there are any) and practices of Indigenous-settler engagement today? Senator Murray Sinclair has noted that "reconciliation" means "coming to terms with the injustices of the past."[3] An examination of the political, social, and ecclesial contexts of the 1970s; the formation and functioning of Project North between 1975 and 1988; and the churches' responses—with a focus on the United Church—may assist in that process of "coming to terms."

The Context: The Unjust Society

In April 1968, just days after the assassination of Martin Luther King Jr., Pierre Elliott Trudeau was elected leader of the Liberal Party of Canada, having run on the theme that "Canada must be a just society." In 1969, Trudeau's minister of Indian affairs and northern development, Jean Chrétien, tabled a White Paper—a policy document—that intended to abolish all previous legal documents pertaining to Indigenous Peoples in Canada, including the *Indian Act* and all treaties, to assimilate all "Indian" people into Canadian society.[4] Harold Cardinal, a brilliant young Cree leader, exposed the cruel irony at work in his book *The Unjust Society*. He drew aside Canada's "buckskin curtain of indifference" to point out that while "our fellow Canadians consider the promise of the Just Society, once more the Indians of Canada are betrayed by a program that offers nothing better than cultural genocide."[5] His indictment of the White Paper, and of the generations of Canadian governance under conditions that could "only be described as colonial, brutal and tyrannical," signalled that a new era was unfolding in Indigenous-settler relations.[6]

Across Canada, Aboriginal communities were organizing. The formation of the Indian Brotherhood of the Northwest Territories (IBNWT) in 1969 and the National Indian Brotherhood (NIB) in 1970 provided the political structure for a "ferocious, united" Indigenous opposition to the White Paper, forcing the Liberal government to rescind its proposals.[7] "We'll keep them in the ghetto as long as they want," Trudeau pouted.[8] In 1970, the Saddle Lake Cree Nation occupied and eventually were granted oversight of the Blue Quills residential school (near St. Paul, Alberta), the first school in Canada to be officially administered by First Nations people.[9] The Nisga'a assertion of territorial rights in the Nass Valley in 1973, the James Bay and Northern Quebec Agreement, and the Dene Declaration's statement of nationhood on July 19, 1975, all put Canada on notice that Indigenous people intended to control their destiny in ways unimagined only a decade before.

Canada's largest churches were slowly shifting in their attitudes too. By the mid-twentieth century, they were largely taking their cues from prevailing government approaches that applied the rhetoric of the social sciences to the suffering of the Indigenous people among whom they ministered. Hugh McCullum described it as "social service rather than social change: Christian hamper syndrome."[10] The churches argued that better education and skills training, housing, health care, and spiritual care would lead to more equal access to the benefits of Canadian life. "A community development approach promises the greatest hope for success,"[11] was a typical refrain. The United Church of the late 1950s and early 1960s, while it asserted that Indians must be granted the vote and otherwise take a larger role in Canadian society, was still mired in an agonizing paternalism. Its 1958 *Report of the Commission to Study Indian Work* stated: "As they move forward to take their rightful places as responsible Canadian citizens, they will need the guiding hands of wise counsellors and friends. This must be part of the church's role in the future."[12] This same report did not blush to aver that the "Residential Schools have, for more than a hundred years, made an incalculable contribution to the lives of the Indian people of Canada."[13]

By the late 1960s, however, the churches had begun to reckon with Indigenous activism and the call for justice. In 1969, the Anglican General Synod received the recommendations of *Beyond Traplines*, the report it had commissioned on its relationship with Indigenous Peoples.[14] Author Charles Hendry (a professor

5. "NOT ALONE IN THIS STRUGGLE FOR JUSTICE"

of social work and a United Church layperson) was blunt in his assessment: the church needed to change its attitudes, and to engage in a partnership of solidarity and equality with its Native constituency. The General Synod accepted the challenge. The United Church did not engage in such an unflinching self-examination, but its leaders in "Indian work" had modified their orientation. Associate Secretary E.E. Joblin began his 1969 report to the Board of Home Missions by noting that 1968 had been the International Year for Human Rights, that the Canadian churches (including the Roman Catholic Church) had pledged to act, that the churches' contributions to Indian welfare had been at best "remedial," and that compassion alone was not enough. Joblin argued that "Parliament and governments will need our support and encouragement as they seek just ways of dealing with the Indian people—in the settlement of long-standing claims and grievances *and* in a revision of the Indian Act, which will guarantee justice for both Indian and non-Indian Canadians."[15]

In the early 1970s, Canadian Christians were forming and participating in resistance movements relating to Indigenous justice, such as Citizens for Public Justice and the Interchurch Task Force on Northern Flooding. By 1975, Canada's Anglican, United, and Roman Catholic churches had made formal statements that the rights of Indigenous people "to participate as equals" took priority "over any development projects being planned for lands which had not been given up through treaties."[16] "Christian hamper syndrome" would not cut it any longer. The stage was set, or at least the denominational corner offices were primed, for a new approach.

"It Will Be of Considerable Help to Us in Our Struggle": Project North in Action, 1975–87

When the Most Reverend Ted Scott, primate of the Anglican Church of Canada, received a proposal in June 1975 for an "ecumenical research, communication, liaison facility with native organizations and churches in Canada," he was no stranger to the authors. Journalist Hugh McCullum had spent the previous seven years as editor of the church's denominational magazine, *The Anglican*

Churchman. McCullum had grown up in the Yukon as the son of an Anglican minister and retained strong ties to the North. Karmel Taylor McCullum, originally from the hamlet of Afton, near Antigonish, Nova Scotia, was a nurse and writer of short stories and poetry. She had travelled extensively with Hugh in the North, where they had been welcomed by Indigenous leaders. They also attended various Indigenous assemblies and resource development hearings. They discussed Indigenous issues with church leaders, especially Scott. He would therefore not be surprised to receive this proposal, in which they assured him as to their motives:

> Quite sincerely, Ted, it is not a need on our part to create a job for ourselves.... Nor do we want to perpetuate some kind of white involvement with native groups that is paternalistic or unwanted, rather, this proposal stems from a real belief, encouraged on us in the last two weeks, that the churches can, if they act ecumenically, do more than any other institution to provide support that Canada's original people require and request.[17]

This overture summarized the approach that Project North would take throughout its mandate. It would be a model of national ecumenical collaboration, and it would act only where requested by Indigenous groups. Only days after the letter to Primate Scott, national staff persons of the United, Anglican, and Roman Catholic churches met at United Church House with the McCullums. There was ready agreement that the churches needed a "liaison" person "across the north" to communicate with church networks, wider public contacts, and the religious and secular press, as "the story of the north is not getting to the south." Further, they acknowledged that they must strategize through connection with local groups, and that the liaison needed to happen with "people whom Natives trust."[18]

The McCullums were in the process of writing *This Land Is Not for Sale*, the first settler-authored book intended for church audiences to address Aboriginal land claims and other justice issues.[19] Their knowledge of the North, their links to northern Aboriginal leaders and to the churches, and their skills in "investigator-journalism," made the McCullums obvious candidates for this "liaison" position. Indeed, it does not appear that any other candidates were invited or considered. James Wah-Shee, president of the IBNWT, gave the project, and the McCullums, a firm endorsement:

> I believe it will be of considerable help to us in our struggle to achieve a just land claim and to establish the principles of our Dene nation to have the support and understanding of the churches and all southern groups. It will also be helpful to the Native people of the north to know that there is a research-liaison-communication facility available, staffed by two persons who know the north and its people.[20]

Within a month, the church representatives had agreed in principal to form an "Interchurch Project on Northern Development" (ICPOND) with four national staff persons as the "Administrative Committee," and the McCullums the "coordinators."[21] Soon after, the name "Project North" emerged (mercifully!) as the "descriptive" shorthand title for ICPOND.[22] The three denominations contributed equally to finance the project, which they intended to run for one year, after which the churches would decide about a further year of sponsorship. A press release in November 1975 announcing the formation of the coalition explained that the project was "designed to increase the capacities of the churches for more effective action on the ethical issues of northern development. At the same time the project will respond to requests for assistance from native organizations especially in the field of communication and southern support."[23] And so it did—not for one year but for twelve.

The eagerness of Canada's three largest churches to work together—despite the failure of church union negotiations between the Anglicans and United Church, and the once impenetrable Catholic-Protestant divide—bears witness to the energy the churches harboured for this project in 1970s Canada. Other Christian denominations quickly came to the table. By late 1977 the Lutheran Church America—Canada Section, the Mennonite Central Committee Canada, the Presbyterian Church in Canada, and the Evangelical Lutheran

Church of Canada had become supporters (the two Lutheran churches merged as the Evangelical Lutheran Church in Canada in 1986). The Society of Friends and the Jesuits were supporting members by 1981. The Baptists could not offer funding but occasionally sat in on Administrative Committee meetings;[24] the Disciples of Christ indicated the desire for a closer relationship with Project North in 1978;[25] and beginning in 1981, the Christian Reformed Church sent a volunteer to the monthly Administrative Committee gatherings.[26] Thus, over 95 percent of Canadians in the 1970s and '80s were connected through their church affiliation to this ecumenical endeavour.[27]

While Project North's specific work shifted over the twelve years of its existence, its three main tasks persisted: to research and document issues facing northern Indigenous Peoples; to communicate these issues to the "South," in part through the development of regional support groups—mostly in southern Canada; and to develop strategies for the churches to act in solidarity with Indigenous communities. To accomplish these many tasks the coordinators maintained an astonishing pace, running the Project North office, until 1980, out of their Toronto home. The McCullums described their activities in their monthly reports to the Administrative Committee (that is, the denominational representatives).

A portion of one of their 1977 reports gives a sense of the work. From April 23 to May 7, one or both McCullums, sometimes in the company of a member of the Administrative Committee, attended a Lutheran Church synod meeting in Manitoba (which included a debate with an Imperial Oil corporate manager); travelled to Washington, DC, for meetings about the American "energy crisis"; and spoke at the Saskatchewan Interchurch Energy Committee conference in Regina. Karmel attended a meeting of the Northern Coordinating Committee of the United Church at Cedar Glen, Ontario—where she encountered "a fair level of disagreement." Hugh, meanwhile, travelled between Edmonton and Calgary bolstering local support groups, speaking at public functions, and addressing the Alberta Federation of Labour, then went to Yellowknife to discuss "immediate strategies" with Dene leaders. Karmel went to Yellowknife a day later on a United Church exchange program with two German pastors who were "anxious to meet the Dene." She used the occasion to meet also with a group of non-Native supporters of Project North and with some Oblate priests. Project North also experienced the rite of passage that signified its true status as an activist organization: the coordinators and chair were summoned to discuss their northern advocacy with the RCMP's internal security branch in Toronto. The RCMP were concerned that Project North's support of the Dene might be subversive.[28] Not included in the McCullums' April 1977 report was the regular work of preparing a monthly newsletter for wide distribution. In 1982, Project North added a "Second Level Newsletter" for support groups, offering further information and action ideas.[29]

While the tasks of research, writing, strategizing, speaking, and connecting with Indigenous leaders, supporters, and other groups continued throughout Project North's mandate, the nature of the work shifted. Its most public project was also its earliest, based on the Berger Commission hearings of 1975–6 on a proposed natural gas pipeline through the Mackenzie Valley. These hearings introduced the public to Indigenous voices that most had never heard before. As Justice Thomas Berger moved from place to place, he and then the rest of Canada heard Georges Erasmus, then a community development worker with the IBNWT, explain that the Dene "have the right to decide when dams are going to be built, when the Mackenzie Highway should be built, if ever; when new cities should be built."[30] They heard an elderly Dene man, Susie Tutcho, say, "The grass and the trees are our flesh; the animals are our flesh."[31] And they heard a young woman, Gabrielle Mackenzie, explain that a pipeline would "destroy our culture of countless generations.... You must understand we are familiar with our surrounding and are content with it."[32]

In May 1977, the Berger Report, titled *Northern Frontier, Northern Homeland*, recommended a ten-year moratorium to settle Indigenous land claims and to set aside conservation areas before commencing pipeline construction. The combined power of these Indigenous voices and the suggestion that Aboriginal rights might trump energy development was electric. It gave Project North profile and focus. Change was afoot, and the media were curious; it was easy to find audiences and cultivate support. Of course, such a profile also brought controversy, but even dissent suggested that the coalition was relevant, in the thick of important issues.

By the 1980s it was difficult for Project North to maintain the momentum the Berger report had unleashed. The federal Liberal government never acted on the report. It approved a pipeline from Norman Wells, Northwest Territories, to Zama, Alberta, and gas and oil exploration continued apace in northern Canada. Indigenous communities ceased to act in concert; some of their organizations splintered into smaller regional groups, and they largely turned their attention to a different battle—to entrench Aboriginal rights in a repatriated Canadian Constitution. This was a new challenge, and made the issues "more conceptual,"[33] harder to interpret to the churches. In mid-1980, Hugh left Project North to become editor of the *United Church Observer*. Around this time, Karmel and Hugh's marriage ended. Karmel offered to resign from Project North but was named director in 1981, and she remained on staff throughout the coalition's life. Several persons moved into and out of staff roles during the 1980s. The denominational staff team (i.e., the Administrative Committee) struggled to determine its work. A staff retreat in late 1980 revealed tension, conflict, and the "hard, hostile treatment of certain individuals."[34] Questions of Project North's mandate, skills, relevance, and fraught internal relationships would persist throughout the decade.

Indigenous leaders, however, continued to seek Project North's partnership. "Project North," wrote Del Riley, president of the National Indian Brotherhood, in 1980, "has played an enormously important role in the past in informing people and mobilizing public support for treating all of the aboriginal peoples of Canada justly and with respect. It is our earnest hope that you may be able to support us by helping Canadians to understand how vital it is for our rights to be entrenched."[35] Thus, Project North staff continued to research, to inform, to travel, to seek media opportunities on behalf of Indigenous concerns. While continuing to support pipeline resistance, especially in Norman Wells, and to work on constitutional rights, the staff moved into new territory, when requested. In Project North's final years, staff spent considerable time assisting the Innu of Labrador in their fight against NATO's low-level flight exercises.

5. "NOT ALONE IN THIS STRUGGLE FOR JUSTICE"

Nonetheless, by the late 1980s the churches were ready to rethink Project North. The United Church had apologized to First Nations communities in 1986. "We tried to make you be like us and in so doing we helped to destroy the vision that made you what you were," the apology stated.[36] The breadth of issues related to Indigenous justice meant it no longer made sense to focus solely on the "North." As one Administrative Committee member put it, the "lens has shifted to Canada as a whole." Links to global Indigenous struggles were growing stronger. Further, Indigenous groups were making their own decisions about resource development, and some gave support to pipeline proposals. The easy equation of Indigenous activism with environmental activism was no longer a given.[37]

In early 1987, Tony Clarke, a Roman Catholic founder of Project North, and its current chair, proposed disbanding the coalition at the end of the year. Karmel Taylor McCullum concurred, naming what she saw as its main flaw: it was a group of settlers telling other settlers the Indigenous story. She felt increasingly uneasy about "telling the story of Aboriginal people."[38] That September, an extensive consultation meeting at—yes—the Bond Place Hotel in Toronto, gathered fifty-one Indigenous leaders, church leaders, and Project North staff and Administrative Committee members to discuss the future of Project North. While many Indigenous participants expressed trepidation about the loss of this long-time ally in the struggle, United Church minister Stan McKay argued for a redevelopment of the team, to include "a number of Native people.... We are looking for a place at the table," he said. "We are asking if the drum has a place at the table."[39]

In November 1987, Project North held its last Administrative Committee meeting and announced that the project would transition to an ecumenical Aboriginal Rights Coalition, and eventually into the work of KAIROS. Peter Hamel, a long-time Anglican staff representative to the committee, offered some reflections, beginning with lyrics from Mahler's "Resurrection" chorus:

...What has come into being
Must perish!

> *What perished must rise again!*
> *Cease from trembling!*
> *Prepare thyself to live!*
> *...What thou hast fought for*
> *Shall lead thee to God!*[40]

Reactions to Project North and the Special Case of the United Church

Project North attracted considerable attention, especially in the 1970s. The sponsoring churches, in their official statements, were supportive,[41] and they continued to "remandate" the coalition every two years—an exhausting process that added to the workload of coalition and denominational staff. Smaller denominations asked to participate even amid public challenges to Project North's positions. Northern Anglican and Roman Catholic church leaders were especially responsive, as this excerpt from a letter written by an Anglican bishop notes:

> We appreciate the clarity of your ministry and we support you in the pressures which we know you are facing.... Project North should never hope to be a popular agency and we know that it will never be easy for the members of the Project. However, we want you to know that you are supported and appreciated by this diocese.[42]

Throughout its dozen years of existence, Project North occasionally encountered disputes among Indigenous communities around their convictions and strategies. While Project North and their Indigenous partners handled these carefully, sometimes the conflict turned up in the press as "evidence" that the coalition was unwanted by Aboriginal organizations.[43] However, the most vociferous challenges to Project North came, not surprisingly, from the oil and gas companies and the press that supported them. The language of the "energy crisis" loomed large, as did the necessity of developing any resources available to avoid a collapse of the Canadian economy and to preserve Canadian sovereignty in the North. Company executives spoke of the need for the Canadian oil industry to "move into our most promising Atlantic and Arctic properties like armies of occupation."[44] They detailed the regulatory processes they faced, and they issued assurances that these "would fully serve the public interest."[45] Oil and gas exploration firms had found a treasure hidden in a field and were not about to let it escape their grasp. Industry supporters accused Project North of being southern do-gooders, unwilling to let northern Aboriginal people develop their economies. Federal cabinet minister Iona Campagnolo accused the Dene of using "public rhetoric ... written by advisors in Toronto who had little in common with, or real understanding of the people they served,"[46] while a *Globe and Mail* article quoted a Cambridge Bay Inuk who called Hugh McCullum and Tony Clarke "Toronto Eskimos."[47] An Alberta Presbyterian Missions superintendent took a similar approach, asserting that because of the pipeline moratorium, "social breakdown is reaching serious proportions," and warned that "there is a group of well-educated and articulate native people, politically astute, and that the church is being used to suit their purposes."[48]

This Presbyterian leader aside, almost all the overt ecclesial suspicion of Project North came from United Church sources. While the denomination remained officially supportive, both at General Council and in the Division of Mission in Canada (DMC), the *Observer* published articles critical of Project North, and the DMC faced tension and dissent from within about its support of Project North. The *Observer* articles tended to take a "Let's Listen to Both Sides" position, accusing Project North (and therefore the church) of failing "to talk to people in the oil and pipeline companies."[49] Within the DMC offices the dissent was stark and pointed. Resistance came from a committee within the DMC, the same division that had oversight of Project North. In 1975, just two months before the founding of Project North, the DMC had convened the first meeting of its "Northern Coordinating Committee" (NCC). The DMC tasked this group of six members, none of whom was Indigenous, with assisting the provision of ministry to the Canadian North, particularly in the many resource-based communities that had sprung up in the past decade. The group discussed ministry leadership options (such as fly-in, or company chaplaincy), dialogued with other denominations, and sent "deputations to the South," (for example, Kingston) to describe the hopes and challenges of northern resource communities and to recruit clergy for northern towns.

From the outset, the NCC was suspicious of the motives of Project North: "We are concerned that this project will produce biased information and information that will have the stamp of approval of the 'United Church of Canada'.... We expect to be informed of the Committee, but we will watch it with grave concern."[50] The NCC refused to support the pipeline moratorium, even after its sponsoring body, the DMC, had passed a motion in support.[51] Its minutes averred that "many in the 'South' do not understand the 'real north' and that many of them are listening to a few Native voices rather than coming to a broad understanding of the true Native concerns of the North and the concerns of the whites who are there."[52]

Meetings between Project North staff and the NCC did not go well. After her April 1977 meeting with the NCC, Karmel suggested that another forum was needed "to discuss the theological and moral imperatives that lie behind our rationale,"[53] even though the NCC noted in its minutes that "it was felt we had begun building a bridge of understanding between the two committees."[54] A subsequent meeting in Calgary between the NCC and Hugh fared even worse. The NCC, having invited Hugh to meet with them, also invited the CBC to be at the meeting room. The CBC were investigating a purported disagreement between Project North and the Métis Association of the NWT. (The Métis Association was in an ongoing dispute with the IBNWT and did not concur with their moratorium stance. Since Project North worked closely with the IBNWT, it was implicated in the dispute.) The NCC delivered to the CBC exactly the story it was seeking: the leader of a major church coalition steeped in conflict with the beleaguered Métis. "There was some hostility, at first," the NCC minutes note, which was perhaps a mild way to describe what was no doubt an angry exchange. The committee members suggested, according to the NCC minutes, that when the media left there could be "some honest discussion." McCullum, however, indicated "this might be a little difficult considering that we seem to have polarized our present situation."[55]

The United Church General Council, meeting in Calgary in 1977, shortly after this altercation, voted to support the pipeline moratorium. The animosity did not end, however. A Project North Administrative Committee member complained in 1978 to the DMC that the NCC received from the DMC nearly double the annual funding it allotted to Project North, despite the NCC vocally opposing a decision of the General Council.[56] The DMC, embarrassed by its renegade committee, renamed and remandated the NCC in 1980. It became the "Forum on the North" in 1980, and DMC leaders expressed the belief that this new group, focused on congregational support, was "trying to understand" the issues.[57] However, the group, under its new "Forum" moniker, continued to criticize Project North, asking, in 1985, "How are northern peoples heard on Project North boards and committees when it appears that all the representatives and staff are located in the south?"[58] (The Forum on the North members might also have asked in reply how their own group could possibly represent the North when it had no Indigenous members.) By 1986, the Forum on the North, at the meeting I attended, included two Indigenous participants and was able, grudgingly, to pass a motion asking the Labrador Presbytery to consult with Project North regarding low-level military flights. The minutes, however, added that Project North did not "know the issue of militarism well enough to be making statements."[59] In 1992, the DMC Executive proposed to replace Forum on the North with "an alternate strategy...focusing on long term strategies for isolated northern congregations."[60]

In the meantime, a different dispute arose between the United Church and Project North. In October 1984, the United Church noted that it had begun to work on "native women's rights" and started to press Project North around Indigenous women's participation in its work. At the November meeting, the United Church representative stated that the church would not participate in future strategy meetings on the Canadian Constitution "between native leaders and church leaders if women were not allowed to be present."[61] This demand threatened Project North's relationships with Indigenous communities, in which it always acceded to the Indigenous groups' decisions around representation. It also played havoc with the delicate ecumenical balance that the coalition maintained. In ecumenical dialogue, it is not for one partner to tell the others whom to appoint or send to meetings and delegations. The Project North team decided to continue in dialogue with the United Church,[62] and the issue was not raised in the minutes again.

Project North and Honourable Reconciliation

Project North belongs to recent history, and yet so much has transpired in the three decades since its official conclusion. What in this new/old story might be relevant in the current search for "honourable reconciliation" between the churches, especially the United Church of Canada, and Indigenous Peoples in Canada? Any assessment must begin with the acknowledgement that northern Indigenous leaders utilized and appreciated Project North. Throughout its mandate, they sent requests for assistance in communicating their concerns to governments, church members, and the wider Canadian public. Occasionally, they asked for help in preparing arguments or letters, and at least once in educating their own people on complex land claims issues.[63] Often they expressed appreciation. In 1977, Georges Erasmus stated: "It is the expression of support from the church constituency which has helped the Dene to realize that they are not alone in this struggle for justice."[64] Ten years later, he wrote to Karmel: "It's good to see the support and encouragement of Project North never diminishes. It makes our days a little easier."[65]

At the conference in late 1987 to determine the future of Project North's work, it was secular Indigenous leaders from First Nations across the North, from the Nisga'a to the Naskapi-Montague Innu, who expressed the gravest concerns about the potential loss that Project North's end would represent. "This message is extremely disheartening," said Richard Sidney, of the Council of Yukon Indians. "How will it be perceived by the public?" "The cards are stacked against the native people," said Nisga'a Chief Rod Robinson. "Project North should continue under the structure it has now." Fred Lennarson of the Lubicon Lake Band relayed the message of Chief Bernard Ominayak to the churches: "I urge you not to go away on a retreat in the middle of a war."[66] Any lessons learned must consider the clear evidence that Project North worked for northern Indigenous leaders.

With that priority in mind, I will list some ways that Project North succeeded in helping the churches take steps toward reconciliation, then some ways that the United Church struggled to embrace it and its agenda. Finally, I will conclude with a suggestion for all who are involved in this challenging, ongoing labour.

Project North as a Catalyst for Honourable Reconciliation

Indigenous Groups Set the Project North Agenda

In 1975, the McCullums explained their motives for the work Project North would undertake in the coming year: "We believe that the future of Canada, the quality of its democracy and its reputation—real or invented—for justice, rests on how it acts on the legitimate demands of its Original People."[67] They, and the staff and denominational representatives who worked with them, remained passionately committed to hearing, and then helping others to hear, these "legitimate demands." The Indigenous groups set the agenda. While they occasionally asked Indigenous groups if they wanted to partner with them,[68] the requests came from Indigenous leaders. Project North's leaders carefully avoided as best they could any triangulation in disputes among Indigenous groups, even the fraught Dene/Métis struggle that brought the CBC to the church meeting room in Calgary.[69] As Lutheran Clifton Monk, a long-time member of the Project North Administration Committee, affirmed to the Council of Yukon Indians, "It is for the native people to do their own thing. We have nothing to say about that, *but* to note whether Native people's proposals are being taken seriously and to criticize publicly the process when proposals are not taken seriously."[70]

Most significantly, Project North moved with these groups into less familiar territory when requested. Their initial commitment had drawn a natural link between Indigenous and environmental issues, grounded in the profound testimonies of the Dene and other Indigenous persons in front of the Berger Commission. When Indigenous leaders shifted the agenda to the complex world of treaties and then constitutional matters, so did Project North. The staff admitted that they needed to learn new information and skills, and they set about doing so.

Project North Was Not a Funding Agency

The coalition operated on a church-funded annual budget of just under $200,000 (adjusted to 2018 dollars). Those funds paid for modest staff salaries, extensive travel, and the printing and distribution of the newsletter and other resource materials.[71] In the early years, Indigenous organizations contributed to the travel budget, but these grants declined in the 1980s.[72] Project North was not a funding organization; at best it appealed to the churches to assist Indigenous groups financially,[73] and it used funds to bring Indigenous partners to "North-South" events. This policy allowed Project North to avoid the challenges of a patron-client relationship—something that can creep into any partnership of persons or groups with unequal wealth.

Project North-Indigenous Relationships Were Rights-Focused

Project North rarely spoke of "reconciliation." The point was Indigenous Rights, always. Addressing the annual meeting of the British Columbia Conference in 1977, Hugh McCullum said:

> Three weeks ago, I was up on the shores of Great Bear Lake at an assembly of the Dene people. We listened to the Dene speak in their own language and in their own way in the tiny settlement of Fort Franklin. One of the old men expressed it best of all—what it is that the Dene want, what it is that we want. He said: "We have chosen to believe in ourselves." That is the issue. The Dene have chosen self-determination and we in the churches have chosen to support them in their rights to self-determination.[74]

5. "NOT ALONE IN THIS STRUGGLE FOR JUSTICE"

The role of southern white Christians, Hugh McCullum told a theological students' conference, was to understand that "the mercy of the gospel is God's standing invitation to repent."[75] The Project North literature does not address questions of friendship. And yet, meaningful Indigenous-settler personal relationships did emerge. As Project North wound down, Georges Erasmus reflected, "There was growth on both sides.... We tried to give, along with the taking.... The relationship was eye-to-eye, an opportunity to learn and share."[76] Rights-based relationships are not simply forensic; they acknowledge personhood, and thereby make possible interpersonal reconciliation between colonizer and colonized, without centring on the redemption of the colonizer.

Project North Involved Settlers Educating Settlers

As I have noted, a significant reason for restructuring the churches' engagement in Aboriginal justice in the late 1980s was the fact that the Project North model called for church staff—who were for the duration of the Project North almost all white and from southern Canada—to describe and interpret Indigenous issues to southern white audiences. The problems with that model were and are clear, but I would like to rescue one learning from it. Indigenous people rightly become annoyed that part of their exhausting battle for justice involves teaching settlers about racism. Sometimes they state that they would like white people to educate *themselves and each other* in these basic lessons. That is what Project North did. It augmented Indigenous voices, and it scripted the issues in ways that southern audiences could grasp.

Furthermore, they did this education broadly and ecumenically. The church staff on the Administration Committee did not simply advise the coordinators; they actively engaged in the work, as we have seen. Up to a third of their denominational positions were devoted to Project North issues.[77] They navigated inter-denominational challenges so that Indigenous leaders did not have to do so. Indigenous groups, so battered by the churches until now, were surprised and encouraged by this ecumenical solidarity. "It is our earnest hope that you may be able to support us by helping Canadians to understand how vital it is for our rights to be entrenched," Del Riley of the NIB wrote to Project North staff person Heather Ross.[78] This settler responsibility persists.

Project North: Unsettling the United Church Ecclesial Identity

The United Church of Canada remained officially supportive of Project North throughout its twelve-year mandate, many of its staff and volunteers devotedly so. In that sense, Project North forms a major part of the United Church's positive first steps in transforming its relationship with Indigenous Peoples. However, there was also vocal resistance to Project North, as we have noted, and even pressure from the United Church on its Indigenous and coalition partners. For once, in their Indigenous relations, the churches seemed to get it right. Why, then, did some things go so wrong in the United Church?

As Canada's largest Protestant denomination, the United Church was founded and grounded in the notion that its mission was not only to unite Protestants, but to unite all of Canada, to be "a church with the soul of a nation."[79] Found in every region of the country, embracing a wide swath of theological perspectives, it had, until the 1970s, reined in its more radical fringes and hung together. Many church leaders assumed they could employ a liberal everyone-has-a-point orientation toward any issue, including that of colonial hegemony. A recent book on northern environmental historiography suggests that Canada's North is "not only a physical but an imagined space, with diverse ideas about where it is, who and what belongs there."[80] The Northern Coordinating Committee had taken up the notion of "many norths," and it was repeated by other church leaders.[81] While the term "many norths" may be evocative and accurate, it can be used to imply that all narratives—all diverse ideas about the North—have equal status.[82]

Yet the narratives were not equal. The "North" of the oil companies and the settler United Church congregations in northern Canada was recognizable to southern Canadians in a way that the Indigenous North was not. In 1974, Patricia Clarke described for *Observer* readers the burgeoning United Church in Yellowknife: "Here on the edge of civilization, the [United] church is crowded with capable, energetic young families." She introduced some of the parishioners—all white persons, including a nurse who travelled by plane to "remote Arctic communities," where she would get "called out at three in the morning to take a loaded gun from a crazed person."[83] One can guess the implied race of the "crazed person." The North of the 1970s Yellowknife United Church—growing, vibrant, populated largely with white transplants—was one that southern United Church readers could grasp. Such congregations were of special interest, in fact, as they represented hope and new life in a church that had begun its long and ongoing decline in membership and social importance.

United Church lay leaders in the settler North were often members of the managerial class in government or the resource industries. Chris Pearson, for example, was a member of the Northern Coordinating Committee[84] and a sometime elder in the Whitehorse United Church. He became the leader of the Yukon Progressive Conservative Party and then premier of the Yukon. In that role he withdrew the Yukon from land claims discussions. A lawyer for the Council of Yukon Indians to wrote to Clarke MacDonald, of the DMC: "You may be assured that the Council for Yukon Indians has appreciated the assistance given to it by the various church organizations in Canada including the United Church through its central office. It is unfortunate the same cannot be said for the local church."[85] The "many Norths" narrative helped to sustain the notion of the United Church as a great national project—to a point. Among the blind spots in this ecclesial identity was its failure to admit its white middle-class orientation. It did not acknowledge the issues of race and class that privileged white settlers over the colonized Indigenous population. As the writer of a letter to the *Observer* put it in 1976, church leaders had embarked on a "too-desperate bid to find a second side to listen to."[86]

Closely related to the "many Norths" image in the United Church social imaginary was the binary language of "prophetic versus pastoral." In describing the United Church's debate in 1977 around support for the pipeline moratorium, Clarke MacDonald spoke of the "tension between pastoral and prophetic concerns in the North. The delegates realized the need for some pastoral care for white congregations in the North but strongly reaffirmed Project North's prophetic role in supporting the struggle of the native people."[87] When a national church staff person reported to Forum on the North in 1988 on the "demise" of Project North, she noted that "a tandem approach (pastoral and prophetic) should be adopted in future."[88] Not surprisingly, those closest to Project North's work had no time for such a narrative. In an address to a meeting of the British Columbia Conference of the United Church in 1977, Hugh McCullum said:

> During the past two or three years the churches...have committed themselves...to see that [the] oppression [of Native people] does not continue.... And that, my brothers and sisters, has put us whether we like it or not clearly on one side of the issue. There are not two sides to the story. The prophet does not dialogue. We live the other side.[89]

"We live the other side." Where is a big-tent, liberal church to go from there? United Church leaders might have begun by dissecting the notion that there is a natural bifurcation between "prophet" and "pastor": prophecy for the colonized, and "pastoral care" for the colonizers. René Fumoleau, an Oblate priest and pastor in the Mackenzie region who ministered for decades among the Dene and who ardently supported Project North throughout its mandate, noted that northern white churches tended to "discuss the issues without any reference to faith."[90] As long as the need to do justice on behalf of the colonized can somehow be mitigated by the need for the colonizer to feel accepted or mollified, there will be no reconciliation, only salving of the colonizer's conscience. Yet "God's standing invitation to repent" is a prophetic *and* a pastoral stance, as liberation theologians have pointed out.[91]

Recent scholarship on reconciliation and reparation gives language to the irony that escaped the United Church three decades ago. It suggests that settlers must live inside the paradox colonialism has constructed. Only when settlers embrace the prophetic indictment to "live the other side" will they find their "pastoral" hope. Adam Barker puts it this way: "Settler people who hope to become effective allies must move past the desire to re-establish comfort and ask the question, 'What do we do?' from a profoundly uncomfortable place."[92] Within a decade of the end of Project North, the United Church—along with other churches that had run Indian residential schools—would indeed be in an uncomfortable place regarding Indigenous relationships. The CBC crews would again be waiting at the door, but this time it would not be for Hugh McCullum. It would be for a church that had not yet been ready, in 1977, to "live the other side." The United Church now lives in more than one "profoundly uncomfortable" place. Its numerical and financial decline continues apace, along with most of Canada's churches, and with that comes considerable loss of morale and optimism. It has apologized to several groups for deep damage committed in both its unwitting and witting proclamation of the gospel. It has committed itself to responding to the Truth and Reconciliation Commission of Canada's Calls to Action. In all this discomfort, the United Church must find an ecclesial identity that takes it beyond despair to useful hope and action. For that it will need courage, faith, and allies.

Conclusion: "Commitment, Patience, Perseverance"

I became uncomfortable over thirty years ago, when I realized I had been allocated a colonizer's ration of "pastoral care." I am grateful that Project North did not pander to my discomfort, or that of my fellow United Church members. As I read more deeply the story of this coalition—its "southern" activists and its Indigenous partners—I was frequently in awe of the sacrifice of self that came with the work. Georges Erasmus once took Tony Clarke to task for the fact that Project North paid its staff low wages. Clarke replied with astonishment: "How does this relate to the values of personal (and collective) commitment and sacrifice which have been essential to social movements for liberation throughout history?"[93]

Along with the sacrifice, however necessary, there was exhaustion, frustration, and interpersonal conflict. Georges Erasmus once admitted to his Project North allies that he did not do "inter-office stuff" as well as he used to; he was "too tired, too busy, and under too much pressure."[94] During the

1980s, Project North staff held ongoing meetings with a personnel mediator.[95] Tension among staff and among the sponsoring denominations was named as a reason for the dissolution of the coalition.[96] Although a goal at the outset had been to include "cultural and spiritual realities" in its work with the churches, it is not clear that the coalition's culture nurtured a sense of wonder or playful joy in its staff and volunteers. At his farewell dinner in 1980, Hugh McCullum told his Project North colleagues, "There is a holy pathos deep in the heart of God that yearns to see justice done to the poor and the weak—those who have no power to press their claims."[97] Did he, and they, imagine that this holy pathos might extend also to the allies of the powerless? It does not seem so. Often, they berated themselves for not doing enough, for not being clear enough in their goals, for failing to communicate well enough.

Yet the work of maintaining what Leanne Simpson calls "strong alliances and coalitions that are impermeable to colonialism's mantra of divide and conquer," surely demands a deep reserve of peace, and a generosity of spirit toward our fellow-travellers. Simpson's Nishnaabeg Elders tell her "that creating good relations takes commitment, patience, and perseverance."[98] In uncovering the Project North story, I found myself wishing that more of this graced spirit had accompanied that challenging coalition journey. I pray that such grace may walk with us now on the reconciliation road.

Notes

This chapter employs extensive archival materials related to Project North. The records of Project North, including minutes, correspondence, reports, and unpublished speeches and articles, are housed at the Archives of the General Synod of the Anglican Church of Canada, Hayden St., Toronto. United Church of Canada files relating to Project North are housed at the United Church of Canada Archives, Oak St., Toronto.

1. Paulette Regan, *Unsettling the Settler Within: Indian Residential Schools, Truth Telling, and Reconciliation in Canada* (Vancouver: UBC Press, 2011).
2. Roger Hutchinson described the role of Project North in the debate over the Mackenzie Valley Pipeline, as part of a study in comparative ethics. See *Prophets, Pastors and Public Choices: Canadian Churches and the Mackenzie Valley Pipeline Debate* (Waterloo, ON: Canadian Corporation for Studies in Religion/Wilfrid Laurier University Press, 1992).

Hutchinson and Alf Dumont reflect briefly on this narrative in a study of the United Church of Canada. See "United Church Goals and First Nations Peoples," in *The United Church of Canada: A History*, ed. Don Schweitzer (Waterloo, ON: Wilfrid Laurier University Press, 2012), 221–38. J.R. Miller mentions Project North as a positive shift in the missionary churches' approach to their relations with Indigenous people. See *Residential Schools and Reconciliation: Canada Confronts Its History* (Toronto: University of Toronto Press, 2017), 27–9.

3   Senator Murray Sinclair, oral presentation, University of Saskatchewan, April 17, 2017.
4   See Naithan Lagace and Niigaanwewidam James Sinclair, "The White Paper, 1969," *Canadian Encyclopedia*, last edited June 10, 2020, http://www.thecanadianencyclopedia.ca/en/article/the-white-paper-1969/.
5   Harold Cardinal, *The Unjust Society: The Tragedy of Canada's Indians* (Edmonton: M.G. Hurtig, 1969), 1.
6   Ibid.
7   Miller, *Residential Schools and Reconciliation*, 24.
8   Lagace and Sinclair, "White Paper."
9   See Blue Quills First Nations College, *Blue Quills First Nations College—30th Anniversary*, accessed April 7, 2021, www.bluequills.ca/wp-content/uploads/2012/02/BQ-30th-Anniversary-Book.pdf.
10 Hugh McCullum, "The Churches and Native Struggles," May 28, 1978. Typescript. General Synod Archives, Anglican Church of Canada, GS89-18, Box 5.4.
11 E.W. Scott, "Some Thoughts Concerning Ang Church Policy in Work among People of Indian Origin," July 8, 1963. Typescript. General Synod Archives, Anglican Church of Canada, GS79-8—Native Affairs.
12 United Church of Canada, *Report of the Commission to Study Indian Work*, 1958, section II(a), 9.
13 Ibid., 14.
14 Charles E. Hendry, *Beyond Traplines: Does the Church Really Care? Towards an Assessment of the Work of the Anglican Church of Canada with Canada's Native Peoples* (Toronto: Ryerson Press, 1969).
15 "Indian Work—1968: A Report to the Board of Home Missions—1969," in *Manual for Those Representing the United Church of Canada Among the Indians of Canada*, vol. 3. Binder of materials.
16 Hutchinson, *Prophets, Pastors, and Public Choices*, 15.
17 Letter from Hugh and Karmel McCullum to Ted Scott, June 1, 1975. General Synod Archives, Anglican Church of Canada, GS89-18, Box 2, Minutes 1975–7 folder.
18 Memo to Primate Scott and Ernie Willie from Russ Hatton, June 13, 1975. General Synod Archives, GS89-18, Box 6, File 0—Background.
19 Hugh McCullum and Karmel McCullum, *This Land Is Not for Sale: Canada's Original People and Their Land—a Saga of Neglect, Exploitation, and Conflict* (Toronto: Anglican Book Centre, 1975).
20 Letter to unknown recipient ("To Whom It May Concern") from James J. Wah-Shee, July 25, 1975. General Synod Archives, GS89-18, Box 6, File 0—Background.

21 Interchurch Project on Northern Development (ICPOND), August 31, 1975. General Synod Archives, GS89-18, Box 2, Minutes Folder 1975-7.
22 Ibid., Minutes, October 16, 1975.
23 Ibid., Minutes, November 28, 1975.
24 Interchurch Project, Minutes, November 29, 1976.
25 Interchurch Project, Minutes Folder 1978-80. Minutes, September 12, 1978.
26 Interchurch Project, Minutes Folder 1981-5. Minutes, February 18, 1981.
27 Brian Clarke and Stuart Macdonald, *Leaving Christianity: Changing Allegiances in Canada since 1945* (Montreal: McGill-Queen's University Press, 2017), 29, 34.
28 General Synod Archives, GS89-18, Box 2, Minutes Folder 1975-7, "Coordinators' Report," April 8–May 12, 1977.
29 Council of General Synod Archives, GS89-18, Box 6, file 3—Second Level Newsletter, March 22, 1982. Project North produced the Second Level Newsletter monthly until January 1986.
30 Patrick Scott, *Stories Told: Stories and Images of the Berger Inquiry* (Yellowknife: Edzo Institute, 2008), 53.
31 Ibid., 87.
32 Ibid., 60.
33 Cliff Monk, quoted in minutes of April 16, 1980. General Synod Archives, GS89-18, Box 2, Minutes Folder, 1978–80.
34 Ibid. Minutes of October 15, 1980.
35 Letter of Del Riley to Heather Ross, November 5, 1980. General Synod Archives GC89-18, Box 14, File 1: AFN.
36 See "1986 Apology to Indigenous Peoples," accessed April 7, 2021, https://united-church.ca/sites/default/files/apologies-response-crest.pdf.
37 General Synod Archives GC89-18, Box 2, Minutes Folder 1981-5. Minutes of November 22-3, 1983, March 20, 1984.
38 Ibid., Minutes Folder 1986-7. Minutes of January 1987 Administration Committee Meeting—Personnel Committee.
39 General Synod Archives GS89-18, Box 1.5.—Remandating (File folder 1987-1), Meeting of September 23, 1987.
40 Ibid., Peter Hamel, "Project North: Rebuilding a Vision," November 20, 1987.
41 See, for example, the affirmations of the churches in the minutes of the Action Reflection Seminar, September 11–13, 1977. General Synod Archives GS89-18, Box 2, Minutes Folder 1975-7.
42 Letter from Douglas Hambidge, Bishop of Caledonia, to Hugh McCullum, March 22, 1977. General Synod Archives, GC 89-18, Box 1.2.
43 NWT Métis break with IBNWT on pipeline (January 18, 1977, minutes). Inuit of Labrador temporarily broke with Project North: Letter from Eric Tagoona, President, Inuit Tapirisat of Canada to Hugh McCullum, March 1, 1979 (General Synod Archives, GS89-18, Box 15—PN—Inuit Files, File 8—Inuit Tapirisat of Canada—Correspondence).
44 Jack Armstrong, Chairman of Imperial Oil, in a speech delivered at the Canadian National Exhibition, 1980, quoted by Karmel Taylor McCullum, in an untitled article, June 21, 1981. General Synod Archives, GS89-18, Box 5.5—Freelance Articles 1977-81.

5. "NOT ALONE IN THIS STRUGGLE FOR JUSTICE"

45 "Meeting of Project North and Polar Gas," December 12, 1977, Toronto. Typewritten notes. General Synod Archives, GC89-18, Box 1.
46 Quoted in *Project North Newsletter* (v. 2:9, November 1978), 5.
47 "Toronto Church Group Disaster for North, Eskimo Leader Says," *Globe and Mail*, February 4, 1978. Clipping in Anglican Church of Canada General Synod Archives, GS98-14, Box 2, File 24.
48 George Johnston, "The North Now," *Presbyterian Record*, October 1980, 19.
49 James Taylor, "Let's Listen to Both Sides," *United Church Observer*, July 1976; W. Clarke MacDonald, "Church Speaks: 'Firmly on the Side of the Poor,'" and Ronald G. Willoughby, "Business Replies: 'Using the Church to Promote a One-sided Economic View," *United Church Observer*, August 1978, 16–18, 19–21.
50 United Church of Canada Archives, Acc. 95.030C, Box 40-7, Northern Coordinating Committee Minutes, Yellowknife, September 6–7, 1975.
51 General Synod Archives GS89-18, Box 2, Minutes Folder 1975–7, Meeting of October 27, 1976.
52 Ibid., Edmonton, Northern Coordinating Committee Minutes, January 23–5, 1976.
53 GS89-18, Box 2, Minutes Folder 1975–7, "Coordinators' Report," April 8–May 12, 1977.
54 UCC Archives, Acc. 95.030C, Box 40-7, Northern Coordinating Committee Minutes, April 28–May 1, 1977, 22.
55 Ibid., Calgary, Minutes of August 18–21, 1977.
56 Letter from Michael Lewis to Howard Brox, 1978. United Church of Canada Archives, Acc. 95.030C, Box 41-2—correspondence relating to Forum on the North.
57 Project North Minutes Folder, 1981–5, Meeting of February 18, 1981.
58 Acc. 95.030C, Box 40-8, Forum on the North, Minutes 1980–5, Minutes of February 8–9, 1985.
59 Project North Minutes, Folder 1986–7, Minutes of March 18–19, 1987.
60 Ac 95.100C, Box 3-8—DMC Mandate for Forum on the North, January 1992.
61 Project North Minutes, Folder 1981–5, October 15–16, 1984, November 20–1, 1984.
62 Project North Minutes, November 20–1, 1984.
63 Letter from Adeline Webber, President, Yukon Indian Women's Association, to Hugh and Karmel McCullum, May 19, 1976. General Synod Archives, GS89-18, Box 14, File 4.
64 Letter from Georges Erasmus (IBNWT) to Tony Clarke, Project North Chair, February 18, 1977. General Synod Archives, GS89-18, Box 1, Remandating, 1976–7.
65 Letter from Georges Erasmus to Karmel Taylor McCullum, May 26, 1987. General Synod Archives, GS89-18, Box 14, File 1.
66 General Synod Archives GS89-18, Box 1.5, Project North Meeting, September 23, 1987, Bond Place Hotel, Toronto.
67 McCullum and McCullum, *This Land Is Not for Sale*, 1.
68 Letter from Noel V Starblanket to Hugh McCullum, November 24, 1976. It indicates that he does not have time to meet with Project North right now as he is focused on "solidification of the NIB [National Indian Brotherhood] itself." GS89-18, Box 14, File 1.
69 NWT Métis break with IBNWT on pipeline (January 18, 1977, minutes). Inuit of Labrador temporarily broke with Project North: Letter from Eric Tagoona, President, Inuit

Tapirisat of Canada to Hugh McCullum, March 1, 1979 (General Synod Archives, GS89-18, Box 15—PN—Inuit Files, File 8—Inuit Tapirisat of Canada—Correspondence).

70 Clifton Monk, Address to Council of Yukon Indians General Assembly, Whitehorse, November 27–December 1, 1978. GS89-18, Box 14, File 4.

71 The minutes rarely included the printed budget but did on June 19, 1979. GS89-18, Box 2, Minutes Folder 1978–80. Inflation adjustment figures can be calculated at https://www.bankofcanada.ca/rates/related/inflation-calculator/.

72 Anglican Church of Canada, Internal Memo from Peter Hamel and others to staff, July 31, 1984. GS89-18, Box 1.5.

73 See letter from Cindy Gilday, Dene Nation, to Karmel Taylor MCullum, December 5, 1985. GS89-18, Box 14, File 5.

74 Speech notes for the morning of BC Conference of the UCC in Trinity Western College, Langley, BC, June 5, 1977. GS89-18, Box 5.1—Speeches 1975–80.

75 Speech Notes for the Ecumenical Forum of Canada: Canadian Theological Students' Conference, February 28, no year. GS89-18, Box 5.1—Speeches 1975–80.

76 Project North Meeting, September 23, 1987.

77 The "team members" (Administrative Committee members) each described their involvement at a meeting of the Administrative Committee. Minutes of January 21–2, 1986. GS89-18, Box 2, Minutes Folder 1986–7.

78 Letter from Del Riley, President, National Indian Brotherhood, to Heather Ross, November 5, 1980. GS89-18, Box 14, File 1.

79 Phyllis Airhart, *A Church with the Soul of a Nation: Making and Remaking the United Church of Canada* (Montreal: McGill-Queen's University Press, 2013).

80 Stephen Bocking, "Conclusion: Encounters in Northern Environmental History," in *Ice Blink: Navigating Northern Environmental History*, ed. S. Bocking and B. Martin (Calgary: University of Calgary Press, 2017), 511.

81 Northern Coordinating Committee Minutes, October 15–17, 1976. See also Hutchinson, *Prophets, Pastors*, 104n46.

82 Hutchinson devotes a chapter of *Prophets, Pastors* to "Competing Rights and Conflicting Ways of Life" (89–110).

83 Patricia Clarke, "Yellowknife: The Suburban Church in Mukluks," *United Church Observer*, October 1974, 23.

84 GS89-18, Box 2, Minutes Folder, 1975–7. Minutes of November 29, 1976.

85 Letter from Allen Lueck to Clarke MacDonald (Associate Secretary of the DMC), November 18, 1976. GC89-18, Box 14, File 3.

86 Bill Richards, Letter to the Editor, *United Church Observer*, 1976.

87 GS89-18, Box 2, Minutes Folder 1975–7. Action Reflection Seminar Minutes, September 11–13, 1977.

88 United Church of Canada Archives, Acc. 95.030C, Box 40–8. Forum on the North Minutes, February 4–7, 1988. In *Prophets, Pastors*, Hutchinson names Project North as the "prophets" in the pipeline debate and their critics as "more pastorally oriented" (121).

89 Hugh McCullum, Speech Notes for the morning of BC Conference.

90 Project North Minutes, June 20, 1978. Minutes Folder, 1978–1980.

5. "NOT ALONE IN THIS STRUGGLE FOR JUSTICE"

91 See, for example, Stephen Pattison, *Pastoral Care and Liberation Theology* (London: SPCK, 1997).
92 Adam Barker, "From Adversaries to Allies: Forging Respectful Alliances between Indigenous and Settler Peoples," in *Alliances: Re/Envisioning Indigenous-non-Indigenous Relationships*, ed. Lynne Davis (Toronto: University of Toronto Press, 2010), 323.
93 Letter from Tony Clarke to Georges Erasmus, March 12, 1981. GS98-14, Box 2.
94 Re: Reactions/reflections on the Denedeh Seminar—July 6–22, 1982. General Synod Archives, GC89-18, Box 14—Project North—Correspondence/Reports with Indigenous Groups. File 7: Dene Seminar—1981-4
95 Minutes Folder, 1986–7. Meetings of January 21–2 and March 18, 1986.
96 Paul DeGroot, "Project North to Disband, Natives Lose Major Advocate," *Edmonton Journal*, October 24, 1987. Reprint in GS89-18, Box 1.5.
97 GS98-14, Box 2.
98 Leanne Simpson, "First Words," in *Alliances: Re/Envisioning Indigenous-non-Indigenous Relationships*, edited by Lynne Davis (Toronto: University of Toronto Press, 2010), xiv.

CHAPTER 6

STORIED PLACES and SACRED RELATIONS
Métis Density, Lifeways, and Indigenous Rights in the Declaration

by

PAUL L. GAREAU

THE UNITED NATIONS DECLARATION ON THE RIGHTS OF Indigenous Peoples serves as a non-legally-binding supranational declaration of rights. It acts as a guide for restitution and justice for Indigenous Peoples around the globe who have experienced systemic oppression and misrecognition at the hands of European colonial powers. The Declaration's preamble recognizes an "urgent need to respect and promote the inherent rights of indigenous peoples which derive from their political, economic and social structures and from their cultures, spiritual traditions, histories and philosophies, especially their rights to their lands, territories and resources."[1] In a settler-colonial country like Canada, this is a powerful tool to help rectify a legacy of erasure and ethnocultural genocide of Indigenous Peoples. Though formally engaged in reconciliation, as evidenced by its eventual endorsement of the Declaration in 2016 (notably, after initially rejecting it) and the ratification into Canadian law of Bill C-15 in 2020, Canada still cannot implement the spirit of the Declaration, largely because of an unwillingness to give up unilateral access to power and resources.[2] Against the consistent ambivalence of the Canadian state, it is understandable that the United Church of Canada—a Canadian Christian denomination known for its strong engagement with social justice, but with its own history of settler colonialism, specifically regarding its participation in Indian residential schools[3]—would embrace the Declaration as an institutional effort toward generating reconciliation between settler society and Indigenous Peoples. However, before we assess the Declaration's potential to promote meaningful relations between settler society and Indigenous Peoples in Canada (i.e., the prerogative of this edited volume), we must first examine how Indigenous Peoples interpret the document.

Settler colonialism and the rise of the nation-state of Canada has done much to destabilize and fragment the cohesiveness of Indigenous relations. This is evidenced in every Indigenous nation and community across Canada by a history of state coercion, dispossession of Indigenous relations and Lands, and repression and erasure of Indigenous language and culture, and by the continued racialization and marginalization of Indigenous Peoples. The values of Traditional Knowledge; perceptions of and relations to the land, mobility, and access; the importance and operationalization of kinship, politicization, traditional economy, and gender perspectives, have been ignored, suppressed, or silenced. The Métis—a post-contact Indigenous People defined by an Indigenous Title to land, extended kinship relations, and a broad sense of mobility—were fractured by dispossession, socio-economic marginalization, and racism brought on by settler colonialism in the early twentieth century. Whether on the road allowances, on farms, in the bush, or in cities, the Métis were caught in the fissures caused by this fragmented settler-colonial landscape. Nevertheless, like all Indigenous Peoples today, the Métis are resilient in maintaining, where possible, places made sacred by a history of usage for ceremony and kinship relations. Though largely lacking ethnocultural, economic, and socio-political recognition by settler society brought on by a racialized mixedness, I argue that Métis have and continue to affirm self-determination at Catholic pilgrimage sites like Lac Ste. Anne near Edmonton—one site within the larger network of storied places making up the Métis Homeland.

The reality of Métis relations at Catholic pilgrimage sites points to a key theme of this edited volume: how to interpret religious/spiritual aspects of sacred territory in light of the Declaration. In an Indigenous context, sacredness has less to do with a binary between sacred and profane, and more to do with how Indigenous Peoples (both individuals and nations) engage in kinship relations with humans and more-than-humans, and where this occurs. For many Métis, this maintenance of relations happens at sites like Lac Ste. Anne. However, there remains a clear problem with the category of religion when it comes to understanding sacred sites for Indigenous Peoples as outlined in the Declaration. Religion (in this case, Christianity) is conflated with the power of institutions that are linked to a legacy of settler-colonial values and world view, through which settlers are naturalized to the land and Indigenous people are erased. An Indigenous interrogation of the category of religion is necessary, therefore, when reading the underlying message of the Declaration in order to account for what is important to Indigenous Peoples. Access to land, for instance, is inextricably tied to Indigenous Rights. But how do Indigenous activists and scholars describe, define, and discuss the religio-spiritual aspects of tradition, ceremony, and knowledge wrapped up in land and place?

This chapter will discuss how, for the Métis, Catholic pilgrimage sites like Lac Ste. Anne operationalize a complex relationality that affirms the Indigenous epistemologies and sovereignty mentioned throughout the Declaration. The discussion will be in three parts. First, I explain how religion and spirituality are problematic concepts for Indigenous people because they are tied to the evolution of Western civilization and are counter to Indigenous Rights. Second, I discuss theoretical frameworks that help communicate and understand Indigenous experiences of religion. And third, I argue that the Métis are not invested in upholding Christian, settler institutionalization as a means of organizing race and culture—rather, they are asserting an ethos of relations or relationality at places made sacred by Métis ways of being and knowing. This work maintains that pilgrimage to Catholic sites helps maintain Métis identity via a storied connection to place and a continued experience of complex social relations, Traditional Knowledge, mobility, socio-religious practice, and a socio-political world view. This discussion helps to affirm that the Declaration's support of Indigenous rights to self-determination and access to sacred lands applies to the Métis.

Reconciling Religion and Indigenous Peoples: Christianity vs. Native Traditionalism and Sacred Sites

The Declaration is a complex and layered document that defines and promulgates the special rights and freedoms of Indigenous Peoples across the globe. It affirms Indigenous sovereignty through self-determination in the areas of culture, governance, land entitlement, treaty recognition, kinship, and safety from harm and oppression. And religion and spirituality are mentioned several times throughout the document. Religion is defined in terms of material culture and practice, and is referred to with regards to cultural revitalization[4] and the rights to unimpeded access, manifestation, and repatriation (rematriation) of stolen items.[5] Spirituality is mentioned with more frequency, and is specifically linked to the personal well-being and development of Indigenous people: individual labour rights and child personal and spiritual welfare,[6] Indigenous connection and access to "sacred" lands and Traditional Territory,[7] the assertion that states must support Indigenous self-determination regarding traditional lands,[8] the right to maintain and develop Indigenous culture and governance systems,[9] and access to transborder communities.[10] Each of these relates to the religio-spiritual connection of Indigenous people to the land and the need for unimpeded access. Religion and spirituality, therefore, are tied in with each of the major themes of the Declaration: Indigenous sovereignty, land rights, and support from the nation-state. The obvious question, then, is why is there so much talk about religion and spirituality in the Declaration?

Religion—Christianity, more specifically—has played a major part in the global history of oppression brought about by European colonization. The project of empire building was pursued in collaboration with Christian churches as a "civilizing force" bringing Western values to foreign shores.[11] Both *terra nullius* (empty lands) and the Doctrine of Discovery have helped European empires and Christian churches justify brutal campaigns of settlement and colonization as acts of attempted civilization.[12] This civilizational defence has long served as a broad justification for engagement in antagonistic relations with Indigenous Peoples, and it still has repercussions today. As a settler-colonial state, Canada has perpetuated grave and heinous acts in the name of the common good, freedom of citizenship (i.e., enfranchisement), and Christian charity.[13] Against this legacy, there have been constructive efforts by both Indigenous and settler scholars intent on fostering dialogue between Christianity and Indigenous ways of seeing and thinking about the world.[14] Yet an important critique—one that ought to be outlined here—is deployed by Indigenous Peoples and scholars regarding the complicity of Christianity in asserting settler-colonial socio-political supremacy while denigrating Indigenous values and perspectives.

The most prominent of these voices is pre-eminent Native studies scholar and Native American activist Vine Deloria Jr.[15] In his seminal book *God Is Red*,[16] Deloria outlines the colonial legacy of Christianity and how Indigenous Peoples have responded. He writes:

> Christianity among Indians has fared rather badly during recent years. When placed next to traditional religions, it has very little to say about responsibilities to family and community; most Christians deal simply with the church as if it were the deity. Indian symbolism is not symbolic in the same way that Christian symbolism is; therefore, mixing liturgical objects has become anathema to many Indians. Indian cultural traditions provided an easy explanation for certain kinds of religious acts whereas Christian religious acts depended primarily upon the acceptance of Western culture. It was this cultural and historical perspective that Indians rejected. The result

we see today is the rapid movement away from secularism and Christianity toward a more serious traditional religious life.[17]

By highlighting socio-cultural and religious difference, Deloria shows how affirming Indigenous traditional ways serves as a rejection of settler-colonial institutionalization as a means of organizing culture. This astute observation points to how religion and secularism are one and the same in terms of the history of Western civilization and settler-colonial values. Deloria critiques Western socio-religious values around hierarchy, dualism, metaphysical transcendence, and teleology as an institutionalization that centres humanity in a sacred/profane binary and hierarchical relationship with the Divine or the Sacred. The problem is that, when deployed, these values diminish Indigenous relations, which are implicit to Tribal Religions or Native spiritualities. This interpretation is not without its problems in attempting to explicate all of Indigenous "religious" experience; nor does Deloria intend it to. Emphasizing the rejection of both Christianity and secularism, however, offers a measure of how Western socio-political values and religion are seen in Indigenous traditionalist circles. Deloria argues that to embrace traditional Native religion/spirituality is to affirm the Indigenous values of relations, land rights, and sovereignty,[18] and that these should be central values for both Indigenous Christians and Native traditionalists.

Deloria's perspective mirrors the substance and spirit of the Declaration with regards to religion and spirituality. The central conflict has always been between the settler notion of sovereignty over access to land and resource extraction, and Indigenous sovereignty over Traditional Territory and Indigenous Rights. This conflict is often played out at different levels of the judicial system. Land becomes the battleground for control, and religion or the right to religious freedom often becomes a primary legal tactic for Indigenous Peoples. Recent examples are plentiful: the Dakota Access Pipeline protest at Standing Rock Sioux Nation in North Dakota,[19] the RCMP "crackdown" on anti-fracking protestors from Elsipogtog First Nation in New Brunswick,[20] and the Canadian Supreme Court ruling against the Ktunaxa First Nation in favour of a proposed ski resort development in British Columbia.[21] Though the underlying concern

6. STORIED PLACES AND SACRED RELATIONS

in each of these cases is the need for consultation with Indigenous Peoples with regards to resource extraction and development, all have been couched in a discourse of religiosity or religious identification for both the settler state and Indigenous communities. A perfect example of this is the case of the Dakota Access Pipeline, whose state-sanctioned developers actively destroyed a sacred burial site at Standing Rock, which antagonized Indigenous Land Defenders/ Water Protectors, resulting in violent escalation and an increasingly militarized police presence in order to push back against the "Indigenous activists."[22] These tactics are part of a long legacy of colonial violence against Indigenous religious and spiritual symbols and sites, as well as possessiveness over Indigenous Lands, names, symbolism, people, and claims.[23]

In light of these many examples, it is unsurprising to see the justification of religious language and the defence of Indigenous land rights in the Declaration. But Deloria accurately assesses the danger of framing these concerns in terms of religious freedom, because courts tend to promote the ideals of objectivity and the power of the law, often claiming they have no jurisdiction over people's religious choices.[24] The Ktunaxa First Nation's defence in the Supreme Court of Canada of its right to the sacred ceremonial grounds of Jumbo Mountain is a perfect example: the ruling stated that the *Canadian Charter of Rights and Freedoms* protects people's right to worship, but not "the spiritual focal point of worship."[25] Though Deloria generalizes the courts' responses in such cases in terms of the philosophical difference between "individual consciousness" in Western perspectives and "communal traditions" in Indigenous perspectives,[26] he effectively demonstrates how this rationalist attitude toward religion imposes a particular definition of the sacredness of the land that ultimately suits the needs of the settler state. As a result, Indigenous people are left out of the circle of justice and restitution at all levels of settler society. Indigenous activists and scholars have therefore focused on drawing out Indigenous definitions of and engagements with the land that can help to disentangle it from settler-colonial discourse with regards to religion.

The sacredness of place and space for Indigenous Peoples has little to do with a sacred/profane binary or the institutional affirmation of a site that acknowledges its importance. Though the language of sacred and profane has much traction in Western religious discourse,[27] for Indigenous Peoples, sacred sites can only be understood in terms of a complex ethos of relations between humans and more-than-humans.[28] In promulgating this definition, Deloria focuses on outlining—in a comparative way vis-à-vis Western frameworks—the importance of Indigenous relations in all religio-spiritual activities, especially religious and spiritual actions/practice in relation to the land. He writes:

> Recognizing the sacredness of lands on which previous generations have lived and died is the foundation of all other sentiment. Instead of denying this dimension of our emotional lives, we should be setting aside additional places that have transcendent meaning. Sacred sites that higher powers have chosen for manifestation enable us to focus our concerns on the specific form of our lives. These places remind us of our unique relationship with the spiritual forces that govern the universe and call us to fulfill our religious vocations. These kinds of religious experiences have shown us something of the nature of the universe by an affirmative manifestation of themselves and this knowledge illuminates everything else that we know.[29]

Indigenous sacred sites are places that attest to the longevity of communal land use and gathering; they are places of communication with more-than-human beings, which is fundamental to the maintenance and creation/generation of knowledge. Control over these sites is therefore absolutely paramount to Indigenous interests, providing a means of divesting power from settler-colonial hegemony and control. Deloria is not alone in his conclusions, as this view regarding the spiritual aspect of land and Indigenous sovereignty is echoed by many other Indigenous people and Native/Indigenous studies scholars.[30] Sacredness involves collective memory through individual and collective action. The repeated actions of ceremony, storytelling, and reciprocal relations at particular meeting places imbue these places with memory; and memory is the embodied and experiential connection to ancestors and knowledge. What makes a place meaningful and sacred is the fact that people are drawn to it, and use it over and over again to feel, sense, listen, think, learn, teach, heal, and remember. But most importantly, these places serve to remind of and reaffirm reciprocal obligations to relations. Only in light of this can we understand how access to sacred sites is an Indigenous Right that must be defended. These are the underlying elements of the Indigenous religio-spiritual aspect of the Declaration.

Density and Lifeways: Expounding Indigenous Socio-religious Perspectives

Deloria's writings on religion help destabilize the hegemony of settler colonialism and affirm Indigenous self-determination with regards to Indigenous Peoples' rights and freedoms as outlined in the Declaration. Indigenous Peoples know too well the tactics and violence used by the settler state in asserting a possessiveness over Indigenous Lands, names, symbolism, and nations. Deloria's approach helps focus our priorities in terms of Indigenous sovereignty over access to and usage of sacred land. However, there remains a rhetorical and epistemological problem regarding the comparative framework that Deloria uses to validate Indigenous ways of thinking and being in resisting and critiquing settler colonialism. In using a framework of difference between Indigenous and settler-colonial world views, Deloria perpetuates a bifurcation of epistemological value wherein Indigenous ways of thinking and being remain marginalized in relation to the power of settler colonialism. In this way, Indigenous perspectives fall short of being communicated, let alone instigating change in settler-colonial society.

Chris Andersen presents an alternative to the conventional discourse on Indigenous scholarship and Native studies and their relationship to what he calls "whitestream society," or the normative structures that support the white-settler colonial world view.[31] Andersen questions the tendency in Indigenous scholarship and Native studies to point to "difference," which, in turn, promotes or assumes the hegemonic power and dominance of settler colonialism. Though Andersen's work asserts the value and overall direction of Native studies as a distinct discipline, it reflects critically on current dynamics in Indigenous epistemology. His critique focuses specifically on the scholarship of American Indian studies professor Duane Champagne and his view that Indigeneity is diametrically different from the hegemonic Western colonial way of thinking. Andersen argues that, "In line with the repressive formulation of power which anchors his understanding of Indigenous studies, for Champagne *colonialism = sameness/assimilation and indigeneity = difference/freedom*."[32] Andersen's retort is that this "analytical tack produces an emphasis on Indigenous difference which vastly oversimplifies the complex set of relations within and through which contemporary Indigenous collectivities and their histories are represented."[33] As a counter to colonial oppression, Champagne and many Native studies scholars essentialize Indigenous identity, which inadvertently denies the discipline the capacity to engage with whitestream academia and society, and lacks reflexivity in terms of power relations. In Andersen's words, Native studies becomes a "guard dog" to defend Indigenous communities and epistemologies. In its focus on the defence of Indigenous ways of thinking and knowing and resisting the settler-colonial attitudes of whitestream society, it inadvertently takes itself out of the ring of debate.

As opposed to a focus on cultural and epistemological "difference," Andersen claims the term/concept of "density" as an assertion of the breadth and diversity of Indigenous epistemology(ies). This idea of density allows for engagement with and critique of settler-colonial society while resisting its hegemonic pull. He explains, "The temporal and epistemological complexity of our relationships with whitestream society means that Indigenous studies must counter hegemonic representations of Indigeneity which marginalise or altogether ignore our density."[34] Density draws on the relational experience of Indigenous people without extracting them from their power relations with whitestream society. This, in turn, affirms an Indigenous capacity to resist normative discourses of settler colonialism. Andersen points to Moreton-Robinson to help examine the problem of how whiteness generates universality by remaining invisible or "unnamed" as it produces normativities that blanket Western societies and define knowledge production.[35] This process occurs through an optic of difference whereby (1) Indigenous people are perceived as objects rather than subjects in knowledge production, and (2) Indigenous scholars stand outside of white knowledge production, and thus are rendered discursively powerless. The idea of Indigenous density asserts a capacity to engage with Western ways of thinking. "Thus, teaching about whiteness, how whiteness frames Indigeneity and how Indigenous people know whiteness should stand as a central component of the discipline of Indigenous studies."[36] Indigenous ways of knowing and being, as defined in the corpus of Indigenous studies scholarship and by Indigenous communities worldwide, inform this notion of density. In other words, through their individual and collective density, Indigenous Peoples have the capacity to critique and resist the forces of settler colonialism on equal terms.

It is essential to note that Andersen's work is not programmatic in terms of outlining what density is and how it should be defined to help scholars and communities resist the legacy of settler colonialism and whitestream society. He leaves it up to Indigenous people to see how language, philosophy, governance, economy, ecology, gender, and kinship serve to fill out this density. Ultimately, density is a baseline principle that emphasizes the complexity of Indigenous epistemologies in a modern engagement with the world.

Another key problem in the discussion of religion and Indigenous ways of knowing and being is that of institutionalization. As pointed out by Deloria in reference to the courts, Indigenous people are forced to deploy religious terms and definitions in order to communicate their rights and needs within settler-colonial systems. The problem is that these terms and definitions are not drawn from Indigenous experiences, but were developed within a settler-colonial world view. In other words, the use of religious language reflects a closed circuit of settler-colonial normalcy. As David Delgado Shorter claims,[37] even the assertion of Native spirituality, or usage of the term "sacred," represents a conceptual affirmation of the settler-colonial dichotomy between the spiritual and the material. He explains, "we know that the term ['sacred'] carries with it the Cartesian notion of a spirit/body divide. We have little evidence that most indigenous people think of the world according to this divide."[38]

Shorter argues that, due to "conceptual slippage," notions of religion and spirituality must be further developed in order to consider the Indigenous frame of relationality.

In response to these inherent problems of definition, John Grim[39] delineates the concept of Indigenous "lifeways," which is based on Indigenous epistemology and the formation of Indigenous knowledge through action and engagement with Indigenous relations. Grim explains:

> Lifeway is an interrogative concept that raises questions about the ways in which diverse indigenous communities celebrate, work towards, and reflect on their wholeness as a people. Indigenous knowledge is a key component in this communal reflection. In their diverse ways of knowing the world, indigenous peoples draw out their identity and meaning-in-the-world in both the presence of ecosystems and the authority of cosmology. These reciprocal ways of knowing in indigenous lifeways manifest differences in expression and underlie the wisdom and specificity of indigenous knowledge.[40]

In correlation with Deloria, Indigenous lifeways as a means of knowledge formation is based on storied interaction with the land. The land, upon which social, political, and economic kinship relations are enacted and reciprocated among humans and with more-than-human beings, is central. The land is made up of material and metaphysical spaces where humanity is not the centre of existence or knowledge production, but one element in contact and in negotiation with many others. These negotiated points of contact are always informed and motivated by an experiential and reciprocal exchange of values and knowledge that happens again and again.

The concept of lifeways is a non-dualistic, non-hierarchical framework that focuses on experience as the key factor in knowledge formation and transfer. Grim writes, "Often, when it is imaged in the immediacy of land, a sacred site may be more like a portal leading to that depth than simply the site of the sacred in and of itself."[41] These performative and experiential aspects form a massive chain of interactive, historical transmission that is cyclical rather than teleological. Grim asserts that "indigenous knowledge in its diverse expressions seeks to integrate an authenticity and originality of knowing by exploring the pervasive, interactive, and process-punctuated characters of time, space, authority, and spiritual presences."[42] Ceremony and sacred space are intersections for this experiential knowledge, which Grim describes as traditional (intergenerational transmission of knowledge), empirical (what one experiences), and revelatory (knowledge that appears through dreams, visions, and intuition—spiritual in nature). Lifeways is a flexible and resilient concept that describes how the confluence of complex Indigenous knowledges form and are informed by relationships through ceremony in storied and collectively significant (i.e., sacred) places.

When considering the religious elements of the Declaration, we can see how sacred places are key to affirming Indigenous Peoples' density and lifeways, and as such must be safeguarded and protected for the sake of Indigenous sovereignty. With an understanding of these Indigenous frameworks, we can now shift our attention to the Métis experience of religion and how the Métis fit within the Declaration. As we will see, conventional conceptualizations of race, religion, and Indigeneity support the portrayal of Métis as mixed-bloods and hybrid/syncretistic Christians, which ends up affirming settler-colonial values and a Eurocentric world view. This presents a challenge to the inclusion of the Métis, who share the political needs for protection and affirmation of sovereignty outlined in the Declaration.

Métis Density and Lifeways: Unpacking Métis Experiences of Religion

The Métis are an Indigenous People who have been defined (which is to say, misrepresented) by their racial mixing à-la-creolization, and their religious syncretism between Christianity (i.e., religion) and Indigenous traditionalism (i.e., spirituality). Sacred sites, which First Nations have done so much political work to gain control over, are equally important to the Métis. The problem is one of neglect or misrecognition of Métis perspectives due to a persistent colonial mindset that affirms the "Métis-as-mixed" trope, and therefore, their religious engagement as inauthentically Indigenous (i.e., Christian). The purpose of this chapter is to provide background on the complex Indigenous ways of knowing and being, and how these relate to the categories of religion and spirituality, so that the Métis can be included without recourse to a homogenizing Indigenous identity and experience. This discussion aims to define and outline Métis density by describing Métis lifeways that encompass religion, land, and kinship structures, and to connect the Métis to the rights spelled out in the Declaration. But we must first address the problems around race and syncretism.

Chris Andersen has done groundbreaking work unpacking and destabilizing the racialized view of Métis-as-mixed in order to assert the Indigenous sovereignty of the Métis. Andersen has described this racialized optic as an "administrative concept" of Aboriginal identity[43] that says more about the racist taxonomies and ontology of the settler state of Canada than it does about how the Métis understand themselves. Harkening back to his concept of density, Andersen asserts that Métis identity is not an ahistorical genealogical fantasy or a legal category (the result, say, of having an Indian ancestor in the distant past or of being from a mixed-race family), but a storied relationship to community(ies) that allows for the occurrence of common experiences that strengthen and affirm shared values. He establishes a pragmatic and effective definition: "I'm Métis because I belong (and claim allegiance) to a set of Métis memories, territories, and leaders who challenged and continue to challenge colonial authorities' unitary claims to land and society."[44] And yet, despite this historical and community-oriented definition, there remains a struggle to view Métis identity in terms of relationships rather than biological descent.

Adam Gaudry effectively breaks through this tension by looking back over Métis history to assert that biological mixing does not make an Indigenous nation. He argues, rather, that "only social and political processes create new human communities."[45] In order to interrupt the deterministic logic of racial mixedness, he points to the work of Indigenous studies scholar Robert Innes,[46] who explains how every Indigenous group on the Prairies, including the Métis, used marriage and kinship relations "as a way of ensuring a large network of

6. STORIED PLACES AND SACRED RELATIONS

relatives to support one another, form military alliances, and provide food and shelter in times of need."[47] Métis identity, Gaudry explains, is formed by political consciousness and collective identity around the buffalo hunting economy and historical events like the Battle of Seven Oaks (1816), the Battle of Grand Coteau (1851), the resistances at Red River (1869–70) and Batoche (1885), and the struggle against the Hudson's Bay Company monopoly in the Sayer trials (1849). But even more significant is the cohesion brought on by a strong identification with kinship relations that effect socio-cultural, economic, and gendered relations. Though Gaudry is not alone in proposing this view of Métis historical identity,[48] his engagement with the historiography decidedly shifts the determinist discourse of biological descent and genetics to socio-cultural and political relatedness. To talk about Métis identity is to talk about Métis relations as the basis for their Indigenous self-determination and nationhood.

The second misrepresentation of the Métis relates to their historical and continued affirmation of Christianity. The Métis experience of religion is framed as either falling within the hegemony of institutional Christianity (e.g., Catholic or Protestant denominations in Canada), or as being an inherently syncretic spirituality, which effectively differentiates it from settler-colonial structures by associating it with "traditional" Indigenous religiosity.[49] Note that these are not erroneous perspectives. As with the critique of Shorter above,[50] the problem is that the definition of religion continues to be dominated by dichotomous thinking that views Métis engagement with religion as mixed between the mutually exclusive civilizational structures of European religion and Native spirituality. This affirms our conceptual dependence on settler-colonial definitions of religion as being either Christian or Native, white or brown. Anything in between is deemed inconsequential; people are either *choosing* to mix and match religio-spiritual dimensions or drifting to one of the diametrically opposed poles of Christian religious orthodoxy and Native spiritual traditionalism. The problem herein is basic: there is no room for Indigenous self-determination.

The idea of syncretism does not leave room for the density of historical and contemporary Métis perspectives, nor does it explicate the substance of Métis experiences of religion. In her seminal book *Lived Religion*, Meredith McGuire claims that all culture, and therefore religion, is inherently syncretic and adaptive, integrating and resisting influences across ethnocultural boundaries. The problem lies with "the Western image of a religion as a unitary, organizationally defined, and relatively stable set of collective beliefs and practices."[51] These definitional boundaries must be contested if we are to develop an understanding of Métis religion based on Métis self-definition and the importance of lived experience. Based on this theoretical insight from McGuire's *Lived Religion*, I have argued elsewhere that conventional definitions of religious experience do not account for the multiple acts and attitudes of Métis resistance to the discourses of power and coercion of institutional Catholicism, in particular; but neither do they account for the flexibility of the institutional Catholic Church.[52] The historical record, especially as derived from the writings of Catholic missionaries, such as those of the Oblates, is ambivalent about the Métis moral/religious character based on racialized logics.[53] By virtue of its civilizational mandate, the message of the institutional Catholic Church was clear: that *white was good* and *brown was bad*. I proffer that by shifting our analytical lens to account for Métis density, we can begin to ask new questions about the historical record that allow for Métis self-determination and sovereignty. As for Métis density, I argue that Métis have always incorporated Catholic institutional power, metaphysics and cosmology, symbols, rituals, and devotions in their deployment of Métis values and a philosophical orientation that revolves around complex relations. We must see past a hegemonic and deterministic view of Catholic institutionalization in order to understand how, and where, Métis operationalize relational values and lifeways. Therefore, we can examine the Catholic pilgrimage site of Lac Ste. Anne as an example of a long-standing site for Métis lifeways.

Lac Ste. Anne, or Manito Sakahigan (nēhiyawēwin/Cree for "Holy Lake" or "God's Lake"), was one of the first Catholic mission sites west of the Red River. According to the historical record, the mission dates back to 1842, when Métis families brought Oblate missionary Father Jean-Baptiste Thibault to their settlement site, which he promptly named Lac Ste. Anne after his personal devotion to Mary's mother, Jesus's grandmother. In 1889, another Oblate,

Father Joseph Lestanc, initiated the pilgrimage to Ste. Anne based on the pilgrimage from his home in Brittany, France.[54] The annual Catholic pilgrimage has remained popular over the past 130 years with thousands of pilgrims, many of them members of various Indigenous Peoples who have travelled significant distances, converging at the lakeshore.[55] This site, however, long predates the Catholic missionary presence as a healing lake and meeting place. Many settler historians see this fact as a sort of prehistory, and so it is difficult to extricate Indigenous experiences of this place from reified settler-colonial understandings of culture, religion, and identity. Indeed, the majority of the literature on Lac Ste. Anne reifies a racialized discourse speaking only of First Nations' experiences of healing[56] and the religious syncretism between First Nations and Europeans, thereby romanticizing Indigenous ways to varying degrees.[57] Much of this historiography serves a settler-colonial narrative of "natural" civilizational processes that have excised the land of its previous inhabitants (Indigenous people and their spirits) to make way for Christian European settlers.[58] Built on these racialized understandings of ethnocultural identity, this literature does little to recognize Métis experiences at Lac Ste. Anne, let alone speak to Métis sovereignty at this site.

The literature on Lac Ste. Anne proves that it is difficult to conceptualize a Catholic pilgrimage site that involves Indigenous people as anything but syncretic, seeing the Catholic institution as "allowing" Native spiritual elements within the structure of the pilgrimage (e.g., the welcoming ceremony, the pipe ceremony, raising flags, and smudging). This institutional thinking leaves little room for understanding Métis density and lifeways, or the density and lifeways of First Nations at Lac Ste. Anne, for that matter. It obfuscates the variety of Indigenous socio-religious experiences, expressions, and interactions occurring at Lac Ste. Anne. The history of Métis presence and engagement at Lac Ste. Anne must therefore be outlined in terms of storied engagements with a sacred place in order to establish the significance of pilgrimage in shaping what it means to be Métis.

Rather than seeing Lac Ste. Anne as a space that has been colonized and assimilated by the power and moral coercion of the institutional Catholic Church, we need to recognize it as a site for ongoing engagement in the lifeways of Métis and other Indigenous nations. It has been a place where different Indigenous Peoples pilgrimage in order to trade medicines, meat, fish, and berries, laugh, sing, drum, dance, practise healing, walk in the lake and soak up its power and presence, light candles, encounter ancestors and higher powers, pray for healing, safety, and comfort, meet with people, buy T-shirts with jokes in Cree (e.g., baby singlets with the provocative and hilarious phrase "Pretty Fly for a Tuguy!"), go on fairway rides, eat candy, get in trouble, and, maybe, fall in love. These dynamic social and religious aspects are part of what makes Lac Ste. Anne special, and what draws Métis to gather there in community and as an Indigenous nation among nations. Returning to Deloria's understanding of sacred sites, Lac Ste. Anne is a sacred site because it was chosen *for us* by higher powers and *by us* in our ongoing pilgrimage to maintain and engender our complex relations.

In order to further develop this picture, we must turn to the storied insight of a relational perspective on how and why Lac Ste. Anne is important for Métis density and lifeways. Remarkably, these stories are not found in history books, but rather in the biographies and reflections of Métis citizens. For the sake of brevity, we will look at two Métis individuals: Herb Belcourt and Marilyn Dumont. The late Herb Belcourt, a prominent businessman and Métis leader in Alberta, speaks fondly in his memoir of his kinship relation to Lac Ste. Anne. He writes:

> To me, the Lac Ste. Anne pilgrimage is a reunion: for friendship and for storytelling, as you walk around the tents and motorhomes. I enjoy listening to the stories and the laughter. People use the opportunity to earn a few dollars, selling hot dogs, hamburgers, pop, ice cream, old clothes—it is like a garage sale, sometimes. Some people are bargaining, and I find it quite humorous. Does it hold any spiritual meaning for me in a Catholic religious sense? No, it does not. There are times when it reminds me of my thoughts as a kid, when the priests played poker. Selling their beads. Selling their holy water. To me it was like gambling. The pilgrimage is important to me, but in my own way. I think of it as an important gathering for Native people.[59]

6. STORIED PLACES AND SACRED RELATIONS

Belcourt asserts that his sacred connection to Lac Ste. Anne has less to do with contemplating "holy visions" within a Catholic framework (i.e., affirming the moral authority of the institutional church), and more to do with engaging the storied aspect of the land itself and its capacity to hold people together through relational acts. This brief excerpt underscores the capacity for stories in connection with the land to traverse history and memory. At the end of his memoir, Belcourt returns to Lac Ste. Anne to help him "remember" the life he has lived and his symbiotic connection to ancestors named and unnamed. Reflecting on all his hard work, his successes and failures in business, his experience of structural racism and the stigma associated with being Métis in Alberta, and the world's loss of relational connections, Belcourt returns to Lac Ste. Anne, the place of his youth and his ancestors, remarking: "I can touch the past."[60] Here, he engages with relational memory that is alive, emotional, experiential, and affirming. Lac Ste. Anne helps frame a Métis experience that is tangible and representative of a Métis world view.

Marilyn Dumont, a Métis activist and award-winning poet, also speaks vividly of a lifetime of pilgrimages to Lac Ste. Anne. In the introduction to her book of poetry *The Pemmican Eaters*, Dumont describes her connection to and disconnection from her own past, and how this relates to the dark side of Métis history and identity vis-à-vis the violence and imposed silence caused by settler colonialism. Her personal experience of pilgrimage and her understanding of her ancestral connection to Lac Ste. Anne are crucial to how she frames the poetry the reader is about to engage with. Through the miasma of forgotten history resulting from the fragmentation and dispossession of Métis territories, Dumont, like Belcourt, points to the embodied experience of remembering that forms a part of the Lac Ste. Anne pilgrimage:

> The Lac Ste. Anne Pilgrimage is one of the foundations of my cultural memory. It is where my parents taught me to remember our relatives through prayer after their passing. Invoking their memory through the place, people, and ritual was a way of affirming ourselves. For a large family with few economic resources, not unlike most of the families there, the affirmation

of belonging—spiritually and ancestrally—was what sustained my parents through their physically demanding work and uneasy life in a southern Alberta town where Aboriginals were a disdained minority.[61]

It is remarkably telling that two influential Métis figures in Alberta point to Lac Ste. Anne as a means of remembering and an expression of Métis identity. The fullness of the experience of being at Lac Ste. Anne makes this a sacred site for Métis that helps us to remember who we are and who our relations are. Lac Ste. Anne's status as a storied place reinforces Métis density and affirms Métis lifeways centred on complex kinship relations. And added to this, Dumont points out that Lac Ste. Anne is a place of resistance to settler colonialism, which seeks to negate, erase, and forget Indigenous ways of being and knowing. In a society that actively obfuscates, marginalizes, and appropriates Indigenous ways of thinking and knowing, Lac Ste. Anne is one of several places across the Métis Homeland that help us remember who we are as Métis. It is therefore important to acknowledge and protect these places as sacred sites meaningful to the Métis and other Indigenous nations, and crucial to our Indigenous identities and sovereignty.

Storied Places and Sacred Relations: Métis Engagement with the Declaration

The Declaration is a vital document that makes known the violent and disruptive legacy of colonialism as well as the importance of Indigenous sovereignty. Throughout the text, religion and spirituality are used to help justify a vision of the rights due to Indigenous Peoples across the globe. However, these conceptions of religion and spirituality, which are linked to key elements like "sacred land," need to be made more relevant to Indigenous ontologies and epistemologies. This involves examining the impact and obduracy of settler-colonial possessiveness over Indigenous bodies, culture, and thought, as well as acknowledging the importance of land as a basis for Indigenous ways of being and knowing. Shifting to concepts like *density* and *lifeways* can help

6. STORIED PLACES AND SACRED RELATIONS

assert Indigenous self-determination and focus on the importance of relations. From this analytical perspective, we see how sacredness has to do with collective memory through individual and collective action. The repeated actions of ceremony, storytelling, and reciprocal relations help generate knowledge and imbue specific places with memory. What makes a place meaningful and sacred is that people are drawn to it, using it over and over again to feel, listen, think, sense, learn, teach, heal, and visit; and most importantly, to remember or be reminded of obligations to our relations, human and more-than-human.

The Métis have fallen victim to the settler-colonial paradigm, defined as we are through the racialized notion of *mixedness*, which has served to obfuscate and negate Métis density and lifeways. This paradigm has conditioned a conventional understanding of Métis identity regarding peoplehood, economy, mobility, and kinship. In terms of religion, it informs an understanding of the sacred that asserts either traditional spirituality or assimilation with institutional forms of religiosity (i.e., the Catholic Church). Both of these concepts are largely misrepresentative of Métis and misaligned with Métis self-definition because they do not account for an Indigenous ethos or Indigenous experiences of relations. Syncretism, in this case, perpetuates the racialized logic that treats Métis as ambivalent, "not-quite-people," which disqualifies Métis—who, it is sometimes implied, are too Christian to be Indigenous—from being part of the discussion on Indigenous Rights. This chapter has argued that the Catholicism of the Métis has less to do with a hegemonic social and moral influence on Indigenous bodies (i.e., a moral compass guiding them to become white citizens), and more to do with Indigenous engagement through the application of relational values as defined in the socio-religious concept of lifeways. The Métis have always interpreted and practised Catholicism in self-determined ways that consistently resist the power of the institutional Catholic Church and the deployment of settler-colonial values through religion.

Rather than partaking in a Catholic syncretism in an attempt to assume settler-colonial values of "whiteness," the Métis deploy a relational ethos that engages the forms of Catholic devotion for the sake of encountering and negotiating human and more-than-human beings and relations—family, friends, ancestors, metaphysical forces, the land and its medicines, and animal relations. This work does not deny the Christian heritage of the Métis; that would be misrepresentative. Instead, it seeks to add a sense of nuance to the category of religion so that it can consider the complex relationships that make up Indigenous kinship and sovereignty. This work is part of the larger project of destabilizing the Christian hegemony of settler colonialism in order to mitigate, resist, and eliminate racialization that leads to reified constructions of Métis, and more broadly, Indigenous identity. With these insights into Indigenous density and lifeways, we can appreciate how pilgrimage to Lac Ste. Anne acts as a way of being and remembering as Métis. It is through storied relationships to places like Lac Ste. Anne that the self-understanding and self-determination of the Métis as a people are shaped. This helps us to see how the Métis are linked to the rights and justice underlined in the Declaration.

Conclusion

The Declaration is a crucial document affirming the rights and sovereignty Indigenous Peoples. Beyond the significance of upholding Indigenous Rights against settler-colonial violence and manipulation, a focus on Indigenous Rights means a focus on Indigenous self-determination regarding "sacred" land, sites, and territories. Sacred sites are intersectional places that allow for the transmission of tradition, experiential knowledge, and revelation. Indigenous Peoples should have unequivocal access to such sites as a matter of course and as part of their basic human rights. However, the framing of sacred sites is almost always based on a settler-colonial conceptualization and definition of religion. Deloria's discussion on Tribal Religions or Native spiritualities has helped uncover how religion is operationalized by settler society to uphold settler-colonial mandates. Though this approach is critical to help mitigate the power of settler colonialism, we have also questioned the view of Indigenous epistemologies and ontologies as being inherently different than or in opposition to setter values and views. By turning to the concepts of Indigenous *density* and religious *lifeways*, we can affirm Indigenous ways of knowing and being as fully capable of critiquing discourses of power and dismantling settler-colonial ideology.

The Métis are often left outside the rights framework because they lack recognition as an Indigenous People. This is due to bifurcated definitions of race wherein the Métis, as mixed, do not fit within the categories of white or brown. Through the concepts of density and lifeways, we can challenge the established category of religion and the resulting racialization and reduction of Indigenous religious engagement. Using Métis engagement in relationality at the pilgrimage site of Lac Ste. Anne as an example, we can see how Métis lifeways resist colonial discourses that seek to erase and silence Indigenous Peoples. This, in turn, confirms the relevance of the Declaration for the Métis as an Indigenous People with rights to protection and political recognition.

Notes

The author would like to thank the Social Sciences and Humanities Research Council and the Rupertsland Centre for Métis Research for financial help in this research. He also thanks Dr. HyeRan Kim-Cragg, Dr. Adam Gaudry, and David Oppenheim for their suggestions and expertise in writing this chapter.

1   UN General Assembly, Resolution 61/295, United Nations Declaration on the Rights of Indigenous Peoples, A/RES/61/295 (October 2, 2007), https://undocs.org/A/RES/61/295, 2.
2   Aileen Moreton-Robinson, *The White Possessive: Property, Power, and Indigenous Sovereignty* (Minneapolis: University of Minnesota Press, 2015); Ken Coates and Carin Holroyd, "Indigenous Internationalism and the Emerging Impact of UNDRIP in Aboriginal Affairs in Canada," in *The Internationalization of Indigenous Rights: UNDRIP in the Canadian Context*, ed. Terry Mitchell, Ken Coates, and Carin Holroyd (Waterloo, ON: Centre for International Governance Innovation, 2014), 5–10.
3   David B. MacDonald and Graham Hudson, "The Genocide Question and Indian Residential Schools in Canada," *Canadian Journal of Political Science/Revue Canadienne de Science Politique* 45, no. 2 (2012): 427–49; Truth and Reconciliation Commission of Canada, *Final Report of the Truth and Reconciliation Commission of Canada, Vol. 1: Summary: Honouring the Truth, Reconciling for the Future* (Winnipeg: Truth and Reconciliation Commission of Canada, 2015).
4   UN General Assembly, Resolution 61/295, article 11.
5   Ibid., article 12.
6   Ibid., article 17.

7   Ibid., article 25.
8   Ibid., article 32.
9   Ibid., article 34.
10 Ibid., article 36.
11 HyeRan Kim-Cragg, *Interdependence: A Postcolonial Feminist Practical Theology* (Eugene, OR: Pickwick Publications, 2018).
12 Robert J. Miller et al., *Discovering Indigenous Lands: The Doctrine of Discovery in the English Colonies* (Oxford: Oxford University Press, 2012); Steven T. Newcomb, *Pagans in the Promised Land: Decoding the Doctrine of Christian Discovery* (Golden, CO: Fulcrum Publishing, 2008).
13 Nancy Christie and Michael Gauvreau, *Christian Churches and Their Peoples, 1840–1965: A Social History of Religion in Canada* (Toronto: University of Toronto Press, 2010); Laura Ishiguro, "Northwestern North America (Canadian West) to 1900," in *The Routledge Handbook of the History of Settler Colonialism*, ed. Edward Cavanagh and Lorenzo Veracini (London: Routledge, 2016), 125–38; Tracey Banivanua Mar and Penelope Edmonds, eds., *Making Settler Colonial Space: Perspectives on Race, Place, and Identity* (New York: Palgrave Macmillan, 2010).
14 Steven Charleston and Elaine A. Robinson, eds., *Coming Full Circle: Constructing Native Christian Theology* (Minneapolis: Fortress Press, 2015); Justin Tolly Bradford and Chelsea Horton, eds., *Mixed Blessings: Indigenous Encounters with Christianity in Canada* (Vancouver: UBC Press, 2016); James Treat, ed., *Native and Christian: Indigenous Voices on Religious Identity in the United States and Canada* (New York: Routledge, 1996); Aparecida Vilaça and Robin Wright, *Native Christians: Modes and Effects of Christianity among Indigenous Peoples of the Americas* (Farnham, UK: Ashgate, 2009).
15 Vine Deloria Jr., *Custer Died for Your Sins* (New York: Norman Press, 1988); Deloria, *For This Land: Writings on Religion in America*, ed. James Treat (New York: Routledge, 1999); Deloria, *Spirit & Reason: The Vine Deloria, Jr., Reader*, ed. Barbara Deloria, Kristen Foehner, and Sam Scinta (Golden, CO: Fulcrum Publishing, 1999).
16 Deloria, *God Is Red: A Native View of Religion*, 3rd ed. (Golden, CO: Fulcrum Publishing, 2003).
17 Ibid., 38.
18 Ibid., 295.
19 Dennis Ward, "Standing Rock: One Year Later," *APTN Investigates*, April 6, 2018, https://www.aptnnews.ca/investigates/standing-rock-one-year-later-2/.
20 Daniel Schwartz and Mark Gollom, "Aboriginal Rights and the N.B. Shale Gas Fracking Protests," *CBC News*, October 19, 2013, https://www.cbc.ca/news/canada/n-b-fracking-protests-and-the-fight-for-aboriginal-rights-1.2126515.
21 Brian Platt, "Supreme Court Ruling Clears Way for B.C. Ski Resort on Sacred Indigenous Land," *National Post*, November 3, 2017, https://nationalpost.com/news/politics/in-key-freedom-of-religion-case-supreme-court-sides-with-b-c-government-over-ski-resort.
22 Larry Buhl, "Sacred Burial Grounds Destroyed, Judge Halts Construction on Portion of Dakota Access Pipeline," *EcoWatch*, September 7, 2016, https://www.ecowatch.com/sacred-burial-grounds-dakota-access-pipeline-1998932006.html; Chip Colwell, "Why

Sacred Sites Were Destroyed for the Dakota Access Pipeline," *EcoWatch*, November 26, 2016, https://www.ecowatch.com/sacred-sites-standing-rock-2103468697.html.

23 Moreton-Robinson, *The White Possessive*, 173–89.
24 Natasha Bakht and Lynda Collins, " 'The Earth Is Our Mother': Freedom of Religion and the Preservation of Indigenous Sacred Sites in Canada," *McGill Law Journal/Revue de Droit de McGill* 62, no. 3 (2017): 777–812; Lori G. Beaman, "Aboriginal Spirituality and the Legal Construction of Freedom of Religion," *Journal of Church and State* 44, no. 1 (January 2002): 135–49; John Borrows, "Living Law on a Living Earth: Aboriginal Religion, Law, and the Constitution," in *Law and Religious Pluralism in Canada*, ed. Richard J. Moon (Vancouver: UBC Press, 2009), 161–92; John Borrows, *Recovering Canada: The Resurgence of Indigenous Law* (Toronto: University of Toronto Press, 2016); Grace Li Xiu Woo, *Ghost Dancing with Colonialism: Decolonization and Indigenous Rights at the Supreme Court of Canada* (Vancouver: UBC Press, 2011).
25 Jim Bronskill, "Ski Resort a Step Closer after High Court Ruling in Grizzly Bear Spirit Case," CTV *News*, November 2, 2017, https://www.ctvnews.ca/canada/ski-resort-does-not-violate-freedom-of-religion-scc-1.3660080.
26 Deloria, *God Is Red*, 274.
27 William Arnal and Russell T. McCutcheon, *The Sacred Is the Profane: The Political Nature of Religion* (New York: Oxford University Press, 2013); Mircea Eliade, *The Sacred and the Profane: The Nature of Religion* (Orlando, FL: Houghton Mifflin Harcourt, 1959).
28 Leroy Little Bear, "Aboriginal Relationships to the Land and Resources," in *Sacred Lands: Aboriginal World Views, Claims, and Conflicts*, ed. Jill Elizabeth Oakes et al. (Edmonton: Canadian Circumpolar Institute/University of Alberta Press, 1998), 15–20; Little Bear, "Jagged Worldviews Colliding," in *Reclaiming Indigenous Voice and Vision*, ed. Marie Ann Battiste (Vancouver: UBC Press, 2000), 77–85; Aileen Moreton-Robinson, "Relationality: A Key Presupposition of an Indigenous Social Research Paradigm," in *Sources and Methods in Indigenous Studies*, ed. Chris Andersen and Jean M. O'Brien (New York: Routledge, 2016), 69–77; Fausto Sarmiento and Sarah Hitchner, *Indigeneity and the Sacred: Indigenous Revival and the Conservation of Sacred Natural Sites in the Americas* (New York: Berghahn Books, 2017).
29 Deloria, *God Is Red*, 282.
30 Isabel Altamirano-Jiménez, *Indigenous Encounters with Neoliberalism: Place, Women, and the Environment in Canada and Mexico* (Vancouver: UBC Press, 2013); John Borrows, *Canada's Indigenous Constitution* (Toronto: University of Toronto Press, 2010); Jeff Corntassel, "Toward Sustainable Self-Determination: Rethinking the Contemporary Indigenous-Rights Discourse," *Alternatives* 33, no. 1 (January 1, 2008): 105–32; Jill Elizabeth Oakes et al., eds., *Sacred Lands: Aboriginal World Views, Claims, and Conflicts* (Edmonton: Canadian Circumpolar Institute/University of Alberta Press, 1998).
31 Chris Andersen, "Critical Indigenous Studies: From Difference to Density," *Cultural Studies Review* 15, no. 2 (2009): 80–100.
32 Ibid., 85. Emphasis in the original.
33 Ibid., 88.
34 Ibid., 82.

35 Ibid., 93.
36 Ibid., 94.
37 David Delgado Shorter, "Spirituality," in *The Oxford Handbook of American Indian History*, ed. Frederick E. Hoxie (Oxford: Oxford University Press, 2016), 433–52.
38 Ibid., 444.
39 John Grim, "Indigenous Lifeways and Knowing the World," in *The Oxford Handbook of Religion and Science*, ed. Philip Clayton and Zachary Simpson (Oxford: Oxford University Press, 2008), 87–107.
40 Ibid., 88.
41 Ibid., 96.
42 Ibid.
43 Chris Andersen, *"Métis": Race, Recognition, and the Struggle for Indigenous Peoplehood* (Vancouver: UBC Press, 2014); Chris Andersen and Tahu Kukutai, "Reclaiming the Statistical 'Native': Quantitative Historical Research beyond the Pale," in *Sources and Methods in Indigenous Studies*, ed. Chris Andersen and Jean M. O'Brien (New York: Routledge, 2016), 41–8.
44 Chris Andersen, " 'I'm Métis, What's Your Excuse?': On the Optics and the Ethics of the Misrecognition of Métis in Canada," *Aboriginal Policy Studies* 1, no. 2 (2011): 165.
45 Adam Gaudry, "Respecting Métis Nationhood and Self-Determination in Matters of Métis Identity," in *Aboriginal History: A Reader*, ed. Kristin Burnett and Geoff Read, 2nd ed. (Oxford University Press, 2016), 153.
46 Robert Alexander Innes, " 'Wait a Second. Who Are You Anyways?' The Insider/Outsider Debate and American Indian Studies," *American Indian Quarterly* 33, no. 4 (2009): 440–61; Innes, *Elder Brother and the Law of the People: Contemporary Kinship and Cowessess First Nation* (Winnipeg: University of Manitoba Press, 2013).
47 Gaudry, "Respecting Métis Nationhood," 153.
48 Michel Hogue, *Metis and the Medicine Line: Creating a Border and Dividing a People*, (Chapel Hill, NC: University of North Carolina Press, 2015); Nathalie Kermoal, "Métis Women's Environmental Knowledge and the Recognition of Métis Rights," in *Living on the Land: Indigenous Women's Understanding of Place*, ed. Nathalie Kermoal and Isabel Altamirano-Jiménez (Edmonton: Athabasca University Press, 2016), 107–38; Brenda Macdougall and Nicole St-Onge, "Métis in the Borderlands of the Northern Plains in the Nineteenth Century," in *Sources and Methods in Indigenous Studies*, ed. Chris Andersen and Jean M. O'Brien (New York: Routledge, 2016), 257–65; Nicole St-Onge et al., eds., *Contours of a People: Metis Family, Mobility, and History* (Norman: University of Oklahoma Press, 2012).
49 Chantal Fiola, *Rekindling the Sacred Fire: Métis Ancestry and Anishinaabe Spirituality* (Winnipeg: University of Manitoba Press, 2015).
50 Shorter, "Spirituality," 433–52.
51 Meredith B. McGuire, *Lived Religion: Faith and Practice in Everyday Life* (New York: Oxford University Press, 2008), 186.
52 Paul L. Gareau, "Mary and the Métis: Religion as a Site for New Insight in Métis Studies," in *A People and a Nation: New Directions in Contemporary Métis Studies*, ed. Jennifer Adese and Chris Andersen (Vancouver: UBC Press, 2021), 188–212.

53   Robert Choquette, *The Oblate Assault on Canada's Northwest* (Ottawa: University of Ottawa Press, 1995); Raymond Huel, *Proclaiming the Gospel to the Indians and the Métis* (Edmonton: University of Alberta Press, 1996).
54   Archives Committee, *West of the Fifth: A History of Lac Ste. Anne Municipality* (Edmonton: Institute of Applied Art, 1959); Eméric O'Neil Drouin, *Lac Ste-Anne Sakahigan* (Edmonton: Editions de l'Ermitage, 1973).
55   Amber Bracken, "Why Thousands Come for the Healing Waters of Lac Ste. Anne," *Globe and Mail*, September 25, 2015, http://www.theglobeandmail.com/news/alberta/why-thousands-come-for-the-healing-waters-of-lac-steanne/article25784853/; Steve Simon, "Waters of the Spirit: Alberta's Lac Ste. Anne Draws Thousands of Pilgrims," *Maclean's*, September 6, 2004.
56   A. Beaver, "Lac Ste. Anne's Healing Powers Attract Many," *Native Journal* 11, no. 9 (September 2002): 15; Yvonne Irene Gladue, "Thousands of Pilgrims Flock Again to Lac Ste. Anne," *Alberta Sweetgrass*, August 2005; Joanne Rediron, "Thousands Gather to Take in the Yearly Lac Ste. Anne Pilgrimage," *Alberta Sweetgrass*, September 2008; Karen Wall, " 'Across Distances and Differences': Aboriginal Pilgrimage at Lac Ste. Anne," *Leisure/Loisir: Journal of the Canadian Association for Leisure Studies* 33, no. 1 (January 2009): 291–315.
57   Maire Kathleen Anderson-McLean, "The Landscape of Identity: Man'tow Sâkahikan or Lac Ste-Anne," *Religious Studies and Theology* 18, no. 2 (December 1999): 5–32; Anderson-McLean, "To the Centre of the Circle: Pilgrimage to Lac Ste-Anne" (PhD diss., University of Alberta, 2005); Alice Simonne Charland, "First Nations and the Lac Ste. Anne Pilgrimage" (MA thesis, St. Stephen's College, 1994).
58   Jessica Anne Buresi, " 'Rendezvous' for Renewal at 'Lake of the Great Spirit': The French Pilgrimage and Indigenous Journey to Lac Ste. Anne, Alberta, 1870–1896" (MA thesis, University of Calgary, 2012); Bonnie Hansen, *Lac Ste. Anne County History, 1913–2006* (Sangudo, AB: Lac Ste. Anne County, 2007); Dianne Meili, "Pilgrimage: Almost a Century of History at Alberta's 'Holy Land,' " *Windspeaker* 5, no. 10 (1987): 12; Audrey Whitson, "Lac Ste. Anne: On Pilgrimage," *Grail* 8, no. 3 (September 1992): 80–6.
59   Herb Belcourt, *Walking in the Woods: A Métis Journey* (Edmonton: Brindle & Glass, 2006), 28.
60   Ibid., 191.
61   Marilyn Dumont, *The Pemmican Eaters* (Toronto: ECW Press, 2015), 5.

CHAPTER 7

The POWER and PRACTISE of INDIGENOUS CHRISTIAN RITUALS and CEREMONIES

by

HYERAN KIM-CRAGG

THIS CHAPTER EXAMINES ARTICLE 12.1 OF THE UNITED Nations Declaration on the Rights of Indigenous Peoples, which states that "Indigenous peoples have the right to manifest, practise, develop and teach their spiritual and religious traditions, customs, and ceremonies; the right to maintain, protect, and have access in privacy to their religious and cultural sites; the right to the use and control of their ceremonial objects."[1]

I am especially interested in how ritual can be a subversive force and serve as a sort of counter-knowledge against colonialism. As a postcolonial scholar, I want to explore how Indigenous Peoples' self-determination vis-à-vis decolonization can be sustained through ritual and spiritual practices. Article 12 states clearly that ritual and ceremony are important to Indigenous communities. In this chapter, I shed light on the role of ritual by drawing insights from performance studies. In particular, I recall two historic events. One is the recent Standing Rock protest, which I use to show how ceremony and everyday ritual were central to the protest at that place. The other is the 1986 General Council of the United Church of Canada (UCC), which saw an official apology from the UCC to its Aboriginal brothers and sisters. I use this to show how the ritual of creating a circle and praying played an important role for those Indigenous commissioners who were waiting for this apology to happen. In this case, creating a circle serves not simply an external or functional role but a profoundly philosophical and relational one as well.

In what follows I also hope to reveal the ways in which Indigenous spiritual and other practices have been oppressed and violated by European Christianity. In particular, I examine the banning of Indigenous dancing, tracing European Christians' fear of mixing Indigenous and Christian practices and the ultimate suppression of the former. The justification of such suppression relied on the notion that Western knowledge is superior to Indigenous ways of knowing. To counter this expression of Christian supremacy, I argue for performance as a valid episteme, a form of knowing and a system for transmitting knowledge that is equal to the European literary system of written knowledge. I contend that an Indigenous episteme as embodied knowledge is not only valid and important, but also aids in subversive resistance because embodied knowledge performed as ceremonial ritual requires the agency of participation.

The chapter then moves on to argue for worship as both embodied and literary knowledge. I claim that worship embraces both literary and performative knowledge—in other words, it is a mixed practice. Hymn lyrics provide a case in point. Lyrics for singing constitute a form of literary knowledge, but they also become performative as they are translated into singing. This is particularly evident when looking at the translation of hymnody by Indigenous Christians in the Methodist (now United) Church. An analysis of a hymn translated into Cree will show how translation involved acts of subversive resistance that were then developed into an Indigenized theology.

7. INDIGENOUS CHRISTIAN RITUALS AND CEREMONIES

Finally, building upon the previous sections, the paper lifts up the Christian hybrid practices of Indigenous and non-Indigenous communities in the United Church. Here I review various indigenous elements included in *Gathering*, a worship resource magazine of the UCC, published since the General Council's apology to the residential school in 1998. These resources evidently demonstrate an effort to recognise Indigenous people's wisdom and spiritual practice. Furthermore, while it names the reality of holding Indigenous and Christian identities together in tension as a challenge and often a cause for conflict and rejection, it demonstrates the wisdom and resilience of Indigenous Christians who are able to embrace Christian traditions as their own while at the same time decolonizing them. The paper suggests that this hybrid identity is for all of us Indigenous and non-Indigenous people to embrace when taking a journey of reconciliation.

The Standing Rock Campsite in 2016

"Wake up! Pipe carriers, sun dancers, water protectors, Christians. Get up! This is what we're here for!"[2] This is the call that went out every morning at the campsite at Standing Rock, where protesters made up of more than ninety different Indigenous Peoples from across North America, Latin America, and Asia led rallies to oppose the construction of a pipeline through Dakota land. The activists began gathering at the site of the Dakota Access Pipeline in April 2016; they say the pipeline that would carry crude oil across four states to Illinois is a threat to sacred land and to the Missouri River, the main water supply for the nearby reservation of the Standing Rock Sioux Tribe.[3] The Standing Rock occupation is about protecting the water for future generations. (Note: at the time of writing, the protest at the site has ended but the fight to stop the pipeline has not.)

Erica Daniels, associate producer with the CBC Radio program *Unreserved*, has been observing Indigenous rituals for her own healing journey, and she spent a few nights at the campsite and participated in various ceremonies there.[4] The camp begins with a sunrise ceremony over the hill. Multiple sacred fires are put on all day and night. These visible symbolic sensory movements of ritual orient people to the purposes of their gathering: to bless, to resist, and to protect. There is water ceremony, led by women. There is pipe ceremony. There is a Round Dance every day. People sing and offer prayers using words and gestures, using bodies, shaking hands, and hugging. The ceremonies at the site are heterogeneous, ranging from rituals reflecting different regions and tribes to performances using different words and non-verbal actions. In their diversity, some ceremonies are shared, such as at the blessing of every meal, a logistically challenging ritual when one considers that approximately 1,500 people are fed at the same time on any given day.

Josh Dini Senior, who works security for the main camp at Standing Rock, Oceti Sakowin, said, "We are a prayer camp, and not a social camp,"[5] highlighting the fact that this gathering is conceived as a spiritual practice as much as a political one. Lisa Grayshield, a member of the Washoe Tribe of Nevada and California and associate professor of educational psychology at New Mexico State University who is working as a medic in the main camp, said in an interview, "We're water protectors and this is a peaceful gathering and it's about prayer and they've been very adamant about that."[6]

The 1986 General Council of the United Church

According to Stan McKay, a former moderator of the UCC, the seed for the apology at the 31st General Council of 1986 was planted when Alberta Billy, a woman from Cape Mudge, British Columbia, and the first Indigenous representative to the General Council Executive (GCE), said to the GCE meeting in 1984: "It is time you apologize to Native people.... You need to apologize to us for the historical injustice."[7] Since this was a verbal request and not in her written report, it was not only unexpected but also came as a shock to other GCE members. But her request was taken seriously, leading to an eighteen-month-long process of prayerful discernment prior to the General Council in 1986; every congregation was informed and asked to engage in spiritual discernment.[8]

7. INDIGENOUS CHRISTIAN RITUALS AND CEREMONIES

Indigenous leaders met four days before the 31st General Council officially began. They discerned and agreed that the apology was something for the rest of the church to discuss. As Stan McKay and Janet Silman later explained, on the day of the vote

> We requested the apology on the floor of General Council, then asked all commissioners who were First Nations people to come with us as we left the room. We went down to the sacred fire where we waited and prayed for two hours. We had a ceremony of tobacco offerings at the sacred fire. Jim Dumont, a traditional teacher, led us in a ceremonial prayer. The most powerful words in the prayers of the people that evening were: "There is nothing more that we can do than ask in a good way, and continue to pray for strength."[9]

The apology at the General Council was lifted up by the offering of prayer through the ritual performed by Indigenous leaders and commissioners.

After the apology took place, Indigenous people in the United Church moved forward to establish a self-determined independent decision-making body. The name chosen for this body in 1987 was "All Native Circle Conference," and the formation of this conference got approved by the next General Council in 1988. The word "Circle" was a powerful signifier in this new name representing Indigenous people in the church. The symbols of the church for Indigenous people was both "the circle and the cross."[10] McKay and Silman write that "the circle is a place where everyone has a voice and everyone is respected and included; where decisions emerge from a wide-open agenda, wide ranging discussion and consensus—all things that empower people."[11]

Creating a circle is a ritual, one that influences how Indigenous people talk, think, and make decisions. Sitting in a circle as a concrete act shapes the way Indigenous people make decisions by consensus. This consensus model embodies their philosophy of respecting everyone. It enhances a sense of self-governance and contributes to a decolonizing culture, resistance to paternalism, and the refusal to be spoken of as a token minority. The UCC Indigenous model of self-governance and decision-making by consensus has spread to other denominations. "The question of self-government is now being raised in the Anglican Church of Canada; and some parishes in Roman Catholic community pulled away from the rest of the diocesan structures to establish their own church life with a form of self-governance."[12]

The genesis of the present book was a gathering of Indigenous and non-Indigenous scholars at St. Andrew's College in the fall of 2017. Those of us who participated created a circle, and we sat together for two days in that circle. We talked, thought, laughed, and made decisions together about how we would write this book. I believe the circle in which we sat influenced each chapter's contents and intention. For example, we decided that we would not select one or two principal editors. Rather, we agreed that we would collectively give each other feedback. This book project reflects Indigenous consensus model. Not only its contents but also the process through which it was written contributed to the Indigenization of academic writing.

McKay further challenges the church to ask "how the structure of the church globally fits the pattern of oppression of the marginalized." In short, creating a circle is not a mere gesture; it serves, rather, as a critical way to reveal the structural pattern of exclusion and oppression. "If the container that carries the gospel is broken, then you have to change the container. That is a very threatening revelation.... It has to do with who has the power and authority to define the gospel, to determine what is true and good, to decide where the lines are drawn and who is inside or outside the fold. The challenge is not just to people on the margins, but also to those at the centres of ecclesial power."[13]

Imposition of Christian Supremacy and Indigenous Subversive Practices

As the two accounts described above demonstrate, rituals are central to the life of Indigenous people and their theology and spirituality. This was obvious to the first European missionaries. John Hines, an Anglican missionary who worked closely with the Ahtahkakoop, noticed the profoundly beautiful

7. INDIGENOUS CHRISTIAN RITUALS AND CEREMONIES

prayer this Indigenous People offered to the Creator, which he determined was true and good. He was also struck by the common ground he found between the ideas of the Ahtahkakoop and his own Christian faith.[14] The late United Church Elder Jessie Saulteaux talked about how her people, the Assiniboine, prayed to the Great Spirit. Their theology was ritualized in the making of a quilt with the symbol of the morning star—the brightest of all stars shining through the darkness, greeting the first light.[15] The Indigenous view of the star as a guiding promise is similar to the Christian understanding of God in Jesus, who is the light coming to shine in darkness, often celebrated during Advent. Yet, Indigenous Peoples' rituals and theologies were dismissed as a result of the colonial conquest. In the words of Harold Cardinal, "the things that we hold sacred, the things that we believe in have been repudiated by the federal government" and the church.[16] Indigenous rituals have been labelled heretical, superstitious, and even malicious.

Most European Christians did not fully appreciate the deeply embodied and holistic nature of Indigenous spiritualty. For example, hair for Indigenous people is not merely a physical feature; rather, it is regarded as a connection to one's ancestors and the earth. That is why the cutting of hair, which was imposed by Christian missions and residential schools upon Indigenous people, was so brutal. Deanna Christensen writes, "Hair cut was an outward sign of conversion to Christianity. This was somewhat painful because they had, before their conversion, believed that the three sections of hair that made up a braid represented the spirit, mind, and body in order to make a strong person. To cut their hair, other than during times of mourning, was unnatural."[17]

Indigenous dance is another example. The Stomp Dance, which belongs to many tribes, was banned by the early missionaries and the American Holiness movement.[18] Cherokee postcolonial scholar Corky Alexander explains the way the demand for order and solemnity that ultimately led to the banning of the Stomp Dance has resulted in lack of Indigenous participation in Christian worship. Similar bans can be found in other parts of the world where Christian missionaries travelled. According to Charles Kraft, who examined Nigerian dances in Africa and their prohibition under Christianity, the decision to ban these dances stems from both a sense of the superiority of solemn worship, as well as from "the fear of syncretism."[19] Furthermore, the notion of mixing local forms of worship with the colonizers' spiritual practices was seen as compromising the superiority and purity of the latter. Many Christian colonial missionaries fiercely rejected and censored any mixing of local ritual practices with Western liturgy. For example, the Sun Dance, which was an important ritual for all Siouan Peoples, continued to be disallowed until 1950s.[20] However, the Sun Dance, along with the Stomp Dance and other practices, embody a profound theology with salvific significance in which the dancer is seen as taking on the suffering of the community.[21] The summer—when the Sun Dance is performed—is a time for spiritual renewal. Wade Davis, an anthropologist who has travelled to various Indigenous communities, both in Canada and around the world, draws attention to the Sun Dance of the Kiowa. He writes, "The teepees went up in a wide circle, the entire encampment oriented to the rising sun. The medicine lodge was the focal point.... On July 20, 1890, the Sun Dance was officially outlawed, and on pain of imprisonment the Kiowa and all the Plains cultures were denied their essential act of faith.... As late as 1871, buffalo outnumbered people in North America.... Within nine years, the buffalo had vanished from the Plains."[22]

The banning of Indigenous dances went along with the destruction of the bison. Indeed, Janet Silman makes an explicit connection between the disappearance of the Sun Dance and that of the buffalo. "Since the buffalo were gone, the pressure was to live in the white agricultural world. You wore Western dress; you opted to be Christian and 'civilized.'"[23] The Indigenous culture on the Prairies was decimated along with the bison herds. Many Christian missionaries saw Indigenous people as "empty vessels," for they "would never contest the loss of their lands, would never organize against them, and would easily take to Christianity."[24]

Silman tells of her Cree grandmother, who became Christian in 1880s. "The mentality in the 19th century of those who were converted as Presbyterians was that you had to choose to live either in the indigenous world or the white world."[25] In this either/or choice for survival lies the dangerous assumption that being Christian is identical to following Anglo-European ways of life. This assumption was so deeply seated that it pressured Indigenous people into giving up their identity. In these moments of vulnerability, the pressure to give up their way of life and spiritual practices was intense. It also fed into the notion that the Anglo-European Christian way of life was superior, and that any intelligent Indigenous person would therefore choose to become Christian and abandon their Indigenous way of life. This internalized racism—a sort of the reverse Orientalism[26]—had a devastating impact within Indigenous Christian circles, where many shy away from hybridity and interculturation at the expense of abandoning their ancestors' wisdom and dismissing their traditional ways. Some regard traditional spiritual practices as the acts of the devil; on the opposite end of this spectrum, others refuse to associate with Christians because of the abuse they have experienced. McKay comments on the impact of internalized racism, offering the following example. If First Nation farmers were good at farming, he says, and especially if they were more capable than white farmers, this became a problem for white settlers because it did not "fit their image of the indigenous people," who were supposed to be inferior to them.[27]

It is imperative that we work to remove this internalized inferiority. As article 12 of the Declaration states, a positive sense of self-worth is necessary for the "dignity, survival, and well-being of indigenous peoples." And yet, the more we work to ensure these rights, the more obvious it is that they have not been maintained. The 1986 UCC apology speaks to this fact: "We imposed our civilization as a condition of accepting the gospel. We tried to make you be like us and in so doing we helped to destroy the vision that made you what you were."[28]

The imposition of Christian supremacy upon Indigenous people was maintained by Western epistemology. The work of Diana Taylor provides a helpful counterbalance to this outlook as it sheds light on "performance" as "an episteme, a way of knowing, as an embodied action" carried out through cultural and ritual agency.[29] As a performance studies scholar and an Indigenous person from Mexico, Taylor demonstrates how performance enables the intersection of ritual practices and Indigenous ways of knowing.

Moving beyond the disciplinary study of written literary and historical documents as a basis of Western and colonial epistemology, she offers the lens of performed ritual, which has the potential to illuminate wisdom that cannot otherwise be conveyed. By elucidating this episteme, Taylor reveals the limit of Western epistemology, in which "writing has become the guarantor of existence itself."[30]

Here performance is understood as embodied practice, including cultural, religious, and spiritual practice that is rehearsed and performed regularly. Being aware of other meanings of performance—for example, the sense of a "put-on," which signals artificiality or superficiality—we intentionally use performance as reiterative and "vital acts of transfer, transmitting social knowledge, memory, and a sense of identity" through particular behaviours.[31] Most of all, we affirm the indefinability of performance that contains various meanings and roles, including "a process, a praxis, an episteme, a mode of transmission, an accomplishment, and a means of intervening in the world."[32]

I focus on performance as an episteme—that is, as a form of knowing and a system for transmitting knowledge—because this particular function is closely related to Indigenous rituals in the context of colonization. Many European philosophers and theologians have considered Western literary-centred epistemology to be superior to non-Western non-literary epistemology.

When European missionaries arrived in the Americas in the fifteenth and sixteenth centuries, they claimed that Indigenous people's past had disappeared because they had no writing, and thus no history and no knowledge.[33] They were certain that history is inseparably connected to writing and that writing is connected to knowledge. However, it is absurd to claim that Indigenous people who inhabited Turtle Island for thousands of years did not have any writing or any knowledge. Marie Battiste, a Mi'kmaw educator, argues that there were sophisticated symbolic forms of Algonkian literacy. "The Mi'kmaq," she writes, "are among those indigenous peoples who have had a unique history of symbolic writing that began well before letters and orthographies were introduced."[34] Though their writings were different from European writings, they had developed a highly valued writing system contained in codices. However, the primary mode of knowing and the chief medium of knowledge transmission for Indigenous people around the world is performance. This embodied culture of performance often involves the ritual of storytelling. Davis describes the brilliance of orality as practised by the Penan people in Malaysia: "Writing, while clearly an extraordinary innovation in human history... permits and even encourages the numbing of memory. Oral traditions [by contrast] sharpen recollection, even as they seem to open a certain mysterious dialogue with the natural world.... The Penan perceive the voices of animals in the forest.... Entire hunting parties may be turned back to camp by the cry of a bat hawk.... This remarkable dialogue informs Penan life in ways that few outsiders can be expected to understand."[35] This largely inaccessible knowledge (to outsiders, at least) offers a potential mode of resistance: it is inaccessible to colonial invaders, and hence difficult to control. Taylor distinguishes written knowledge as "the archive" and embodied knowledge as "the repertoire."[36] The former is easily stored, controlled, and even erased, which results in the numbing of memory that Davis describes. Embodied knowledge—the repertoire—is non-reproducible; once it is performed it cannot be repeated in exactly the same way. It relies on the agency of participants, their memory and their performance, and within these practices there is a possibility of resistance and subversion. When we appreciate the repertoire of the ritual, we begin to understand how ritual as embodied knowledge can act as a form of subversive agency. It is to this agency that we now turn.

Translation of Hymnody: The Subversive Hybrid Practices of Indigenous Christians

Maintaining Indigenous people's agency involves maintaining their language, which, as we have seen, could be used as a tool for subversion and resiliency. McKay writes, "the Cree language was strong, the missionary was never able to break the leadership style of the people. Whenever he made a statement, it had to be interpreted; and the elders could interpret it as they saw fit. I imagine there was a bit of subversion at times. The elders maintained control."[37]

Kahontakwas Diane Longboat, an Elder, traditional healer, and senior project manager in Aboriginal engagement and outreach at the Centre for Addiction and Mental Health in Toronto, argues that "culture, language, heritage, ceremonies, connection to community and to the land, are all resiliency factors."[38] As long as people kept their language and ceremonies, "their cultural identity was never completely destroyed even though cultural genocide had been practiced everywhere around them from the beginning of contact."[39] In this sense, the Christian evangelization of Indigenous people was never seamless; it was contested with "the insurrection of subjugated knowledge"[40] through Indigenous languages. The act of translation involved a process of constant negotiation, and this negotiation enabled the mixing of Christianity and Indigenous cultures.

If language is power, the loss of language represents a concomitant loss of power. Silman talks about this loss of power as a form of forgetting. "Many of the indigenous cultural ways, as the traditional elders say, have not been lost but forgotten. Yet that 'forgetting' was imposed by an intentional policy of colonial powers to abolish Aboriginal culture and religion."[41] In this regard, colonialism is an oppressive system of "structural forgetting."[42] This structural forgetting took the form of non-recognition as a colonial way of dismissing Indigenous people's languages and values. This non-recognition was in turn manifested in the form of "cultural genocide."[43] The most obvious example of cultural genocide in the Canadian context is found in the history of residential schools. Christians who ran the schools did not recognize Indigenous children as full and dignified human beings with their own languages, traditions, cultures, and family backgrounds. Non-recognition was carried out as structural forgetting and systematic institutionalization. Residential schools were "a place of incarceration" and were ran like "prisons." Their purpose was to "separate children from the influence of their family, culture and language"[44] so that these children would forget who they were. Longboat contends that if any of these pieces of "culture, language, heritage, ceremonies, connection to community and to the land" are removed, people are "lost in the world."[45]

This removal from the family, the community, and the land was devastating not only in terms of the emotional and physical trauma it caused but also its pedagogical effect. Indigenous ways of teaching are carried out predominantly through the process of young people observing Elders and parents. McKay and Silman note that "the young ones would be learning by observation."[46] Aural learning chiefly happened through the ritual of storytelling. For the Cree, winter is the primary time for teaching through storytelling. Education takes place through intergenerational community ritual rather than the solitary reading of books or learning among peer groups. Removing children from their family and community made such education impossible, thereby further alienating Indigenous children from their communities.

Not only were the Indigenous children in residential schools unable to maintain and practise their languages, but they "were given a constant drilling in English, and spent much of their time memorizing and reciting religious texts and hymns."[47] The singing of Christian hymns was part of a broader pattern of colonial teaching in which missionary hymnody was itself used to subjugate, discipline, and control Indigenous children. Hymns operated as "text[s] inscribing the act of colonialism itself."[48] However, while being colonized, Indigenous people did not often accept colonial rules and imposition passively or without resistance. Elders and leaders who could speak Indigenous languages inverted these colonial techniques, and in this way language became a force with which they could reassert their own cultural traditions and self-determination. There was resilience and resistance.

The case of translation in the hymn "O for a Thousand Tongues to Sing" reveals how Cree Christians were able to subvert colonial messages. It is a well-known hymn among Methodist and United Church Christians.[49] Written by Charles Wesley in 1739, it has been published in 1,368 different hymnals around the world and has appeared in most Cree hymnals from the time they first came into existence. Erin McIntyre offers the translation and its analysis of the doxology of the hymn.[50] She notes that the first stanza of Wesley's original hymn was not included in *A Collection of Hymns for the Use of People Called Methodists*.[51] Yet it is the eighth stanza in the 1971 version of the Cree hymnal.[52]

Wesley's original stanza 1	1971 stanza 8
Glory to God, and praise and love	*Praise great God*
Be ever, ever given	*Today/now and forever*
By saints below and saints above,	*With all the ones that are living in this world/*
The church in earth and heaven	*this earth and also the ones in heaven.*

The doxology is the first stanza in Wesley's original hymn. In Cree, it is only included in the 1971 hymnal. The Cree translation omits "glory" and "love." The main difference in this translation comes in the subject of those praising. In English, the ones who are praising are the "saints," while in Cree this refers to "all." McIntyre considers this an example of how we can find the subversive wisdom of Cree translators, who contested Christianity's exclusive view of salvation, by inserting and altering the wisdom represented by God's salvation and love.[53] Indigenous translators had an ability to subvert meanings by amending and omitting certain words.[54]

When the Bible was first translated into Cree in the nineteenth century, it was really the Cree who translated it, since they were the only ones who knew the language. So the translation embedded many Indigenous understandings and philosophies. The missionary translators depended on Indigenous people to find the right words, including those for key biblical terms such as sin, salvation, or heaven.[55] However, one should not jump to the conclusion that missionaries and Indigenous translators were equal. "As a practice," Robert Young asserts, "translation...always involves questions of power relations. If translation involves the power structure of acts of appropriation, it can also invoke power through acts of resistance."[56]

In the case of Cree hymnody, it is very easy to see two distinct groups and their power differentials: missionaries and Cree. While the two groups are easily identifiable, they are not themselves homogenous. For example, we have no way of knowing the possible categories (race, language, ethnicity) that each translator fell into. We cannot know the extent to which certain hymns were used in internalize and form an identity for individuals and the church. That is why we can see hybridity at play in the process of translation, with its heterogeneous acts of subversive and playful resistance. Translation is in and of itself a locus of heterogeneous meaning, as neither original author nor translator write in complete isolation; they draw from their own contexts and canons; and readers do likewise in their reading.[57]

Indigenous Christian translators were guides on a cross-cultural and hybrid journey. This journey brings with it a mix of emotions, ranging from celebration and wonder to grief and hurt. Conflicts can also arise from the crossing of cultural and linguistic borders. Kwok writes such transgression involves both "desire and doubt, affirmation and rejection, projection and identification, management and dysfunction."[58] This creative tension rings true for many Indigenous Christians today as they continue to simultaneously affirm and negotiate their hybrid Indigenous and Christian identity. This also rings true for the United Church of Canada as it continues along a journey of repentance and reconciliation, a journey that both Indigenous and non-Indigenous people must take, reshaping the denomination as they strive to create and imagine a space of coexistence. It is to this space that I now turn.

Toward Reconciliation: Indigenous and Christian Hybrid Identities and Practices

In affirming and negotiating hybrid identity and practice, we should not underestimate the magnitude of the struggles faced by many Indigenous Christians as they sort out for themselves what it means to be both Indigenous and Christian. It is a delicate issue to raise because, as McKay and Silman point out, "it has not always been possible to bring the two together."[59] The difficulty lies partly in the church's past insistence that many Indigenous traditions be dismissed as a result of the internalized racism and reverse Orientalism discussed earlier. The difficulty also lies in the fact that most non-Indigenous Christians do not know how to honour a Medicine Bundle while "participating in sweat lodge and other sacred ceremonies, were evil."[60] Among Plains Cree people, for example, there were "rifts developed within families, among friends, and between bands as denominations competed with each other" and between converts and non-converts.[61]

Indigenous Christians often ask, "How can I be a Christian? How can I be a member in a church that has wreaked so much havoc on my people?" Indigenous Christians sometimes direct this anger at themselves. McKay and Silman recall "the anger some Aboriginal people expressed after the apology by the United Church of Canada." They said, "We have learned this European way....Why do you want us to change back?"[62] The movement between gospel and culture is awkward and unbalanced, a difficult dance to say the least. Reclaiming traditional Indigenous practices and proclaiming Christian gospel—holding these two in a creative tension—is hard. "Some have been excluded from involvement in their band councils because they are Christian and not Traditional; others, who have been rediscovering their Traditional culture, have been excluded from involvement in the Christian church."[63]

The work of easing this tension should not be the sole responsibility of Indigenous Christians; non-Indigenous people have a role to play as well. *Gathering: Resources for Worship Planners*, a national worship resource of the UCC, however modest, demonstrates some of the efforts that non-Indigenous Christians have made to celebrate and recognize Indigenous Christian practices in the United Church. It has featured a number of prayers and liturgies that directly address Indigenous people and issues, especially since the church issued its apology for survivors of residential schools in 1998. Over the last two decades, as a way of marking National Aboriginal Day (June 21), *Gathering* has made an intentional attempt to incorporate Indigenous elements in its summer/autumn issues. For example, the 2003 summer/autumn liturgy introduces an Indigenous prayer in the Four Directions that addresses the wound inflicted by residential schools.[64] After the "Sisters in Spirit" campaign was launched in 2004, *Gathering* featured this collaborative attempt to address violence against Indigenous women. Both the United Church of Canada and the Anglican Church of Canada participated in this initiative, along with the Women's Inter-Church Council and the Native Women's Association of Canada. A liturgy including Indigenous practice was included in 2005. The Four Direction prayer was featured again in 2008–9 as "gifts" from Aboriginal traditions. Then, an interfaith service recognizing "diversities" in Aboriginal traditions was included in the summer/autumn issues in 2015 and 2016. Here, the UCC recognizes that Indigenous traditions are not homogenous, and for this reason it highlights ways of respecting "differences" among Indigenous Peoples. A creed in the volume captures this: "God is colour seen in different ways by many different people. God is unconditional love: though we may come in various unique packages, God loves us all, just the same. After the storm, God is the rainbow of differences."[65] Article 12 of the Declaration states that along with the maintenance of Indigenous language, the question of how Indigenous people "ensure their right to control their ceremonial objects and to keep their privacy" is also important. Here, the danger of cultural misappropriation needs to be raised. To that end, *Gathering* in 2017 addressed cultural appropriation, which it described as "the use of symbols, rituals, and other elements of one culture by people of a different cultural background without permission, invitation, or instruction, as if those symbols, ritual, and other elements are one's own."[66]

All of these services show us how to honour and learn from Indigenous Peoples' cultural traditions and spirituality in the UCC while recognizing the harm that was done to them, including misappropriation. While these services are mainly created for non-Indigenous members, they indirectly support article 12's assertion that "indigenous people have the right to manifest, practise, develop and teach their spiritual and religious traditions, customs and ceremonies."

The other insight that can be gleaned from *Gathering* is the hybrid nature of the service. That certain elements of Indigenous tradition are incorporated into a typical European-style Christian service that is to be used for non-Indigenous members is evidence of such hybrid practice. It implies that this hybrid worship is not just for Indigenous people but for all non-Indigenous people, white and non-white, who live under the tent of the UCC.

A review of *Gathering* in this light affirms that ritual process is neither static nor homogeneous. It changes with the passage of time and as different people are engaged. Ritual, while marking one's own identity, is not exclusive to a certain group because it "historically undergoes change, [and is] often responsive to changed historical and social circumstances." And when ritual goes through these types of changes, existing "forms are constantly contested, and the open-ended nature of this challenge makes the integration of ritual and sincerity an endless project."[67]

The act of worship has always depended on a juggling of continuity and change. This involves both honouring founding traditions and being responsive to historical and social circumstances. The question of how worship can be relevant to and reflective of the changing context is key to understanding worship in the United Church. Bill Kervin calls this "the dialectical ethos of United Church worship."[68] This dialectical dynamic involves a creative, and often difficult, tension between the desire to honour founding traditions and the challenge of responding to new emerging contexts. Our engagement with this tension does not end in some binary opposition between "order and liberty, form and freedom, catholicity and particularity, ecumenism and denominationalism...continuity and change."[69] Instead of choosing one pole exclusively, the UCC, while it is never perfect, has continued to maintain an inclusive and liberal theological tradition without derailing its founding traditions. However, at the same time, UCC worship has a strong tendency to be Eurocentric and to legitimate the hegemony of white Eurocentrism. Pay a visit any UCC congregation, big or small. Look around at your own church worship. Worship in its order, its music, and its use of language, its prayer and preaching, and its movement (or lack thereof) reflects a white Anglo-European tradition. The dialectic pendulum still swings unsymmetrically. The polarization of UCC worship between "centre and periphery, mainstream and margins, colonial and post-colonial" is wide and deep.[70] Thus, it requires painstaking work to pull it back into balance. This demands a radical shift—a shift that must include the agency of Indigenous communities and an affirmation of their ritual practices and ceremonies that contest colonial assumptions and teachings. Their hybrid practices can offer a powerful corrective if non-Indigenous worshipping communities allow it to.

Indigenous-Christian hybrid practices have always existed where there have been Indigenous Christians responding to the faith in a way that makes sense to them. Sasakamoose, a brother of Ahtahkakoop, a shaman, was converted

7. INDIGENOUS CHRISTIAN RITUALS AND CEREMONIES

to Christianity. Many Indigenous people who adopted Christianity had more practical reasons, but for Sasakamoose this new-found religion opened up a whole new world. As a head of the Ahtahkakoop band, he also sought to support Christian mission. On one occasion, he instructed the people on the importance of kneeling when canoeing:

> When you wish to make a journey across your lake in your Birch bark canoes, you don't throw your things in anyhow, & get in yourself in the same careless way, & then paddle out into the deep, because a canoe is a difficult thing to manage. It must be evenly balanced, and you must take your place carefully, so that when you launch out you may devote all your attention to the work of propelling your craft and not be troubled with the unsteadiness with which it rides on the water caused by the careless and uneven way.[71]

Sasakamoose's appreciation of kneeling while canoeing seems to integrate his traditional life with a new way of Christian life. Christensen writes, "To make their new venture [as an Indigenous Christian community] work, everyone had to pull and work together. It was like rowing a canoe. In Sasakamoose's view, kneeling and praying to the Christian God was one way to keep focused on and in balance."[72]

Like kneeling, certain Christian rituals and liturgical elements were better received than others among Indigenous Christians. For example, a more liturgical ceremonial style of worship and dress appealed to Indigenous people. As McKay and Silman write, "there were colours used in worship and smudging (incense). It is not surprising that the Roman Catholic Church became the largest mission church, and the Church of England was next," when we consider their visual and sensory liturgical worship practices in the nineteenth and twentieth centuries.[73] On the contrary, Methodists had a challenge attracting Indigenous people to their churches when they focused on solemnity and order, denying Indigenous Peoples' music, their styles of singing and playing drums.[74] On the one hand, Indigenous Christians welcomed highly liturgical styles of worship, but one the other, non-liturgical churches exerted a strong appeal because of their emphasis on the Holy Spirit, including visions and prophecy.[75] To Indigenous people, God is the Great Spirit. Recognition of this fact is fundamental to Indigenizing Christian theology. McKay and Silman add another possible reason for the appeal of non-liturgical Pentecostal styles of worship to Indigenous people: the church allowed dance! "The Methodists especially did not permit you to move your feet when you were praising God."[76] Within Indigenous tradition, however, dance has always been linked to healing and spiritual renewal, as discussed earlier.[77] In Indigenous traditions, dancing is often combined with drumming: "The drum is the heartbeat of Mother Earth. In order to dance, to celebrate our spirituality, we had to have a drum," writes Reverend James Isbister, a member of the Plains Cree and the chairperson of the Council for Native Ministries within the Anglican Church of Canada.[78] That is why banning dance and drum has contributed to the literal and figurative killing of Indigenous people's spirits. Christian worship that seeks reconciliation with Indigenous people should therefore not dismiss dance and drum but recognize and incorporate them as gifts in worship.

Conclusion: Listening to the Elders

When the first Europeans came to Canada and asked, "What is this place?" the Indigenous people who were already here answered, "*khanatum*," which in Cree means "sacred place," holy ground. The name "Canada" comes from this word. Indigenous people had a sense of the sacredness of this land, Canada, as a place where white and non-Indigenous settlers could live with them to celebrate the sacredness of life.[79] Celebrating an Indigenous-Christian hybrid ritual is thus to create this sacred place as a shared space. Not only do Indigenous Peoples have "the right to manifest, practise, develop and teach their spiritual and religious traditions, customs, and ceremonies" (in the words of article 12); they also have wisdom to offer non-Indigenous people concerning the sacredness of life and the importance of coexistence and reconciliation.

Elder Dominic Eshkakogan, a Roman Catholic deacon and Medicine Man, wishes for a day when Indigenous people may use the most beautiful prayer

7. INDIGENOUS CHRISTIAN RITUALS AND CEREMONIES

of their traditions, the Sunrise Ceremony that incorporates the Sun Dance, in Sunday worship. To him, this ceremony is the most beautiful because it captures the heart of the thanksgiving prayer, which urges us, as "the light of the sun touches each of the elements of the earth, [to] give thanks for each element that we see.... Our prayers are said in freedom at the beginning of each day—and each day is new."[80]

For the late Jessie Saulteaux, being both Indigenous and Christian is not only possible but desirable. It was obvious that she held her Christian heritage and practice dearly. However, she never forgot her grandmother and her traditional teaching as a Medicine Woman. Describing Saulteaux's funeral, Carlson and Dumont capture this hybrid form: "For the hundreds of people at her funeral, the power of the Holy Spirit was present in the outpouring of grief, in the sharing, in the feast, and in the reconciliation that happened in her community. It was even present in the symbols and imagery, both Christian and traditional, that intertwined at her wake and funeral."[81]

Notes

1. UN General Assembly, Resolution 61/295, United Nations Declaration on the Rights of Indigenous Peoples, A/RES/61/295 (October 2, 2007), https://undocs.org/A/RES/61/295, 5.
2. "Unreserved: A Day in the Life at Standing Rock," CBC Radio, November 18, 2016, http://www.cbc.ca/radio/unreserved/something-extraordinary-is-happening-at-standing-rock-1.3850506/a-day-in-the-life-at-standing-rock-1.3857469.
3. "The Current: No End in Sight for Standing Rock Protest against Dakota Access Pipeline," CBC Radio, November 1, 2016, http://www.cbc.ca/radio/thecurrent/the-current-for-november-1-2016-1.3829419/no-end-in-sight-for-standing-rock-protest-against-dakota-access-pipeline-1.3829421.
4. "Unreserved: Something Extraordinary Is Happening at Standing Rock," CBC Radio, November 16, 2016, https://www.cbc.ca/radio/unreserved/something-extraordinary-is-happening-at-standing-rock-1.4203594.
5. "Unreserved: Close Quarters: Disagreements over Protocol, Security and Entertainment at Standing Rock," CBC Radio, November 17, 2016, http://www.cbc.ca/radio/unreserved/something-extraordinary-is-happening-at-standing-rock-1.3850506/close-quarters-disagreements-over-protocol-security-and-entertainment-at-standing-rock-1.3855223.
6. Karen Pauls, " 'We Must Kill the Black Snake': Prophecy and Prayer Motivate Standing Rock Movement," CBC News, December 11, 2016, http://www.cbc.ca/news/canada/manitoba/dakota-access-pipeline-prayer-1.3887441.

7   Stan McKay and Janet Silman, *The First Nations: A Canadian Experience of the Gospel-Culture Encounter* (Geneva: WCC, 1995), 31–2.
8   Stanley McKay and Janet Silman, "A First Nations Movement in a Canadian Church," in *The Reconciliation of Peoples: Challenge to the Churches*, ed. Gregory Baum and Harold Wells (Maryknoll, NY: Orbis Books, 1997), 172–83.
9   McKay and Silman, *The First Nations*, 33.
10 Ibid., 37.
11 Ibid., 36.
12 Ibid., 38.
13 Ibid., 39–40.
14 Deanna Christensen, *Ahtahkakoop: The Epic Account of a Plains Cree Head Chief, His People, and Their Struggle for Survival, 1816–1896* (Shell Lake, SK: Ahtahkakoop Publishing, 2000), 556.
15 Joyce Carlson and Alf Dumont, *Bridges in Spirituality: First Nations Christian Women Tell Their Stories* (Toronto: United Church Publishing House, 1997), 41.
16 Harold Cardinal, *The Unjust Society*, rev. ed. (Vancouver: Douglas and McIntyre, 1999), 138.
17 Christensen, *Ahtahkakoop*, 467.
18 Corky Alexander, "The Cherokee Stomp Dance: A Case Study of Postcolonial Native American Contextualization," in *Liturgy in Postcolonial Perspectives: Only One Is Holy*, ed. Cláudio Carvalhaes (New York: Palgrave Macmillan, 2015), 268.
19 Charles H. Kraft, *Anthropology for Christian Witness* (Maryknoll, NY: Orbis Books, 1996), 259–60.
20 Carlson and Dumont, *Bridges in Spirituality*, 59.
21 Clara Sue Kidwell, Homer Noley, and George E. Tinker, *A Native American Theology* (Maryknoll, NY: Orbis Books, 2001), 42–3.
22 Wade Davis, *The Wayfinders: Why Ancient Wisdom Matters in the Modern World* (CBC Massey Lectures) (Toronto: Anansi Press, 2009), 168–9.
23 McKay and Silman, *The First Nations*, 16.
24 Diana Taylor, *The Archive and the Repertoire: Performing Cultural Memory in the Americas* (Durham, NC: Duke University Press, 2003), 59.
25 McKay and Silman, *The First Nations*, 16.
26 For the classic analysis of Orientalism, see Edward W. Said, *Orientalism* (New York: Vintage Books, 1978).
27 McKay and Silman, *The First Nations*, 17.
28 See "1986 Apology to Indigenous Peoples," accessed April 7, 2021, https://united-church.ca/sites/default/files/apologies-response-crest.pdf.
29 Taylor, *The Archive and the Repertoire*, xvi.
30 Ibid., xix.
31 Ibid., 2.
32 Ibid., 15.
33 Ibid., 16.

34 Marie Battiste, "Mi'kmaw Symbolic Literacy," in *Visioning a Mi'kmaw Humanities: Indigenizing the Academy*, ed. Marie Battiste (Sydney, NS: Cape Breton University Press, 2016), 124.
35 Davis, *The Wayfinders*, 175.
36 Taylor, *The Archive and the Repertoire*, 19.
37 McKay and Silman, *The First Nations*, 23.
38 Kerry Clare, "Healing the Human Spirit," *Vic Report*, Winter 2018, 9.
39 McKay and Silman, *The First Nations*, 25.
40 This is Michel Foucault's term, cited in Kwok Pui-lan, *Postcolonial Imagination and Feminist Theology* (Louisville, KY: Westminster John Knox Press, 2005), 32.
41 McKay and Silman, *The First Nations*, 1.
42 Melinda Sharp, *Misunderstanding Stories: Toward a Postcolonial Pastoral Theology* (Eugene, OR: Pickwick Publications, 2013), 86.
43 McKay and Silman, *The First Nations*, 1.
44 Ibid., 15.
45 Clare, "Healing the Human Spirit," 9.
46 McKay and Silman, *The First Nations*, 4.
47 Truth and Reconciliation Commission of Canada, *Final Report of the Truth and Reconciliation Commission of Canada, Vol. 1: Canada's Residential Schools: The History, Part 1, Origins to 1939* (Winnipeg: Truth and Reconciliation Commission of Canada, 2015), 86.
48 Philip V. Bohlman, "World Musics and World Religions: Whose World?," in *Enchanting Powers: Music in the World's Religions*, ed. Lawrence E. Sullivan (Cambridge, MA: Harvard University Press, 1997), 71.
49 For the complete lyrics, see "O for a Thousand Tongues," *Hymnary.org*, accessed November 17, 2017, https://hymnary.org/text/o_for_a_thousand_tongues_to_sing_my.
50 Erin McIntyre, "United Church of Canada Cree Hymnody in Translation: A Theological Locus of Hybridity" (STM thesis, Saskatoon Theological Union, 2018). As her thesis adviser, I am grateful for Erin's permission to use her work here.
51 John Wesley, *A Collection of Hymns for the Use of the People Called Methodists* (London: John Mason, 1874), 8–9.
52 McIntyre, "United Church of Canada Cree Hymnody in Translation," 87.
53 Ibid., 85.
54 HyeRan Kim-Cragg, *Story and Song: A Postcolonial Interplay between Christian Education and Worship* (New York: Peter Lang, 2012), 89.
55 McKay and Silman, *The First Nations*, 42.
56 Robert J.C. Young, *Postcolonialism: A Very Short Introduction* (Oxford: Oxford University Press, 2003), 140–1.
57 Lawrence Venuti, *Translator's Invisibility: A History of Translation*, 2nd ed. (Abingdon, UK: Routledge, 2008), 13.
58 Kwok Pui-lan, "A Theology of Border Passage," in *Border Crossings: Cross-Cultural Hermeneutics*, ed. D.N. Premnath (Maryknoll, NY: Orbis Books, 2007), 112.
59 McKay and Silman, *The First Nations*, 40.

60   Christensen, *Ahtahkakoop*, 556.
61   Ibid.
62   McKay and Silman, *The First Nations*, 52.
63   Joyce Carlson, ed., *Dancing the Dream: The First Nations and the Church in Partnership* (Toronto: Anglican Book Centre, 1995), 79.
64   *Gathering: Resources for Worship Planners*, Summer/Autumn (2003), 45–6.
65   *Gathering*, Advent/Christmas/Epiphany (2015–16), 84.
66   *Gathering*, Lent/Easter (2017), 71.
67   Adam B. Seligman, Robert P. Weller, Michael J. Puett, and Bennett Simon, *Ritual and Its Consequences: An Essay on the Limits of Sincerity* (Oxford: Oxford University Press, 2008), 129–30.
68   William S. Kervin, "Worship on the Way: The Dialectic of United Church Worship," in *The United Church of Canada: A History*, ed. Don Schweitzer (Waterloo, ON: Wilfred Laurier University Press, 2012), 197–8.
69   Ibid., 197.
70   Ibid., 198.
71   Christensen, *Ahtahkakoop*, 554–5.
72   Ibid., 555.
73   McKay and Silman, *The First Nations*, 9.
74   Ibid., 9.
75   Ibid., 10.
76   Ibid.
77   Carlson, *Dancing the Dream*, 40.
78   Ibid., 41.
79   Ibid., 73.
80   Ibid., 82.
81   Carlson and Dumont, *Bridges in Spirituality*, 70.

CHAPTER 8

JUSTIFICATION by GRACE as a SPIRITUAL RESOURCE

Non-Indigenous Christians Adopting the Declaration as the Framework for Reconciliation with Indigenous Peoples in Canada

by

DON SCHWEITZER

On March 30, 2016, the United Church of Canada and seven other Canadian churches adopted the United Nations Declaration on the Rights of Indigenous Peoples as the framework for reconciliation between Indigenous and non-Indigenous Peoples in Canada.[1] This was in compliance with Call to Action 48 of the Truth and Reconciliation Commission of Canada (TRC), which called churches to do this and to say how they would implement the Declaration as a framework for reconciliation. The latter part of this request can be read on two levels. A first level is that of the actions the churches will undertake to comply with the Declaration. But there is a second level to this "how." The Declaration sets high moral standards for non-Indigenous Canadians. Living up to these will involve far-reaching changes in Canadian society and in many non-Indigenous Canadians' sense of identity. People need strong moral sources to live up to high moral standards.[2] So this request can also be read as a question that churches need to ask themselves. What spiritual/moral resources will they draw upon to empower and sustain their commitment to the Declaration as the framework for reconciliation?

In what follows, I argue that justification by grace provides some of the spiritual resources that non-Indigenous Christians need for this task. This doctrine could be called a neglected part of the United Church's spiritual heritage. It is not central to recent United Church faith statements or to United Church apologies and statements concerning its involvement in residential schools. But I argue that it should be. Justification by grace addresses issues arising from spoiled social identities.[3] A person's or institution's identity becomes spoiled when they fail to realize, or they violate outright, the moral norms central to what they profess to be.[4] This failure discredits and taints their identity and creates within them a need for acceptance.[5] Justification by grace also addresses the need for hope for a better future despite past failures and provides a basis for living with ethnic, religious, and cultural differences. These issues are central to the United Church's apologies and statements made in regard to its involvement in residential schools. The United Church's commitment to the Declaration presents an opportunity to rediscover some of the meaning and value of justification by grace. If the United Church is to pursue reconciliation with Indigenous Peoples in Canada, it will need the transcendent acceptance, ultimate hope, and openness to others that this doctrine conveys.

The United Church and Its Canadian Context

The United Church has issued two apologies to Indigenous people. The first, in 1986, apologized for its participation in Western colonialism and its attempts to assimilate Indigenous Peoples into the dominant white culture. The second, in 1998 was addressed to former students of residential schools, their families,

8. JUSTIFICATION BY GRACE AS A SPIRITUAL RESOURCE

and their communities, and apologized for the damage, suffering, and loss that the United Church's involvement in these schools caused.[6] With these two apologies the United Church confessed its guilt in these matters and the need for the church as a whole to repent of the colonial mindset and the practices that led to its adoption. There is a collective dimension to this guilt. As the identities of members and adherents of the United Church are bound up with its traditions and history—both of which inform its present—they share this guilt. The United Church describes itself in its "A New Creed" as called to "seek justice and resist evil."[7] This identity of seeking justice and resisting evil has been spoiled by the church's involvement in Western colonialism and residential schools. When the United Church affirms its calling to seek reconciliation with Indigenous Peoples in Canada, it simultaneously affirms its guilt for its involvement in this history of colonialism. As a result, a sense of shame has entered into the United Church's identity.[8] Its 2006 faith statement, "A Song of Faith," speaks of being "touched by...the toxins of religious and ethnic bigotry," and of "the covert despair that lulls many into numb complicity with empires and systems of domination."[9] This collective guilt extends to all non-Indigenous Canadians who inherit and benefit from the residual effects of colonial oppression, which continue to shape Canada's economy and culture.

Confessing this guilt is an important first step on the road to reconciliation, for this acknowledges that harm has been done and that the United Church bears some responsibility for it. However, this confession is traumatic for a denomination like the United Church, which is proud of its social activism.[10] The trauma caused by this guilt and shame needs to be addressed if it is not to fester and undermine the church's commitment to reconciliation. Guilt destroys one's self-respect,[11] which is crucial to working toward reconciliation; reconciliation is ultimately based on mutual respect, and only those who respect themselves will respect others. Unaddressed guilt and shame can lead to self-justification and the scapegoating of others. Guilt points to the past, which cannot be undone. It also raises doubts about the future. During the 1990s, a parishioner said to me words to this effect: "We used to be asked to give to help support these schools. Now we are being asked to give to compensate for the damage they did." Implied here was doubt that present efforts will be any more successful or beneficial than those of the past. There is an element of risk in every moral act. A spoiled identity can destroy the courage and confidence needed to undertake such risks. The United Church's collective guilt for its involvement in residential schools raises the question, if this is what our forebears in the church did in seeking to live their faith in their time, what harm might we be doing now as we try to live our faith in our time? What gives us the hope that we can do any better? An "honest recognition of guilt and genuine remorse is necessary for the healing of perpetrators,"[12] but by itself this can be debilitating. As I will argue, the capacity to act responsibly in the quest for reconciliation can be restored if confession of guilt is matched by an acknowledgement that one is justified by grace.

The United Church's apologies did not specify what steps it would take so that its sin of participation in Western colonialism would not be repeated. The TRC came to the aid of it, other churches, and the Canadian government, by calling upon all to accept the Declaration as the framework for reconciliation and emphasizing the importance of this step.[13] The Declaration lays out a much-needed understanding of Indigenous Rights that must be respected by non-Indigenous Canadians, their institutions, and their governments, for reconciliation to occur. At present, a number of the Indigenous Rights that it specifies, such as the right to self-determination, are not fully upheld in Canada. Honouring the stipulations of the Declaration will necessitate fundamental changes in the relationships of non-Indigenous Canadians and institutions to Indigenous Peoples. In accepting it as the framework for reconciliation, churches have committed themselves to seeking radical social change, to struggling to overcome the colonial oppression that still exists in Canada.

What will empower the churches and others to undertake this social struggle? The success of the TRC and Canadian historians in establishing a new common story[14] regarding the history of residential schools, one that has been widely accepted in Indigenous and non-Indigenous circles alike, gives some hope and much impetus to this struggle. But provincial and federal governments have lacked the will to undertake the work required for reconciliation, and many

Canadians still seem attached to "attitudes that are fundamentally assimilationist."[15] In this ambivalent situation, a transcendent principle of expectation, a source of hope and courage that comes from beyond this situation, is needed to empower the struggle for radical social change to which the churches have committed themselves. Justification by grace conveys such a principle of expectation.

To the extent that this struggle succeeds, it will dramatically change the nature of Canadian identity space and of the ethical space between Indigenous Peoples and the Canadian state. To date, both have been dominated by the Eurocentric beliefs and values of non-Indigenous peoples.[16] Accepting the Declaration as the framework for reconciliation will require free, creative self-withdrawal for the sake of others on the part of non-Indigenous people, to make room for the world views, practices, and self-determination of Indigenous people in Canadian public life. The Declaration's stipulations require that the sharing of ethical space by Canada with Indigenous Peoples and of Canadian identity space by non-Indigenous people with Indigenous people be greatly deepened. In order to sustain this greater sharing of ethical and identity space, non-Indigenous Canadians will need to find within their own cultural and religious traditions the basis for a self-relativization that does not lapse into ethical relativism.[17] For Christians, justification by grace can provide just such a tradition. Paul employed it to this end in his letter to the Galatians.[18]

I now turn to justification by grace, looking first at what it is based on and what it means. I will then relate this to the guilt the United Church has incurred and its need for empowerment in the struggle for social change. Finally, I look at justification by grace as a basis for the recognition of others that commitment to the Declaration as the framework for reconciliation requires.

Justification by Grace

Justification by grace describes a change in a person's relationship to God that happens as a result of Jesus's death and resurrection and the work of the Holy Spirit. Through justification by grace, one is reconciled to God. Justification is unconditional.[19] The reality it speaks of was created by what God has done for all in Jesus Christ. Through Christ's life and death, God has entered into communion with all, taking on the human realities of alienation and suffering, guilt, oppression, and marginality. In so doing, God took the burden of these upon God's self in Jesus Christ, who underwent the sufferings that afflict people, most radically in dying on the cross. The love of God proved to be greater than evil, sin, and death, and overcame these alienations and afflictions in principle, raising Christ to new life as a sign of hope and acceptance for all. Through Christ's death and resurrection, "the new world of eternal life is thrown open for the victims and perpetrators of evil,"[20] and a new identity of being justified before God is available to all, regardless of what one has experienced at the hands of others, what one has done, or what one is implicated in.

Justification by grace is sometimes criticized as engendering ethical passivity. It can give rise to a moral hazard for Christians, the temptation to slough off the demands of discipleship because one's identity is secured through God's grace regardless of what one does. But this misinterprets justification by grace. Such a misinterpretation fails to recognize the intrinsic relationship between justification and sanctification. Sanctification is the renewal of a person's life by participation in Christ through the power of the Holy Spirit. Through justification, one's identity is secured by God regardless of what one does or fails to do. But as one is justified by grace, one is called to God's service and sanctified to undertake it. Justification by grace is not invalidated as a moral source by misinterpretations that fail to recognize this. This criticism also overlooks the importance of justification by grace in the Reformed tradition of the church, and how Reformed interpretations of the gospel have moved people to undertake all sorts of ethical and missionary endeavours over the years. How could this happen if justification by grace automatically engenders ethical passivity? Finally, within the United Church since the 1960s, few twentieth-century Christians have been more influential than Lutheran theologian Dietrich Bonhoeffer. Justification by grace was central to Bonhoeffer's understanding of responsible action and Christian discipleship, and it helped empower his costly witness. If Bonhoeffer's life is an example of the ethical passivity that justification by grace gives rise to, let there be more of it!

8. JUSTIFICATION BY GRACE AS A SPIRITUAL RESOURCE

A person who is justified by grace is accepted by God even though they have a spoiled identity. The conscience of those who confess their guilt declares that they are unacceptable. In the case of churches that ran residential schools, the voices of former students and public opinion do the same, with good reason. Yet central to the message that Jesus who was crucified is risen is the meaning that one is forgiven by God in spite of one's sin or guilt.[21] This acceptance does not disregard the sin that is the source of one's guilt. But as God in Christ has taken the burden of one's guilt upon God's self through Christ's death on the cross, and as God has overcome in principle the destructive power of sin through Christ's resurrection, one's guilt is no longer the final word on who one is. Justification by grace does not change the past, but it does grant one a new future. Through Jesus's death on the cross, God has entered into communion with everyone at their lowest point and in relation to their greatest need.[22] In Christ, God, the ultimate source of the moral demand that gives rise to one's guilt, has accepted us. One's guilt remains, but it no longer defines one's identity. As one is justified by grace, one is affirmed by God. This affirmation includes an acknowledgement of one's guilt but reaches beyond it, giving one a new identity as at once guilty, and yet in spite of this, paradoxically accepted by God.[23] This acceptance by God frees us from the debilitating and destructive despair of guilt.[24] The concern of atoning for one's sin has been taken over by God. Christ's resurrection promises that the victims of one's sin will ultimately be set right. With this comes the call to participate in this reparation and to seek reconciliation with those we have wronged.

Sinful acts harm the perpetrators as well as their victims. Forgiveness helps overcome this harm.[25] Sin can so threaten one's sense of self-worth that it is too much to face. For example, the harm done to Indigenous children and their communities through residential schools has been downplayed or denied by some non-Indigenous Canadians despite being well-documented.[26] When white Canadians deny or downplay this harm, their white identity becomes "a structure of denial."[27] As justification conveys forgiveness of sin, it overcomes the threat one's sin poses to one's sense of self and enables one to face it. People seek self-knowledge. But they also fear it, particularly when it threatens their sense of self-worth.[28] Then they often defend themselves against the truth, unless they experience a word addressed to them that exposes the truth that stains their identity and yet also brings a greater truth that can sustain them in receiving this.[29] Justification by grace is the latter kind of word. In justification, a sense of worth based upon one's own self is relinquished. Its place is taken by a self-worth based upon being loved and accepted by God.

As well as enabling one to acknowledge one's guilt, justification empowers one to undertake moral action. Perpetrators of sin or their spiritual descendants can be incapacitated by knowledge of what they are implicated in, particularly when the sin was committed in the name of doing good. As noted above, the experience of guilt can undermine the confidence needed to undertake the risks of moral action. Seeking reconciliation with Indigenous Peoples has become a moral crusade for many Canadian churches and non-Indigenous Christians. But many "early [residential] school staff members believed they were participating"[30] in a moral crusade too. It didn't go so well. What makes non-Indigenous Christians think that their current crusade will be different?

Accepting the Declaration as the framework for reconciliation provides an immanent principle of expectation that things can be different. The Declaration is a word from Indigenous to non-Indigenous people that provides a framework of recognition and respect for the former. This was largely missing in Canada in the residential school era. However, this immanent principle of expectation needs to be matched by a transcendent principle of expectation. The Declaration is a pivotal statement, a powerful tool in the struggle for Indigenous liberation and well-being, a word for its time. But it is a human document. Its framers didn't claim it was perfect, only that it provides a structure for just relations between Indigenous and non-Indigenous people by articulating a minimum standard of human rights pertaining to Indigenous Peoples.[31] It requires the co-operation of nation-states to be fully implemented—something about which successive Canadian governments have been ambivalent. This ambivalence reflects the profound alienation that colonialism and residential schools have created between Indigenous and non-Indigenous people. This alienation is radical, going to the roots of the identities of both. Adhering to the

Declaration will require non-Indigenous Canadians to ponder their own pain and fear as well as their involvement in the ongoing oppression of Indigenous Peoples.[32] Reconciliation between the two will require fundamental conversions on the part of the former in addition to the repentance that churches and the Canadian government have already expressed. It is questionable whether non-Indigenous Canadians are willing and able on their own to undergo these conversions. For these reasons, non-Indigenous Christians need a transcendent principle of expectation, something greater than themselves that brings hope that they can change and that the future can be different, to match the immanent principle of expectation that the Declaration provides. Justification by grace provides this transcendent basis for hope. It brings a foretaste of the coming universal salvation and provides assurance that this salvific future will come to be regardless of one's failures in pursuing it.

For those burdened by guilt, justification marks a new beginning. The divine acceptance and promise it conveys create a new courage and confidence based on God's transcendent love. Knowing that one is accepted by God regardless of what one has done, along with the experience of the presence of the Holy Spirit, which conveys both peace and empowerment, gives one the capacity to engage in moral action without denying past failures or one's current sinful state and limitations. In this way, justification by grace enables one to accept the risks of ethical action even though one is stained by guilt. It also provides hope for the future.

Implicit in every struggle for justice is the belief that goodness will ultimately triumph over evil.[33] Guilt throws this belief into question, for it points to a wrong that cannot be undone. The experience of irrevocable guilt thus creates anxiety about the future. It leads to a questioning of the above-mentioned belief that is crucial for sustaining one's commitment to reconciliation. Justification restores a sinner's faith that goodness will ultimately triumph over sin and evil. In justification, a person "is accepted by that which infinitely transcends one's individual self."[34] In this acceptance, one experiences God's love as a transcendent source of goodness that has overcome the sin and evil separating one from God and from who one should be. As this experience helps restore the belief that goodness will triumph over evil, it provides a source of ultimate hope that can empower struggles for justice and reconciliation.

Justification by grace opens a new future before a person, a future based on the resurrection of the crucified Christ. Because Christ "has been raised inclusively, as the head of the new humanity and as the first-born of the whole creation,"[35] Jesus's resurrection is the beginning of a cosmic redemption. All of Creation is included in the scope of its saving significance. Justification is a foretaste of this coming salvation, the universal dimensions of which include reconciliation with others. Through justification, people are brought into this coming new reality. The foretaste of salvation that it brings creates an impetus to work toward the coming of this salvation in fullness, a desire to seek its actualization in the present as far as possible. The cosmic scope of the teleology of justification means that reconciliation with God becomes an impetus and calling to seek reconciliation with others. As justification is based on Jesus's resurrection, one's reconciliation with God is based upon a source of transcendent expectation for the whole cosmos, that in the end "all will be well and every kind of thing will be well."[36] Justification by grace thus connects us to a transcendent principle of expectation concerning the coming of justice and reconciliation with others. It also frames our participation in this struggle for justice and reconciliation as occurring in response to God's love and as empowered by it.

A person justified by grace has a complex identity. Through Christ they are reconciled to God and in principle to themselves and others even though they remain a sinner, subject to temptation and prone to sin in any number of ways. The struggle between God's grace and sin and evil runs right through them. The fullness of their redemption remains outstanding, a future that beckons to them. The coming of this future is not something they will achieve. Like their justification, it comes as a gift from God. The fullness of salvation will be something radically new created by God, something that people cannot bring into being themselves.[37] Yet though those who are justified by grace still remain sinners, as they are justified they receive the Holy Spirit. It is experienced paradoxically, as acceptance that produces peace, hope, and joy, even though one's identity has been spoiled. In relation to justification, the Holy Spirit has two main aspects. Justification brings a sense of peace about oneself and the surrounding world, in the midst of the conflicts of the present and struggles for justice and reconciliation. This peace comes from the experience in justification received through faith that God's love is greater than sin, evil, and death, and that it will ultimately overcome these. At the same time that the Holy Spirit is experienced as peace, it is also a passion for the possible,[38] the desire to work for the coming of God's reign, for reconciliation with others. It tends to create within us a desire to further express in history the reconciliation to God and the hope of the coming fullness of salvation that we have received.

These contrasting aspects of the experience of the Holy Spirit received in justification—on the one hand peace, and on the other a passion for what is possible—come together to form what Dietrich Bonhoeffer called *hilaritas*,[39] the sense that one is participating in something worthwhile and of lasting benefit to the world. With the restoration and renewal that justification brings comes a sense of meaning, purpose, and joy in life. This sense does not depend upon the success of one's own endeavours. It comes from the experience of God's love, and from that love providing a transcendent principle of expectation for the commitment to seeking reconciliation and working for justice and peace. This has important implications for how non-Indigenous Christians go about working for reconciliation with Indigenous Peoples.

Charles Taylor notes that in the twentieth century there have been repeated instances of people's commitment to philanthropy becoming "invested with contempt, hatred, [and] aggression"[40] toward those they claimed to love as their efforts failed to meet their goals of improvement for those they aimed to help. As a result, these would-be benefactors became "progressively more coercive and inhumane"[41] in their dealings with those they claimed to serve. Taylor mentions residential schools as an example of this.[42] Churches, and many Christians who staffed these schools, often became involved in them out of idealistic motives of love and a desire to help the students. Yet the TRC was inundated with testimony about the violence, abuse, and humiliating punishment that students at residential schools experienced from teachers, principals, and staff.[43] Here, the degeneration of philanthropy into violence and abuse was facilitated by racist and colonial attitudes. However, Taylor argues that wherever "action for high ideals is not tempered, controlled, ultimately engulfed in an unconditional love for the beneficiaries, this ugly dialectic risks repeating itself."[44] This kind of degeneration remains a permanent danger for philanthropic endeavours, and by extension, for the commitment to working toward reconciliation.

As mentioned here, Taylor sees a possible antidote to this tendency for philanthropy to degenerate into contempt and violence toward those it claims to serve. Work for the good of others or toward reconciliation can avoid this if it is motivated by "a love/compassion which is unconditional."[45] That is, work for reconciliation with others needs to be based on a love that values these others simply as they are, unconditionally, not for how well they respond to one's efforts or for what one's efforts toward them are able to achieve. This is the kind of love conveyed in justification by grace, and the kind of acceptance and love for others that justification should give rise to.

Simply believing in justification by grace is no guarantee that it will prevent this kind of degeneration from happening.[46] Justification was part of the doctrinal heritage of the Protestant churches that ran residential schools. However, doctrines, like the religious traditions they are part of, can be interpreted and lived out in different ways. Much depends on how they are appropriated. Justification conveys that God loves all of us unconditionally. As this understanding enframes and motivates the work of non-Indigenous Christians toward reconciliation with Indigenous Peoples so that this work is based on this love and reflects it, it can be an antidote to the danger that the commitment of churches to reconciliation may become poisoned by disappointments and failures. Non-Indigenous Christians in Canada have many motives for seeking reconciliation with Indigenous Peoples. Justification by grace indicates that vindicating oneself or proving one's righteousness should not be foremost among these. In light of the experience of justification, the ultimate motives for seeking reconciliation with those we have wronged are gratitude for what one has been given in justification, love, and respect for others, and delight in doing the good, seeking to further express in one's own life what one has received

8. JUSTIFICATION BY GRACE AS A SPIRITUAL RESOURCE

from God. Justification by grace teaches that through Christ we belong to one another, and that those who have wounded others will find fullness of life through seeking reconciliation with them.

Justification understood in this way should create within non-Indigenous Christians a passion for reconciliation with Indigenous Peoples that moves them to work for this. It also gifts them with a sense of peace and joy, of *hilaritas*, following Bonhoeffer, that enables them to learn from criticism and mistakes, to accept rejection and failure as they work toward reconciliation, without becoming defensive or contemptuous and violent toward those they seek to be reconciled with. The Declaration has been described as "a framework to guide a listening"[47] by non-Indigenous Canadians to Indigenous Peoples. Accepting the Declaration as a framework for reconciliation commits settlers to "investing significant amounts of time and resources into substantive engagement"[48] with Indigenous cultures: their legal orders, traditional narratives, spiritual teachings, et cetera. Christian theologians need to put dialogue with Indigenous spirituality, religious teachings, and practices on their agendas, along with the development of dialogical theological proposal in conversation with Indigenous spiritualities and proposals.[49] This listening should never end, as listening to one another is part of sharing identity and ethical space.

The road to reconciliation with Indigenous Peoples will involve many conversions for non-Indigenous Christians. The apologies that churches have already issued were a turning point signalling their recognition, in theory at least, that their attitudes and orientations toward Indigenous Peoples and their traditions needed to change, and that this had to be publicly acknowledged. This need was brought to their attention through dialogues with Indigenous Peoples and Indigenous church members. If the Declaration is followed as a guide to continued listening to Indigenous Peoples, there will be many more corrections to come for non-Indigenous Canadians as they seek reconciliation. A sense of obligation as Christians, a sense of pride in one's Christian identity, can orient us toward following the Declaration as a guide to the listening that reconciliation requires. However, the empowerment needed to sustain this will not come from one's willpower, but from faith in God's presence, from the acceptance that salvation and holiness result ultimately not from one's works and righteousness, but from the justifying grace of God, which accepts us even as we are. As non-Indigenous Christians work toward reconciliation with Indigenous Peoples they will need to undergo many conversions through which they again and again die to previously held self-understandings, economic arrangements, and social practices, in order to enter into others that will bring reconciliation closer. The road to reconciliation that the Declaration maps out for non-Indigenous Christians is the way of the cross. It will require repeatedly facing the colonial settler within,[50] and being willing to let that identity die for the sake of justice, reconciliation, and a fuller life for all. To sustain such a commitment to reconciliation without it degenerating into self-hatred or contempt for Indigenous people, non-Indigenous Christians will need to see that they and the Indigenous people they seek reconciliation with are all encompassed within the unconditional love of God. This is the message of justification by grace.

Justification is a transitional moment in a Christian's life, the means by which one moves from alienation to reconciliation with God. But justification is also a permanent moment in the Christian life. It places one on a journey toward cosmic reconciliation and renewal. But that journey will not be completed within history. Christians are always in need of justification and sanctification. This is known as the eschatological reservation. It should prevent Christians from ever confusing their present achievements with the reign of God that is to come. Yet it should not tempt Christians to resignation and shirking the work of reconciliation. While justification is a permanent moment in the Christian life, it brings with it the gift of the Holy Spirit. Justification by grace tells us that we are able to seek reconciliation, to walk the way of the cross, through the power of a love that upholds us come what may, that in Christ's death and resurrection has shown itself to be greater than the sin, suffering, and evil that we face and that lies hidden in our hearts. Justification teaches that as we commit to working for reconciliation, our hope and strength lie in a power not our own. We are summoned and empowered by a transcendent love that has already accepted us, even as we are.

Justification by Grace as a Basis for Ethical and Shared Identity Space

I turn now to the Declaration as the framework for reconciliation between Indigenous and non-Indigenous Peoples in Canada. Article 3 of the Declaration states the following: "Indigenous peoples have the right to self-determination. By virtue of that right they freely determine their political status and freely pursue their economic, social and cultural development."[51]

This right to self-determination is "the centralizing principle from which all other [Indigenous] rights flow,"[52] and at the present time the "crucial issue in the *Declaration*."[53] It underlies many of the Calls to Action contained in the fifth volume of the TRC's final report.[54] It is the basis for "the exercise of spiritual, territorial, social, cultural, economic, and political rights, as well as for practical survival"[55] for Indigenous Peoples. During the deliberations and negotiations that forged the Declaration, some nation-states sought to remove this right, place it in the preamble, or water it down. Indigenous delegates refused to allow this. Recognition by others of Indigenous Peoples' right to self-determination is necessary for ending centuries of colonialism, racism, and the domination of Indigenous Peoples by nation-states.

In Canada, the ramifications of Indigenous Peoples' right to self-determination are far-reaching. For instance, at present, determinants "of health, safety, and well-being for Indigenous children fall well below the national average for Canadian children, and remain one of the most significant human rights challenges that Canadians must address."[56] Child-welfare services for Indigenous children in Canada—including federally funded on-reserve social services, which are supposed to help address this—remain bound by provincial legislation.[57] Adherence to the right to self-determination requires that Indigenous Peoples have full jurisdiction over these services[58] and adequate funding to support them. This is but one example of how, as mentioned earlier, many Canadian laws, including the *Indian Act*, "still do not permit the effective exercise of indigenous self-government,"[59] and need to be changed to comply with Indigenous Peoples' right to self-determination. Self-determination also requires material support and reparations. Rights without the means to exercise them are empty. James Anaya, United Nations special rapporteur on the rights of Indigenous Peoples, noted that in Canada, the "most jarring manifestation of these human rights problems is the distressing socio-economic conditions of indigenous peoples in a highly developed country."[60] Fulfilling the right to self-determination requires addressing "the structural/economic aspects of colonialism at its generative roots"[61] and overcoming the economic structures of oppression that Indigenous people in Canada face within a "racially stratified capitalist economy."[62] Implementing the Declaration will thus require economic reparations as well as political, institutional, and juridical reform.

Another kind of change is also needed to bring about reconciliation between Indigenous and non-Indigenous Peoples in Canada. Reconciliation requires "a fundamental shift"[63] in the underlying attitudes of former enemies. However, "Beliefs and attitudes that justified residential schools...continue to animate much of what passes for Aboriginal policies today."[64] This reflects the fact that these beliefs and attitudes continue to be present in the non-Indigenous population that elect the governments that frame these policies. Reconciliation will require that these demons be exorcised from the hearts of white and other non-Indigenous Canadians and replaced by acceptance, respect, and admiration for Indigenous Peoples.

Justification by grace can be a source for non-Indigenous Christians of such acceptance and respect. If those who have been justified by grace consider the full implications of Jesus's death and resurrection,[65] they know that all others have been justified by God in the same way. This makes these others deserving of respect as persons, with all the rights that personhood entails. The common identity of having been justified by God provides non-Indigenous Christians with a basis for respecting Indigenous Peoples that reconciliation requires and necessitates that Indigenous Peoples' rights to self-determination be adhered to. Justification can also empower the kind of change on the part of non-Indigenous Canadians that adhering to these rights will require.

The Royal Proclamation of 1763 and the 1764 Treaty of Niagara are important benchmarks in the history of treaty making in Canada. Indigenous leaders

8. JUSTIFICATION BY GRACE AS A SPIRITUAL RESOURCE

entered into the latter "with the understanding that they would remain free and self-determining peoples."[66] Mutual recognition and respect between Indigenous and non-Indigenous Peoples were basic principles of these two treaties. The history of residential schools provides glaring evidence that these principles have not been upheld by non-Indigenous peoples and their governments. Honouring article 3 of the Declaration require changes that will redress this in Canada's shared identity space and in the ethical space within which Indigenous Peoples and non-Indigenous Canadians encounter each other.

Charles Taylor has defined shared identity space as one in which two or more peoples with different cultures, histories, and understandings of the world live together under the same democratic governance, with each group contributing their understanding of reality to a shared collective identity.[67] Indigenous Peoples and non-Indigenous Canadians exist within the shared identity space of Canada. However, their space of encounter also extends beyond this. Many Indigenous people in Canada are divided regarding participation in Canadian municipal, provincial, and federal politics. The signing of treaties represented "an agreement to interact" that established what Willie Ermine calls an ethical space between Indigenous Peoples and non-Indigenous Canada.[68] This exists beyond the governance structures of each and is the space where they meet.

The encounters and interactions of Indigenous Peoples with non-Indigenous Canadians happen at both levels: within the structures of Canadian democratic governance and in nation-to-nation encounters. Even as sovereign nations with their own governments, Indigenous Peoples share identity space within provinces and Canada as a whole through overlapping, intersecting, and deeply intertwined economies, health care, legal jurisdictions, shared education facilities, participation in sports, et cetera. Recognition of this has led a number of Indigenous people to enter federal, provincial, and municipal politics, so as to represent their people in these spaces where decisions are made that affect their communities. Yet Indigenous Peoples in Canada also rightly insist that they have their own governance structures and political identities, and that they relate to Canada on a nation-to-nation basis. Indigenous people have also participated in the shared identity space of the overarching governing structures of the United Church, though they have also insisted on their own space, managed by themselves, from which they have at times addressed the larger church as Indigenous people speaking to non-Indigenous people. In so doing, they, too, have constituted something like the ethical space that Ermine describes.

The shared identity space that is Canada has never been properly shared by white settlers with Indigenous Peoples. Lingering colonial attitudes of cultural and racial superiority on the part of the former continue to undermine the ethical space that should exist between settler society and Indigenous Peoples.[69] White Canadians have historically taken up too much space in both these domains, and they continue to do so. Recognizing the right of Indigenous Peoples to self-determination requires changing this. White settlers need to learn from the horrific impact of residential schools if they are to relativize their own forms of life and take the universalist bases of their own traditions[70] as grounds for a more just sharing of identity space and the creation of an authentic ethical space between themselves and Indigenous Peoples. Justification by grace provides a universalist base by which white Christians can accept the differences of Indigenous Peoples and recognize and respect their human rights. It empowers free, creative self-withdrawal for the sake of others, which can in turn open up space for "mechanisms that will promote aboriginal political voice and leverage"[71] that reconciliation requires.

Human life requires adequate space to flourish.[72] This includes room for a people's culture, self-governance, and self-determination. One of the reasons why Indigenous communities have tended not to flourish in Canada is that they have been denied this space. Honouring article 3 of the Declaration will require that they have much more room to contribute to the collective Canadian identity, and that they have much more room as sovereign peoples within the ethical space where they encounter non-Indigenous Canada on a nation-to-nation basis.

White and non-Indigenous Canadians need to practise free, creative self-withdrawal in order to help create this space for Indigenous people. Free, creative self-withdrawal does not require us to leave others alone, but creates space in which they can flourish, exercise their agency, and so contribute to the common project of building Canada and engaging with it in a nation-to-nation exchange.[73] Free, creative self-withdrawal can be costly. It involves sacrifices of power and control. It is risky and always ambiguous. Yet it is the way to a new relationship with those who have been denied the living space they need, and it can create the possibility of a qualitatively different future for those who withdraw and those they withdraw for.

Justification by grace helps empower us to take this step by enabling us to accept our limited and perishable nature and the perishability of the social order we are at home in and comfortable with.[74] Justification reveals one's eschatological destiny, so that one does not need to defend one's present status at a cost to others, or grasp all that one can, but instead can make way for others, for the sake of a common good, knowing that one's final destiny is safe with God. It enables us to go beyond ourselves, not by colonial expansion or by assimilating others, but, paradoxically, through free, creative self-withdrawal for others' sake. Article 3 of the Declaration has a remedial function at present. It was perceived to be a threat to the status quo by many nation-states because at present Indigenous Peoples do not have space to exercise their right to self-determination. To provide this, white settlers will have to relinquish some of the excessive power, control, and material wealth they currently have, so that Indigenous people can take their rightful place within Canada's shared identity space, and so that the power imbalances and colonial attitudes that distort the ethical space between Indigenous Peoples and non-Indigenous Canada can be rectified.

Conclusion

The road to reconciliation that the Declaration charts will be long and difficult for white-settler Canadians. As we walk it, we will need something that can help us accept ourselves, despite our spoiled identities and the further mistakes we will make on the way. We will also need something that enables us to accept and respect those who are different from us. Justification by grace can be a moral source that helps non-Indigenous Christians do just that.

Notes

I thank Alison Jantz, formerly librarian for the Saskatoon Theological Union Libraries, for locating several articles referenced in this chapter.

1. See "An Ecumenical Statement on the *United Nations Declaration on the Rights of Indigenous Peoples*," released March 30, 2016, https://www.kairoscanada.org/wp-content/uploads/2016/03/Ecumenical-Statement-EN.pdf. The statement is also reproduced in appendix A of this volume.
2. Charles Taylor, *Sources of the Self* (Cambridge, MA: Harvard University Press, 1989), 516.
3. The term "spoiled identity" comes from the subtitle of Erving Goffman's *Stigma: Notes on the Management of Spoiled Identity* (Toronto: Simon & Schuster, 1963).
4. Ibid., 6.
5. Ibid., 8–9.
6. See "1986 Apology to Indigenous Peoples" and "To Former Students of United Church Indian Residential Schools," United Church of Canada, accessed March 10, 2021, https://united-church.ca/social-action/justice-initiatives/reconciliation-and-indigenous-justice/apologies.
7. United Church of Canada, "A New Creed," in *The Manual*, 2016 (Toronto: United Church Publishing House, 2016), 20.
8. Phyllis Airhart, "A Letter from Phyllis Airhart to Arnprior Assembly Participants," October 19, 2005. In possession of the author.
9. United Church of Canada, "A Song of Faith," in *The Manual*, 2016, 22.
10. Brian Thorpe, "A Loss of Innocence," *Ecumenism*, no. 155 (September 2004): 21.
11. Jürgen Moltmann, *History and the Triune God* (London: SCM Press, 1991), 49.
12. John De Gruchy, *Reconciliation: Restoring Justice* (Minneapolis: Fortress Press, 2002), 197.
13. J.R. Miller, *Residential Schools and Reconciliation: Canada Confronts Its History* (Toronto: University of Toronto Press, 2017), 240.
14. For the importance for reconciliation of groups in conflict developing a shared story of their history together, see Gregory Baum, "A Theological Afterword," in *The Reconciliation of Peoples: Challenge to the Churches*, ed. Gregory Baum and Harold Wells (Maryknoll, NY: Orbis Books, 1997), 190–1.
15. J.R. Miller, *Lethal Legacy: Current Native Controversies in Canada* (Toronto: McClelland and Stewart, 2004), 260, 210. See also Miller, *Residential Schools and Reconciliation*, 266–8.
16. Willie Ermine, "The Ethical Space of Engagement," *Indigenous Law Journal* 6, no. 1 (2007): 198.
17. Rainer Forst, *Toleration in Conflict: Past and Present* (New York: Cambridge University Press, 2013), 403.
18. Frank Matera, *Galatians* (Collegeville, MN: Liturgical Press, 1992), 29–32.
19. George Tavard, *Justification: An Ecumenical Study* (New York: Paulist Press, 1983), 73.
20. Jürgen Moltmann, *In the End—The Beginning: The Life of Hope* (Minneapolis: Fortress Press, 2004), 75.

21 Edward Schillebeeckx, *Jesus: An Experiment in Christology* (New York: Seabury, 1979), 391.
22 Jürgen Moltmann, *The Crucified God* (London: SCM Press, 1974), 275-7.
23 Paul Tillich, *The Courage to Be* (New Haven, CT: Yale University Press, 1952), 166.
24 Jürgen Moltmann, "Das Geheimnis der Vergangenheit," in *Das Geheimnis der Verganenheit*, ed. Jürgen Moltmann (Göttingen: Neukirchener Theologie, 2012), 115.
25 Ibid., 112.
26 In the summary of its final report, the TRC concluded that "these children were sent to what were, in most cases, badly constructed, poorly maintained, overcrowded, unsanitary fire traps. Many children were fed a substandard diet and given a substandard education, and worked too hard. For far too long, they died in tragically high numbers. Discipline was harsh and unregulated; abuse was rife and unreported. It was, at best, institutionalized child neglect." See Truth and Reconciliation Commission of Canada, *Honouring the Truth, Reconciling for the Future: Summary of the Final Report of the Truth and Reconciliation Commission of Canada* (Winnipeg: Truth and Reconciliation Commission of Canada, 2015), 43.
27 James Perkinson, *White Theology: Outing Supremacy in Modernity* (New York: Palgrave Macmillan, 2004), 175.
28 Gregory Baum, *Man Becoming: God in Secular Experience* (New York: Herder and Herder, 1970), 155-6.
29 Ibid., 156.
30 Truth and Reconciliation Commission of Canada, *Honouring the Truth, Reconciling for the Future*, 122.
31 James (Sa'ke'j) Youngblood Henderson, *Indigenous Diplomacy and the Rights of Peoples: Achieving UN Recognition* (Saskatoon: Purich Publishing, 2008), 75.
32 Letty Russell, *Household of Freedom: Authority in Feminist Theology* (Philadelphia: Westminster Press, 1987), 71.
33 This is a paraphrase of Max Horkheimer, quoted in Moltmann, *The Crucified God*, 223-5.
34 Tillich, *The Courage to Be*, 165.
35 Moltmann, *In the End—The Beginning*, 75.
36 *Julian of Norwich: Showings*, ed. Edmund Colledge and James Walsh (New York: Paulist Press, 1978), 225.
37 Walter Brueggemann, *An Unsettling God: The Heart of the Hebrew Bible* (Minneapolis: Fortress Press, 2009), 170.
38 Jürgen Moltmann, *Theology of Hope* (London: SCM Press, 1967), 212.
39 Dietrich Bonhoeffer, *Letters and Papers from Prison, Dietrich Bonhoeffer Works Vol. 8* (Minneapolis: Fortress Press, 2010), 319.
40 Charles Taylor, *A Secular Age* (Cambridge, MA: Belknap Press of Harvard University Press, 2007), 697.
41 Ibid.
42 Ibid.
43 Truth and Reconciliation Commission of Canada, *Honouring the Truth, Reconciling for the Future*, 101-5. While the TRC summary report noted the abuse, humiliation, and violent punishment that many residential school students endured, it also noted that "many staff

members spent much of their time and energy attempting to humanize a harsh and often destructive system" (128–9).

44 Taylor, *A Secular Age*, 697.
45 Ibid., 701.
46 Ibid., 697.
47 James Perkinson, "Unsettling Whiteness: Refocusing Christian Theology on Its Own Indigenous Roots," in *Wrongs to Rights: How Churches Can Engage the United Nations Declaration on the Rights of Indigenous Peoples*, ed. Steve Heinrichs (Winnipeg: Mennonite Church of Canada, 2016), 98.
48 Hannah Askew, "UNDRIP Implementation, Intercultural Learning and Substantive Engagement with Indigenous Legal Orders," in *UNDRIP Implementation: More Reflections on the Braiding of International, Domestic and Indigenous Laws* (Waterloo, ON: Centre for International Governance Innovation, 2018), 85.
49 I thank an anonymous reader of this chapter for making this latter point.
50 Paulette Regan, *Unsettling the Settler Within: Indian Residential Schools, Truth Telling, and Reconciliation in Canada* (Vancouver: UBC Press, 2010).
51 UN General Assembly, Resolution 61/295, United Nations Declaration on the Rights of Indigenous Peoples, A/RES/61/295 (October 2, 2007), https://undocs.org/A/RES/61/295, 4.
52 Truth and Reconciliation Commission of Canada, *Canada's Residential Schools, Vol. 6: Reconciliation* (Montreal: McGill-Queen's University Press, 2015), 74.
53 Adelfo Regino Montes and Gustavo Torres Cisneros, "The United Nations Declaration on the Rights of Indigenous Peoples: The Foundation of a New Relationship between Indigenous Peoples, States and Societies," in *Making the Declaration Work: The United Nations Declaration on the Rights of Indigenous Peoples*, ed. Claire Charters and Rodolfo Stavenhagen (Copenhagen: International Workgroup for Indigenous Affairs, 2009), 154.
54 Truth and Reconciliation Commission of Canada, *Canada's Residential Schools, Vol. 5: The Legacy* (Kingston: McGill-Queen's University Press, 2015), 182.
55 Henderson, *Indigenous Diplomacy*, 71.
56 Mary Ellen Turpel-Lafond, "More Than Words," *Realizing the UN Declaration on the Rights of Indigenous Peoples*, ed. Jackie Hartley, Paul Joffe, and Jennifer Preston (Saskatoon: Purich Publishing, 2010), 170.
57 Hugh Shewall, "Why Jurisdiction Matters: Social Policy, Social Services and First Nations," *Canadian Journal of Native Studies* 36, no. 1 (2016): 185.
58 Ibid., 187–90.
59 James Anaya, "The Situation of Indigenous Peoples in Canada. Report of the Special Rapporteur on the Rights of Indigenous Peoples," Human Rights Council, United Nations General Assembly (July 4, 2014), https://www.ohchr.org/documents/issues/ipeoples/sr/a.hrc.27.52.add.2-missioncanada_auv.pdf, 13.
60 Ibid., 7.
61 Glen Coulthard, "Subjects of Empire: Indigenous Peoples and the 'Politics of Recognition' in Canada," *Contemporary Political Theory*, no. 6 (2007): 446.
62 Ibid.

63 De Gruchy, *Reconciliation*, 25.
64 Truth and Reconciliation Commission of Canada, *Canada's Residential Schools, Vol. 5*, 4.
65 Hans Küng, *Justification: The Doctrine of Karl Barth and a Catholic Reflection*, 40th ann. ed. (Louisville, KY: Westminster John Knox Press, 2004), 231.
66 Truth and Reconciliation Commissions of Canada, *Honouring the Truth, Reconciling for the Future*, 196.
67 Charles Taylor, "Sharing Identity Space," in *Québec—Canada: What Is the Path Ahead?*, ed. John Trent, Robert Young, and Guy Lachapelle (Ottawa: University of Ottawa Press, 1996), 121–2.
68 Ermine, "The Ethical Space of Engagement," 196.
69 Ibid., 198–9.
70 Jürgen Habermas, *The New Conservatism: Cultural Criticism and the Historians' Debate* (Cambridge, MA: MIT Press, 1989), 258.
71 Courtney Jung, "Canada and the Legacy of the Indian Residential Schools: Transitional Justice for Indigenous People in a Non-transitional Society," *Social Science Research Network*, March 18, 2009, 25.
72 Jürgen Moltmann, *The Spirit of Life: A Universal Affirmation* (Minneapolis: Fortress Press, 1992), 276.
73 The concept of free, creative self-withdrawal was developed by Michael Welker. An issue of *Touchstone* (35, no. 3, October 2017) offers discussions and case studies of this from the United Church's history.
74 Michael Welker, *God the Spirit* (Minneapolis: Fortress Press, 1994), 282.

CHAPTER 9

THE DECLARATION *and the* COMMON GOOD

by

JENNIFER JANZEN-BALL

A SIGN NEAR THE WEIR ON THE SOUTH SASKATCHEWAN RIVER where it flows through Saskatoon, on Treaty 6 territory and the Métis Homeland, reads as follows:

For centuries, life-giving margins along the river's edge have been attracting and sustaining wildlife and people. Today, these green zones or riparian areas, are one of the most diverse and productive ecosystems in our urban landscape. Not only are they pleasing to our senses, but they also regulate the movement of water, sediments, nutrients, and energy. We share this natural zone with a wide variety of wildlife who depend upon it for food, shelter, water, and space.

This sign, for me, is evocative as well of the diversity and life that can be found on the margins of church and society. Too often in a white-dominant, predominantly middle-class, liberal church like the United Church of Canada (UCC), the assumption is that being at the centre is the goal to which we all aspire. We sometimes fail—especially those of us who are white and middle-class—to recognize that the centre is where power can be concentrated and where differences are erased, to the detriment of all. Decolonizing ourselves, and moving to embrace the margins, is part of a journey of living into right relations and is key to recognizing and valuing the diversity and richness of life on the margins. The United Nations Declaration on the Rights of Indigenous Peoples seeks to establish globally the conditions for this diversity and richness of life to thrive. Too often, those who are marginalized do not enjoy the conditions necessary to thrive, and in fact have systematically and deliberately been denied abundant life. Too often, theology, ethics, and the church have been part of that systematic denial of abundant life. In this chapter, therefore, I seek to deconstruct and decolonize the concept of the "common good," which itself has often been used to minimize and erase difference, even as it has been upheld as a theo-ethical vision of abundant life for all.

I suggest, therefore, that it is necessary to problematize the concepts of the "common good" and universal norms, given the context of a globalized and pluralistic world. These concepts can fail to consider, or can even erase, the needs and rights of particular, contextual societies and individuals. In doing so, these ethical constructions fail to acknowledge and honour diversity and complexity in human communities (as well as ecological communities). I suggest that, in a Christian ethics framework that situates itself in a liberative world view, we need to hold together both universal and particular norms. I will examine how the Declaration could be an example of this dialectic tension by looking at so-called general human rights (primarily understood to be universal and applicable to *individual* human beings) and Indigenous Rights (also understood to be universal, in addition to also being *collective* and particular/contextual). This approach gives rise to particular questions about the UCC's adoption of the Declaration as the framework for reconciliation. Consider the following:

9. THE DECLARATION AND THE COMMON GOOD

- What does it mean to adopt the Declaration as a framework for reconciliation in a liberal/settler society that has insisted on not privileging one group over another?

- What does it mean to take seriously the harm done by one group (white settler/colonial Euro-Canadians) to other groups (the Indigenous Peoples of Turtle Island), and how does that lived reality (historic and ongoing) influence a liberative theo-ethical understanding of *the* common good?

- What does it mean to look at collective/communal human rights through a liberationist perspective, and how does that perspective both critique and augment a nuanced and intentionally limited conception of *the* common good as both a means and an "end" (goal) for pluralistic societies?

This raises two further questions:

- How does adopting a human rights framework for reconciliation work based in a Christian denomination help the church (and, potentially, wider society) create (the/a) common good?

- How does the Declaration as a framework for reconciliation offer appropriate challenges to the notion of a universal common good— namely, challenges of pluralism, decolonization, and contextual and particular needs and interests? How might the Declaration thus decentre, or even decolonize, the universalizing concept of the common good and move us toward concepts of common *goods*, which would seek to recognize the particularities of contexts, especially in relation to seeking justice and reconciliation?

While I argue that these challenges lead to a revised understanding of *a* common good (or common goods), I also suggest that there is an ongoing need to hold some universal norms. The tension between universal and particular, contextual norms is a creative tension that I think the Declaration, as a human rights instrument, illustrates. Therefore, a third question arises:

What will it mean for a liberal (universalizing) church such as the UCC to take seriously a collective human rights framework that decentres the individual (the liberal ideal of a "universal human") and focuses on particular and collective groups and cultures?

Articles Matter: Seeking *the* or *a* Common Good in a Pluralized World?

The concept of the common good has its roots in Catholic social teaching. Over the centuries, this concept has been revitalized through vigorous dialogue and debate. Much of the more recent theo-ethical discussions of the concept of the common good have particularly focused on economics and the ways in which economic structures can hinder or contribute to the common good. In more general discourse, however, the common good is a contested term. For example, it can imply the domination of the majority by a few or the imposition of one way of viewing the world upon all people,[1] or, as Augustine put it in *City of God*, it can be the notion of "the advantageousness, the common participation in which makes a people."[2]

The common good, particularly as a Catholic social teaching (developed in large part by Thomas Aquinas in the thirteenth century and modified and amplified over the last several centuries by Catholic moral theologians), is a teleological concept in Christian ethics. That is, the ideal of the common good is an end result that Christians are called to create. The common good should be a result of faithful and moral living by Christians, both individually and collectively in society.

Creating the conditions for the common good involves not only ideals but also material resources, as is reflected in the writings of Thomas Aquinas. For Thomas Aquinas, the common good involved holding together both "temporal" and "non-temporal" aspects. The temporal aspects of the common good included a combination of physical goods (food, clothing, shelter); "relational

9. THE DECLARATION AND THE COMMON GOOD

social goods" (peace, security); and "goods of the heart and soul" (love, pleasure, friendship). Non-temporal components of the common good include truth and virtues. As Susanne DeCrane explains, "the truth is a common good to which people have a right and which is vitally important for a person to grow in the goodness possible to her in this life.... Aquinas names virtues themselves as part of the common good. When one acts virtuously one gives good example and does good, and this contributes to the good of everyone."[3]

Other theologians note that the common good is both holistic and particular. Jacques Maritain, a Catholic theologian, wrote that the common good "is therefore common to both the whole and the parts into which it flows back and which, in turn, must benefit from it."[4] The Second Vatican Council also offered a definition of the common good: "the sum of those conditions of social life which allow social groups and their members relatively thorough and ready access to their own fulfillment."[5]

This same impulse toward love and justice realized on earth can be found in the Protestant equivalent of the social gospel. The common good is the way in which God's realm on earth is to be realized—materially, politically, socially, culturally, and economically. The common good is the manifestation of these goods for all people within a society, just as it can also be considered the process by which these goods come to be realized. It must also consider the good of being a community or society together. The "common good," therefore, is both a means and an end.

Ada María Isasi-Díaz also suggests that the common good is both the common vision of a just society and the means by which such a vision is achieved.[6] For Isasi-Díaz, justice is the norm of the common good. She names four elements necessary for the achievement of justice, and thus for the creation of the common good:

1. Equal power in decision-making;

2. Being committed, making room for ambiguity. Differences have to be embraced... and have to be understood as relational: as ambiguous, as shifting, without clear borders that keep us separate from each other;

3. Recognizing power dynamics;

4. Living in history, being free from history's constraints.... The future [is] not simply dependent on the possibilities inherent in the past.⁷

Isasi-Diaz identifies the need for equal power in decision-making and recognizes power dynamics. This recognition points to a requirement to acknowledge the particularities of social contexts and the ways in which social systems and institutions, including the common good, can act to marginalize and exclude some people and peoples who do not fit the ideal of the liberal concept of the universal human being. These are necessary steps in order to create an understanding of "common good" that does not erase or exclude difference, nor offers a totalizing world view that negates the lived realities of people who do not fit the image of a so-called universal human being (who in reality was, and is, a particular kind of human being: white, cis-male identified, heterosexual, educated, and economically well off).

I suggest that an ethics of common good cannot be the domination of a simplistic "majority rules" but rather needs to be a participatory democratic *process* seeking to hear all voices. Christian social ethics names the ways in which socially constructed systems can create inequalities and therefore acknowledges and takes seriously the need to seek ways in which to hear those who are silenced by a dominant society/ethos. In attending to particularities, *the* common good can shift to *a* common good or common goods that are negotiated based on the lived realities of those who have been most marginalized and excluded in dominant Western societies and institutions.

Human Rights and Common Good

One of the challenges to the common good has come from the conception of universal human rights, one of the great achievements of a modern, liberal paradigm. The realization of universal human rights (in theory, if not always in lived, concrete reality) is based on liberal ideals of respect and tolerance.

9. THE DECLARATION AND THE COMMON GOOD

Each human being is worthy of *respect* because of their humanness; *tolerance* for different perspectives, world views, and lifestyles flows from that respect. If society is to respect and tolerate each person, then it becomes almost impossible to uphold a concept like the common good, which carries connotations of uniformity of perspective, a singular conception of what is "good," and an erasure of differences for the "good of the whole." The assumption is that *the* common good refers to one, and only one, common good to which everyone must subsume themselves, even if it denies some or all of their individual human rights. Therefore, modern Western societies have become rightly suspicious of *the* common good as a totalizing concept—at the same time that modern Western societies, on Turtle Island and elsewhere, have also relied on this totalizing concept as part of the project of colonization. The lived consequences of *the* common good as a universal concept can be seen in the effects of colonization upon Indigenous Peoples around the world, and—relating more directly to the context of this book—in the realities of church-run and government-sponsored Indian residential schools whose purpose was to perpetrate the cultural genocide of Indigenous Peoples. Even when a body such as the United Nations addressed "the concerns of colonized peoples" after the Second World War, it did so without including the Indigenous Peoples "whose territories lay *within* the borders of the colonizers."[8]

Human rights discourse has tended to focus on the individual. As the Western European Enlightenment spread, so did the focus on the individual, to the detriment of community. Kidwell, Noley, and Tinker note that "this shift devalued human communities and notions of the common good; but, more important, it displaced spiritual beings as a part of that community. In the Indian intellectual tradition and in cultural practice, human beings are not privileged over the rest of the world, nor are individuals privileged over the good of the whole community."[9] The Declaration unsettles this Western, liberal focus on the individual by identifying collective rights for Indigenous Peoples and communities throughout the world.[10] This shift in focus and agency, to communities rather than individuals, calls those of us who are inheritors of a Western, liberal Christian tradition to look more closely at key theological and ethical concepts through this lens of community or collectivity. What difference might this understanding of collective human rights make to the concept of the/a common good?

David Hollenbach notes the need for persons (individuals) to have freedom (rights) to pursue their conceptions of "the good life." At the same time, he also suggests that each person is located within a community (or communities) that shapes, sustains, and supports us as persons in realizing our freedoms/rights. However, the pursuit of these freedoms and rights relies upon our access to economic and material resources.[11] Hollenbach thus seeks to hold together particularity and universality, individual freedoms and community formation. Ethna Regan also argues that human rights must be universal—in order to "protect and provide for the conditions in which concrete human beings can flourish in a multiplicity of contexts."[12]

The critique that arises out of the lived realities of particular peoples in particular social contexts applies to both *the* common good and the idea of individual human rights. The collective and particular nature of the human rights espoused in the Declaration becomes another avenue for critique and theo-ethical reflection in relation to the concept of "common good." I follow Traci West's liberative social ethics methodology to engage in such critique and ethical reflection.[13] In *Disruptive Christian Ethics*, West outlines an ethical methodology that holds together the particular and the universal while privileging the moral agency of those who are most marginalized within (US) society. She writes,

> Christian social ethics will remain inadequately formed without a primary concern for socially and economically marginalized people that shapes both core notions for conceiving ethics as well as overarching goals for practicing it.... Formulating a Christian ethical method that comprehensively addresses [concrete] injustices... also requires attention to concrete social practices.... A liberative method allows for the consideration of multiple layers of subjugating assumptions related to gender, race/ethnicity, socio-economic class, and sexuality.... It also prompts a critique of the web of public moral assumptions.[14]

West deliberately turns away from the classic liberal ideology that states that all people are equal regardless of background. She does so because she recognizes the ways in which societal structures have operated to limit the equality of some people and privilege the equality of others. The particularities of marginality are important to a liberative social ethics, not because they carry some special virtue in and of themselves, but because these particularities help us to identify the social practices and structures that lead to such marginalization, and thus help us to identify strategies of resistance.

Experiences of marginality are therefore significant sources for Christian ethical reflection (including critical reflection on Christian norms) and for the ongoing construction of norms that take seriously social location and experiences of marginalization and oppression. Universal moral norms are necessary to help judge social practices and structures within particular contexts; particular contexts are necessary to help interrogate the validity of universal moral norms.[15] In light of this methodological and praxiological commitment, the concept of the common good needs to be examined critically using the particular experiences of oppression of Indigenous Peoples throughout the world.

As I follow West's methodological commitment, the voices and experiences of Indigenous Peoples must be the primary source for evaluating the validity of any universal or universalizing ethical or theological concept. For West, the particularities of perspective and experience that shape the identities of women of colour give rise to a particular ethical claim. This is not a claim of virtue based on social location, but rather a privileged epistemological position where liberative ethics must stand in order to be able to include all—that is, to make concrete the claim of the universal. Liberative ethics, according to West, must be able to account for the experiences of "even" such a moral agent as a Black female sex worker who is addicted to drugs.[16] West thus sets forth an ethics that attends to the concrete voices and needs of female others. In this chapter, my revision of an ethics of the common good must be able to account for the experiences of the moral agency of Indigenous Peoples who have experienced the brunt of racist colonization and ongoing systemic racism. An ethic of common good will attend to the concrete voices and needs of these Indigenous Peoples.

Indigenous theological reflection on "the good life" as portrayed in Kidwell, Noley, and Tinker's *A Native American Theology* identifies the tension stemming from the need to hold together the universal and the particular as an integral aspect of ethics in Indigenous communities. The authors pose the question "What is good?" They respond by noting that in Indigenous communities, "good" comes through responsibility "to kin and the community. Spirituality is a way of gaining access to power that can then be used for the good of one's relatives and the rest of the community.... While Indian communities respect the integrity of the individual, they expect the individual to exercise the responsibility to act according to the expectations of family and community. Ella Deloria noted that for the Lakota the worst thing that could be said of an individual was that he or she acted 'as if they had no relatives.' "[17]

And finally, Kidwell, Noley, and Tinker remind us that community and ethical behaviour extends beyond solely human relationships: "The maintenance of appropriate social relationships is essential to good behavior. These relationships are not only human ones but those with the other-than-human persons who live in the natural world, and whose presence constitutes the spiritual world. God is called upon as grandfather, thus developing a sense of the importance of intergenerational relationships."[18] What is good, then, must be good for all beings, not just human beings.

The project of colonization in Canada (and around the world) may not have specifically referenced "common good." Its aim, however, was to make Indigenous people into the so-called universal human being: more like white Europeans culturally, religiously, socially, politically (and at the same time, to deny Indigenous people their rights, voices, power, full participation, and equity because they were never white enough).[19] Given the history of colonization, the forcible imposition of Euro-Christian cultural values and norms upon Indigenous Peoples, and the resulting cultural genocide, it behooves Christian theologians, ethicists, and churches to examine critically any "universal" ethic or doctrine. The stated goal of residential schools, for instance, was to erase Indigenous cultures and differences so that Indigenous people could participate fully in society (read "white, middle-class society").

Education was seen as key to this process of assimilation (i.e., genocide); residential schools were set up for the "good" of Indigenous people. While not specifically a reference to "common good," these racist systems of domination certainly relied upon Western Christian theologies and ethics, including the beloved social gospel movement. In particular, the social gospel movement emphasized education (meaning white, Western, Christian education) as a primary method for addressing social ills and issues—and it included Indigenous Peoples in that category.

Taking the history of colonization and the diversity of Indigenous Peoples seriously means that the idea of *the* common good can no longer be credible. This is borne out in a critique of the use of the term "the commons" by Rita Wong and Dorothy Christian. They acknowledge that the use of that term (by which they refer specifically to the enclosure of the commons during the Industrial Revolution in England and to the notion of the "common good") is important in resisting capitalism and, in particular, commodification. However, they also note that the idea of "the commons" "cannot be used to yet again ignore the very real cultural differences and power imbalances that restrict some people's access to it, as well as the historical violence that threatens to erase Indigenous naming and protocols with the land."[20] They note that "the commons" is a "contingent settler term" that could be helpful in relation to Indigenous leadership and Protocols as long as it is not "used to elide histories or evade responsibilities.... A use of the commons as a term needs to articulate how the specificity of local knowledges matter, starting first and foremost with the names, stories, and places that Indigenous communities have long cultivated through oral and now written traditions."[21]

However, the ideal of *a* common good—understood as always negotiated,[22] partial, situated, attentive to particularities—can still be valid today, I believe. In this conception, "common good" becomes a universal ideal that is determined by, and lived out in, particular contexts by particular peoples (communities, groups, societies). At the same time, particular peoples must have access to the material and socio-politico-cultural goods that they need in order to participate fully in decision-making and the creation of social institutions (all of which are crucial to common good). As Tonya Gonnella Frichner writes (prior to the adoption of the Declaration but still relevant today),

> while using the language of reconciliation, Canada, the United States and other nations continue to challenge basic human rights of Indigenous peoples, in particular, our right to self-determination. This right, *a fundamental right of all peoples*, is a prerequisite to being able to exercise all our other human rights. To deny us this right is discriminatory, perpetuates poverty, and is not an action of partnership or good faith.[23]

Material/temporal and non-temporal resources must be held together in order to achieve common good for all peoples, not just for some. Human rights and the ability to achieve human rights in full requires access to material goods.

The work of Seyla Benhabib, a feminist critical social theorist, in outlining a process of dialogue among many different moral agents by which universal norms can be arrived,[24] is particularly applicable to the project of re-visioning an ethics of the common good. A revised ethics of the common good must incorporate the global realities of pluralism and diversity (complicating the liberal Enlightenment notion of the common good) while at the same time encompassing universal norms that uphold justice, dignity, compassion, and sustainability for humankind and the entire Creation. A revised ethics of the common good will need to assume many different public spaces and thus a plurality of common *goods* suited to multiple lives, contexts, and publics.

Collective Human Rights in Common Good(s)

The Declaration seeks to recognize the truth that Indigenous communities are the primary or foundational agents or actors with regard to human rights, by acknowledging the particular experiences of Indigenous communities and addressing the lived and ongoing injustices experienced by those communities. Therefore, the Declaration is an example of how both particularity and universality can be held together. It is a universal human rights statement that

9. THE DECLARATION AND THE COMMON GOOD

applies to a multitude of Indigenous Peoples globally;[25] at the same time, it is up to each Indigenous People to determine how their fundamental collective, universal human rights are to be lived out in ways that are authentic to their particular cultural-spiritual practices and world views. For instance, article 7 holds together individual and collective human rights:

1. Indigenous individuals have the rights to life, physical and mental integrity, liberty and security of person.

2. Indigenous peoples have the collective right to live in freedom, peace and security as distinct peoples and shall not be subjected to any act of genocide or any other act of violence, including forcibly removing children of the group to another group.[26]

In this way, we can see how common *goods* could be a reconstructed ethical framework that holds together both a universal claim (seeking the good life together) and a particularist approach (each community or group determines the nature and shape of that good life together, in such a way as to allow for differing visions even within the community or group). For instance, the authors of *A Native American Theology* note how "rights, obligations, and responsibilities" of individuals and groups are balanced: "Kin relationships structure" these interactions. They add, "In Indian communities, people are valued not for what they achieve for themselves but for what they contribute to the stability and continuity of the group. At the same time, tribal societies recognize the uniqueness and personal identity of individuals. These sources of individual identity and power are found in the relationship between the individual and the spiritual world."[27] Ultimately, one could even understand the Declaration as a framework for creating common good, through its important safeguards and annotations on the specific rights of Indigenous Peoples. The Declaration, after all, identifies the conditions that Indigenous Peoples need in order to thrive, not just survive. These conditions include a land base, political authority, economic agency, the ability to engage in spiritual and cultural practices, and self-determination. All of these aspects of life together are foundational to an ethic of common good. This is echoed by Alannah Young Leon and Denise Marie Nadeau when they write that "Indigenous nations on Turtle Island lived by protocols, diplomacy, and laws that were specific to each nation and linked to the land and waters on which they lived. These traditions guided governance, family life, and relationship with the land, water, and its creatures, as well as trade and relationships with other nations. Our obligations are grounded in relationships that are affirmed in these legal traditions."[28] Ultimately, any conception of a common good/common goods must be attentive to relationality and to the ways in which relationships, both among individuals and among different communities, are structured. A revised concept of common good must take as foundational the following norms: all relationships are based on "respect" and "reciprocity," "the balancing of the world and living in reciprocity."[29]

As part of the journey toward reconciliation, the UCC has adopted the Declaration as the framework for reconciliation, as laid out in the Calls to Action from the Truth and Reconciliation Commission of Canada (TRC). The UCC has indicated its understanding that foundational principles, norms, and standards of the Declaration are as follows:

- The right to self-determination
- The right to cultural and spiritual identity
- The right to participate in decision-making
- The right to lands and resources
- The right to free, prior, and informed consent
- The right to be free from discrimination

These norms are universal in nature, in that they apply to all Indigenous Peoples in all contexts. They are particular in how they are lived out, sustained, and challenged in the relationships among Indigenous Peoples, nation-states, and the systems and institutions that are part of such nation-states and Indigenous communities. These norms help create the conditions and parameters for the possibility of co-creating common good together, as

Indigenous and non-Indigenous people. However, the primary focus for these norms is for Indigenous people to determine the ways in which these norms can function to hold space for their own common goods to be determined. The Caretakers of Our Indigenous Circle, in a recent document entitled "Calls to the Church," reference exactly this focus: "the Indigenous faith community must exercise a truly Indigenous self-determination and possess a sustainable land-based support."[30]

As the UCC continues the journey of living into right relationships and reconciliation, the particularities of living out the Declaration as a framework for reconciliation must be front and centre. The Caretakers note that it is the Indigenous church that will teach the "broader United Church" "who we are, what our values are, and place into practice how we want to work among ourselves and with others."[31] No reconciliation is possible without attention to the real, material consequences for actual Indigenous human bodies and the body of the earth. (As Indigenous Peoples continue to remind those of us in the white-dominant, liberal church and society, land shapes and forms identities and is foundational aspect of Indigenous life.) Seeking to redress these consequences leads into thinking about reparations, in terms of real, material resources and time shared with/given to Indigenous Peoples.[32] In part, the work of reconciliation through material reparation is already happening in various ways. For instance, the UCC established the Healing Fund in partial response to the church's involvement in colonization and residential schools. As a signatory to the Indian Residential Schools Settlement Agreement, the UCC has also made particular financial commitments as well as commitments of personnel and time (for instance, by providing residential school Survivors with access to the UCC archives throughout the TRC process, and having archivists compile information on the UCC's involvement in the schools). In addition, the national church allocates donations from the UCC's Mission and Service Fund to Indigenous governing bodies and theological-spiritual centres in the church (for instance, the National Indigenous Council and Elders' Council and the Sandy-Saulteaux Spiritual Centre).[33] As the Caretakers remind the broader church, "reconciliation is not just heads and hearts that feel bad but hands and feet that do tangible good."³⁴ As we continue to work at reparations and reconciliation, we must maintain a sense of the ongoing need for tangible, material evidence that these relationships are in fact being rebuilt. Another way that this can happen—indeed, it already is—is for churches and wider church bodies to engage in reparations by sharing with the Indigenous church the proceeds from the sale of church buildings and from bequests.³⁵

The Declaration as a framework for reconciliation applies to the UCC's relations with Indigenous Peoples in Canada, but it also must apply to the UCC's relationships with Indigenous Peoples around the world, given the document's scope and the ongoing colonization that Indigenous Peoples in various parts of globe continue to experience. For example, Indigenous Peoples in Guatemala (through one of our global partners) have asked us to address the divestment of the UCC pension plan from a resource-extraction company, Goldcorp, that did not honour the "free, prior, and informed consent" enshrined in the Declaration. Given the UCC Pension Board's refusal to divest from Goldcorp— even though proposals to that end have been passed by the church's national decision-making body—one might question how the UCC is living into the Declaration as a framework for reconciliation.³⁶ The UCC's stated intention, outlined in its March 31, 2016, statement adopting the Declaration as a framework for reconciliation, to "assess the church's current alignment with the Declaration in all areas of its institutional life" and to "provide mechanisms for addressing non-alignment"³⁷ is thus a reminder that we still have work to do.

The UCC continues to engage in the challenge of living into its promise to draw upon the Declaration as a framework for reconciliation. While a framework provides the outlines or shape of the work to be done, it remains empty unless it is filled with concrete goods and actions. Therefore, I suggest that the TRC's Calls to Action and the Caretakers of Our Indigenous Circle's "Calls to the Church" are both helpful, concrete supplements to the Declaration. The Calls to Action provide practical suggestions for achieving reconciliation and reparation. Particular calls pertaining to the churches and theological schools provide clear guideposts for the journey to reconciliation and right relationship. For instance, theological colleges are asked to commit real material resources (the dedication of faculty time and resources) to teaching about residential schools, colonization, and the histories, cultures, and spiritualities of Indigenous Peoples in Canada. The Caretakers' "Calls to the Church" also address these priorities, with concrete and specific references to theological education and formation for ministry, church governance, material reparations, Indigenous leadership and development, and the range and diversity of human sexuality (particularly as was known in Indigenous communities prior to colonization).[38]

Conclusion

In this chapter, I have sought to explore critically an ethics of the common good through the lens of the collective rights outlined in the Declaration. In so doing, I take seriously the marginalization and oppression that Indigenous Peoples have experienced for centuries, particularly as this has been manifest in the project of colonization undertaken by the nation-state of Canada here on Turtle Island. The realities of marginalization and oppression exist in part because Indigenous people were not deemed to be human and therefore did not have access to the same privileges, power, and rights that white settlers did. Indigenous people were not considered to represent the "universal human" of the Enlightenment. This reality has led me to critique an ethics of the common good that assumes a universal common good that is equally applicable to all people, without attention to the ways in which systems of oppression have served to devalue, limit, exclude, and even kill Indigenous people and nations. I have argued that attending seriously to the particularities of Indigenous people's experiences means critiquing universal concepts such as the common good. I also note that Indigenous people's particular experiences and realities are foundational to any revised ethics of a common good or goods. The particular and the universal can be held together as long as the particular informs, challenges, and corrects the universal. The Declaration thus becomes an example of the way in which universal human rights for Indigenous people can be lived out in particular contexts by particular Indigenous Peoples, creating a framework for the establishment of a common good in and among different Indigenous communities, with particular attention to the right to self-determination. Embracing a revised, nuanced, and partial ethics of a common good or goods can serve to help the UCC navigate its journey of reconciliation with Indigenous Peoples in Canada. The journey toward reconciliation is an uneven, uncertain, sometimes fragmented and challenging one, and it will extend beyond the present generation. But it is a journey that encourages the UCC to commit to seeking abundant life for those it has marginalized and to decentre and decolonize the church, so that common goods may be realized.

Notes

1   See, for example, David Hollenbach, *The Common Good and Christian Ethics* (Cambridge: Cambridge University Press, 2002), 9–12.
2   Cited in John Langan, "Common Good," in *The Westminster Dictionary of Christian Ethics*, ed. James F. Childress and John Macquarrie (Philadelphia: Westminster Press, 1986), 102.
3   Susanne M. DeCrane, *Aquinas, Feminism, and the Common Good* (Washington, DC: Georgetown University Press, 2004), 64.
4   Jacques Maritain, *The Person and the Common Good* (Notre Dame, IN: University of Notre Dame Press, 1966), 49–51. For Maritain, the common good is just that because "it is received in persons, each of whom is as a mirror of the whole....The end of society, therefore, is neither the individual good nor the collection of the individual goods of each of the persons who constitute it. Such a conception would dissolve society as such to the advantage of its parts, and would amount to either a frankly anarchistic conception, or the old disguised anarchistic conception of individualistic materialism in which the whole function of the city is to safeguard the liberty of each; thus, giving to the strong full freedom to oppress the weak."
5   United States Catholic Bishops, *Economic Justice for All: Catholic Social Teaching and the U.S. Economy* (Washington, DC: National Conference of Catholic Bishops, 1986), par. 79, quoted in Eric Mount, *Covenant, Community, and the Common Good: An Interpretation of Christian Ethics* (Cleveland: Pilgrim Press, 1999), 42.
6   Ada María Isasi-Díaz, "To Be Fully Alive Is to Work for the Common Good," *Church and Society* 89, no. 1 (September–October 1998): 13.
7   Ibid., 17.
8   Tonya Gonnella Frichner, "A Perspective from North America," in *Reconciliation in a World of Conflicts*, ed. Luiz Carlos Susin and Maria Pilar Aquino (London: SCM Press, 2003), 40.
9   Clara Sue Kidwell, Homer Noley, and George E. "Tink" Tinker, *A Native American Theology* (Maryknoll, NY: Orbis Books, 2001), 40.
10 Article 1 of the Declaration states: "Indigenous peoples have the right to the full enjoyment, as a collective or as individuals, of all human rights and fundamental

freedoms as recognized in the Charter of the United Nations, the Universal Declaration of Human Rights and international human rights law." See UN General Assembly, Resolution 61/295, United Nations Declaration on the Rights of Indigenous Peoples, A/RES/61/295 (October 2, 2007), https://undocs.org/A/RES/61/295, 3. The Declaration also attends to spiritual realities in its many references to cultural practices.

11 David Hollenbach, *The Global Face of Public Faith: Politics, Human Rights, and Christian Ethics* (Washington, DC: Georgetown University Press, 2003), 15.

12 Ethna Regan, *Theology and the Boundary Discourse of Human Rights* (Washington, DC: Georgetown University Press, 2010), 12.

13 West states that "method matters because it represents the pathway that we follow when reflecting on societal concerns and making decisions about 'what's wrong here?' It allows us to assess how that wrong can be addressed constructively. A basic yet crucial factor to remember is that whatever approach is chosen to interpret social problems, it determines the entire focus and definition attached to those problems." Traci West, *Disruptive Christian Ethics: When Racism and Women's Lives Matter* (Louisville, KY: Westminster John Knox Press, 2006), xiv.

14 Ibid., xvi.

15 Ibid., 61–2. While not sharing precisely the same methodological and ethical commitments, other authors also suggest the need to hold particularity and universality together as "situated" or "dialogic" universalism, including (but not limited to) Hollenbach, *The Common Good*; Richard Amesbury and George M. Newlands, *Faith and Human Rights: Christian and Global Struggle for Human Dignity* (Minneapolis: Fortress Press, 2008); and Regan, *Theology and Boundary Discourse of Human Rights*.

16 West, *Disruptive Christian Ethics*, 68–70.

17 Kidwell, Noley, and Tinker, *A Native American Theology*, 106.

18 Ibid. The authors also note that "the goal of life is maintaining a proper relationship with the spiritual world in order to achieve the ultimate goals of human life. If Christianity explores the notion of God, the study of ethics asks the question, What is good? The answer in Indian communities lies in two dimensions. For the individual, good is long life, good health, and happiness. It is achieved by remaining in proper relationship to all people, all beings in the physical world, and the spirits.... The ideal of harmony entails fulfilling one's responsibilities to the community and to the spirit world" (109).

19 The preamble to the Declaration notes these realities, albeit in general terms: "Concerned that Indigenous peoples have suffered from historic injustices as a result of, inter alia, their colonization and dispossession of their lands, territories and resources, thus preventing them from exercising, in particular, their right to development in accordance with their own needs and interests, [and] recognizing the urgent need to respect and promote the inherent rights of Indigenous peoples which derive from their political, economic and social structures and from their cultures, spiritual traditions, histories and philosophies, especially their rights to their lands, territories and resources…" UN General Assembly, Resolution 61/295, 2.

20 Rita Wong and Dorothy Christian, "Re-storying Waters, Re-storying Relations," in *Downstream: Reimagining Water*, ed. Dorothy Christian and Rita Wong (Waterloo, ON: Wilfrid Laurier University Press, 2017), 17.
21 Ibid.
22 See, for instance, Seyla Benhabib, *Situating the Self: Gender, Community and Postmodernism in Contemporary Ethics* (New York: Routledge, 1992), and Nancy Fraser, *Justice Interruptus: Critical Reflections on the "Postsocialist"* (New York: Routledge, 1997). Discourse ethics, or communicative ethics, stands within the modern philosophical tradition and relies on the concepts of autonomy and social contracts. As Benhabib writes, "Only those norms and normative institutional arrangements are valid, it is claimed, which individuals can or would freely consent to as a result of engaging in certain argumentative practices" (24). According to Benhabib, Karl-Otto Apel and Jürgen Habermas are the two foremost thinkers in the area of communicative or discourse ethics:

> Apel maintains that such argumentative practices can be described as "an ideal community of communication"...while Habermas calls them "practical discourses." Both agree that such practices are the only plausible procedure in the light of which we can think of the Kantian principle of "universalizability" in ethics today. Instead of asking what an individual moral agent could or would will, without self-contradiction, to be a universal maxim for all, one asks: what norms or institutions would the members of an ideal or real communication community agree to as representing their common interests after engaging in a special kind of argumentation or conversation? The procedural model of an argumentative praxis replaces the silent thought-experiment enjoined by the Kantian universalizability test. (24)

Kwok Pui-lan also notes that a multiplicity of voices can provide enriching dialogue and action together "if we understand that identity is always constructed in relation to others." Kwok, *Postcolonial Imagination and Feminist Theology* (Louisville, KY: Westminster John Knox Press, 2005), 60.
23 Gonnella Frichner, "A Perspective from North America," 41.
24 In *Situating the Self*, Benhabib writes that the core of communicative ethics is "the processual generation of reasonable agreement about moral principles via an open-ended moral conversation" (37).
25 I note the deliberate use of the word "peoples" in the Declaration as a recognition of particularities of diversity—of lived experiences, of socio-political constructions of Indigenous Peoples, and of the diversities of the socio-cultural-religious world views of Indigenous Peoples throughout the world.
26 UN General Assembly, Resolution 61/295, 4.
27 Kidwell, Noley, and Tinker, *A Native American Theology*, 15.
28 Alannah Young Leon and Denise Marie Nadeau, "Moving with Water" in *Downstream: Reimagining Water*, ed. Dorothy Christian and Rita Wong (Waterloo, ON: Wilfrid Laurier University Press, 2017), 134.
29 Kidwell, Noley, and Tinker, *A Native American Theology*, 34.

9. THE DECLARATION AND THE COMMON GOOD

30 Caretakers of Our Indigenous Circle, "Calls to the Church," United Church of Canada General Council 43, July 2018, Oshawa, Ontario, https://united-church.ca/sites/default/files/06_caretakers_of_our_indigenous_circle_report_-_revised.pdf, 1.

31 Ibid., 3.

32 For more on the connection between reconciliation and reparation, see Jennifer Harvey, *Dear White Christians: For Those Still Longing for Racial Reconciliation* (Grand Rapids, MI: William B. Eerdmans, 2014), especially chapters 4–6, in which Harvey describes a "reparations paradigm." In Harvey's work, "reparations" is a multi-faceted and ongoing process, not simply a lump-sum payment for evils done in the past (or present).

33 See, for instance, the short summaries at "Indigenous Communities and Leadership," United Church of Canada, accessed June 29, 2018, https://www.united-church.ca/community-faith/being-community/Indigenous-communities-and-leadership.

34 Caretakers of Our Indigenous Circle, "Calls to the Church," 3.

35 For instance, the former Saskatchewan Conference shared the revenue from a bequest on a fifty-fifty basis with the former All Native Circle Conference, as one tangible and material way to begin repairing broken relationships. The Caretakers' also note this needs to become an ongoing and regular practice at all levels of the UCC. See "Calls to the Church," 3, 10.

36 Debate within the UCC on this issue has centred on the Pension Board's fiduciary responsibility and the importance of having shares in companies so that the UCC can engage in shareholder action. At the same time, the UCC chooses not to purchase shares in companies that deal in weapons or tobacco (for instance)—which, arguably, it could also do in order to engage in shareholder action. All of these examples have in common the reality of violence enacted against certain groups of people. While I argue in this chapter that universal norms also need to be critiqued and examined in particular contexts, I am not convinced that the reasoning behind this decision not to divest offers a sufficient critique to deny the application of universal norms of love, justice, and mutuality in mission and partnership, along with the living out of reconciliation in concrete and particular ways.

37 The UCC's "Statement on UN Declaration on the Rights of Indigenous Peoples as the Framework for Reconciliation" is reproduced in appendix B of this volume.

38 Caretakers of Our Indigenous Circle, "Calls to the Church," 4–11.

CHAPTER 10

WORKING FROM THE HEART
Considering Reconciliation/Mīnwastamātowin through the Lenses of Miýo-Wāhkōtowin, Miýo-Pimātisiwin, and Gender

by

ISKWEWUK E-WICHIWITOCHIK/
WOMEN WALKING TOGETHER

This chapter is dedicated to our IE Sister and reconciliation activist Mary Ann Assailly.

A culturally relevant gender-based analysis can and must guide the process of reconciliation in Canada.
—Native Women's Association of Canada,
Culturally Relevant Gender Based Models of Reconciliation

> *The issue of missing and murdered Indigenous women is an ongoing, painful issue for the Indigenous community that needs resolution in order for us to be able to move forward with a better relationship in this country. Those families that have lost women to violence... need to have some answers because they will be unwilling to engage in dialogues around reconciliation until that issue is addressed.*
> —Murray Sinclair, former Truth and Reconciliation Commission chair cited in *Our Women and Girls Are Sacred*

ALL MY RELATIONS, AHĀW. We use this bilingual version of a traditional Indigenous oral formula for opening an address to establish Cree philosophy and nēhiyawēwin/Cree language as foundational parts of the vision of reconciliation that we wish to share. Cree has no single word for reconciliation, but alternative translations include mīnwastamātowin ("setting things to rights for one another")[1] and miýo-wāhkōhtowin ("good relationship").[2] We intend for this opening formula to be further read as a linguistic gesture of reconciliation between Cree and English in response to the invitation to contribute to discussion of the United Church of Canada's (UCC) adoption of the United Nations Declaration on the Rights of Indigenous Peoples as a framework for the church's reconciliation efforts. The bilingual formula verbally encapsulates the principle of miýo-wāhkōhtowin/good relationship, which entails an understanding of all beings, including the land we live on and its non-human inhabitants, as relations. If all in Canada/the northern part of Turtle Island—an English-language name widely used by First Nations Peoples in lieu of the settler term "North America"—are to live together in miýo-pimātisiwin/a good way of living on the territory we share, the process and outcome of reconciliation will need to be informed by the cultural values of both Indigenous and non-Indigenous populations. Non-Indigenous Canadians will also need to let go of what Marie Battiste (Mi'kmaw) and Sa'ke'j Henderson (Chickasaw) refer to as "the Eurocentric illusion of benign translatability."[3] This concept entails recognizing that Indigenous values cannot, without the loss of important cultural context and nuance, be carried over into English or French, the languages in which the most widely published discourses of reconciliation in Canada have to date been exclusively framed.

Despite the Declaration's explicit mention of Indigenous Peoples' language rights in articles 13, 14, and 16, it lacks words in any Indigenous language or translated Indigenous idioms, and is framed instead in the European-derived language of international law.[4] Because that language would be alien to many Indigenous people, we contend that the Declaration, for all its potential to improve the lives of Indigenous people, is not fully *culturally* relevant to them.[5] Yet *Culturally Relevant Gender Based Models of Reconciliation* (henceforth referred to as CRGB *Models of Reconciliation*), a report published by the Native Women's Association of Canada (NWAC) and prepared to help guide the Truth and Reconciliation Commission's (TRC) vision and processes, argues the need for a model of reconciliation that attends to both culture and gender. The latter is necessary because colonization differentially impacted—and continues to impact—males, females, and Two-Spirits.[6]

Members of Iskwewuk E-wichiwitochik/Women Walking Together (henceforth referred to as "IE"; the Cree name is pronounced isk-WAY-wuk ee-wich-i-WI-to-chik), a Saskatoon-based activist group that works on the issue of missing and murdered Indigenous women, girls, and Two-Spirits (MMIWG2S), endorses NWAC's call for culturally relevant, gender-based reconciliation. To create a future in which everyone thrives and in which non-Indigenous and Indigenous people can live in harmony, we require an honourable reconciliation that would fully respect the differences between non-Indigenous and Indigenous societies in terms of culture, economy, social and political organization, and governance—all aspects of Indigenous lifeways addressed in the Declaration. Additionally, we contend that honourable reconciliation requires ongoing and active work toward healing and decolonization *on both sides*. Reverend Stan McKay warns against "perpetuat[ing] the paternalistic concept that only Aboriginal peoples need healing" because "the perpetrators are wounded and marked by history in ways that are different from the victims, but both groups require healing."[7]

We contend that healing comes from decolonization and that without dual efforts toward healing and decolonization, official reconciliation will become just another neo-colonial strategy that benefits Indigenous people far less than those of settler-Canadian ancestry. Thus, some Indigenous people and their allies will persist in thinking that reconciliation and decolonization are by strict definitions incompatible.[8]

Walking a reconciliatory path that focuses only on addressing the impact of residential schools rather than taking in the larger "set of relationships that generated policies, legislation, and practices aimed at assimilation, and political genocide" risks a problematic outcome. Many Canadians could unjustly think that "the legitimacy of Indigenous resistance" has been "neutralize[d]" by the official TRC process and the perceived "righting" of the historical "wrong" of residential schools so that "further transformation is not needed."[9] Such a credible risk acutely concerns anti-violence activists in the Indigenous context precisely because the violence is ongoing. Honourable reconciliation cannot duck settler colonialism's having been a matter of settlers coming to make a new home on Indigenous Land, and then "insist[ing] on settler sovereignty over all things in their new domain."[10] Moreover, such reconciliation needs vigorously to pursue prosperous Indigenous futures, which can only proceed from systemic transformations of colonial power relations, including gendered ones. United Church feminist ethicist Marilyn Legge contends that dominant theologies have themselves been obstacles to what she calls "right relations," a term that we understand as giving ethical emphasis to miýo-wāhkōhtowin: "If religious institutions are to advocate for social, political, and economic resolutions adequate to restore right relations with those most wounded and burdened," Legge argues, "they must learn to acknowledge that dominant theologies are not only racist but also implicated in state, nation, gender, class and sexual systems."[11]

Common traditional Indigenous ideas of gender balance (rather than hierarchy) and respect for women's power and wisdom as complementary to those of men were devastatingly undermined in Canada by the imposition of the *Indian Act* and Indian residential schools.[12] As NWAC's CRGB *Models of Reconciliation* states:

The Indian Act and residential school education were designed to destroy women's traditional roles within clan, kinship and governance systems, preparing them instead to become the "property" of individual men as good "Christian" wives and mothers, dependent upon and submissive to male authority, and isolated within nuclear families. The sacredness of women's bodies, honoured through ceremonies celebrating menstruation and the capacity to create life[,] were replaced with the belief that the bodies of women and girls are inherently savage, dirty, impure and sinful [and] therefore violable.[13]

Non-Indigenous Canadians concerned with effecting reconciliation need to be aware of the many ways in which colonizing effects have extended well beyond what most think of as the colonial period. For example, the Sixties Scoop and the contemporaneous apprehension of Indigenous children into state care continue the work of earlier legislation and assimilative institutions, which have severely impacted Indigenous males as well as females. As settler scholar and Indigenous ally Allison Hargreaves remarks, "In communities wracked by generations of dislocation and loss, such social issues as poverty, addiction, and lateral violence have become increasingly normalized. In this environment, women are the targets of gendered violence in family settings and in their communities more broadly."[14] She adds, Indigenous women also face an equally normalized violence from settler men along with "economic disadvantage [and] discriminatory treatment in the justice system."[15] Thus "in this complex history of colonial disenfranchisement, gender has become a determinant of one's health and safety, of one's access to land and other community resources, and of one's official claim to Indigenous identity."[16] Moreover, the homophobic character of European-derived and Canadian-perpetuated attitudes, legislation, policies, and practices has similarly lethally subverted the place in Indigenous and larger Canadian society of those Indigenous people whose sex and/or gender orientation is outside the hetero-normative frame.

In the face of these realities, IE urges that after consultation with Indigenous women, girls, and Two-Spirits, through NWAC and/or Reconciliation Canada,[17] and with the modifications set out near the end of this chapter, CRGB *Models of Reconciliation* be adopted as a complement to the Declaration to guide the UCC's reconciliation efforts. We do so in accord with the understanding of Alex Neve, former director general of Amnesty International Canada, that when a group has been shown to have a heightened vulnerability to human rights violations—as we argue Indigenous women, girls, and Two-Spirits have—they require "extra attention, different... or more detailed attention."[18] The formulation of such United Nations documents as the Convention on the Elimination of All Forms of Discrimination against Women (1979), the Convention on the Rights of the Child (1989), and the Convention on the Rights of Persons with Disabilities (2008) as supplements to the Universal Declaration of Human Rights (1948) attests to the UN's acting on this understanding.

While we understand and value human-rights-focused work, such as getting in place the Declaration, which is primarily concerned with remedying what James (Sa'ke'j) Youngblood Henderson refers to as "oppression of [the] legal personality"[19] of First Nations people, IE believes that for the reconciliation process to succeed, a speaking from and to the heart and a complementary engaged listening and reading are necessary. As Legge argues of "right relations": "Face to face relations are key... especially because religious interaction is meaningful precisely when it draws upon our capacity to engage communicatively with each other."[20] Indeed, as the model of reconciliation enacted by the Ottawa Children's Aid Society—which is based on the four stages outlined by Cindy Blackstock (Gitxsan)—teaches us, "Reconciliation... [is] a relational process; therefore [in that process], time was structured-in for communal eating, talking and laughter which are the central activities around which healthy relationships are built. Providing refreshments and sharing food creates a human bond and sustains energy levels during times of emotionality."[21] IE has made central to its work listening to the accounts of grieving family members of MMIWG2S and providing occasions for them to tell their stories to the wider public in contexts where food sharing and informal conversation are also typical. To accord with the practice of bearing witness and to give readers a heart-sense of one family's experiences, we offer below the story of one woman and her daughter, who was missing for five and a half years before she was found murdered.

One Grieving but Resilient Mother's Story of Un-reconciled Canada[22]

The last time Carol Wolfe of the Muskeg Lake Cree Nation in Saskatchewan saw her daughter, Karina Beth-Ann Wolfe, was July 2, 2010, just after twenty-year-old Karina had completed a drug rehabilitation program and moved back home to live with her mother and younger brother, Desmond. Carol related in an interview with us that Karina had told her before going out that July day that she would be home again that night. She never returned. "In the following days," Carol told us, "I got feeling worse and worse, so I sent out messages to her pink phone." Karina "was crazy about pink," Carol told us. Not, however, until Karina missed Carol's July 19 birthday—something she'd never done before—did Carol's fears turn to strong conviction that something was seriously wrong. What followed was nearly five and a half agonizingly long years of what psychologists refer to as ambiguous loss. This is a condition of unresolved grief, caused in this case by Karina's physical absence but her strong emotional presence in the lives of her family, especially those of Carol and Desmond, the latter of whom was close to his only sister. Karina's remains were finally discovered on November 14, 2015, dumped into a swampy area just northwest of Saskatoon by a man later convicted of her murder and of offering an indignity to human remains. A temporary memorial at the wintry site included pink flowers and a pink stuffed animal.

Carol had known intense suffering even before Karina was taken and murdered. As an adult Carol had two brothers die prematurely, but she was only five when her mother died. Her father chose to put Carol into foster care: "My father had five kids when my mom died. He took care of the other four. He did not want me, because I was deaf," she says. Her world after her mother's death consisted of foster homes and the residential Saskatchewan School for the Deaf in Saskatoon. "It was confusing not having a place to call home," she adds.[23] The longest-lasting foster home was "bad," she emphasizes over coffee following her first IE interview. She explains that both foster parents were cruel and yelled and drank a lot; and, she adds, "My foster parents beat me." They also tossed Carol around by her hair. She was beaten again at the School for the Deaf. "Teachers, students, the principal, all were cruel to me. I was afraid, couldn't sleep," Carol adds.[24] "That one almost killed me," she recounted. Worse still, when she reported her abuse more than once, her then foster parents did not believe her. "You are a liar," she remembers them telling her, so she ran away. "Bumping around in grade 8 and 9, never [having] a counsellor," she said, "I didn't feel I had an ally. I went to every person I could think of and got nothing."

Repeated and extreme violence to body and spirit deprived Carol of high school graduation as a youth, but, determined to model resilience to her children, she twice enrolled in academic upgrading as an adult. Ill-health subverted both attempts. Now she reads to self-educate and self-empowers by adjusting the way she interacts when communication problems arise. These are just two examples of "what a wonderful mother Carol is," said Dorthea Swiftwolfe.[25] Carol spoke recurrently of her lack of education as a barrier to improving life for her children and herself: "I felt I lacked the things I needed, so my children will lack them too." She is haunted by the sense that her children blame her for this situation and says she wishes they "had been able to see counsellors, stop the cycle of abuse so things could be better for the family." Looking about today, she often sees people in the community around her as happy and, by painful contrast, feels devalued by those who ignore or dismiss her because of communication barriers. She says she feels "stuck...because I don't have the tools I need to change my circumstances. She adds, "I think education is the biggest factor here."

Karina was born May 7, 1990, and a proud Carol observed that her infant daughter lifted her head at two or three days old and quickly recognized her mother's face. At three years old Karina already loved painting, and she would later develop a passion for reading and journaling as well as drawing and sketching. "She wanted to become a recognized artist," Carol says of the daughter she called "her beautiful butterfly,"[26] and adds that Karina grew into a sociable young woman who loved going out with her friends and playing cards with her family. Carol's maternal aunt Josephine Longneck confirms that Karina "could talk [in sign language] and laugh with her mother for hours."[27] Karina and Desmond helped to break the isolation Carol so often experienced because of being deaf, and because her literacy skills—her only significant means of communication with those unable to sign—were weak. Carol reports of Karina, "she would tell me about some of the things she was reading and writing. She liked to laugh. She was serious about school, more than the others." In fact, she was registered to return to school when she disappeared. When away from the family home, Karina was, Carol relates, "usually coming by daily, texting me or using the TTY [telephone teletype terminal][28] ... she always had a lot to say."

Sometime before Karina went into rehabilitation, Carol knew that her daughter was being hurt and victimized: "She told me about it, but she was very independent," and would say, "Mum, I'm fine." Over coffee, Carol relates that her daughter was also brave, standing up for her mother in the face of communication difficulties when she thought Carol might be hurt. Unsurprisingly, then, Carol felt particularly bereft when her daughter went missing. She repeatedly speaks of Karina as her only daughter. Precisely because Karina had been so communicative, when there was suddenly silence at her end, the change seemed to Carol "very abrupt."

Carol responded to Karina's disappearance by walking the streets of Saskatoon to the point of exhaustion, at first for three days straight and then sometimes twenty-two hours a day, going into bars, asking in written notes if people had seen the young woman whose photograph Carol showed them. Carol relates that growing more desperate and unable to sleep, "I walked and walked and walked just looking for my daughter. ... And then when I got back home ... I'd just be wondering, 'Where is she?' 'Where are you, Karina; where are you?' ... And I'd yell out and I'd cry ... 'Where are you, Karina?' "[29] Lacking speech, Carol nevertheless signs in the documentary *My Only Daughter* that she felt compelled to "become her daughter's voice." Longneck often served as spokesperson in this situation.

She, Carol, Desmond, and others put up missing person posters around Saskatoon, made placards announcing Karina's disappearance, and had printed both a banner asking the public for help in bringing Karina home and T-shirts with her picture, the word "Missing," and a heart to indicate how well loved she was. In 2013, Carol and supporters, including Muskeg Lake Cree Nation and the then Federation of Saskatchewan Indians, helped erect, at a prominent Saskatoon intersection, a billboard with Karina's picture, the text "Missing / Talented Painter & Writer / Karina Beth Ann Wolfe / Age at Disappearance: 20 years old," the date of her disappearance, and contact information for the Saskatoon Police and Crime Stoppers. Carol and her circle continued to organize fundraisers to support the search for Karina and later to buy a headstone for her grave. Vigils and memorial walks designed to keep Karina as much in the foreground of Saskatonians' minds as possible were held on the anniversary of her disappearance until her remains were discovered. At the third-anniversary vigil, held at the street corner where Karina was last seen, a grieving Desmond, vexed at the lack of progress in finding his sister or the person who had taken her, spoke about his sister to a group that included several reporters, emphasizing, "She is very important. She needs to come home."[30] Carol's statement for the fourth-anniversary vigil included the comments "Every second of every minute of every day I struggle because I miss her so much. It's like a piece of my heart and soul and life is missing.... To not know where she is makes me panic. Not knowing is the most devastating thing I've struggled with."[31]

Holidays when people tend to gather with loved ones are particularly difficult for Carol, but she told documentarian Smith that while days like Christmas are always painful, "It's more painful on Mother's Day because that's a time for family." Nonetheless, Carol's gritty determination and her resilience are evident in her statement four years after Karina went missing: "I'm going to keep going. I am never going to give up. I am not going to give up. I am going to keep fighting and keep looking. Keep having these walks. I am not going to just sit back and wait.... We need to find her. I mean, she is my daughter. I gotta find her."[32]

The family's interactions with police after Karina's disappearance got off to a terrible start but shifted over time. Thus, Carol would acknowledge in testimony before the National Inquiry on MMIWG2S (or NIMMIWG2S)[33] the support of now retired Saskatoon Police Service (SPS) chief Clive Weighill, and her perception that the police, Victim Services, and the women who walked in search and in honour of Karina, "were the voice for my daughter."[34] On July 20, 2010, however, the day after Carol's birthday, the distraught mother went, photo in hand, to the SPS to report her daughter missing. Wolfe told the NIMMIWG2S that she brought to the station an image of her daughter and a note explaining she couldn't find her, but the uniformed officer "just looked and acted like it was not important. He ignored me. I was so angry as he was not helping me, I slammed my hand hard on the counter. That is when he looked at me and handed me a witness statement," Wolfe said.[35] When she returned to the police station, Carol told us, "they assigned a detective. He was better."

Following Carol's testimony to the NIMMIWG2S, a CBC journalist reported that Carol "found it tough to get answers to her questions—partly due to her deafness"—and her first contact with the Saskatoon police, Carol said, left her feeling "like I did something wrong."[36] Things really changed, however, soon after the SPS missing persons liaison, Dorthea Swiftwolfe, was assigned to support and help the family in interactions with police. Though communication even with her was initially difficult, and Carol originally mistrusted her, Swiftwolfe persisted and gradually earned Carol's confidence. Communication deepened after Swiftwolfe learned a few American Sign Language signs.

Carol, when asked how being a person who communicates primarily in sign language affected her experiences of having her daughter go missing and attempting to keep up the pressure to have her both found and remembered in the way Carol wanted, made clear that her whole life has been made more difficult by her disability: "It's so hard to communicate. I always wanted to write, but I don't understand written English that well. It was so much better when I had an interpreter." Sign language translation is, however, a scarce and costly resource, and was unavailable to Carol when she first met with Swiftwolfe and when she tried to get a headstone made for Karina's grave. Carol told us, "I had been saving [and fundraising for two years with the help of family and friends, Swiftwolfe added] to make sure that I had the money for the stone. I had been told that I'd be responsible for half." Things changed after Carol had given her half to a company that makes memorial markers. Staff could not seem to find the money when Carol texted them because things seemed to be taking a long time. She reported to us, "I wanted my money back. They [the company paid for the gravestone] weren't returning my texts." She turned to Swiftwolfe for help getting things straightened out because, she said, "I would have no ability to communicate things like that."

When Karina's murderer, already a convicted sex offender, walked into the SPS, reportedly hearing voices,[37] he said he had information about Karina's disappearance. Soon after, he led police to the swampy site of Karina's remains. Carol was of course devastated when a few days later DNA tests confirmed those remains, scattered by animals, were Karina's. In her impact statement, made June 17, 2016, before Karina's killer was sentenced to life in prison with no chance of parole for fourteen years,[38] Carol addressed the man, saying, "What you did shattered my family, shattered me, my heart, my spirit, my soul. You took my only daughter and then left her like she was garbage.... Karina was not garbage.... Each day that goes by is still a struggle."[39]

Part of that struggle had to do with how bereft and alone Carol felt after losing her daughter, and being unaware that Karina's disappearance was part of a national epidemic of Indigenous women and children going missing.[40] "When my daughter was missing, I didn't really understand the term 'missing and murdered Indigenous women.' I knew that the people got together, but I never really understood. They had posters and walks, but I really couldn't get my head wrapped around what that actually meant.... And I thought I was the only one, and there were so many other people who had the same experience across Canada."[41] When Karina was murdered, Carol lost the chance to support her daughter's dreams of graduating and taking art classes, and to see her daughter "working and having her own home" so that Carol "could go over and visit with her, and just have a relationship with [her] daughter, just hav[e] that family life."[42] The list of losses Carol reports in *My Only Daughter* includes the promise of grandchildren through Karina, but Carol also had to watch her son Desmond suffer with unresolved anger and grief, before and after his sister was found and her murderer convicted. Carol told us that in his depressed state, Desmond seems uninterested in a job or further education.

10. WORKING FROM THE HEART

The way some media reports described Karina has also been problematic. A CBC report of June 17, 2016, for example, introduced the young woman in a way hardly calculated to cultivate respect for her: "Karina Beth Ann Wolfe was 20 years old and struggled with crystal meth and relationships."[43] The report unaccountably foregrounds Karina's coloured hair, perhaps suggesting to some that she was trashy: "It would be five years before [her family] learned what happened to the young woman with the dyed hair, who her family described as a talented painter and writer." It was to counter such constructions of Karina, and those asserting that she lived a high-risk lifestyle—rather than acknowledging that she struggled against overwhelming conditions—that the billboard with the family's description of Karina was erected.

Despite Carol's pain, her participation in numerous events related to MMIWG2S, such as NWAC's annual nationwide Sisters in Spirit vigils held on October 4, the 2016 Ottawa roundtable on MMIWG, the official Saskatoon openings of Christi Belcourt's curated moccasin installation *Walking with Our Sisters*, and Jaime Black's REDress installation have educated others and helped Carol. As she told us, "I'm not healed, but my pain is less," explaining that meeting with others concerned about MMIWG has "helped her manage her trauma." She now advocates united action by Indigenous families and others on the survivor families' behalf. Encountering reporters in her fresh grief after hearing the horrifying details of her daughter's murder during the trial of Karina's killer, making her victim impact statement, and taking in Desmond's statement, she reminded people that many Indigenous people continue to live with the agony of missing or murdered loved ones.[44] She says, "We need to be supportive to everybody that's out there."

Stories of the Missing and Murdered as Prompts to Honourable Reconciliation

Stories of the way individual families have been impacted by their loved ones going missing and later being found murdered can potentially move listeners or readers to work toward producing the kinds of radical social change necessary for honourable reconciliation. Family stories correct misperceptions like the ones Eberts reports: "Indigenous victims of violence are not seen as women with families and communities, or rounded human lives; they are all too often reduced to the stereotype of women who frequent bars or dangerous urban areas, engage in prostitution or have 'high-risk' lifestyles."[45] Similarly, Lavell-Harvard and Brant point out that rather than recognizing that Indigenous victims of violence are put "at risk" by historical and contemporary legal, political, social, and economic forces, victims are often branded as leading "high risk lifestyles."[46] Police, media, and public commentary often represents Indigenous women in these terms, effectively blaming victims for their victimization.[47] Indeed, Karina was repeatedly described in these terms. Hearing family stories is also an important way to counter the idea that MMIWG2S are "ungrievable," when the reality is that their loss is deeply felt.[48] Listening to family stories has additionally taught us that traumatized families have trouble eating, sleeping, and, at times, thinking clearly.

The reason we tell Carol and Karina Wolfe's story here is to help Carol memorialize her daughter in a way that focuses on Karina's gifts and strengths, and that counters the flattening effect that results from prejudicial descriptions of so many Indigenous victims of lethal violence. Our recounting also aims to evoke fellow feeling among readers and to stir others to become allies in the struggle to free Indigenous women—and by extension girls and Two-Spirits—from violence. However, we wish to caution non-Indigenous people against naive empathetic identification with the Wolfes' story. The *Concise Oxford Dictionary* defines empathy as "the power of identifying oneself mentally with (*and so completely comprehending*) a person or object of contemplation" (our emphasis). Thus, politically naive empathetic response to the Wolfes' story could well prompt non-Indigenous readers to imagine themselves as having understanding they simply do not possess. Moreover, as IE member and United Church minister Helen Smith-McIntyre explains, the work of the church is the work of the heart. Thus, congregants may feel particularly called upon in their faith practice to be empathetic.

Yet as settler scholar and Indigenous ally Amber Dean warns, focusing on our common humanity across racialized, ethnic, gender, class, ability, and other dividing lines may be dangerous. It could lead non-Indigenous people to imagine "that the disappeared women could have been *any* woman, including ourselves or other women we know and care about."[49] She explains that the result of positioning ourselves in this way within Indigenous females' stories risks "repudiation of how we might each be in th[ese] stor[ies] quite differently… [and] how settler colonialism is connected to the violence [Indigenous women] experienced."[50] Thus, settler Canadians may understand and represent themselves as innocent of oppressive actions rather than confronting the reality that they inherit a privilege based on past and ongoing Indigenous dispossession.

Individual stories of MMIWG2S are undoubtedly important for UCC members and other Canadians to understand victims' full humanity as well as both the depth of the suffering of those left behind and their determination to find their loved ones, bring them home, and see them respectfully remembered. Such stories also inform people about some of the many ways Canada has dispossessed and devalued the taken ones, their families, and friends, and help us to perceive the yawning gulf between the concrete details of individual stories and the abstractions of the Declaration. However, some sense of how *many* Indigenous people have lived stories like Carol's is also necessary and is best conveyed through statistics.

The Statistical Context of MMIWG2S in Canada

NWAC's Sisters in Spirit project began documenting cases of MMIWG across Canada in 2005 and provided the first published report of cases across Canada: 582 between 1980 and 2010.[51] Most victims were less than 31 years old and many were mothers. Further analysis by Human Rights Watch shows that 39 percent of the 582 went missing and/or were found murdered after 2000.[52] This means that the rate of violence against Indigenous women increased from under 18 incidents per year on average before 2001 to almost 22 per year after. Using police records from across Canada, the Royal Canadian Mounted Police in 2015 reported 1,181 cases of missing and murdered for roughly the same time period covered in NWAC's report.[53] Even this figure likely understates the horrifying reality.

After the NIMMIWG2S's review of the available evidence, its interim report concludes: "No one knows for sure how many Indigenous women and girls have been murdered or gone missing in Canada."[54] What is known is that 1,859 families and survivors have registered with the inquiry, clearly indicating higher numbers of the missing and murdered than have previously been reported.[55] The inquiry's analysis also clearly shows that Indigenous females are dramatically overrepresented among Canada's female victims of violence, comprising 9 percent of female homicides in 1980 and 24 percent in 2015, despite making up only 4 percent of women in Canada.[56] Analysis by academic researchers Maryanne Pearce and Tracey Peter reported in the same document reveals that Indigenous women are twelve times more likely to be murdered than other Canadian women and sixteen times more likely than Caucasian women. In Manitoba and Saskatchewan, the situation is most dire, with Indigenous women nineteen times more likely to be murdered. This heightened vulnerability to violence can be attributed in part to the fact that Indigenous women are less able than their non-Indigenous counterparts to leave violent situations due to "precarious housing, lack of access to shelters, and transiency."[57]

Sadly, violence against Indigenous people who are LGBTQIA or Two-Spirit is compounded by "homelessness, homophobic and transphobic biases in the health care system, and a lack of expertise in LGBTQ services for Two-Spirit and other Indigenous gender or sexual minorities," as well as by police abuse.[58] Although data are limited, the NIMMIWG estimates that "people who identified as lesbian, gay, or bisexual are violently victimized nearly five times as often as people who identified as heterosexual."[59] Two-Spirit activists have begun to compile statistics related to violence against Indigenous LGBTQ2S people. Cree Two-Spirited education professor Alex Wilson reports that, based on data from the United States, "in comparison to the general population two-spirit women are four times more likely to be sexually or physically assaulted, and they are 50 per cent more likely to be assaulted than Indigenous women who are heterosexual."[60] Wilson provides anecdotal evidence from her own circle of friends: "Over the past few years, five of my Indigenous, trans[gender]and two-spirit-identified friends have been murdered."[61] Although she does not specify what nationality these people are, the fact that one person in Canada is reporting that five friends have been murdered surely indicates that the losses are staggering, and Canadians would be naive to assume such violent loss of Two-Spirit lives does not occur in our country. Indeed, we know from volume 5 of the TRC's final report that "Two-Spirit people in residential schools were particularly vulnerable to violence and abuse," and that survivors reported others' consequent suicides.[62]

MMIWG2S, Reconciliation, and Iskwewuk E-wichiwitochik's Work

While stories can record the impact on families of a loved one's disappearance and death, and statistics can document the wider scope of such losses, stories and statistics rarely if ever communicate "what this loss means as a lived sense of 'fear, frustration and sorrow' permeating whole [Indigenous] communities."[63] Just how the stories told by families of the missing and murdered and the statistics about violence relate to reconciliation in Canada is made clear by former TRC chair Murray Sinclair in the statement that serves as the second epigraph to this chapter. He asserts that the painful and ongoing problem of MMIWG needs to be resolved before Indigenous people are able to take Canada's reconciliatory plans seriously. IE members are painfully aware of the ways in which ongoing violence against Indigenous women, girls, and Two-Spirits undermines reconciliatory initiatives, and are keenly interested in Indigenous healing and resurgence after the suppressive effects of colonization.[64] Three IE members, Mary Ann Assailly, Darlene Okemaysim-Sicotte, and Helen Smith-McIntyre, have additionally been particularly active in reconciliation work, both locally and nationally. And could there be a more convincing indicator of the pressing need to work energetically toward reconciliation between Indigenous and non-Indigenous people in Canada than the disproportionately high level of often fatal violence experienced by Indigenous females, males, and Two-Spirits in this country?[65]

While solving this dire situation will require a multi-pronged approach, Iskwewuk E-wichiwitochik/Women Walking Together came into existence in

2005 as an activist coalition to tackle one dimension of this national epidemic of violence. The Saskatoon-based group gives highest priority to supporting the families of missing and murdered Indigenous women and girls, particularly in Saskatoon and area, but IE networks with similar groups and like-minded individuals across Canada and beyond. Allying with other social justice–seeking groups like Amnesty International Group 33 and, especially in the context of reconciliation, churches, IE educates the public about the larger issue of MMIWG2S. Our group also lobbies all levels of government, including Indigenous ones, to urgently and effectively address this issue. It supports government efforts in this area by actively participating in such work as the NIMMIWG.[66]

The collaborative work of IE's Indigenous and non-Indigenous members could serve as a model for reconciliation as articulated by the TRC and defined in NWAC's CRGB *Models of Reconciliation*. In its final report, the TRC describes reconciliation as "an on-going individual and collective process" whose guiding principles include "mutual respect, coexistence, fairness, meaningful dialogue, and mutual recognition."[67] The report further states that "reconciliation, in the context of Indian residential schools, is similar to dealing with a situation of family violence. It's about coming to terms with events of the past in a manner that overcomes conflict and establishes a respectful and healthy relationship among people, going forward."[68] Moreover, reconciliation "implies a solemn duty to act, a responsibility to engage, and an obligation to fulfill the promises inherent in an advanced democratic and ethical citizenship.... [It] must mean real change for all of our people in all the places we choose to live, change that addresses the [past and present] wrongs in a way that brings all of us closer together."[69]

NWAC's CRGB *Models of Reconciliation* argues that a culturally relevant and gender-responsive reconciliation must rest on an Indigenous conceptualization of gender inclusive of Two-Spirits and characterized by "balance, reciprocity, interdependence and respect" among genders.[70] The type of reconciliation that IE envisages presupposes an end to forms of colonialism still at work at the time of our writing, and entails supporting Indigenous people in their healing from harms inflicted by such colonialisms, as well as recognizing and acting on the understanding that the non-Indigenous inheritors of colonialism also need to heal because racism, sexism, and homophobia damage the full humanity of the colonizers and colonized.[71] IE's work is, however, specifically focused on what the NWAC report sets as its bottom line for reconciliation: "restoring Indigenous women's [and girls'] dignity, safety, authority and agency."[72]

Assessing the UCC's Decision to Adopt the Declaration as a Framework for Reconciliation

Positives of the Decision to Adopt the Declaration

Few things—if any—can be more important in the reconciliation process than for Indigenous people to know that they are finally being truly heard and to see the calls to non-Indigenous people in the context of reconciliation acted upon. We cannot, then, underestimate the importance of the UCC's decision to act on the TRC's Call to Action 48. This call asked churches that are parties to the Indian Residential Schools Settlement Agreement "to formally adopt and comply with the principles, norms, and standards of the United Nations Declaration on the Rights of Indigenous Peoples as a framework for reconciliation," and to "[engage] in ongoing public dialogue and actions to support [the Declaration]."[73] Together, the UCC's national-level decision and the St. Andrew's College faculty's choice to create opportunities for dialogue about that decision—of which the current book and the November 23–24, 2017, colloquium from which it emerged are an outgrowth—are, then, encouraging movements toward reconciliation.

Certainly, to those who worked hard and long to give the Declaration its present powers, IE sends out gratitude and respect for this dedicated work and the degree of gender-sensitive Indigenous diplomacy entailed in arriving at a consensual text and getting most nations (including, belatedly, Canada) to adopt the Declaration.[74] Even one of the Declaration's most forceful critics, Peter Kulchyski, recognizes it as a "worthy document," waves off any suggestion that it will be of no use in Indigenous Peoples' struggles, and reminds readers that Indigenous Peoples *do* need their human rights respected and that getting

Indigenous Peoples recognized at the United Nations is a lasting achievement.⁷⁵ Several of the Declaration's articles specifically direct attention to the rights of Indigenous women, though girls are subsumed under the category of children despite girls' heightened vulnerabilities to sexual assault and being trafficked. Articles 21.2 and 22.1 both assert the obligation to attend particularly to "the rights and special needs of indigenous elders, women, youth, children, and persons with disabilities" when taking measures to improve Indigenous Peoples' economic and social conditions and when implementing the Declaration.⁷⁶ Additionally, article 22.2 explicitly enjoins states to act with Indigenous Peoples to ensure Indigenous women and children are fully protected and have guarantees against "all forms of violence and discrimination," while article 44 guarantees equally to Indigenous women and men all of the rights set out in the document. Indeed, the Declaration in the context of reconciliation offers a counterweight to two threats: the entrenchment of a neo-colonial business-as-usual model of reconciliation (which would benefit the Canadian state and, by some understandings, settler Canadians, at the expense of the Indigenous Peoples of Turtle Island), and the misperceived neutralization of legitimate Indigenous resistance to unjust relations, as discussed above.

There is, then, much to recommend the Declaration as a framework for reconciliation. However, with our work on the issue of MMIWG2S and our broader knowledge of the historical and contemporary treatment of Indigenous females and people who are gay or identify outside dominant ideas of gender conformity, we do want to articulate some concerns.

Cautions about the Limitations and Drawbacks of the Declaration

In sounding a cautionary note about the UCC's choice of the Declaration as a framework for reconciliation, we identify what we believe to be limitations to the Declaration's ability to protect *all* Indigenous people's human rights (and hence those of all Indigenous females and Two-Spirits). In what follows, we describe more fully our sense of the Declaration's limitations and drawbacks that are specific to Indigenous women, girls, and Two-Spirits.

The many critiques of the Declaration that settler scholar and Indigenous ally Peter Kulchyski articulates in his book *Aboriginal Rights Are Not Human Rights* are well worth considering, though he shows minimal interest in the gender-specific violations of Indigenous women's rights. He critiques the idea that Aboriginal Rights (that is, rights specific to Aboriginals and not held by all humans) are the same thing as human rights, and argues that the Declaration risks subordinating Aboriginal Rights to overarching human rights, like equality, guaranteed to all people.[77] However, Joyce Green (English, Ktunaxa, and Cree, Scottish, and Metis) counters that Indigenous Rights are ultimately indivisible from human rights, and that "the human rights of Indigenous people are injured when their rights as Indigenous peoples are violated."[78]

Our concerns about the Declaration's limited ability to protect Indigenous people's human rights are wide-ranging. As a UN declaration, the Declaration is not legally binding, while UN conventions, which have the status of treaties, legally bind states that sign them. The Declaration is also rooted in Enlightenment-era "universalisms" that are Eurocentric, so only time will tell whether Indigenous Peoples will be able to "make the concept of human rights authentically their own in the process of analyzing their conditions and making their claims," as John-Andrew McNeish and Robyn Eversole's work suggests Indigenous people will do.[79] That the Declaration's conception of self-determination is framed exclusively in terms of non-interference, separation, and independence (rather than relationally, in line with Indigenous values) indicates that those values may be overwritten in the process of defending the rights asserted in the Declaration. It problematically frames Indigenous Rights as exclusively a matter between nation-states and Indigenous Peoples rather than recognizing that these rights can also be a matter of violations by one individual of another's rights.[80] The Declaration is written in the language of international law, which speaks to the head rather than the heart, and thus is not fully appropriate for formulating a framework for churches' reconciliatory actions. Moreover, as noted above, that language is alien or even incomprehensible to most of the people whose interests the Declaration is meant to serve.

Our concerns about the Declaration arising from problems that specifically disadvantage Indigenous females and Two-Spirits include its privileging of collective over individual identities when, as noted in the *Mairin Iwanka Raya* report, Indigenous women often experience human rights violations at the intersection of their individual and collective identities.[81] That the Declaration's clauses lack specificity about women's and girls' rights is seriously concerning given the many gender-specific ways these groups experience discrimination and violence, including sexual slavery, enforced prostitution and sterilization, and forced pregnancy.[82] This list focusses entirely on various forms of sexual violence, but it is by no means exhaustive. Other commentators have, for example, reported Indigenous women's heightened vulnerability to state agents' seizure of their children[83] and assaults on their health, safety, and well-being in the context of resource-extraction projects.[84] Furthermore, the Declaration sometimes problematically subordinates Indigenous women's group and individual interests to those of Indigenous Peoples as a whole, despite the document's avowed interest in ensuring equality of rights to men and women. University of Toronto professor Rauna Kuokkanen (Sámi) points out that the wording of articles 21.2 and 22.1 "renders Indigenous women inherently vulnerable [by] categorizing them with children and elders."[85] She further maintains that "the UNDRIP ought to have acknowledged that in most cases, women's vulnerability stems from the prevalent gender discrimination and subjugation in society." And, additionally, that the Declaration ought not to have "turn[ed] a blind eye to the intragroup difference and oppression that exists in Indigenous communities."[86] Xanthaki asserts that "the history of the Declaration on the Rights of Indigenous Peoples reflects the reluctance to touch upon issues related to women's rights."[87] She reports that, despite article 44's offering a guarantee of equal rights to male and female Indigenous persons, "the article was never really discussed in depth during the elaboration of the Declaration and was the focus of very little attention." Even "Indigenous female representatives repeatedly said, when asked informally, that [negotiations around the text of the Declaration] was not the forum to discuss the issue."[88] Kim Anderson (Cree-Métis) and Rob Innes (Cree) follow Anishinaabe lawyer Joan Jack by identifying Indigenous male violence against Indigenous females as "the moose in the room" in many of the discussions of violence against Indigenous women and girls.[89] At the same time, Anderson and Innes carefully contextualize this problem by explaining the power of the colonial state to prompt and enforce Indigenous internalizing of colonial values.[90]

However, if the Declaration fails to recognize the specific vulnerabilities of Indigenous women, it also reinforces a deficit model of them rather than recognizing that colonial laws, policies, and practices uniquely sought to disempower the leadership that Indigenous women nonetheless continue to show. Additionally, that model works to obscure their gender-specific knowledges. For example, Val Napoleon (Saulteau) notes, "men and women often have different traditional knowledge of natural resources in relation to 'habitat, conservation, management, use, storing, and processing'.... This includes knowledge relating to access to, and control and use of, natural resources, which are basic elements of indigenous law."[91] Moreover, as Nathalie Kermoal and Isabel Altamirano-Jiménez assert, "to ignore the specific ways in which Indigenous women know is to undermine them as active producers of knowledge that participate in complex socio-environmental community processes."[92] Thus Brenda L. Gunn (Métis) contends that in implementing the Declaration, "a gendered approach is necessary not only because Indigenous women have special needs, but also because Indigenous women have particular knowledges that contribute to Indigenous nations and laws, and that need recognition and protection."[93]

Our final point about the Declaration's limitations is that it does not clearly and specifically articulate rights for Indigenous people who are outside the hetero-normative frame. However, Henderson asserts that nation-states' discrimination on the basis of sexual orientation and gender identity, including transgender identity, "were raised in different ways every year at the UNDRIP meeting."[94] Such matters were discussed as part of "the right to have an identity and as part of the diversity of Indigenous peoples," and "enfolded in the provisions in the *Declaration* about non-discrimination and the right to have an identity and the diversity of Indigenous peoples." Henderson adds, "The existing and developing standards of protection of their identity human rights in the

UN [are] incorporated in parts 1 and 2." Notably, Henderson points out that the origin of these gender problems lay with the colonizers, not with Indigenous Peoples: "In general, the Indigenous meetings had trouble with the issue of gender because many Indigenous languages did not have an emphasis on gender nor did they have any limitation of the scope of love in their knowledge systems and world views." Indigenous meetings about the Declaration, he notes, developed a consensus view of "the categories of gay, queer, and transsexual identity as part of the discrimination and oppression of the homophobic and transphobic Eurocentric knowledge system toward Indigenous peoples, but made the collective decision not to highlight the discrimination and oppression."[95] Much of Henderson's discussion has the potential to be broadly enlightening, but given that Indigenous people now exist in a world pervaded by often violently enforced limitations to the scope of love, and given our argument about the need for special protections for those who experience heightened vulnerability to human rights violations, we remain committed to the view that the Declaration's failure to specifically articulate gender-identity rights limits its efficacy.

Closing Words to the United Church of Canada

The UCC has made an important and welcome commitment in adopting the Declaration as a framework for reconciliation with Indigenous Peoples in Canada. As Green writes, "Somewhere between the universality of our humanity and the particularity of our social, political, cultural, gendered and historical experiences, the lives of human beings are lived in specific, often inequitable and unjust contexts that benefit from human rights protection."[96] While, as Andrea Smith argues, "the ultimate goal of Indigenous liberation is decolonization rather than human rights protection, the human rights framework can potentially be used as part of a strategy for decolonization."[97]

So, what are IE's suggestions to the UCC for pursuing the goals of reconciliation and decolonization? First, as our inclusion of the story of Carol and Karina Wolfe suggests, work from the heart to encourage church members to listen to the stories of Indigenous people in general, being careful to include those of women, girls, and Two-Spirits about the effects of the imposition of the dominant culture's values and practices on their lives and about what has enabled them to be resilient. No one can truly reconcile with what they do not know. Finding ways to engage face-to-face and to work alongside Indigenous people in projects in which they have identified the priorities is strong reparative medicine. Second, retain the Declaration framework but understand and act on its limitations for the UCC's pastoral mission. Third, adopt NWAC's CRGB *Models of Reconciliation* (with the adaptations we outline below to give fuller attention to girls and Two-Spirits) as a supplementary framework. Fourth, consult with groups such as NWAC, Two-Spirit organizations, and Indigenous scholars for advice about adaptations for the specific church context.

NWAC's CRGB *Models of Reconciliation* presents a checklist of indicators designed to move people in Canada toward culturally relevant, gender-responsive reconciliation, and pairs these indicators with related questions that could potentially be useful to the UCC for discerning whether the reconciliation process being developed is likely to achieve its goals. The NWAC report states that the word "gender" as used "in this context refers to gender roles and identities that people live [and is] expressly inclusive of Two-Spirit people."[98] Thus, for reconciliatory gender relations to be respectful, the report states, "they must address how effectively Two-Spirit people are welcomed and treated in the process of reconciliation." However, in the list of indicators, Two-Spirit people are not mentioned where we believe they should be. Where appropriate, we have, therefore, interpolated them in indicators 1, 2, 4, and 5, and we recommend that the UCC check its reconciliatory practices against the adapted checklist:

1. Restore and respect Indigenous women's [and Two-Spirits'] agency, authority, leadership and decision-making capacity.

2. Restore safety and the human right to security of the person for Indigenous women and girls [and Two-Spirits]—physically, mentally, emotionally, spiritually, politically and economically.

3. Reclaim and revitalize Indigenous knowledge, worldviews, and traditions of gender balance in ways that are relevant to the contemporary context.

4. Share the truth about the gendered impacts of colonization, human rights violations, and ethnocide/genocide such as tragically high levels of violence against Indigenous women and girls [and Two-Spirits], and exclusion of women[, girls, and Two-Spirits] from leadership and decision-making.

5. Promote personal and social responsibility for ending neocolonial attitudes and practices that devalue Indigenous women[, girls, and Two-Spirits] and create social conditions that put women and girls [and Two-Spirits] in harm['s] way.[99]

CRGB *Models of Reconciliation* also lists the purposes of truth and reconciliation commissions that Priscilla Hayner identifies in *Unspeakable Truths: Confronting State Terror and Atrocity*, purposes that we believe could usefully guide the UCC in its own vision for reconciliation—that is, if they were adapted to be fully inclusive of Two-Spirted people and to recognize specifics of the Canadian situation.[100] In the following list, Hayner's wording is silently integrated into the NWAC document's wording wherever doing so produces greater clarity. We have added in square brackets our clarifications and further considerations relevant for the Canadian context:

1. Clarify and acknowledge the gendered impacts of colonialism, residential schooling, [the Sixties Scoop, and ongoing child apprehensions].

2. Respond to the needs and interests of victims/survivors by creat[ing] an enabling environment for truth telling through inclusion of ceremony, gendered safety protocols; adequately trained staff;

engagement of community supports;...the promotion of healing [and post-reconciliation health remedies].

3. Contribute to justice and accountability by recognizing ways in which women[, girls, and Two-Spirits] are marginalized and dispossessed within their communities and in the broader society as a result of colonialism while also recognizing their achievements and gender-specific approach to cultural continuity, healing, leadership, community development, and legislative reform.

4. In outlining institutional responsibility and recommending reforms, address gendered impacts, especially in governance... [101]

5. Prioritize ending violence against Indigenous women and girls [and Two-Spirits] as a key element in healing and reconciliation; recognize the leadership role of women in politicizing this issue and their expertise in addressing it.

6. To meet the [right] of victims/survivors and society to the truth, [use] education and communications strategies... [to] promote mass public engagement in reconciliation.

As the call to recognize Indigenous women's and Two-Spirits' achievements (see indicator 3 above, "Contribute to justice and accountability...") suggests, remembering to celebrate the resilience of those who have survived the oppressions that the families and communities of MMIWG2S, Two-Spirits, and Indigenous female survivors of violence have exhibited is crucial to honourable reconciliation. The UCC's enacting of such reconciliation therefore demands both the recognition, honouring, and supporting of resilient Indigenous leadership and non-Indigenous UCC members becoming active allies to Indigenous people in their struggle for just relations with the Canadian state and individual citizens. Both fellow feeling and rigorous self-examination about settler privilege are also crucial if non-Indigenous Canadians are to be effective allies. The guidance offered in this context by an Australian Aboriginal activist group in Queensland during the 1970s (but often attributed to Lilla Watson alone) offers a potent formulation with which to close: "If you have come here to help me, you are wasting your time. But if you have come because your liberation is bound up with mine, then let us work together."[102]

ēkosi/that is all.

Notes

Deep gratitude and respect, Carol Wolfe, for your strength in reopening the pain entailed in sharing your and Karina's story with us and for giving us permission to tell it in this chapter. Thank you, Dorthea Swiftwolfe, for active participation in a follow-up session and revision stages that allowed us to enhance the accuracy and depth of the Wolfes' story presented here, and to translators Tyler Burgess, Carla Klassen, and Sue Schmid of Saskatchewan Deaf and Hard of Hearing Services, without whom the original interview and two follow-up sessions with Carol Wolfe could not have been conducted. kinanāskomitinān, Dr. Arok Wolvengrey, for your translation of the word "reconciliation"; for providing, along with Darren Okemaysim and First Nations University of Canada professor and author of *mâci-nêhiyawêwin/Beginning Cree*, Solomon Ratt, commentary on other Cree translations of the term "reconciliation" that were forwarded to us; for instructing us how the Cree words we have used should be accented when presented in text; and for explaining component elements of others' translations. Thanks are also due to Rhett Sangster of the Office of the Treaty Commissioner, Saskatchewan, both for directing us to the interview in which Chief Littlechild discusses and gives Cree translations for "reconciliation," and for consulting with other Cree speakers about translations of the English word.

Susan Gingell and Darlene Okemaysim-Sicotte are the primary authors of this chapter, but we owe thanks to Andréa Ledding, who was instrumental in formulating the proposal for IE's chapter in this book. Louise Clarke and Helen Smith-McIntyre enriched discussion when IE met with St. Andrew's College faculty about the proposed book; Louise offered editing suggestions and helped format the article; and reconciliation activist Mary Ann Assailly has animated a reconciliatory spirit in IE's work and provided important support and information to our present project.

1   After consultation with colleagues, Arok Wolvengrey, First Nations University of Canada professor and compiler of the two-volume bilingual dictionary *nēhiýawēwin: itwewina/ Cree: Words*, provided this translation in an email of August 17, 2018, to Susan Gingell. "The term was," he wrote, "the one we seem to favour most in terms of simply the most common notion of 'reconciliation.'" He added, "This term was suggested by Alvin Grieves of Oxford House in Manitoba in a response to a Cree Word of the Day Facebook

post (and I have edited the spelling—this term should actually cross-cut dialect nicely). My colleague Darren Okemaysim and I felt it made sense."

2 The original source of this translation is "Lift Each Other Up: An Interview with Chief Wilton Littlechild, Commissioner for the Truth and Reconciliation Commission of Canada," *Cultural Survival Quarterly*, March 2011, https://www.culturalsurvival.org/publications/cultural-survival-quarterly/lift-each-other-interview-chief-wilton-littlechild. In the interview, Littlechild says of reconciliation:

> I look at it from two different places. One is from a cultural perspective. In my language, in Cree, when you say "reconciliation" it's called Miyowahkotowin. It means "having good relations." That's what reconciliation is in my view, and I have a cultural support for that in our ceremonies, where we have protocol: Waypinasun, which can mean "letting go" when it is offered in that spirit. Whether it's letting go of a bad experience to find a place where you can forgive, or, once you've let go, regaining your own self, your strength as an individual so you can start to get back to the balance that you were first blessed with. That is from a cultural perspective, but I've also said that for me it's a feeling when I have a good relationship with someone else. That can be you with the Creator, you with God, you with your family, or with your community. Personally, [f]or me reconciliation is actually a spiritual feeling, a good feeling.

We were directed to this interview by Rhett Sangster, director of reconciliation and community partnerships in the Office of the Treaty Commissioner, Saskatchewan. He told Susan Gingell in an email on July 13, 2018, that "there are numerous definitions of what reconciliation means in English—so it stands to reason that there are also numerous definitions in Cree or other languages as well." Sangster "received from a colleague who in turn reached out to a local Elder" an additional translation for the concept "mindfully set aside." We have not included the Cree words suggested for this concept because the spelling was not in accord with the standardized Cree script and thus we received only educated guesses about what the Cree words were meant to be.

Darlene Okemaysim-Sicotte consulted the Internet about the Cree for "restoring good relations," and then conferred with her uncle, Robert Spence, a fluent Cree speaker, to confirm the translation "ka mīnosihtahk miyo-pimātisiwin itahkomitiwin." Asked about the meaning of the component parts of the phrase, Wolvengrey included in his August 17, 2018, email the following reply: "Perhaps what is intended here is something like…'to remake a good life through (kin) relationship.'"

3 Marie Battiste and James (Sa'ke'j) Youngblood Henderson, *Protecting Indigenous Knowledge and Heritage: A Global Challenge* (Saskatoon: Purich Publishing, 2000), 79.

4 Peter Kulchyski, *Aboriginal Rights Are Not Human Rights: In Defence of Indigenous Struggles* (Winnipeg: Arbeiter Ring Publishing, 2013), 60. Kulchyski calls the lack of Indigenous discursive practices and concepts in the Declaration "a travesty" (60) and notes its use of the Latin phrase *inter alia*, meaning "among other things," the most obvious example of the European-derived character of international law's language.

5   Littlechild, who in the March 2011 interview "Lift Each Other Up," said of the Declaration, "In my view, it is a framework for reconciliation," is himself a lawyer, as is Commissioner Murray Sinclair, so two if not all three TRC commissioners—Marie Wilson, the third, is a journalist—would have been familiar with the legal language used in the Declaration.

6   "Two-Spirit" is the term by which, since its coinage in 1990, some Turtle Island Indigenous people choose to identify themselves, "rather than, or in addition to, identifying as lesbian, gay, bisexual, trans or queer." See "Two Spirits, One Voice," Egale, accessed March 11, 2021, https://egale.ca/awareness/two-spirits-one-voice/. Spellings of the term are as yet variable. Cree education professor Alex Wilson writes, "As a self-identifier, *two-spirit* acknowledges and affirms our identity as Indigenous peoples, our connection to the land, and values in our traditional cultures that recognize and accept gender and sexual diversity." See Wilson, "Skirting the Issues: Indigenous Myths, Misses and Misogyny," in *Keetsahnak: Our Missing and Murdered Indigenous Sisters*, ed. Kim Anderson, Maria Campbell, and Christi Belcourt (Edmonton: University of Alberta Press, 2018), 167–8. The interim report of the National Inquiry into Missing and Murdered Indigenous Women and Girls states that " 'Two-Spirit' describes a societal and spiritual role that people played within traditional societies, as mediators [and] keepers of certain ceremonies, and...a role as an established middle gender." See *Our Women and Girls Are Sacred: Interim Report* (Vancouver: National Inquiry into Missing and Murdered Indigenous Women and Girls, 2017), 85. Egale's "Two Spirits, One Voice" (cited earlier in this note) is a valuable resource for those wishing to understand more about Two-Spirits, including how to be an ally.

7   Quoted in Truth and Reconciliation Commission of Canada, *Final Report of the Truth and Reconciliation Commission of Canada, Vol. 1: Summary: Honouring the Truth, Reconciling for the Future* (Toronto: James Lorimer, 2015), 9.

8   Eve Tuck and K. Wayne Yang, "Decolonization Is Not a Metaphor," *Decolonization: Indigeneity, Education and Society* 1, no. 1 (2012): 3. Tuck and Yang theorize "an ethic of incommensurability, which recognizes what is distinct, what is sovereign for project(s) of decolonization in relation to human and civil rights based social justice projects" (28). The Declaration is, of course, one of the former.

9   Leanne Simpson, *Dancing on Our Turtle's Back: Stories of Nishnaabeg Re-creation, Resurgence and a New Emergence* (Winnipeg: Arbeiter Ring Publishing, 2011), 22.

10 Tuck and Yang, *Decolonization Is Not a Metaphor*, 5.

11 Marilyn Legge, "Seeking 'Right Relations': How Should Churches Respond to Aboriginal Voices?" *Journal of the Society of Christian Ethics*, no. 22 (Fall 2002): 13. In using the verb "restore," Legge does assume the prior existence of right relations, a position a number of Indigenous people would contest.

12 We cannot here rehearse the ways in which the provisions of the Victorian-era *Indian Act* (1876) and its many subsequent amendments have entailed the imposition and maintenance of Victorian patriarchal ideas of proper femininity and family values, dangerously, and often lethally, subordinating women to men. We do note, however, that it put Indigenous females in double jeopardy because the legislation was further expressly

designed to subjugate all Indigenous Peoples in Canada to people of European ancestry. Indigenous ally and legal scholar Mary Eberts distills the results of this process by saying it rendered Indigenous women "legal nullities," situated them "outside the rule of law," and made of them "a population of prey for those who would harm and abuse them." See Eberts, "Victoria's Secret: How to Make a Population of Prey," in *Indivisible: Indigenous Human Rights*, ed. Joyce Green (Winnipeg: Fernwood Publishing, 2014), 144.

13   Native Women's Association of Canada, *Culturally Relevant Gender Based Models of Reconciliation* (Ohsweken, ON: Native Women's Association of Canada, 2010), https://www.nwac.ca/wp-content/uploads/2015/05/2010-NWAC-Culturally-Relevant-Gender-Based-Models-of-Reconciliation.pdf, 11.

14   Allison Hargreaves, *Violence against Indigenous Women: Literature, Activism, Resistance* (Waterloo, ON: Wilfrid Laurier University Press, 2017), 13.

15   Ibid.

16   Ibid.

17   The Native Youth Sexual Health Network and 2-Spirited People of the 1st Nations might also usefully be consulted.

18   Cited in Kulchyski, *Aboriginal Rights*, 52.

19   James (Sa'ke'j) Youngblood Henderson, *Indigenous Diplomacy and the Rights of Peoples: Achieving UN Recognition* (Saskatoon: Purich Publishing, 2008), 37.

20   Legge, "Seeking 'Right Relations,'" 20.

21   Native Women's Association of Canada, CRGB *Models of Reconciliation*, 24.

22   Unless otherwise attributed, all quotations in this section are from an interview with Carol Wolfe by Susan Gingell and Darlene Okemaysim-Sicotte through American Sign Language interpreter Tyler Burgess conducted June 19, 2018, at Station 20 West in Saskatoon. To ensure accuracy and receive further detail and explanation, Susan conducted two follow-up sessions. The first, on August 23, 2018, at Susan's house, included Carol's close friend Dorthea Swiftwolfe and interpreter Carla Klassen. The second, on October 17, 2018, again at Susan's house, included interpreter Sue Schmid.

23   During the October 17, 2018, follow-up session, Carol revealed this impact and that her foster parents tossed her about by her hair.

24   Also at the October 17 follow-up, Carol provided this statement about the multiple sources of cruelty she experienced at the School for the Deaf and the effect these had on her.

25   The comment came during IE's August 23, 2018, follow-up.

26   Jacqueline Wilson, "Jerry Constant Pleads Guilty to Second-Degree Murder of Karina Wolfe," *Global News*, June 17, 2016, https://globalnews.ca/news/2770836/man-pleads-guilty-to-the-second-degree-murder-of-karina-wolfe/.

27   Janet French, "Vigil Marks Four Years since Wolfe's Disappearance; 'We're Not Going to Stop Looking for Her,' Family Vows," *Saskatoon Star Phoenix*, July 3, 2014, https://thestarphoenix.com/uncategorized/saskatoon/vigil-marks-four-years-since-wolfes-disappearance-were-not-going-to-stop-looking-for-her-family-vows.

28   A telephone teletype terminal is a telecommunication device for the deaf.

29   Grace Rebecca Smith's documentary film *My Only Daughter* is available at https://gracesmithdocumentary.com/portfolio/my-only-daughter/.

30 See "Karina Wolfe," Missing & Murdered: The Unsolved Cases of Indigenous Women and Girls, CBC News, accessed March 15, 2021, http://www.cbc.ca/missingandmurdered/mmiw/profiles/karina-wolfe.
31 Swiftwolfe, who helped Carol write her statement, provided in the follow-up session this corrected version—which in Swiftwolfe's view is more faithful to Carol's suffering—of what was reported in French, "Vigil."
32 "Vigil and Walk Held for Missing Karina Wolfe in Saskatoon," CBC News, July 2, 2014, https://www.cbc.ca/news/canada/saskatoon/vigil-and-walk-held-for-missing-karina-wolfe-in-saskatoon-1.2693912.
33 The national inquiry was commissioned with looking into missing and murdered Indigenous women and girls, but in their interim report, the commissioners stated that they had heard the urgings of Two-Spirited people, so the inquiry came to encompass missing and murdered women, girls, and Two-Spirits. Hence, we and others now often refer to the inquiry acronymically as NIMMIWG2S.
34 "From Mistrust to Gratitude: Karina Wolfe's Mother Thanks Police for Help," CBC News, November 24, 2017, https://www.cbc.ca/news/canada/saskatoon/ mistrust-to gratitude-mother-indigenous-woman-police-thanks-mmiw-1.4417192.
35 Laura Woodward, "Deaf Woman Whose Daughter Was Murdered Calls for More Interpreters," CTV News, November 23, 2017, https://saskatoon.ctvnews.ca/deaf-woman-whose-daughter-was-murdered-calls-for-more-interpreters-1.3691743?autoPlay=true.
36 CBC News, "From Mistrust."
37 Dan Zakreski, "Convicted Sex Offender Jerry Constant Charged in Karina Wolfe's Death," CBC News, November 30, 2015, https://www.cbc.ca/news/canada/saskatoon/convicted-sex-offender-jerry-constant-charged-in-karina-wolfe-death-1.3343183.
38 Wilson, "Jerry Constant Pleads Guilty."
39 Transcribed by the authors from "Moments from Day 3 of the National Inquiry Hearings in Saskatoon," APTN News, November 23, 2017, YouTube video, 0:44, https://www.youtube.com/watch?v=RsXctH2dpJE.
40 For statistics indicating the scope of the violence, see "The Statistical Context of MMIWG2S in Canada" below.
41 Smith, *My Only Daughter*.
42 Ibid.
43 Dan Zakreski, "Saskatoon Murder Victim Karina Wolfe Troubling Symbol of Missing and Murdered Indigenous Women," CBC News, June 17, 2016, https://www.cbc.ca/news/canada/saskatoon/saskatoon-karina-wolfe-missing-1.3640484.
44 "Judge Delivers Sentence after Saskatoon Man Pleads Guilty to 2010 Murder of Karina Wolfe," CKOM News, June 17, 2016, http://www.ckom.com/2016/06/17/judge-delivers-sentence-after-saskatoon-man-pleads-guilty-to-2010-murder-of-karina-wolfe.
45 Eberts, "Victoria's Secret," 147.
46 D. Memee Lavell-Harvard and Jennifer Brant, "Introduction: Forever Loved," in *Forever Loved: Exposing the Hidden Crisis of Missing and Murdered Indigenous Women and Girls in Canada*, ed. D. Memee Lavell-Harvard and Jennifer Brant (Bradford, ON: Demeter Press, 2016), 5.

47 Eberts, "Victoria's Secret," 147.
48 Amber Dean, *Remembering Vancouver's Disappeared Women: Settler Colonization and the Difficulty of Inheritance* (Toronto: University of Toronto Press, 2015), xxviii.
49 Ibid., 130.
50 Ibid.
51 Native Women's Association of Canada, *What Their Stories Tell Us: Research Findings from the Sisters In Spirit Initiative* (Ottawa: Native Women's Association of Canada, 2010), https://www.nwac.ca/wp-content/uploads/2015/07/2010-What-Their-Stories-Tell-Us-Research-Findings-SIS-Initiative.pdf.
52 Human Rights Watch, *Those Who Take Us Away: Abusive Policing and Failures in Protection of Indigenous Women and Girls in Northern British Columbia, Canada* (Amsterdam: Human Rights Watch, 2013).
53 Royal Canadian Mounted Police, *Missing and Murdered Aboriginal Women: A National Operational Overview*, 2014, https://www.rcmp-grc.gc.ca/wam/media/460/original/0cbd8968a049aa0b44d343e76b4a9478.pdf.
54 National Inquiry into Missing and Murdered Indigenous Women and Girls, *Our Women and Girls Are Sacred*, 7.
55 This figure was taken from the website of the National Inquiry into Missing and Murdered Women and Girls at the time of writing. Further information is available at www.mmiwg-ffada.ca.
56 National Inquiry into Missing and Murdered Indigenous Women and Girls, *Our Women and Girls Are Sacred*, 7.
57 Ibid., 7–8, 4.
58 Ibid., 50, 54.
59 Ibid., 8.
60 Alex Wilson, "Skirting the Issues: Indigenous Myths, Misses and Misogyny," in *Keetsahnak: Our Missing and Murdered Indigenous Sisters*, ed. Kim Anderson, Maria Campbell, and Christi Belcourt (Edmonton: University of Alberta Press, 2018), 161.
61 Ibid., 165.
62 Truth and Reconciliation Commission of Canada, *Final Report of the Truth and Reconciliation Commission of Canada, Vol. 5: Canada's Residential Schools* (Montreal: McGill-Queen's Press, 2015), 148.
63 Hargreaves, *Violence against Indigenous Women*, 45.
64 For a discussion of Indigenous resurgence as the result of long-term visioning of social transformation that continually and creatively enacts more just realities, see Simpson, *Dancing on Our Turtle's Back*, especially chapter 1.
65 See Robert Innes and Kim Anderson, "The Moose in the Room: Indigenous Men and Violence against Women," in *Keetsahnak: Our Missing and Murdered Indigenous Sisters*, ed. Kim Anderson, Maria Campbell, and Christi Belcourt (Edmonton: University of Alberta Press, 2018), 6; Wilson, "Skirting the Issues," 161, 172.
66 Darlene Okemaysim-Sicotte, Susan Gingell, and Rita Bouvier, "Iskwewuk E-wichiwitochik: Saskatchewan Community Activism to Address Missing and Murdered Indigenous Women and Girls," in *Keetsahnak: Our Missing and Murdered Indigenous*

Sisters, ed. Kim Anderson, Maria Campbell, and Christi Belcourt (Edmonton: University of Alberta Press, 2018), 264–5.
67 Truth and Reconciliation Commission of Canada, *Final Report, Vol. 5*, 217.
68 Ibid., 6.
69 Ibid., 217.
70 Native Women's Association of Canada, CRGB *Models of Reconciliation*, 5.
71 See Reverend Stan McKay's statement about the mutual need for healing, quoted in Truth and Reconciliation Commission of Canada, *Final Report, Vol. 1*, 9.
72 Native Women's Association of Canada, CRGB *Models of Reconciliation*, 3.
73 Truth and Reconciliation Commission of Canada, *Final Report, Vol. 5*, 5.
74 See Henderson, *Indigenous Diplomacy*, for a detailed account.
75 Kulchyski, *Aboriginal Rights*, 58.
76 See UN General Assembly, Resolution 61/295, United Nations Declaration on the Rights of Indigenous Peoples, A/RES/61/295 (October 2, 2007), https://undocs.org/A/RES/61/295. All subsequent citations to the Declaration come from this source.
77 The mainly, but not exclusively, Indigenous essayists anthologized in *Indivisible: Indigenous Human Rights*, in contradistinction to Kulchyski, all take the position that Indigenous Rights *are* human rights.
78 Joyce Green, "Introduction: Honoured in Their Absence: Indigenous Human Rights," in *Indivisible: Indigenous Human Rights*, ed. Joyce Green (Winnipeg: Fernwood Publishing, 2014), 11.
79 Ibid., 4.
80 Sámi scholar Rauna Kuokkanen notes that feminist philosopher Iris Marion Young, in *Global Challenges: War, Self-Determination, and Responsibility for Justice* (Cambridge: Polity Press, 2007), recognizes the interdependence and overlapping character of human communities in the world as the foundation of theories and conceptions of relational self-determination. Kuokkanen also notes that Young sees "the dominant understanding of self-determination as non-interference, separation, and independence [as] a dangerous fiction." See Kuokkanen, "Confronting Violence: Indigenous Women, Self-Determination and International Human Rights," in *Indivisible: Indigenous Human Rights*, ed. Joyce Green (Winnipeg: Fernwood Publishing, 2014), 128.
81 International Indigenous Women's Forum, *Mairin Iwanka Raya: Indigenous Women Stand against Violence: A Companion Report to the United Nations Secretary-General's Study on Violence against Women* (New York: International Indigenous Women's Forum, 2006).
82 Native Women's Association of Canada, CRGB *Models of Reconciliation*, 4.
83 Amnesty International, *No More Stolen Sisters: The Need for a Comprehensive Response to Discrimination and Violence against Indigenous Women in Canada* (Ottawa: Amnesty International, 2009), 16; Brenda L. Gunn, "Bringing a Gendered Lens to Implementing the UN Declaration on the Rights of Indigenous Peoples," in *UNDRIP Implementation: More Reflections on the Braiding of International, Domestic and Indigenous Laws. A Special Report*, ed. Oonagh E. Fitzgerald and Larry Chartrand (Waterloo, ON: Centre for International Governance Innovation, 2018), 38.

84 UN Human Rights Council, "Report of the Special Rapporteur on the Rights of Indigenous Peoples, James Anaya: Extractive Industries Operating within or Near Indigenous Territories," A/HRC/18/35 (July 11, 2011), https://undocs.org/en/A/hrc/18/35, 10; Sarah Morales, "Canary in a Coal Mine: Indigenous Women and Extractive Industries in Canada," in *Indigenous Peoples and the Law: Comparative and Critical Perspectives*, ed. Benjamin J. Richardson, Shin Imai, and Kent McNeil (Oxford: Hart Publishing, 2018), 74.
85 Why Kuokkanen leaves out persons with disabilities, as mentioned in articles 21.2 and 22.1, is not clear. See Kuokkanen, "Confronting Violence," 130.
86 Ibid.
87 Alexandra Xanthaki, "The UN Declaration on the Rights of Indigenous Peoples and Collective Rights: What's the Future for Indigenous Women?," in *Reflections on the UN Declaration on the Rights of Indigenous Peoples*, ed. Stephen Allen and Alexandra Xanthaki (Oxford: Hart Publishing, 2011), 422.
88 Ibid.
89 Innes and Anderson, "The Moose in the Room," 175.
90 Ibid., 181.
91 Val Napoleon, "Aboriginal Discourse: Gender, Identity and Community," in *Indigenous Peoples and the Law: Comparative and Critical Perspectives*, edited by Benjamin J. Richardson, Shin Imai, and Kent McNeil (Oxford, UK and Portland, OR: Hart Publishing, 2009), 243.
92 Nathalie Kermoal and Isabel Altamirano-Jiménez, *Living on the Land: Indigenous Women's Understanding of Place* (Edmonton: Athabasca University Press, 2016), 4.
93 Gunn, "Bringing a Gendered Lens," 35.
94 Sa'ke'j Henderson, email to Susan Gingell, July 25, 2018.
95 Ibid.
96 Green, "Honoured in Their Absence," 1.
97 Andrea Smith, "Human Rights and Decolonization," in *Indivisible: Indigenous Human Rights*, ed. Joyce Green (Winnipeg: Fernwood Publishing, 2014), 83.
98 Native Women's Association of Canada, *CRGB Models of Reconciliation*, 27.
99 Ibid.
100 Priscilla B. Hayner, *Unspeakable Truths: Confronting State Terror and Atrocity* (New York: Routledge, 2001), 24.
101 We have elided Hayner's phrase "and justice," which we feel is more appropriate to a state than a church context.
102 Cited in Marie McMahon, " 'Liberation' and 'You Are On Aboriginal Land,' " Sovereign Union—First Nations Asserting Sovereignty, accessed March 11, 2021, http://nationalunitygovernment.org/content/liberation-and-you-are-aboriginal-land.

AFTERWORD

by

SA'KE'J HENDERSON AND DON SCHWEITZER

The preceding chapters bring together various disciplines in Indigenous and theological studies, along with concrete work on honourable reconciliation, to generate, establish, and maintain mutually respectful relationships between Indigenous and settler Canadians. The authors have revealed an awareness of the harms of the past, the beneficial efforts of yesterday and today, and the framework for reconciliation in the future. Their reflections are intended to aid the United Church and other denominations in living out their commitment to the United Nations Declaration as the framework for honourable reconciliation. What do they say to us?

The opening chapter, by Sa'ke'j Henderson, lifts up Indigenous people's inherent human dignity and underscores the need for this to be respected all down the line by churches, and particularly in seminary education. Indigenous people need to be welcomed in seminaries, and their knowledge, traditions, and spiritualities respected. Christine Mitchell focuses on troubling biblical texts, such as Deuteronomy 20:10–18, that authorize God's people to colonize a land and act violently toward its original inhabitants. Her chapter reminds church members that in addition to being an inspiration to many, the spiritual visions of Christianity can also represent "poisoned chalices, the causes of untold misery and even savagery."[1] Christians must take responsibility for how these texts are read and take effect in society. Lynn Caldwell warns settler Christians against confusing education about colonial oppression and current injustice with achieving reconciliation. Education may be a salutary first step, but reconciliation requires concrete structural change and material reparations. Adrian Jacobs's chapter recounts much of the journey that the United Church has taken toward reconciliation while emphasizing that it is essential that settlers recognize that Indigenous communities have their own traditions, structures, and ways of doing things. The United Church must make space within itself for these Indigenous traditions, structures, and practices. Sandra Beardsall explores what the United Church did in the past to be in solidarity with Indigenous Peoples through its participation in Project North. She notes the importance for reconciliation of settlers educating themselves about Indigenous issues and working to move beyond a purported objectivity that seeks always to hear "both sides" to a stance of solidarity with the oppressed. Paul L. Gareau notes the centrality of Indigenous understandings of spirituality, the land, and community to any interpretation of the Declaration. Self-determination, these chapters show us, includes the right of self-definition on the part of Indigenous Peoples. HyeRan Kim-Cragg argues for the importance of ritual in sustaining identity and as a source of knowledge, and for the need to respect Indigenous spiritual traditions and to allow them to enter into settler worship and ritual. Don Schweitzer points to the need for spiritual resources to empower and sustain settlers in the United Church as they seek to live out their church's commitment to the Declaration, and in particular, he identifies justification by grace as just such a resource. Jennifer Janzen-Ball lifts up the idea of the common good as an ethical guide, arguing that reconciliation will depend upon notions of the common good, including the flourishing of Indigenous Peoples. Finally, the collectively written chapter by Iskwewuk E-wichiwitochik highlights the importance of basic respect for others. It notes that reconciliation will depend upon settlers having respect for Indigenous Peoples and rigorously examining how they express this.

— AFTERWORD —

Together, these chapters sketch out the extent of the commitment that the United Church, other Christian denominations, and Canadians more broadly have undertaken in accepting the Declaration as the framework for honourable reconciliation. Now, the question becomes: What do we need to fulfill this commitment? The Declaration provides principles that will guide the United Church and other denominations toward reconciliation. But what will enable their members to follow them? Martin Luther King Jr. once observed that principles and legal enforcement can break down unjust laws and bring people together physically, but something must enter into their hearts that moves them to come together spiritually.[2] Reconciliation depends on people becoming "possessed by the invisible inner law which etches on their hearts the conviction"[3] that all people are worthy of respect. Ultimately, reconciliation will be achieved by people "who are willingly obedient to [the] unenforceable obligations"[4] that spring from their hearts. What must we breathe in to create these obligations within us?

In both Indigenous and non-Indigenous spiritualities, these questions regenerate the force of spirit contained within human reconciliation that cries out for atonement, accommodation, and trust. No cognitive feature of honourable reconciliation is more important than the recognition of people's ability to go beyond the particular regimes of religion, thought, and society in which they are embedded. This reflects the central role of the visions developed by the historical religions of salvation and most Indigenous spiritualities, which is to set us on the quest for an exemplary experience of the possibilities of personal connection—of intense and transfiguring relationships among peoples and individuals. Through actualizing the possibilities of personal connection and reconciliation, we can always do, feel, think, or create more than religion, thought, and society bless, allow, or make sense of. No past or present scheme of religious or social organization can accommodate all the activities that we have reason to value or all the abilities that we have reason to exercise and develop. This potential abundance, one that exceeds all the determinate circumstances of existence—over the historical destructiveness of colonization and racism and the belittlement, extremes of economic deprivation, and nihilism they have generated—should excite in our spirit and mind the idea of achieving our collective greatness, or of our share in the attributes that some of the world religions have ascribed to God, others to Nature. What we are to do about the legacy of indignity and oppression has always been a central theme in the spiritual and religious consciousness of humanity.

The generic antidote is political, legal, and education empowerment—institutionally, collectively, and individually—through legislation that reflects a justifiable consensus about expected behaviour. In July 2017, the Government of Canada promised to fulfill its commitment to implementing the Declaration by reviewing laws, policies, and other collaborative initiatives and actions. Eeyouch (James Bay Cree) Romeo Saganash led the Aboriginal Peoples of Canada in a multi-year effort to integrate the Declaration into federal law. His private member's bill, *An Act to Ensure that the Laws of Canada are in Harmony with the United Nations Declaration on the Rights of Indigenous Peoples* (Bill C-262), passed both the House of Commons and the Senate but languished after the end of that parliamentary session. In 2019, the British Columbia legislature enacted the *Declaration on the Rights of Indigenous Peoples Act*, which integrated the Declaration into BC provincial law. In 2020, the Government of Canada renewed its effort to integrate the Declaration into federal law. It introduced Bill C-15, *An Act Respecting the United Nations Declaration on the Rights of Indigenous Peoples*, to ensure that the government take all measures necessary to make the laws of Canada consistent with the Declaration and that it prepare and implement an action plan to achieve the Declaration's objectives.

As is usually the case with any proposed legislation, the political parties have in the past and will continue to robustly debate its merits. However, they do not comprehend the harms to both Aboriginal Peoples and Canadians caused by their resort to degrading and divisive rhetoric. Such discourse reflects the unresolved aspects of colonialism and racism, which continue to hamper the application of universal human rights.

The lingering problem with this legislative antidote is its reliance on coercive authority and power worship, rather than humanity and the spirit of life-giving empathic love that makes a dignified life, justice, and reconciliation possible. Despite its best intentions, the Declaration is not self-fulfilling. It requires determined commitment and collaboration on the part of individuals and institutions to maximize its promise and potential. Our understanding of the embodied spirit and inherent dignity of the Declaration imagines a better penumbra of adjacent possibilities derived from and through the grace of others and the reorientation and enhancement of the conduct of life. The vision, principles, and teachings of the Declaration reveal a path that can help make all of us greater by reflecting our potential greatness through honourable reconciliation and generating an equitable and inclusive society. The greatness of being human lies in our future relationships and in finding new ways of living together more than in the healing of past wrongs. Human greatness by reconciliation is built on our ability to connect with other people and the natural environments outside of our artificial social and political regimes, to reveal and to nourish the invisible circle of empathic love that generates the spiritual justice by which we are all bound. That is the underlying vision that runs through and unites the voices contained in this book. It is crucial that we hear theses voices, deliberate on their message, and practise the constructive action for which they call.

The Declaration is a very encompassing international human rights instrument, the companion of other United Nations human rights instruments. But it is more than that. It is a statement about the inherent dignity of Indigenous people produced by a spiritual movement that struggled for over twenty years to have the rights of Indigenous Peoples recognized in an international forum. The spirit animating this movement was one of "respect for others and their differences."[5] This guided the representatives of sovereign nations and Indigenous Peoples and generated every right in the Declaration. In reflecting on the Declaration as the framework for reconciliation, the authors of this book have breathed in this spirit. To fulfill their commitment to the Declaration as the framework for honourable reconciliation, settler members of the United Church will also need to breathe in this spirit of respect for others. The Declaration provides principles to guide us in seeking reconciliation and building better relationships. But we will need this spirit to uplift and empower us.

ēkosi.

Notes

1. Charles Taylor, *Sources of the Self* (Cambridge, MA: Harvard University Press, 1989), 519.
2. Martin Luther King Jr., *Where Do We Go from Here: Chaos or Community?* (New York: Harper & Row, 1968), 118.
3. Ibid.
4. Ibid.
5. James (Sa'ke'j) Youngblood Henderson, *Indigenous Diplomacy and the Rights of Peoples: Achieving UN Recognition* (Saskatoon: Purich Publishing, 2008), 50.

APPENDIX A

AN ECUMENICAL STATEMENT on the UNITED NATIONS DECLARATION on the RIGHTS OF INDIGENOUS PEOPLES

Responding to the Truth and Reconciliation Commission's Call to Action 48

March 30, 2016

The Truth and Reconciliation Commission of Canada (TRC) released 94 Calls to Action in June 2015 "to redress the legacy of residential schools and advance the process of Canadian reconciliation." The Calls to Action provide multiple opportunities to address and overcome more than a century of systemic discrimination and abuse in the residential school system, and to create a transformed relationship between Indigenous and non-Indigenous peoples.

The Government of Canada acted on behalf of all Canadians when it created the residential schools system. Some churches and religious communities ran the federally-funded schools as part of a national policy of assimilation spanning 160 years. The TRC has described the outcome of this policy as cultural genocide.

The church parties to the Indian Residential Schools Settlement Agreement received and promised to work with these Calls to Action. Other churches, faith communities, and ecumenical organizations have signaled their intent as well. In addition to the many statements released by churches and other faith groups in response to Call to Action #48, we the undersigned, jointly commit to Call to Action #48, to implement the principles, norms, and standards of the *United Nations Declaration on the Rights of Indigenous Peoples* as the framework for reconciliation.

The UN *Declaration* is an international human rights instrument adopted by the UN General Assembly on September 13, 2007. It affirms the inherent or pre-existing collective and individual human rights of Indigenous peoples. It does not create new rights. It provides a framework for justice and reconciliation, applying existing human rights standards to the specific historical, cultural and social circumstances of Indigenous peoples. The rights affirmed in the UN *Declaration* constitute the minimum standards for the survival, dignity, security, and well-being of Indigenous peoples worldwide.

In an executive summary of its final report, the TRC emphasized that "Canadians must do more than just talk about reconciliation; we must learn how to practise reconciliation in our everyday lives—within ourselves and our families, and in our communities, governments, places of worship, schools, and workplaces."

Settlers in Canada have benefited, directly or indirectly, from the occupation and usurpation of Indigenous lands and resources. Indigenous peoples, however, have experienced impoverishment, oppression, dispossession from their lands, and the destruction of their cultures and spiritual practices. The root causes of this ongoing impoverishment and oppression of Indigenous peoples must be identified and, then, we must be willing to make it right.

The UN *Declaration*, with its emphasis on self-determination and consent, freedom from discrimination, and rights to spirituality, culture, lands, and

APPENDIX A

resources, helps us to address the root causes of this inequity, and provides the means for us to correct it.

Call to Action #48 necessitates a fundamental reordering of our relationship, and a significant change in our identity as a country. It requires us to truly respect Indigenous peoples' right of self-determination and to acknowledge and respect nation-to-nation relationships based on mutuality and respect.

Implementing the UN *Declaration* includes examining the Doctrine of Discovery, which some faith bodies have repudiated. We acknowledge that this doctrine has had and continues to have devastating consequences for Indigenous peoples worldwide. All doctrines of superiority are illegal in international and domestic law, and immoral, and we affirm that they can never justify the exploitation and subjugation of Indigenous peoples and the violation of their human rights.

As churches and religious organizations, we have acknowledged our failures to respect the rights and dignity of Indigenous peoples. We acknowledge the harm done and are committed to journeying together towards healing and reconciliation. Many of us are on different places in that journey: some have been engaged in these questions for decades; for others, it is new terrain. But we are all committed to responding to this call.

We are strengthened in this journey by Indigenous peoples, both inside our faith communities and more broadly across Canada, who have chosen to journey with us. In these relationships, respect and understanding are strengthened, and we see the possibility for transformation.

We undertake this work in our communities of worship and beyond through educational initiatives. We support growing social, political, and legal efforts that promote the UN *Declaration*. As well, we welcome working alongside governments in Canada as they live into their stated commitments to the implementation of the UN *Declaration*.

Today we embrace the opportunity that Call to Action #48 offers faith communities to work for reconciliation and to fully respect the human rights and dignity of Indigenous peoples in Canada.

APPENDIX A

Signed by:
Anglican Church of Canada
Christian Reformed Church
Evangelical Lutheran Church in Canada
The Presbyterian Church in Canada
Religious Society of Friends (Quakers)
The Salvation Army
The United Church of Canada

APPENDIX B

STATEMENT on UN DECLARATION on the RIGHTS OF INDIGENOUS PEOPLES as the FRAMEWORK for RECONCILIATION

by

**THE UNITED CHURCH OF CANADA/
L'ÉGLISE UNIE DU CANADA**

March 31, 2016

On June 2, 2015, The United Church of Canada, along with the other church parties to the Indian Residential Schools Settlement Agreement, welcomed the Calls to Action of the Truth and Reconciliation Commission (TRC). These calls include the adoption of the United Nations Declaration on the Rights of Indigenous Peoples as the framework for reconciliation. Call to Action #48 specifically calls on the churches to do this work, and to report by March 31, 2016.

— APPENDIX B —

UN Secretary-General Ban Ki-moon has previously said of the Declaration, "It provides a momentous opportunity for States and Indigenous Peoples to strengthen their relationships, promote reconciliation and ensure that the past is not repeated." The TRC Commissioners have offered the churches that same "momentous opportunity," giving us a concrete way to transform a relationship of colonization and exclusion into one of mutuality, equity, and respect.

Today, The United Church of Canada expresses publicly our commitment to honouring Call to Action #48, adopting and complying with the principles, norms, and standards of the United Nations Declaration on the Rights of Indigenous Peoples as the framework for reconciliation.

Today is also an important moment in the life of the United Church, as the Aboriginal Ministries Council, accompanied by the non-Indigenous (settler) church, begins a process of consultation to determine its vision and future structure.

The United Church has been on a journey towards reconciliation for more than 30 years. In 1986 the settler church responded to the long-standing call of Indigenous Peoples to apologize for its role in colonization and the destruction of their cultures and spiritual practices. This Apology was acknowledged by the Indigenous church two years later, with the expressed hope that the church would live out the Apology in "action and sincerity."

We have adopted the United Nations Declaration on the Rights of Indigenous Peoples as a commitment to honouring that expectation of Indigenous Peoples in the United Church.

We understand the principles, norms, and standards of the Declaration to be reflected in:

- The right to self-determination
- The right to cultural and spiritual identity
- The right to participate in decision-making
- The right to lands and resources
- The right to free, prior, and informed consent
- The right to be free from discrimination

APPENDIX B

Indigenous Peoples are self-determining and engaged in the church's decision-making processes. One key structure for this is the Aboriginal Ministries Council and its constituent parts. But we also understand that our practices "for many years resulted in the exclusion of Indigenous Peoples from visioning, leadership and decision-making."[1]

The United Church recognizes Indigenous Peoples' right to their own cultural and spiritual practices, and acknowledges how as an institution it continues to be enriched by Indigenous wisdom and ways of knowing. But it would be misleading to say that these principles are fully understood and lived out in the church, or that Indigenous Peoples in the church are free from discrimination.

The United Church has a tradition of advocating for Indigenous justice on issues such as land and treaty rights; clean water; murdered and missing Indigenous women; and equitable funding for social welfare, education, and health care. Yet the church still struggles to understand how important the resolution of these issues will be in achieving true reconciliation.

These gaps between intention and results demonstrate that there is still much for us to do as we seek to make the Apology tangible and real. Adopting the United Nations Declaration on the Rights of Indigenous Peoples as the framework for reconciliation sets us a new standard for that journey. It requires us to review all aspects of our life as a church, from how we worship and build community to our human resources and finance policies to how we practise advocacy. It requires us to revisit our identity as a church, and how that identity does or does not foster relationships of mutuality, equality and respect, both within and beyond the walls of the church.

To that end, the United Church has created a task group on implementing the United Nations Declaration on the Rights of Indigenous Peoples. Comprising representatives from the Indigenous church, the Conference structure, and committees of General Council, the task group will develop a process to:

- Engage the church in learning more about the UN Declaration on the Rights of Indigenous Peoples and the meaning of its "principles, norms, and standards"

APPENDIX B

- Assess the church's current alignment with the Declaration in all areas of its institutional life
- Provide mechanisms for addressing non-alignment
- Provide a mechanism with which to assess its progress
- Establish a mode of accountability

We acknowledge that this work will be neither quick nor easy. The settler church is only beginning to absorb the shock of its complicity in creating the inequities facing Indigenous Peoples. The Indigenous church is also facing the challenge of decolonization. The 1986 Apology shifted us as a denomination; it impacted our identity in ways that we couldn't understand at the time. Adopting the UN Declaration as the framework for reconciliation brings us to a similar moment now.

Yet we know, not just in our hearts and minds, but where our faith resides, that this is the path we are meant to be on together. "All this is from God, who reconciled us to himself through Christ, and has given us the ministry of reconciliation; that is, in Christ God was reconciling the world to himself…and entrusting the message of reconciliation to us" (2 Corinthians 5:18–19). We are not sure what lies ahead as we complete this turn towards justice and deepen our commitment to a new identity, a new relationship, and a new way of being, both in the church and in the world. A new relationship is waiting, and we turn our faces towards it.

Note

1 United Church of Canada, *The Manual* (Toronto: United Church Publishing House), 4.

INDEX

A
Aboriginal educational institutions, 16–18, 21, 24
Aboriginal History: A Reader, 156
Aboriginal Ministries Council, 81, 89–90
Aboriginal Peoples. *See* Indigenous Peoples
Aboriginal Rights Are Not Human Rights: In Defence of Indigenous Struggles, 249, 257, 259, 262
Aboriginal Rights in Canada–Ecumenical Coalition, 111
abundant life, 204, 224
abuse, of Indigenous Peoples: by Christians, 167; cycle of, 236; from police, 244; in residential schools, 193, 203; vulnerability to, 28, 245, 259. *See also* oppression
activism: as call to justice, 63, 104, 133; and education for reconciliation, 56, 59, 70; for the environment, 111, 117; as form of Indigenous resistance, 137; international solidarity for, 64; participation of white settlers in, 60; against racism, 63–65
Adese, Jennifer, 156
Ahmed, Sara, 58–59, 69, 72
Ahtahkakoop, 164–165, 176–177

Ahtahkakoop: The Epic Account of a Plains Cree Head Chief, His People, and Their Struggle for Survival, 180, 182
Airhart, Phyllis, 128
Alberta Federation of Labour, 108
Alberta Presbyterian Missions, 113
Alexander, Corky, 165
Allen, Stephen, 263
Alliances: Re/Envisioning Indigenous-non-Indigenous Relationships, 129
allies/allyship: and concept of goodness, 58; with Indigenous Peoples through Project North, 102; need for, 123–124, 232, 242; as outcome of social justice education, 60, 66; in settlers, 56, 122; through education/self-awareness, 54, 65, 256
All Native Circle Conference (ANCC), xxxii, 82, 87–89, 163, 227
Altamirano-Jiménez, Isabel, 155–156, 251, 263
American Declaration on the Rights of Indigenous Peoples, 4
American Holiness movement, 165
Amesbury, Richard, 225
Amnesty International, 33, 234, 246, 262
Anaya, James, 198

INDEX

Andersen, Chris, 139–141, 144, 155–156
Anderson, Kim, 250–251, 258, 261–262
The Anglican Churchman, 105
Anglican Church of Canada: Council for Native Ministries, 178; General Synod, 104–105; as incorporating Indigenous rituals, 177; Indigenous communities of faith in, 164; and Project North, 106, 112, 124; and support for Indigenous women, 174
Anthropology for Christian Witness, 180
anti-racism: and activism, 63–65; and concept of goodness, 58; and education, 56, 60–62, 64, 70; white-settler approaches to, 56, 71
Applebaum, Barbara, 67–68
Aquinas, Feminism, and the Common Good, 224
Aquinas, Thomas, 210–211
The Archive and the Repertoire: Performing Cultural Memory in the Americas, 180
Arendt, Hannah, 64
Arnal, William, 155
Assailly, Mary Ann, 229, 245, 256
assimilation, forced: as antithesis to Jesus' teaching, 84; effects of, 83; as policy, 76, 80, 92, 97; as prohibited in the Declaration, 11, 15; redress/reparations for, 20–21, 25; survival of through ceremony, 94
Assiniboine people, 165

B
Barker, Adam, 122
The Basis of Union, 79, 85, 98
Battiste, Marie, xxiv, xxxii, 12, 28, 30, 155, 168, 181, 230, 257
Battle of Batoche, 145
Baum, Gregory, 180, 202–203
BC Native Ministries, 89
Beardsall, Sandra, xxvii, 266
The Beautiful Risk of Education, 72
Belcourt, Christi, 241, 258, 261–262
Belcourt, Herb, 148–149, 157
Benhabib, Seyla, 218, 226
Berger Commission/Report, 109–110, 118
Betcher, Sharon V., 49, 51
Beyond Traplines: Does the Church Really Care? Towards an Assessment of the Work of the Anglican Church of Canada within Canada's Native Peoples, 104, 125
Bible/biblical conquest stories, 32–34, 36; as enabling colonialism, xxv, xxx, 14, 36–37, 43, 92, 135, 147, 152; ideological effects of, 38; as justifying genocide, 43; reading of, 45–46, 49; as a resource for reconciliation, xvii, 47, 49; translations of, xx, 83, 172
Biesta, Gert J.J., 72
Bill C-15 *An Act Respecting the United Nations Declaration on the Rights of Indigenous Peoples,* xxiv, 132, 268
Bill C-262, 268
Billy, Alberta, xxii, xxxii, 89, 94, 97, 162
Black, Jaime, 241
Black Elk (Lakota holy man), xxi
Black Lives Matter movement, 83
Blackstock, Cindy, 234
Blue Quills First Nations College–30th Anniversary, 125
Blue Quills residential school, 104
Board of Home Missions, 105
Bocking, Stephen, 128
Bonhoeffer, Dietrich, 188, 193, 195, 203
Border Crossings: Cross-Cultural Hermeneutics, 181
Borrows, John, 155
Bourgeois, Michael, xxxii
Bradford, Justin Tolly, 154
Brant, Jennifer, 242, 260
Bridges in Spirituality: First Nations Christian Women Tell Their Stories, 180, 182
Brueggemann, Walter, 203
Burnett, Kristin, 156

C
Caldwell, Lynn, xxvi, 266
Calling Lakes Retreat Centre, 86
The Calling of the Nations: Exegesis, Ethnography, and Empire in a Biblical-Historic Present, 49, 51
Campagnolo, Iona, 113
Campbell, Maria, 258, 261–262
Canaan/Canaanites, 32, 37–38, 45–46
Canada: distressing conditions of Indigenous Peoples in, 198; engagement in

INDEX

reconciliation, 132; as entrenching Aboriginal rights in Constitution, 5, 11, 110, 115; history of Indigenous rights, xix–xx, 68; as implementing the Declaration, 247, 268; as *khanatum* (sacred place), 178; and Métis people, 6; and nation-to-nation exchange with Indigenous Peoples, 34, 201; policy of cultural genocide, 35; as settler-colonial country, 46, 67, 70, 131, 135, 144, 186, 216, 223; as shared identity space, 187, 199–200; as stolen Indigenous land, 45, 47; and violence towards Indigenous Peoples, 67, 70

Canada's Indigenous Constitution, 155

Canada's Residential Schools, 204–205

Canadian Broadcasting Corporation (CBC), 114, 117, 123, 161, 239, 241

Canadian Charter of Rights and Freedoms, 6, 20, 27–28, 137

Cantwell, Jordan, 88

Cardinal, Harold, 103, 125, 165, 180

Caretakers of Our Indigenous Circle, 77, 221–222

Carlson, Joyce, 179–180, 182

A Carnival of Science: Essays on Science, Technology and Development, 29

Carry-the-Kettle First Nation, 86

Carvalhaes, Cláudio, 180

Catholic Church (Catholicism). *See* Roman Catholic Church

Cavanagh, Edward, 154

Centre for Addiction and Mental Health, 170

Centre for International Governance Innovation, xxv

ceremonial objects, 175

ceremony, 92, 132, 138, 143, 257; as imbuing places with memory, 151; as maintaining cultural identity, 170; preservation of, 93; and truth telling, 254. *See also* memory; pipe ceremony; tobacco ceremony

Champagne, Duane, 140

Charleston, Steven, 154

Charters, Claire, 204

Chartrand, Larry, 262

Childress, James F., 224

Chipewyan nation, 27

Choquette, Robert, 157

Chrétian, Jean: White Paper on Indian policy 1969, 103

Christensen, Deanna, 165, 177, 180, 182

Christian, Dorothy, 217, 226

Christian Churches and Their Peoples, 1840–1965: A Social History of Religion in Canada, 154

Christian hamper syndrome, 104–105

Christian Island Reserve, 86

Christianity: as aiding oppression, assimilation, xxix, 52, 80, 135, 216, 266; colonial legacy of, xxx, 14, 135, 167; doctrine used to justify discriminatory actions, 15, 232; ethical reflection of, 215; held in tension with Indigenous identities, 161; Indigenizing of theology, 177; Métis experience of, 145, 147; as mixed with Indigenous cultures, 16, 170; as prohibiting Indigenous ceremonies/dance, 92, 160, 165; seen as superior to Indigenous way of life, 167; social ethics of, 212, 214. *See also* Bible/biblical conquest stories

Christie, Nancy, 154

A Church with the Soul of a Nation: Making and Remaking the United Church of Canada, 128

circle, creating: as ritual to counter exclusion, 163–164. *See also* Learning Circle model

Citizens for Public Justice, 105

City of God, 210

Clarke, Brian P., 51, 126

Clarke, Louise, 256

Clarke, Patricia, 120

Clarke, Tony, 111, 113, 123

Clayton, Philip, 156

Coalitions for Justice, xxxii

Coates, Ken, 153

Coetzee, J.M., xix

cognitive justice: in educational systems, 12–13; and inherent human dignity, 8, 13; as recognizing all knowledge systems, 12, 29

Cognitive Justice in a Global World: Prudent Knowledges for a Decent Life, 29

A Collection of Hymns for the Use of People Called Methodists, 171

collective human rights, 213, 219; and concept of common good, 214, 223; framework for, 209–210. *See also* human rights
Colledge, Edmund, 203
colonialism/colonization, xxviii; as alienating Indigenous and non-Indigenous Peoples, 124, 132, 190; as attempting to assimilate Indigenous Peoples, xx, 92, 98, 135, 184; as cause of intergenerational trauma, 87, 149; destructive effects of, 54, 150, 198, 213, 225, 231, 233, 245, 267–268; as exerting sovereignty over domain, 232; as facilitated by Christian religion/biblical texts, xxx, 14, 36–37, 92, 135, 147, 152; forms still in existence, 246; gendered impacts of, 243, 254; legacy of, 133, 141, 150; and racialization of Métis Peoples, xxviii; solidarity against, 56, 63, 65, 139–141, 197; as system of structural forgetting, 170; teaching about to promote understanding, 61–62, 70, 223; as transformed to ensure Indigenous futures, 25, 79, 232; United Church of Canada's involvement with, xvi, 122, 185–186; white settlers as benefiting from, xxv, 185
Coming Full Circle: Constructing Native Christian Theology, 154
common good: decolonizing of, 208–209, 215; definitions of, 211, 224–225; as ethical guide for reconciliation, 212, 215, 218, 220, 223–224, 266; as manifestation of good for all people, 211, 218; roots of in Catholic social teaching, 209–210; that includes all world views, contexts, 212–213, 217–219, 224
The Common Good and Christian Ethics, 224–225
Concise Oxford Dictionary, 242
Conflicted Commitments: Race, Privilege, and Power in Solidarity Activism, 73
conquest. *See* Biblical conquest stories
Constitution Act, 1982, 6, 30
Contours of a People: Métis Family, Mobility, and History, 156
Convention on the Rights of Persons with Disabilities, 27

Cormier, Raymond, 46
Coulthard, Glen, xxxii
Council of Yukon Indians, 116–117, 121
The Courage to Be, 203
Covenant, Community, and the Common Good: An Interpretation of Christian Ethics, 224
Cree people (nêhiyewak): hymnody of, 171–172; language of, 172, 230; philosophy of, 230
The Crucified God, 203
cultural appropriation, 175
cultural genocide, 8, 34–35, 103, 132, 170, 213, 216. *See also* genocide
Culturally Relevant Gender Based Models of Reconciliation (CRGB Models of Reconciliation), 229, 231–232, 234, 246, 253–254, 259, 262–263
cultural values, translatability of: as Eurocentric illusion, 230
culture. *See* Indigenous cultures
Culture, 72
Custer Died for Your Sins, 154

D
Dakota Access Pipeline protest, 136–137, 161
dance: banning of by colonizers, 160, 165–166; as linked to healing and spiritual renewal, 178
Dancing on Our Turtle's Back: Stories of Nishnaabeg Re-creation, Resurgence and a New Emergence, 258, 261
Dancing the Dream: The First Nations and the Church in Partnership, 182
Daniels, Erica, 161
Daum, Robert A., 49, 51
Davis, Lynne, 129
Davis, Wade, 166, 169, 180–181
Dean, Amber, 242, 261
Dear White Christians: For Those Still Longing for Racial Reconciliation, 73, 227
decision-making: consensus model for, 95, 163–164; to create the common good, 217; power/right to, 211–212, 220; as role of Indigenous women, 253–254
decolonization, 3, 57, 66, 103; and common good, 209; as enabling Indigenous liberation, 252; and healing, xxxi;

INDEX

needed by both Indigenous and non-Indigenous, 231; as a spectrum of actions, 92; and white-settler approaches, 56
Decolonization: Indigeneity, Education and Society, 258
Decolonizing Education: Nourishing the Learning Spirit, 28–29
Decolonizing Methodologies: Research and Indigenous Peoples, 29
DeCrane, Susanne, 211, 224
De Gruchy, John, 202, 205
Deloria, Barbara, 154
Deloria, Ella, 216
Deloria Jr., Vine, 135–136, 138–139, 141–142, 154–155
Dene people, 109, 113, 116–117, 122; Declaration on nationhood, 104; land claims of, 107; testimonies of, 118
Deschooling Society, 72
Designated Lay Ministry (DLM) Program, xxx
determinants of health: and Indigenous children, 197
Dini Senior, Josh, 162
Dion, Léon, 52
Discovering Indigenous Lands: The Doctrine of Discovery in the English Colonies, 154
discrimination: on basis of gender identities, 250–252; combatting of, 20; against Indigenous knowledge systems, 14–15; against Indigenous Peoples, 6–7, 23, 273, 279; as prohibited in Declaration, 9, 19, 33, 89, 220, 248, 250, 274, 278
Disruptive Christian Ethics: When Racism and Women's Lives Matter, 214, 225
diversity: in ceremonies, 93, 162; in human sexuality, 91, 223, 258; of Indigenous cultures, 11, 20–21, 140, 208, 217–218, 226, 251; of knowledge systems, 29, 140; policy initiatives for, 58–59
Division of Mission in Canada (DMC), 113–115, 121
Doctor Jessie Saulteaux Resource Centre (DJSRC), 86
Doctrine of Discovery, 33–34, 42, 68, 78, 82, 135; biblical bases of, xxv, 37
Donaldson, Laura E., 39, 51
Douglas, Mary, 36

Downstream: Reimagining Water, 226
Drouin, Eméric O'Neil, 157
drumming: as celebrating spirituality, 178
Dumont, Alf, 179–180, 182
Dumont, Jim, 163
Dumont, Marilyn, 148–150, 157
Durham College, 91
Dwellings: A Spiritual History of the Living World, 1

E

Eberts, Mary, 242, 259
Economic Justice for All: Catholic Social Teaching and the U.S. Economy, 224
An Ecumenical Statement on the *United Nations Declaration on the Rights of Indigenous Peoples*, xv–xvi, xxxii
ecumenism/ecumenical, xxvi, 176. *See also* Ecumenical Statement; Project North
Edmonds, Penelope, 154
education: as anti-racist, 56, 60–62, 64, 70; decolonizing of Eurocentric systems, 12–13, 92, 217; as essential for reconciliation, xxiii, 2, 57–58, 60, 65, 255, 266; Indigenizing of, 9, 11–13, 16, 20, 68; on oppression and social inequities, 58, 266; as promoting human dignity and equal access, 9, 11, 104; for social change/justice, 53–57, 59, 61, 64, 66, 69, 71; through intergenerational community ritual, 171; through Project North, 119. *See also* seminaries; settler education; universities
Elder Brother and the Law of the People: Contemporary Kinship and Cowessess First Nation, 156
Eliade, Mircea, 155
Elikawake Treaty of 1726, 27
Elsipogtog First Nation: anti-fracking protest, 136
Emmanuel College, xxix
empty land. *See* terra nullius (empty lands)
Enchanting Powers: Music in the World's Religions, 181
Epistemologies of the South: Justice against Epistemicide, 28–29
Erasmus, Georges, 109, 116, 119, 123
Ermine, Willie, 10, 29, 199–200

285

INDEX

eschatological reservation, 196, 201
Eshkakogan, Dominic, 178
ethical space, 10–11, 16, 197; as having no room for colonial attitudes, 201; between Indigenous Peoples and Canada, 187, 195, 199–200
ethics: and the common good, 210, 212, 214–215, 217–218, 223–224; Indigenous perspective on, 216; that deny abundant life, 208; that reject domination, 57, 70, 214
Eurocentric (Western) knowledge systems: on inherent human rights/dignity, 8, 13, 17, 252; place in education, 14, 16–17; in relation to Indigenous knowledge systems, xix, 10, 12. *See also* Indigenous knowledge systems
Evangelical Lutheran Church of Canada, 108
Eversole, Robyn, 249
extermination: of Canaanites, 38–39; as commanded in biblical texts, 36; of Indigenous inhabitants, 40, 94

F
Fairbairn, Brett, 2
Faith and Human Rights: Christian and Global Struggle for Human Dignity, 225
Federation of Saskatchewan Indians, 238
feeling, structure/restructure of: to become allies, 242, 255; as form of reconciliation, 54, 257; through reconciliatory education, 60, 65, 67–68, 70
Fennell, Robert C., xxxii
Final Report of the Truth and Reconciliation Commission of Canada, 4, 26, 30, 153, 181, 258, 261–262
Fiola, Chantal, 156
First Nations, xix–xx, 6; density and lifeways at Lac Ste. Anne, 147; viewed as non-persons, xx. *See also* Indigenous Peoples
The First Nations: A Canadian Experience of the Gospel-Culture Encounter, xxxii, 180–182
First Nations University of Canada, 256
First White Frost: Native Americans and United Methodism, xxxii
Fitzgerald, Oonagh E., 262
Five Oaks Retreat Centre, 86
Flowers, Rachel, 63, 65–66

Flying Dust First Nation, xxvi
Foehner, Kristen, 154
Fontaine, Tina, 46–47
Forever Loved: Exposing the Hidden Crisis of Missing and Murdered Indigenous Women and Girls in Canada, 260
forgiveness: and action, 48; Christian notions of, 52; for colonization, 47; for harm of residential schools, 189
Forst, Rainer, 202
For This Land: Writings on Religion in America, 154
Forum on the North, 101–102, 115, 122
Francis Sandy Theological Centre (FSTC), 86
Fraser, Nancy, 226
Frichner, Tonya Gonnella, 218
From Jerusalem to Irian Jaya: A Biographical History of Christian Missions, 99
Fumoleau, René, 122

G
Gabowitsch, Mischa, 50, 52
Galatians, 202
Gareau, Paul L., xxviii, 266
gas and oil exploration, 110
gathering: for resistance, 161–162; at sacred sites, 138, 148; and self-governance, 87; as spiritual practice, 162. *See also* Lac Ste. Anne (Manito Sakahigan); pilgrimage
Gathering: Resources for Worship Planners, 174–175, 182
Gaudry, Adam, 144, 153
Gauvreau, Michael, 154
gender: balance upended by *Indian Act*, 232; as basis for discrimination, 250–251; as determinant of health and safety, 233; and sexual minorities, 244
gender binary, 96–97, 99
General Council Archives Guide to Holdings Related to Residential Schools, 99
genocide, xxv, 78, 219, 232, 254; biblical bases of, 37; definition of, 34–36; ideology for, 49; moral justification in biblical texts, 43. *See also* cultural genocide
Genocide, the Bible, and Biblical Scholarship, 51–52
George, Chief Dan (Tsleil-Wauthth), 1

Ghost Dancing with Colonialism: Decolonization and Indigenous Rights at the Supreme Court of Canada, 155
Global Challenges: War: Self-Determination, and Responsibility for Justice, 262
The Global Face of Public Faith: Politics, Human Rights, and Christian Ethics, 225
Globe and Mail, 113
God Is Red: A Native View of Religion, 135, 154–155
God the Spirit, 205
Goffman, Erving, 202
Goldcorp, 222
goodness: and the importance of truth, 211; as outcome of settler education, 58–60; as triumphing over evil, 191–192
good relations. *See* right/good relationships
Grayshield, Lisa, 162
Green, Joyce, 249, 252, 259, 262–263
Grim, John, 142–143
guilt: as allayed by justification by grace, 185–191; felt by United Church, 185–187; for involvement in colonialism, 47; as needing to be addressed, 185
Gunn, Brenda L., 251
Guswentah/Two Row Wampum Belts, 80–81

H
Habermas, Jürgen, 205
hair cutting: as sign of Christian conversion, 165
Hamel, Peter, 111
Hamilton, Charles, 49
Hanke, Lewis, xxxii
Hansen, Bonnie, 157
Hargreaves, Allison, 233, 259, 261
Hartley, Jackie, 204
Harvey, Jennifer, 73, 227
hate speech, 20, 24
Haudenosaunee Confederacy, 80–81
Hayner, Priscilla B., 254, 263
healing, xxvii, 84, 87, 93, 186, 269; as coming from decolonization, 232; experiences of, 147–148, 161, 178; as part of honourable reconciliation, 231–232, 245–246, 255, 275; through ceremony, 255
Healing Fund (United Church of Canada), 221
Heinrichs, Steve, 204

Henderson, James (Sa'ke'j) Youngblood, xxiv, xxxi; on benign translatability, 230; cited as author in Notes, xxxii, 30, 203–204, 257, 259, 262, 270; on diverse sexual identities, 251–252; on face-to-face relations in reconciliation, 234; on respect for Indigenous Peoples' inherent dignity, 265
Hendry, Charles, 104, 125
higher education. *See* universities
hilaritas, 193, 195
Hines, John, 164
History and the Triune God, 202
Hitchner, Sarah, 155
Hogan, Linda, 1
Hogue, Michel, 156
Hollenbach, David, 214, 224–225
Holroyd, Carin, 153
Holy Spirit, xviii–xix, 84, 178–179; as enabling moral action, 191; role in justification by grace, 187, 192, 196
homophobia, 233, 244, 247, 252
Honouring the Truth, Reconciling for the Future: Summary of the Final Report of the Truth and Reconciliation Commission of Canada, xxxi–xxxii, 28, 203, 205
Horton, Chelsea, 154
Household of Freedom: Authority in Feminist Theology, 203
Hoxie, Frederick E., 156
Hudson's Bay Company, 145
Huel, Raymond, 157
human dignity, as inherent, 6, 25, 27–28; and cognitive justice, 13; as foundation of global justice, 8
human rights: as affirmed in the Declaration, 3–4, 33, 190, 218, 247, 249, 252; as affirming knowledge systems, 12; as ensuring access to sacred sites, 152; of Indigenous Peoples, 33, 152, 249, 262; as inherent, 6; and kin relationship structure, 219; recognition of, xxxi, 27, 200; as universal, 208–209, 212, 214, 219, 223, 268; violations of, based on gender, xxi, 234, 250, 254. *See also* collective human rights
Human Rights Watch, 243, 261
Hutchinson, Roger, 124–125, 128

hybrid (religious) practices, 161, 169, 175–176
hymnody, 88; as inscribing colonialism, 171; translations of, 160, 169, 172

I
Ice Blink: Navigating Northern Environmental History, 128
identity space, 187, 195, 219, 266; as shared, 197, 199–201. *See also* space, creating
Idle No More movement, 67
Illich, Ivan, 72
Imai, Shin, 263
incommensurability, ethic of, 57, 71, 258
Indian Act, 103, 105, 197, 232–233, 258
Indian Brotherhood of the Northwest Territories (IBNWT), 103, 107, 109, 114, 126–127
Indian Ministry Training Program, 94
Indian residential schools: as agents of cultural genocide, 34–35, 170–171, 213, 216; aimed at assimilation, 76, 80, 93, 165, 232; attitudes justifying them, 56, 104, 198, 217; as constituting spiritual violence, 14–15, 193, 245; gendered impacts of, 232–233, 254; guilt/regret/apology for, xxii, xxx–xxxi, 52, 97, 123, 132, 161, 184, 186, 189, 194, 246; harms done by, 14, 189–190, 193, 199–200, 232; and loss of traditional language and culture, 93, 171; survivors of, xxii, 21, 221; teaching about to promote understanding, 68, 223; as violation of UN Convention on Genocide, 50
Indian Residential Schools Settlement Agreement, xv, xxii, 221, 247
Indigeneity: as different from colonial way of thinking, 140
Indigeneity and the Sacred: Indigenous Revival and the Conservation of Sacred Natural Sites in the Americas, 155
Indigenization: as priority for education, 2–3, 5, 9, 11–13, 16, 20, 68; of seminary/university curricula, 7–8, 12–15, 19–20, 58, 70, 223; of theology, 160, 177–178
Indigenous Christians: in either/or choice for survival, 166; and hybrid rituals, 161, 176, 178; ministry of, xxvi–xxvii; as welcoming liturgical worship styles, 177

Indigenous churches/communities of faith: as called for in Declaration, 78; consensus methodology in, 95; requirements for, 76, 94; self-governance by, 77, 89; as sharing in proceeds from reparation sales, 222; and stories of exclusion, resistance, 92–93; as teaching broader church, 221; in the United Church of Canada, 85–87, 90, 93–94
Indigenous Community Leadership and Consensus Building, 91
Indigenous cultures: and church culture, 84, 124, 136, 146–147, 161, 174, 184; and colonialism, 51, 61, 76, 78–79, 83, 150, 166, 170, 185, 200; as expressed in biblical texts, 34, 46–47; and inherent human rights, 11; legacies of, 9, 19; as maintained/restored, 79, 92–93, 96, 170; as protected in the Declaration, 17, 22, 24, 76, 195; respect for, xviii, 86, 89, 231, 274. *See also* diversity
Indigenous density: as challenging established religion, 153; and Indigenous epistemologies, 140–141; Métis perspective on, xxviii, 143–148, 150–152
Indigenous diplomacy, xxiv, 3–4, 247
Indigenous Diplomacy and the Rights of Peoples: Achieving UN Recognition, xxiv, xxxii, 26, 203–204, 259, 262, 270
Indigenous Encounters with Neoliberalism: Place, Women, and the Environment in Canada and Mexico, 155
Indigenous episteme, 167; as embodied knowledge, 160
Indigenous epistemologies, xxviii–xxix, 133, 139–142, 150, 152. *See also* Eurocentric (Western) epistemologies
Indigenous knowledge systems: as based on storied interaction with the land, 142; historically seen as inferior, xxix, 160; and importance of ethical space, 10; inherent dignity of, 2; need for education on, xix, 12–13, 23; as protected in the Declaration, xxii; revitalization of, 254; as traditional, empirical, and revelatory, 143; and trans-system reconciliation, 11, 14, 17, 25

INDEX

Indigenous Land Defenders/Water Protectors, 137

Indigenous Lands: as basis for Indigenous ways of knowing and being, 76, 150; benefits from natural resource extraction, 21; claims on/title to, 82, 105–106, 109, 116, 121, 132; dispossession of, xvi, 33, 48, 132, 225; as indigenous right, 82, 102, 133; redress/reparations for dispossession, 23, 79, 82, 137; repatriation of, 57; sacredness of, 134, 137–139; settlers' possessiveness over, 37, 78, 139. *See also* Promised Land; *terra nullius*

Indigenous languages: as not emphasizing genders, 252; as protected in the Declaration, 23–24; as resiliency factor, 169–170; rights to, 231; suppression of, 132

Indigenous lifeways, xxviii, 10, 150, 152–153; as based on storied interaction in sacred places, 142–143

Indigenous Ministry Formation, 85–86, 90, 93; decolonizing of, 87; development of, 86, 89, 91

Indigenous Peoples: and attempts to assimilate/exterminate, 70, 76, 78, 80, 83–84, 92, 97, 103; as cultural "Others," 60; as displaced from the land, xvi, 33, 48, 68, 132, 225; diversity of, 226, 251; forms of governance, xxvii, 68, 71, 199; inherent human dignity of, 2, 9, 269; oppression of, xv–xvi, 122, 131–132, 140, 191, 198, 215, 223, 234, 250, 274; relationships to non-indigenous people, 65, 82; self-worth of, xxix, 167. *See also* Indigenous Land; Indigenous Rights; Métis people/Métis identity

Indigenous Peoples and the Law: Comparative and Critical Perspectives, 263

Indigenous Peoples in Guatemala: and church divestment in Goldcorp, 222

Indigenous Peoples Programme of the World Council of Churches, 2003, xxii

Indigenous Rights: and access to sacred sites, 139; as affirmed in Native religion, 136; to be affirmed in seminaries/universities, 15–16, 19; and church respect/support for, xvii, xxiii, 105; as constitutional, 13; and gender bias, 30; and northern development, 109; and Project North, 118; as protected in the Declaration, xxix, 5, 11, 22, 24, 30, 131, 269; to self-determination, xvi, xxvii, 186; as universal, 208. *See also* collective human rights; human rights

Indigenous self-governance. *See* Indigenous sovereignty (self-determination)

Indigenous sovereignty (self-determination): as applying to Métis Nation, xxviii, 133–134, 145, 151–152; as asserting resilience and resistance, 171; to be assisted by seminaries/universities, 6; as centred on Indigenous values/lands, 75–76, 78, 136, 138, 220–221, 249; and forms of self-governance, 68, 71, 75–76, 85, 199; as manifested in reconciliation, 2; as principle of international law, 8; as protected in the Declaration, xvi–xvii, 4, 139, 150, 187, 197; as relational, 152, 262; as requiring support and reparations, 198; as a right, 9, 118, 186, 197–198, 218, 220, 224, 266; and sharing identity space, 200, 266; as supported through education, 68; as sustained through ritual, sacred places, 143, 159; traditional systems as destroyed through colonialism, 145, 233

Indigenous spiritualities/theologies: to be affirmed in seminaries/churches, 14–16, 195; as envisioning Indigenous rights, 150; and experience of personal connection, 142, 267; as protected in the Declaration, 6, 10–11, 25, 134; regarding the common good, 216; respect for, 95, 266; as syncretic, 145; teaching about to promote understanding, 12, 16, 223; as violated/dismissed by European Christianity, xvi, 15, 137, 141, 160, 165, 167, 174–175

Indigenous stories, xxviii, 80, 94, 148–149, 217, 234, 241–243, 245, 252. *See also* storytelling

Indigenous Studies, 135, 138; as a distinct discipline, xxviii, 139, 141

Indigenous Testamur, 90, 93

289

Indigenous women and girls: bodies as sacred, 233; as harmed by imposition of dominant culture, 253; human rights of, 115, 234, 248, 250; as legal nullities, 259; and limitations of Declaration, 248; as marginalized by colonialism, 255; as missing and murdered, xxxi, 231, 240, 244–246, 260; power, wisdom, knowledge of, 232, 251; restoring dignity and security of, 247, 253; as subjugated to men, 258; as targets of gendered violence, 233, 242–245, 248–251, 254–255; traditional leadership role of, 233, 251, 253–255. See also Two-Spirit people

Indivisible: Indigenous Human Rights, 259, 262–263

Innes, Rob, 144, 156, 250–251
Innu of Labrador, 110
intention, good, subjectivity of, 64–65
Interchurch Project on Northern Development. See Project North
Interchurch Task Force on Northern Flooding, 105
Interdependence: A Postcolonial Feminist Practical Theology, 154
International Convention for the Protection of All Persons from Enforced Disappearance, 27
International Convention on the Protection of the Rights of All Migrant Workers and Members of Their Families, 27
International Covenant on Civil and Political Rights, 7, 28
International Covenant on Economic, Social and Cultural Rights, 7, 28
International Indigenous Women's Forum, 262
The Internationalization of Indigenous Rights: UNDRIP in the Canadian Context, 153
International Labour Organization, 10; Indigenous and Tribal Peoples Convention, xxi, 4
International Year for Human Rights, 105
In the End–The Beginning: The Life of Hope, 202–203
Inuit Peoples, 6
Irinici, Angelina, 49
Isasi-Díaz, Ada María, 211–212
Isbister, Reverend James, 178

Iskwewuk E-wichiwitochik (IE) (Women Walking Together), xxx, 231, 233, 236, 242, 245–247, 252, 256, 266

J

Jack, Joan (Anishinaabe), 250
Jacobs, Adrian, xxvi, 266
Jacobs, Peter, 94
James Bay and Northern Quebec Agreement, 104
Janz, Alison, 202
Janzen-Ball, Jennifer, xxx, 266
Jesus: An Experiment in Christology, 203
Jesus Christ: as anonymous Indigenous person, 96–97; as assuming human suffering, 188; discipleship of, 84; as enabling justification by grace, 192, 198; message of forgiveness of, 189
Joblin, E.E., 105
Joffe, Paul, 204
Johnson v M'Intosh, 78
Jones, Peter, 94
Jourdain, Cheryl, 88
Julian of Norwich: Showings, 203
Jumbo Mountain: as ceremonial grounds, 137
justice: struggles for, xviii, xxii, 111, 116, 119, 185, 191–193, 209. See also cognitive justice; social justice
Justice and Reconciliation Fund (United Church of Canada), xxiii
Justice Interruptus: Critical Reflections on the "Postsocialist," 226
Justification: An Ecumenical Study, 202
justification by grace, 186–187, 189, 266; and acceptance of "Others," 194, 198; as bringing restoration and renewal, 193, 195; as bringing salvation and holiness, 196; as empowering reconciliation, 184, 201; as enabled by Holy Spirit, 193; and ethical passivity, 188; and hope for a better future, 184, 191–192; and renewed self-worth, 190
Justification: The Doctrine of Karl Barth and a Catholic Reflection, 205

K

KAIROS, 111; blanket exercises, 70
Kanesatake Resistance (Oka Crisis), xxii

INDEX

Keetsahnak: Our Missing and Murdered Indigenous Sisters, 258, 261
Keewatin Presbytery, 85, 87
Kelley, Shawn, 49, 51–52
Kermoal, Nathalie, 156, 251, 263
Kervin, Bill, 176
Kidwell, Clara Sue, 180, 213, 216, 224–226
Kim-Cragg, HyeRan, xxix, 153–154, 181, 266
King Jr., Martin Luther, 103, 267, 270
kinship relations, xxviii, 132–133, 141–142, 144–145, 148, 233; at sacred places, 134, 149, 153; structure for individual and collective rights, 219
Kiowa people, 166
knowledge, embodied: as relying on memory and performance, 169; as requiring agency of participation, 160. *See also* Indigenous knowledge systems
Knox United Church (Regina), 82
Kraft, Charles H., 165, 180
Ktunaxa First Nation, 136–137
Kulchyski, Peter, 247, 249, 257, 259, 262
Küng, Hans, 205
Kuokkanen, Rauna, 250
Kwok, Pui-Lan, 173, 181, 226

L

Lachapelle, Guy, 205
Lac Ste. Anne (Manito Sakahigan): Catholic pilgrimage to, xxviii, 133, 146–147, 149, 152–153; as engagement/sacred site for Métis, 147–150, 152; as place of resistance to colonialism, 150
Lac Ste. Anne County History, 1913–2006, 157
Lac Ste. Anne Sakahigan, 157
Lakota people, 92, 216
Lakota Seven Ceremonies and Directions, 92
Landsdowne, Dolly, 94
Lavell-Harvard, D. Memee, 242, 260
Law and Religious Pluralism in Canada, 155
Learning Circle model, 86–87
Leaving Christianity: Changing Allegiances in Canada since 1945, 51, 126
Ledding, Andréa, 256
Legge, Marilyn, 232, 234
Lennarson, Fred, 116
Leon, Alannah Young, 220
Lestanc, Joseph, 147

Lethal Legacy: Current Native Controversies in Canada, 202
Letters and Papers from Prison, Dietrich Bonhoeffer Works, 203
LGBTQ persons, 91, 244
liberation: of Indigenous Peoples, 4, 39, 123, 190, 252, 256; as modeled by Jesus, 84
liberation theology, 85, 122
Lind, Christopher, xxxii
Littlechild, Chief Wilton, 256–258
Liturgy in Postcolonial Perspectives: Only One Is Holy, 180
Lived Religion: Faith and Practice in Everyday Life, 146, 156
Living on the Land: Indigenous Women's Understanding of Place, 156, 263
Li Xiu Woo, Grace, 155
Longboat, Kahontakwas Diane, 170
Longneck, Josephine, 237
Lubicon Lake Band, 116
Lutheran Church of America–Canada Section, 108; and Project North, 107

M

MacDonald, Clarke, 121
Macdonald, Stuart, 51, 126
Mackenzie, Gabrielle, 109
Mackenzie Valley pipeline, 109, 124; moratorium on, 109, 113–115, 121
MacKinnon, Peter, 2
Macquarrie, John, 224
Mahrouse, Gada, 58, 63–65, 70, 73
Maier, Harry O., 49, 51
Mairin Iwanka Raya: Indigenous Women Stand Against Violence: A Companion Report to the United Nations Secretary-General's Study on Violence against Women, 262
Making Settler Colonial Space: Perspectives on Race, Place, and Identity, 154
Making the Declaration Work: The United Nations Declaration on the Rights of Indigenous Peoples, 204
Man Becoming: God in Secular Experience, 203
The Manual. See United Church of Canada (UCC) *Manual*
Manual for Those Representing the United Church of Canada Among the Indians of Canada, 125

INDEX

Mar, Tracey Banivanua, 154
marginalization, 15, 188, 214–215, 223
Maritain, Jacques, 211, 224
Martin, B., 128
Matera, Frank, 202
McCullum, Hugh, 102, 104–110, 113–114, 117–119, 122–125
McCutcheon, Russell T., 155
McGuire, Meredith, 146, 156
McIntyre, Erin, 171–172
McKay, Reverend Stan, xxxii, 91, 164, 180–182; on apology of the United Church of Canada, 162–163; on hybrid Christian identities, 173–174, 177–178; on importance of language, 169; on importance of storytelling, 171; on internalized racism, 167; on mutual need for healing, 231, 262; on Project North, 111
McMurtry, Reverend Doug, 85
McNeil, Kent, 263
McNeish, John-Andrew, 249
Medicine Bundle, 173
Memnook, Edith, xxxii
memory: as collective, 151; as connection to ancestors, 138; as invoked at sacred places, 149; through performance, 168–169
Methodist Churches, 79, 160, 171, 177–178
Métis and the Medicine Line: Creating a Border and Dividing a People, 156
Métis Association of NWT, 114
Métis Homeland, 133, 150, 207
Métis people/Métis identity: connection to sacred sites, xxviii, 143; as considered hybrid/syncretistic Christians, 143, 151–152; and density and lifeways, 144–148, 151; dispossession of their territories, 149; historical identity of, 80, 145; homeland of, xvii, xxx; importance of kinship relations, 144–145, 150–151; and Indigenous self-determination, xxviii, 133, 144, 146, 152; marginalization of, 132; as misrepresented by racial mixing, 143–144, 151, 153; in NWT, 126–127; and storied connection of places, 134
"Métis": Race, Recognition, and the Struggle for Indigenous Peoplehood, 156
Mihevc, Joe, xxxii

Mi'kmaq people, 27, 92
Miller, J.R., xxxii, 125, 202
Miller, Robert J., 154
mīnwastamātowin (reconciliation), 230
Missing and Murdered Aboriginal Women: A National Operational Overview, 261
Mission and Service Fund (United Church of Canada), 221
Misunderstanding Stories: Toward a Postcolonial Pastoral Theology, 181
Mitchell, Christine, xxv, 265
Mitchell, Terry, 153
Mixed Blessings: Indigenous Encounters with Christianity in Canada, 154
miýo-wāhkōhtowin (good relationship), 230, 232, 257
Moltmann, Jürgen, 06, 202–203, 205
Monk, Clifton, 117
Moon, Richard J., 155
Moreton-Robinson, Aileen, 140, 153, 155
Moses and the Deuteronomist: A Literary Study of the Deuteronomic History, 51
Mount, Eric, 224
Muskeg Lake Cree Nation, 235, 238
My Only Daughter (film), 237, 240, 259–260

N

Nadeau, Denise Marie, 220
Napoleon, Val, 251
Naskapi-Montague Innu people, 116
National Aboriginal Day, 174
National Indian Brotherhood (NIB), 103, 110, 120
National Indigenous Council, 221
National Indigenous Organization for Fellowship and Support, 90
National Inquiry into Missing and Murdered Indigenous Women, Girls and Two Spirit People (NIMMIWG2S), 231, 234, 238–239, 241–244, 248, 255, 260
National Inquiry into Missing and Murdered Indigenous Women and Girls (NIMMIWG), 241, 243, 246, 258, 261
nationhood: and Indigenous self-governance, 78, 104, 145; as preserved within church governance, 84
A Native American Theology, 180, 216, 219, 224–226

INDEX

Native and Christian: Indigenous Voices on Religious Identity in the United States and Canada, 154
Native Christians: Modes and Effects of Christianity among Indigenous Peoples of the Americas, 154
Native spirituality. *See* Indigenous spiritualities/theologies
Native Studies. *See* Indigenous Studies
Native Women's Association of Canada (NWAC), xxxi, 174, 229, 231–233, 241, 243, 246–247, 253–254, 259, 261–263
Neve, Alex, 234
Newcomb, Steven T., 154
The New Conservatism: Cultural Criticism and the Historians' Debate, 205
A New Covenant: Towards the Constitutional Recognition and Protection of Aboriginal Self-Government in Canada, 30
"A New Creed" (United Church of Canada), 85, 185
Newlands, George M., 225
Nisga'a people, 116; assertion of territorial rights, 104
Nishnaabeg people, 124
Noley, Homer, xxxii, 180, 213, 216, 224–226
No More Stolen Sisters: The Need for a Comprehensive Response in Discrimination and Violence against Indigenous Women in Canada, 262
non-Indigenous Canadians: collective guilt of, 185; high moral standards for, 184; and illusion of benign translatability, 230; as seeking reconciliation with Indigenous Canadians, 186, 190–191, 193–196; self-withdrawal by, 200–201; spoiled identity of, 186, 189, 201. *See also* allies/allyship
Norman Wells pipeline, 110
Northern Coordinating Committee (NCC), 108, 113, 115, 120–121; and suspicions about Project North, 114
Northern Frontier, Northern Homeland, 109
Numbered Treaties. *See* Treaties

O

Oakes, Jill Elizabeth, 155
The Oblate Assault on Canada's Northwest, 157

O'Brien, Jean M., 155–156
Odora Hoppers, Catherine A., 12, 29
oil and gas exploration, 112–113
Okenmaysim-Sicotte, Darlene, 245
Ominayak, Chief Bernard, 116
On Being Included: Racism and Diversity in Institutional Life, 72
ON QC Native Ministries, 89
Ontario Institute for Studies in Education, xxvi
Oppenheim, David, 153
oppression, 48, 64, 255; as based on gender identities, 250, 252; as based on the notion of inferiority, xxix; of Indigenous Peoples, xv–xvi, 122, 131, 134, 140, 191, 198, 223, 234, 274; as legacy of colonialism, 185–186, 268; role of Christianity/churches in, 135, 164, 188, 215, 266; teaching/learning about, 54, 58, 69, 266
oral traditions, xxi, 22; as a multi-community conversation, 94; right to use and transmit, 12; as sharpening recollection, 169
Orientalism, 167, 173
Orientalism, 180
Ottawa Children's Aid Society, 234
Our Women and Girls Are Sacred, 230, 258, 261
The Oxford Handbook of American Indian History, 156
The Oxford Handbook of Religion and Science, 156

P

Pagans in the Promised Land: Decoding the Doctrine of Christian Discovery, 154
paranoid reading, of biblical texts, 45
Pastoral Care and Liberation Theology, 129
Pattison, Stephen, 129
Pearce, Maryanne, 244
Pearson, Chris, 121
The Pemmican Eaters, 149, 157
Penan people (Malaysia), 169
Pension Board (United Church of Canada), 222, 227
A People and a Nation: New Directions in Contemporary Métis Studies, 156

performance: as embodied practice, 168; as episteme, 160, 167–168; as medium for knowledge transmission, 168–169. *See also* ceremony; ritual/ritual practices; worship
Perkinson, James, 203
The Person and the Common Good, 224
Peter, Tracey, 244
philanthropy, 193–194
Pilar, Maria, 224
pilgrimage, xxviii, 133–134, 146–149, 152–153. *See also* gathering; Lac Ste. Anne (Manito Sakahigan)
pipe ceremony, 92, 162
place. *See* storied connection, to place
plain reading: of biblical conquest stories, 49
Plains Presbytery, 82
Polzin, Robert, 51
Postcolonial Imagination and Feminist Theology, 181, 226
Postcolonialism: A Very Short Introduction, 181
post-colonial vision, xx–xxi, 176; and critique of education, 72
Prairie Christian Theological Centre, 86
Premnath, D.N., 181
Presbyterian Church, xxix, 79, 166; Council of Elders, 77, 87, 97; and Project North, 107
Preston, Jennifer, 204
Proclaiming the Gospel to the Indians and the Métis, 157
Project North (Interchurch Project on Northern Development): criticisms of, 113, 115, 120; as ecumenical coalition, xxvii, 102, 105–108, 115, 119; mandate of, 106, 108–110; as a non-funding organization, 118–119; reformation of, 111–112; relationships with northern Indigenous communities, 103, 109–112, 115, 117–118, 120; relationship to United Church of Canada, 102, 115, 120, 266; success of, 117, 123
Promised Land, 37, 39–40, 42, 48
Prophets, Pastors and Public Choices: Canadian Churches and the Mackenzie Valley Pipeline Debate, 124–125, 128
Protecting Indigenous Knowledge and Heritage: A Global Challenge, xxiv, xxxii, 30, 257

Puett, Michael J., 182
Purify and Destroy: Political Uses of Massacre and Genocide, 35, 50, 52

Q

Québec–Canada: What Is the Path Ahead?, 205
Quebec: The Unfinished Revolution, 52
Questions on the Heptateuch, 33

R

racialization, xxviii, 132, 152–153
racialized people, as settlers, xxix, 63
racism, 25, 37, 60–61, 71, 119, 132, 149, 247; destructiveness of, 267; difficulties in countering, 65; harms caused by, 268; as internalized, 167, 173; legacy of, xxii, xxxi; as systemic, xx, xxviii, 215; and whiteness, 70
Ratt, Solomon, 256
Raya, Marian Iwanka, 250
Read, Geoff, 156
reading with empathy and love: of biblical texts, 46
Realizing the UN Declaration on the Rights of Indigenous Peoples, 204
Reclaiming Indigenous Voice and Vision, 155
reconciliation: as built on mutual respect and trust, 15, 185; and common good, 266; Cree translations of, 256–257; as culturally relevant, gender-based, 229–231, 246, 253; as educational outcome, 17, 54, 58, 71, 73; empowerment needed to sustain efforts, 195; as ending violence towards Indigenous women, 255; as honourable, 116, 231–232, 242, 255, 265, 267, 269; between Indigenous and non-Indigenous, xvi, xxiii, 65, 245; as interpersonal and relational, 119, 234; as journey, xviii, 14, 46, 124, 161, 186, 192, 196, 201, 220–222, 224, 230, 246; as making structure change, 266; model for, 234, 246, 248; and recognition of Indigenous communities, 89; as requiring work, 186, 191, 193, 198, 200, 209, 222; and structuring settler feelings, 54, 57, 257; through Indigenous-Christian hybrid ritual, 178
Reconciliation Canada, 233

INDEX

Reconciliation in a World of Conflicts, 224
The Reconciliation of Peoples: Challenge to the Churches, 180, 202
Reconciliation: Restoring Justice, 202, 205
Recovering Canada: The Resurgence of Indigenous Law, 155
Red Man's Land/White Man's Law: The Past and Present Status of the American Indian, 50
redress. *See* reparations/redress
REDress installation, 241
Red River resistance, 145
Red Skin, White Masks: Rejecting the Colonial Politics of Recognition, xxxii
Reflections on the UN Declaration on the Rights of Indigenous Peoples, 263
Regan, Ethna, 214, 225
Regan, Paulette, 124, 204
Rekindling the Sacred Fire: Métis Ancestry and Anishinaabe Spirituality, 156
relations (relationality), xxviii, 133–134, 142, 153, 220. *See also* kinship relations; right/good relationships
religion, tribal (Native spiritualities). *See* Indigenous spiritualities/theologies
religions/religious values (Western): as enabling racist systems of domination, 217; as problematic concept for Indigenous Peoples, 133, 136; settler-colonial definitions of, 25, 145; as supporting sacred/profane binary, 136; as unitary, collection of beliefs, 146
religious syncretism, 143–147, 151, 166
Remembering Vancouver's Disappeared Women: Settler Colonization and the Difficulty of Inheritance, 261
reparations/redress: church participation in, 21, 76, 189, 222; as including material support, 198, 221–223, 266; for loss of spiritual property and customs, 11; mechanism for in Declaration, 20, 199; models for in biblical texts, 47, 49; as part of road map for reconciliation, xxv, 93, 122, 227; for past land dispossessions, 23, 25, 79, 82, 137; for reconciliation, 47, 221, 227; as working alongside Indigenous Peoples, 253. *See also* reparative reading, of Biblical texts

reparative reading, of Biblical texts, 45–46
repatriation: of cultural objects, 22, 134; of human remains, 12; of Indigenous lands and life, 57
Replicating Atonement: Foreign Models in the Commemoration of Atrocities, 50, 52
Report of the Commission to Study Indian Work (United Church of Canada), 104, 125
residential schools. *See* Indian residential schools
Residential Schools and Reconciliation: Canada Confronts Its History, xxxii, 125, 202
resilience, 236, 238, 253, 255; culture, language, ceremonies as factors, 170; of Indigenous cultures and languages, 78; through maintaining cultural traditions, 171
resistance: to anti-racist education, 64; to colonization, 67, 70, 93, 150, 163, 171; legitimacy of, 232, 248; of Métis people to Catholicism, 146; to pipelines, 110, 113, 120; relating to Indigenous justice, 105; as response to genocide, 35; as subversive, xxix, 160, 169, 173; through translation, 172
resource extraction, 136–137
Richardson, Benjamin J., 263
Ricoeur, Paul, 45
right/good relationships: as needed in reconciliation, 93, 208, 221–222, 230, 234, 257–258; and recognizing dominant theologies as racist, 232; as requiring reparations, 48; as symbolized in Wampum Belt, 81; as taking time, commitment, 124. *See also* relations (relationality)
Riley, Del, 110, 120
Ritual and Its Consequences: An Essay on the Limits of Sincerity, 182
ritual/ritual practices: as central to Indigenous spirituality, 164; as dismissed by colonizers, 165; as embodied knowledge, requiring participation, 160, 168–169; as enabling Indigenous ways of knowing, 159, 167; mixing of, 166, 178; as promoting healing/sustaining identity, 161, 266; as subversive activity, 159, 169. *See also* ceremony; worship

Robinson, Chief Rod, 116
Robinson, Elaine A., 154
Roman Catholic Church (Catholicism): influence of on colonization, 50; Métis resistance to, 146, 151; and Project North, 106, 112; and regard for Indigenous Peoples, xx, 105, 164, 177; and syncretism, 151
Ross, Heather, 120
Round Dance, 162
The Routledge Handbook of the History of Settler Colonialism, 154
Royal Canadian Mounted Police, 109, 136, 243, 261
Royal Commission on Aboriginal Peoples, xxii
Royal Proclamation of 1763, 78, 198
Russell, Letty, 203

S

The Sacred and the Profane: The Nature of Religion, 155
The Sacred Is the Profane: The Political Nature of Religion, 155
Sacred Lands: Aboriginal World Views, Claims, and Conflicts, 155
sacred places/sites, 132–134, 137–138, 142, 148, 150, 152, 178; access to as indigenous right, 139; as affirming Indigenous density and life ways, 143; and sacred fires, 162–163; storied engagements with, 147
sacred/profane binary, 133, 136–138; as settler-colonial dichotomy, 141
the sacred/sacredness, xxviii, 133, 151
Saddle Lake First Nation, 104
Saganash, Eeyouch Romeo, 268
Said, Edward W., 180
sanctification, 196; as renewal through the Holy Spirit, 188
Sandy, Francis, 86, 94
Sandy-Saulteaux Spiritual Centre (SSSC), xxvi, 82, 86–87, 89, 93, 96, 221; as promoting trans-systemic knowledge systems, 16; as teaching reconciliation, 17
Sangster, Rhett, 256–257
Santos, Boaventura de Sousa, 28–29
Sarmiento, Fausto, 155

Sasakamoose, Fred, 176–177
Saskatchewan Interchurch Energy Committee, 108
Saskatchewan School for the Deaf, 235–236
Saskatoon Crime Stoppers, 238
Saskatoon Police Service (SPS), 238–240
Saulteaux, Jessie, 86, 165, 179
Schick, Carol, 58, 60–62, 64, 70
Schillebeeckx, Edward, 203
Schweitzer, Don, xxix, xxxi–xxxii, 125, 182, 266
Scinta, Sam, 154
Scott, Patrick, 126
Scott, Reverend Ted, 105–106
Second Vatican Council, 211
A Secular Age, 203–204
Sedgwick, Eve Kosofsky, 45–46, 48, 52
self-determination. *See* Indigenous sovereignty (self-determination)
self-withdrawal: as needed for reconciliation, 187, 200–201, 205
Seligman, Adam B., 182
Semelin, Jacques, 35–36, 49–50, 52
seminaries: core responsibilities towards Aboriginal Peoples, 5, 19–23; as guiding realization of Declaration, 4, 14–15; as Indigenizing curricula and practices, 7, 13–15, 18–20, 22, 58, 70, 223; to make reparation for benefiting from dispossessions, 20–21, 23, 25; to revitalize Indigenous knowledge systems, 13, 17, 21, 265. *See also* universities
settler-Christian education. *See* settler education
settler colonialism. *See* colonialism/colonization
settler conscientization, 57
settler education: focus/outcomes of, 54–55, 58, 62, 66–70; measure of, 57, 62, 266; nonperformativity of, 69, 71; pitfalls in, 58, 63, 65, 71; for social justice, 56, 58, 61, 71. *See also* education; feeling, structure/restructure of
settler institutionalization, 133
settlers/white settlers: as benefiting from occupation of Indigenous lands, xvi; colonial world view of, 139; as cultural norm, 61; desire for recognition in

non-racist actions, 65; as displacing/ destroying Indigenous communities, 98; harm done by colonialism, xvii, 170, 209; and image of Indigenous people, 167; as interfering in Indigenous freedom, 66; as needing to share identity space with Indigenous Peoples, 200; as privileged colonizers, 121, 223, 243; self-perceptions from social justice education, 60–61. *See also* whiteness (whitestream)
Sharp, Melinda, 181
Shaw, Martin, 35, 50
Shorter, David Delgado, 141–142, 145, 148
Sidney, Richard, 116
Silman, Janet, xxxii, 163, 166, 170–171, 173–174, 177–178, 180–182
Simon, Bennett, 182
Simpson, Leanne Betasamosake, 66–67, 124, 258, 261
Simpson, Zachary, 156
Sinclair, Jim, xxxii
Sinclair, Justice Murray, xxxi, 50, 103, 230, 245, 258
Sisters in Spirit (part of NWAC), 241, 243
Situating the Self: Gender, Community and Postmodernism in Contemporary Ethics, 226
Six Nations Haudenosaunee Confederacy, xxvii
Sixties Scoop, xxx, 233, 254
Smith, Andrea, 252
Smith, Grace Rebecca, 238, 259–260
Smith, Linda Tuhiwai, 29
Smith-McIntyre, Helen, 242, 245, 256
social change, 54, 104, 186–187, 241, 261
social ethics, as liberative, 214–215
social gospel movement, 211, 217
social justice, 12, 33, 72, 246, 258
social justice education, xxvi, 55–56, 59, 61, 64, 66; and notion of goodness, 58; outcomes of, 60, 69; performativity of, 60; relation to reconciliation, 57
Society of Friends, 108
solidarity: against colonialism, 56, 63, 65, 139–141, 197; and concept of goodness, 58; with Indigenous Peoples, xvii, xxvii, 4, 65, 105, 108; as outcome of social justice education, 60, 66; over Indigenous land rights, 102; against racism, 61; through activism/ education, 54, 63–64, 70; white-settler approaches, 56
"A Song of Faith" (United Church of Canada), 85, 185
Sources and Methods in Indigenous Studies, 155–156
Sources of the Self, 202, 270
sovereignty. *See* Indigenous sovereignty (self-determination)
space, creating, 221, 266; on campuses, 23; for co-existence, 173; for connections on the land, 142; as safe, 95; through treaties, 199; for youth, 14. *See also* ethical space; identity space
The Spanish Struggle for Justice in the Conquest of America, xxxii
The Spirit of Life: A Universal Affirmation, 205
Spirit & Reason: The Vine Deloria, Jr., Reader, 154
spirituality. *See* Indigenous spiritualities/ theologies
spoiled identity (stigmatized person), 186, 189, 201–202
Standing Rock Sioux Nation, 136–137, 161; protest by, 160–162
St. Andrew's College, xxiii, xxv–xxvii, xxix–xxx, 164, 247
Statement of Faith, 1940 (United Church of Canada), 85
Statement on UN Declaration on the Rights of Indigenous Peoples as the Framework for Reconciliation (United Church of Canada), 53–54, 56, 60–62, 64, 67–73, 98, 227
Stavenhagen, Rodolfo, 204
St. Denis, Verna, 58, 60–62, 64, 70
Steinhauer, Henry Bird, 94
Stigma: Notes on the Management of Spoiled Identity, 202
Stoicheff, Peter, 3
Stomp Dance, 165–166
St-Onge, Nicole, 156
storied connection: to place, xxviii, 133, 142, 150; to relationship/engagement, 144, 147–149, 152

INDEX

Stories Told: Stories and Images of the Berger Inquiry, 126
Story and Song: A Postcolonial Interplay between Christian Education and Worship, 181
storytelling, 138, 148; as imbuing places with memory, 151; as ritual, 169, 171. *See also* Indigenous stories
Sullivan, Lawrence E., 181
Sun Dance, 166, 179
Sunrise Ceremony, 179
surface reading, of biblical texts, 46
Susin, Luiz Carlos, 224
suspicion, hermeneutics of, 45–46
sweat lodge, 173
Swiftwolfe, Dorthea, 236, 239–240, 256, 259

T

Tavard, George, 202
Taylor, Charles, 193–194, 199, 202–204, 270
Taylor, Diana, 167–169, 180
Taylor McCullum, Karmel, 102, 106–111, 114, 116–117, 125–126
Teilhard de Chardin, Pierre, 25, 30
terra nullius (empty lands), 33–34, 135; as rationalized in biblical texts, xxv, 37, 43
Theology and the Boundary Discourse of Human Rights, 225
Theology of Hope, 203
The Theology of The United Church of Canada, xxxii
Thibault, Jean-Baptiste, 146
This Land is Not for Sale: Canada's Original People and Their Land–a Saga of Neglect, Exploitation, and Conflict, 106, 125
Thompson, Reverend John, 85
Those Who Take Us Away: Abusive Policing and Failures in Protection of Indigenous Women and Girls in Northern British Columbia, 261
Thunderchild First Nation, xxx
Tilley, Leonard, 40
Tillich, Paul, 203
Tinker, George E., 180, 213, 216, 224–226
tobacco ceremony, 163
Toleration in Conflict: Past and Present, 202
Touching Feeling: Affect, Pedagogy, Performativity, 52

Toward the Future, 30
Traditional Knowledge, xxi, xxvii, 22, 132, 134, 251; right to maintain and control, 12. *See also* Indigenous epistemologies; Indigenous knowledge systems
Traditional Territories, 9, 25, 134. *See also* Indigenous Lands
traditional values/ways of thinking/being, 150, 153, 226; and importance of intergenerational relationships, 216; as informing concept of density, 141; as marginalized in colonization, 135, 139; as rejecting settler institutionalization, 136; and religion and spirituality, 136, 144
transformation: as educational effect/outcome, 53–54, 57–59, 67–69, 71; as fundamental structural change, xxi, 92–93, 232, 261, 275
translation: of hymnody, 160, 169, 172; sign language, 239; as subversive activity, 172
Translator's Invisibility: A History of Translation, 181
trans-systemic knowledge systems, xix, 17, 28
Treat, James, 154
treaties, xxx, 80, 93, 103, 105, 118, 199; colonial records of, 82; commitments of, 9; Numbered Treaties, 33
Treaty of Niagara, 1764, 198
Treaty Rights of Aboriginal Peoples, 6, 15, 17, 19
Treaty territory, xvii, xxvi, xxx, 207
Trent, John, 205
Tribal Religions/Native spiritualities, 136, 152. *See also* Indigenous spiritualities/theologies
Trudeau, Pierre Elliott, 103–104
Truth and Reconciliation, xxxiii
Truth and Reconciliation Commission of Canada (TRC): call to implement the Declaration, 34, 48, 186; and models of reconciliation, 246; principles/standards for Indigenous survival, xxiii, 2, 10, 246; vision, process, outcomes of, 232; vision, processes, outcomes of, 231
Truth and Reconciliation Commission of Canada: Calls to Action, 50, 99
Truth and Reconciliation Commission of Canada (TRC) Calls to Action: call to

compliance by churches, seminaries, xv, xvii, 76, 88–89, 183, 247; commitment by United Church of Canada, 75, 92, 123, 220; as enjoining faith and justice groups to adopt Declaration, xv, xxxi, 33; as informing educational practice, xxvi, xxix, 58, 222; as minimum standards for Indigenous survival, 197

Tuck, Eve, 57, 59, 66, 70, 258

Tucker, Ruth, 83, 99

Tutcho, Susie, 109

Two-Spirit people, 233–234, 246; as impacted by colonialism, 231; meaning of, 258; as targets and survivors of violence, xxxi, 242, 244–245, 255, 260; and UN Declaration, 248, 250, 253

U

UN Convention on Biological Diversity, xxi

UN Convention on Genocide, 50

UN Convention on the Elimination of All Forms of Discrimination Against Women, 234

UN Convention on the Rights of Persons with Disabilities, 234

UN Convention on the Rights of the Child, 27, 234

UN Declaration on the Rights of Indigenous Peoples (UNDRIP): as applying to Métis people, 134, 143, 150, 152–153; Article 12, xxix, 12, 22, 159, 167, 175, 178; as call to listen to Indigenous Peoples, 195, 266; as creating a new relationship with Indigenous Peoples, xvii–xviii, 6, 9, 23, 62; as decolonizing the common good, 209, 219; as framed in language of international law, 4, 218, 231, 249, 257; as framework for education, 69, 71; as framework for reconciliation, 3–5, 33, 54–55, 88, 183, 190, 220, 222, 230, 247, 265, 267, 269; implementation of, 59, 248, 268; as Indigenous/human rights statement, 4, 48, 131, 208, 214, 218, 223, 252, 269; limitations and drawbacks of, 209, 231, 248–253; as referring to religion and spirituality, 22, 136–137, 139, 143; and right to self-determination, 75, 92, 186, 197; and right to shared identity space, 199–201, 219; and sharing of ethical space, 10, 187; and women's rights/gender identities, 248, 250–252. *See also* Indigenous sovereignty (self-determination)

UNDRIP *Implementation: More Reflections on the Braiding of International, Domestic and Indigenous Laws*, 204, 262

UN Economic and Social Council (UNESCO), 10, 28; Canadian Commission for, xxv; World Declaration on Higher Education in the Twenty-First Century: Vision and Action, 4–5, 19, 26

United Church Observer, 110, 113, 120–121

United Church of Canada (UCC): as adopting TRC Calls to Action, 75, 123, 243, 247; as allies/partners to Indigenous Peoples, 105, 123, 255; apologies of, xxii, 62, 80, 97, 111, 160–163, 167, 174, 184–186, 195; challenges faced in northern communities, 101; as committed to embracing the Declaration, xvi, xxiii, 3, 88, 183–184, 208, 230, 252; as denouncing Doctrine of Discovery, 82; as following conciliar model of governance, 77; as guarding rights of IWG2S, xxxi; Indigenous ministries of, 89, 161, 163, 174; involvement/collective guilt in colonization, xvi, xviii, 58, 132, 186–187, 221; and journey to reconciliation, xxx, 95, 116, 173, 220, 224, 234, 265–266, 269; liberal theological tradition of, 176; and paternalism towards Indigenous Peoples, 104

The United Church of Canada: A History, 125, 182

United Church of Canada Archives, 99, 124

United Church of Canada (UCC) General Councils, xxvii, xxxii, 77, 79, 81, 87, 89, 91–92, 113, 115, 160–163

United Church of Canada (UCC) *Manual*, xvi, xxxii, 85, 87–88, 92, 202

United States Catholic Bishops, 224

Universal Declaration of Human Rights, 1948, 7, 28, 234

universal human rights. *See* human rights

INDEX

universal norms: for moral issues, 215; as needing to account for diversity, 208, 210, 216, 218, 227; to support the common good, 211, 220–221, 226
universities: access to by Indigenous Peoples, 30; as guiding realization of Declaration, 14, 25; as Indigenizing curricula, 7–8, 12–13, 15, 70; not to condone benefits from dispossession or assimilation, 20; responsibility to protect Indigenous human rights, 5. *See also* seminaries
University of Alberta, xxviii
University of Saskatchewan, 3; Aboriginal education at, 2; Native Law Centre of Canada, xxiv
The Unjust Society: The Tragedy of Canada's Indians, 103, 125, 180
UN Permanent Forum on Indigenous Issues, xxii, 10
Unreserved (CBC Radio program), 161
An Unsettling God: The Heart of the Hebrew Bible, 203
Unsettling the Settler Within: Indian Residential Schools, Truth Telling, and Reconciliation in Canada, 124, 204
Unspeakable Truths: Confronting State Terror and Atrocity, 254, 263

V

Venuti, Lawrence, 181
Veracini, Lorenzo, 154
Vessey, Mark, 49, 51
Vickers, Patricia, 92
Victorian Treaty 8, 27
Vienna Declaration and Programme of Action, 1993, 27
Vientie, Truija, 29
Vilaça, Aparecida, 154
Violence against Indigenous Women: Literature, Activism, Resistance, 259, 261
Visioning a Mi'kmaw Humanities: Indigenizing the Academy, 181
Vision Keepers, 86
Visvanathan, Shiv, 29

W

Wabung Group, 86
Wabung process, 87
Wah-Shee, James, 107, 125
Waiting for the Barbarians, xix
Walking in the Woods: A Métis Journey, 157
Walking with Our Sisters installation, 241
Walsh, James, 203
Wampum Belts: as symbol for Indigenous communities of faith, 94; as treaty symbols, 80
Warick, Jason, 49
Warrior, Robert Allen, 32
Washburn, Wilcomb E., 50
Washoe Tribe (Nevada), 162
Watson, Lilla, 256
The Wayfinders: Why Ancient Wisdom Matters in the Modern World, 180–181
Weighill, Clive, 238
Welker, Michael, 205
Weller, Robert P., 182
Wells, Harold, 180, 202
Wesley, Charles, 171–172
Wesley, John, 181
West, Traci, 214–215, 225
Western European Enlightenment, 213
Western knowledge systems. *See* Eurocentric (Western) knowledge systems
Western/settler epistemologies, 57, 167–168
The Westminster Dictionary of Christian Ethics, 224
West of the Fifth: A History of Lac Ste. Anne Municipality, 157
What is Genocide?, 50
What Their Stories Tell Us: Research Findings from the Sisters In Spirit Initiative, 261
What We Have Learned: Principles of Truth and Reconciliation, xxxiii, 50, 52
Where Do We Go from Here: Chaos or Community?, 270
White, Jim, 94
White, Sophie, 79, 98
Whitehorse United Church, 121
whiteness (whitestream): as assigning cultural "Others," 65; examining of in anti-racist education, 61–62; fragility of, 83; in history of race and racism, 70; identification with Christianity, 62, 71, 146; and knowledge production, 141; legacy of, 139–141; as privileged identity,

17, 63–64, 189, 256; as settler-colonial value, 151
The White Possessive: Property, Power, and Indigenous Sovereignty, 153, 155
White Self-Criticality beyond Anti-racism: How Does It Feel to Be a White Problem?, 72–73
White Theology: Outing Supremacy in Modernity, 203
Wild Frenchmen and Frenchified Indians: Material Culture and Race in Colonial Louisiana, 98
Williams, Raymond, 54, 72
Wilson, Alex, 244
Wolfe, Carol, 235–243, 252, 256, 259
Wolfe, Desmond, 235, 237
Wolfe, Karina Beth-Ann, 235–236, 252, 256; disappearance of, 237–240; reputation as maligned, 241–242
Wolvengrey, Arok, 256
women. *See* Indigenous women and girls
Women's Inter-Church Council, 174
Wong, Rita, 217, 226
Wood Cree nation, 27
World Conference on Indigenous Peoples, 4
World Health Organization (WHO), 10
worship: ceremonial style of, 177; hybrid nature of, 160, 175; as reconciling with Indigenous Peoples, 178, 266; as reflecting Anglo-European tradition, 176; as solemn, superior, 166. *See also* ritual/ritual practices
Wright, Robin, 154
Wrongs to Rights: How Churches Can Engage the United Nations Declaration on the Rights of Indigenous Peoples, 204

X
Xanthaki, Alexandra, 250, 263

Y
Yancy, George, 67–68, 72
Yang, K. Wayne, 57, 59, 66, 70, 258
Yellowknife United Church, 121
Young, Robert J.C., 172, 181, 205

www.ingramcontent.com/pod-product-compliance
Lightning Source LLC
Chambersburg PA
CBHW032027290426
44110CB00012B/698